# Lessons of the
# Venezuelan Experience

# LESSONS OF THE VENEZUELAN EXPERIENCE

Edited by
Louis W. Goodman, Johanna Mendelson Forman,
Moisés Naím, Joseph S. Tulchin, Gary Bland

The Woodrow Wilson Center Press
Washington, D.C.

The Johns Hopkins University Press
Baltimore and London

F
2328
L48
1995

Editorial Offices
The Woodrow Wilson Center Press
370 L'Enfant Promenade, S.W.
Suite 704
Washington, D.C. 20024-2518
Telephone 202-287-3000, ext. 218

Order from
The Johns Hopkins University Press
Hampden Station
Baltimore, Maryland 21211
Telephone: 1-800-537-5487

Printed in the United States of America
⊗ Printed on acid-free paper

9 8 7 6 5 4 3 2 1

Library of Congress Cataloging-in-Publication Data

Lessons of the Venezuelan experience / edited by Louis W. Goodman . . .
[et al.].
    p.    cm.
Includes bibliographical references and index.
ISBN 0-943875-65-X (alk. paper)—ISBN 0-943875-66-8 (pbk. : alk. paper)
    1. Venezuela—Politics and government—1974-    2. Political
stability—Venezuela—History—20th century.    3. Venezuela—Economic
conditions.    4. Venezuela—Social conditions.    I. Goodman, Louis
Wolf.
F2328.L48    1994
320.987—dc20                                                94-42552
                                                              CIP

# CONTENTS

# PREFACE

In February 1992, a failed coup put Venezuelan politics in a new light. A seeming bastion of democracy was now under siege. Venezuelan politics became the subject of questions from both policymakers and social scientists. Since February 1992, events have moved at a dizzying pace: Other coups have been attempted, a sitting president has been impeached, formerly nonexistent or marginal political parties have won seats in municipal and national elections.

In the November 1993 Venezuelan elections, the candidates of the two major parties were defeated by a former president who ran on an anti-party, anti-reform platform. The new administration promptly reversed the prior administration's economic policies, which had stressed privatization and open markets, and reimposed controls over prices and foreign exchange, and in general took an adversarial, restrictive stance toward the private sector. Nostalgic for past prosperity, Venezuelan leaders and citizens turned inward, looking for scapegoats.

When will Venezuela abandon inward-looking politics and old political leaders? This is hard to predict. While Venezuela has lessons to learn from its other national experiences, other nations can see in Venezuela clear warnings for their own political and economic systems. Mistakes were made in a country where democratic institutions had achieved great legitimacy. The lessons of emerging success stories in Latin America indicate that new leadership is important for democratic consolidation. In an economy prosperous by world standards, what happened in Venezuela can illustrate for other countries that the struggle to balance economic well-being with the effort to create representative political systems requires that leaders pay attention to citizen preferences and that citizens be allowed—even stimulated—to take an active interest in and participate in affairs of state.

An edited volume always carries a history of its own. This one is no exception. It brings together five individuals as volume editors and two institutions, all of whose interests in Latin America converged due to the Venezuelan events of February 1992. The failed coup presented two of the editors with an occasion to take a hard look at the Venezuelan military as part of a larger project on civil-military relations in the hemisphere. Two others were engaged in a broad inquiry into the democratization process and the notion of consolidated democracy, a term that once described Venezuela. The fifth editor, a key player in the economic development of Venezuela, had sought answers to why the programs of reform had unleashed harsh responses from Venezuela's citizens.

These interests converged in Washington as policymakers, scholars, and political figures took stock of Venezuela's problems. Once a country hits the "radar screen" of the U.S. Congress, its salience can rise to unprecedented levels. Placing Venezuela in this new light was an opportunity for individuals studying democratization to look with a new perspective at what was once considered a closed chapter of Latin America's democratic success stories. The challenges facing Venezuela's government also afforded opportunities for forums and dialogue about how the petroleum-based economy had failed to develop alternative sources of revenue to support the comfortable, state-supported structures that so many middle-class Venezuelans had come to expect.

In the summer of 1992 the editors of this volume proposed a conference on the subject of the current crisis in Venezuela. In October 1992, a few weeks before the second coup attempt, the conference convened a large number of policy officials, Venezuelan government representatives, political leaders, scholars, and military officers from Venezuela, the United States, and other countries to learn more about the specific issues facing the failed consolidation of democratic government in Venezuela. The papers presented new research on a wide range of subjects, bringing fresh views to the discussion, and adding the case of Venezuela to the new perspective on democratization in the region. The dialogue and research presented at this event revealed how profound a democratic unraveling had taken place in Venezuela.

The papers written for the conference form the basis of the chapters in this book, although some were commissioned after the event to create a comprehensive work. Revising and editing the papers was the work of all of us and the editors at the Woodrow Wilson Center Press. This volume represents current thinking on a wide range of issues that will long affect not only the future of Venezuela's political and economic development, but also the future of Venezuela's leadership in the hemispheric quest for a more open, just, and democratic region.

No such project is possible with the work of editors and authors alone. At the American University, staff associates Betty Sitka and Beth Wachs played key roles in assisting with the October 1992 conference and later in coordinating the compiling and editing of the papers. The Woodrow Wilson Center's Latin American Program staff played the major role, overseeing copyediting, final preparation, and delivery of the manuscript. Program Associate Allison Garland and Program Assistant Lucy Hetrick were most helpful in organizing the conference, as were staff assistants Susan Roraff and Paul Psaila. Co-editor Moisés Naím was assisted by his staff at the Carnegie Endowment for International Peace in coordinating the task of working with four other individuals in making this volume complete. In particular, the able assistance of Deborah Hudson was crucial in freeing him from other work to focus on this project. The Carnegie Endowment also provided the environment conducive for developing many of the ideas that found their way into Naím's writings in this volume.

Financial support is essential in undertaking a project as large and complex as a conference and book. The United States Agency for International Development (USAID), through support for the American University's Democracy Projects, by the Office of Democratic Initiatives, Latin America and Caribbean Bureau, provided major funding. Deputy Director and Project Officer Debra McFarland and Office Director Kenneth Schofield were of great assistance throughout our work. We are also deeply grateful to Roma Knee, now retired program officer at USAID, who provided the initial impetus for the project. Assistant Administrator Mark Schneider and Deputy Assistant Administrator Norma Parker have continued their encouragement to make this project an ongoing part of USAID support for building democratic institutions.

At the Woodrow Wilson Center, the support of the Gran Mariscal de Ayacucho Foundation for programming on Venezuela in recent years was essential. The Ayacucho Foundation provided key funding at a critical juncture of Venezuela's history. Leopoldo López Gil, president of the foundation, demonstrated his extraordinary vision in encouraging the project. Andrés Stambouli, senior adviser to the foundation, provided invaluable support in shaping the event. We are deeply grateful for the support of the Ayacucho Foundation in making Venezuela a major part of the program's broader focus on Latin America.

We also owe great thanks to the North-South Center at the University of Miami. Through its initial interest in this project we were able to fund some of the conference participants and papers. Ambassador Ambler Moss and professors Bill Smith and Robin Rosenberg were instrumental in this early effort.

Editing a volume with five individuals is a test of collaboration, teamwork, and friendship. We retain our diverse and deep interest in a hemisphere economically secure and respectful of the rights of its citizens. The complex process of producing this book, often done after "normal" working hours, represents our commitment to the search for new knowledge and for an understanding of a process fundamental to improving the human condition. Finally, as with any book, the ultimate responsibility for its contents lies with the editors alone.

# ABBREVIATIONS

| | |
|---|---|
| AD | Democratic Action |
| | Acción Democrática |
| ADLAF | German Association of Research on Latin America |
| | Asociación Alemán de Investigación sobre |
| | América Latina |
| ALADI | Latin American Integration Association |
| | Asociación Latinoamericana de Integración |
| AVEX | Venezuelan Association of Exporters |
| | Asociación Venezolana de Exportadores |
| BAP | Agrarian Bank |
| | Banco Agrario Popular |
| BCV | Central Bank of Venezuela |
| | Banco Central de Venezuela |
| CACM | Central American Common Market |
| | Mercado Común Centroamericano |
| CARICOM | Caribbean Community |
| CEN | National Executive Committee |
| | Comité Ejecutivo Nacional |
| CEPAL | Economic Commision for Latin America and the |
| (or ECLAC) | Caribbean |
| | Comisión Económica para América Latina y el |
| | Caribe |
| CESAP | Center for Service to Popular Action |
| | Centro al Servicio de la Acción Popular |
| CMA | Agricultural Marketing Association |
| | Corporación de Mercadeo Agrícola |
| CONACOPRESA | National Commission of Costs, Prices, and Salaries |
| | Comisión Nacional de Costos, Precios e Salarios |
| CONIA | National Council of Agricultural Research |
| | Consejo Nacional de Investigación Agricultura |
| CONINDUSTRIA | Council of Industries |
| | Consejo Nacional de la Industria |
| COPEI | Committee for Political Organization and Independent Election |
| | Comité de Organización Política Electoral Independiente |
| COPRE | Presidential Commission for the Reform of the State |
| | Comisión Presidencial para la Reforma del Estado |

| | |
|---|---|
| CORDIPLAN | Central Office of Planning and Coordination |
| | Coordinador de Planificación |
| CPN | National Political Committee |
| | Comité Político Nacional |
| CSE | Supreme Electoral Council |
| | Consejo Supremo Electoral |
| CTV | Confederation of Venezuelan Workers |
| | Confederación de Trabajadores de Venezuela |
| CVF | Venezuelan Development Corporation |
| | Corporación Venezolana de Fomento |
| CVG | Venezuelan Guyana Corporation |
| | Corporación Venezolana de Guyana |
| ECLAC | *See* CEPAL |
| EVV | School of Neighborhood Communities of Venezuela |
| | Escuela de Vecinos de Venezuela |
| FAC | National Guard of Venezuela |
| | Fuerzas Armadas de Cooperación |
| FACUR | Federation of Urban Community Associations |
| | Federación de Asociaciones de Comunidades Urbanas |
| FCA | Agricultural Credit Fund |
| | Fondo de Crédito Agropecuario |
| FCV | Peasant Federation of Venezuela |
| | Federación Campesina de Venezuela |
| FD | Democratic Factor |
| | Factor Democrático |
| FEDEARGRO | National Farmers' Federation |
| | Confederación Nacional de Asociaciones de Productores Agropecuarios |
| FEDECAMARAS | Federation of Chambers of Commerce and Production |
| | Federación Venezolana de Cámaras y Asociaciones de Comercio y Producción |
| FEDEINDUSTRIA | Federation of Small and Medium Enterprises |
| | Federación de Industria |
| FEDENAGA | National Cattlemen's Federation |
| | Federación Nacional de Ganaderos |
| FIV | Venezuelan Investment Fund |
| | Fondo de Inversiones Venezolanas |
| FONAIAP | National Fund for Agricultural Research |
| | Fondo Nacional de Investigación Agropecuario |

| | |
|---|---|
| FUNDACREDESA | Venezuelan Foundation for Growth and Development of Food Supplies |
| | Fundación para el Crecimiento y Desarollo Alimentario |
| GATT | General Agreement on Tariffs and Trade |
| IAEDN | Institute for Advanced Studies in National Defense |
| | Instituto de Altos Estudios de la Defensa Nacional |
| IAN | National Agrarian Institute |
| | Instituto Agrario Nacional |
| IDB | Inter-American Development Bank |
| | Banco Interamericano de Desarollo |
| IEA | International Energy Agency |
| IESA | Institute for the Advanced Study of Administration |
| | Instituto de Estudios de Administración |
| ILDIS/AVECA | Latin American Institute for Social Research/ Venezuelan Association for Caribbean Studies |
| | Instituto Latinoamericano de Investigaciones Sociales/Asociación Venezolana de Estudios del Caribe |
| IMF | International Monetary Fund |
| INAVI | National Housing Institute |
| | Instituto Nacional de Vivienda |
| INCE | The National Institute for Vocational Education |
| | Instituto Nacional de Cooperación Educativa |
| INVESP | Venezuelan Institute for Social and Political Studies |
| | Instituto Venezolano de Estudios Sociales y Político |
| IRELA | Institute for European-Latin American Relations |
| | Instituto de Relaciones Europeo-Latinoamericanas |
| MAS | Movement Toward Socialism |
| | Movimiento al Socialismo |
| MBR-200 | Bolivarian Revolutionary Movement |
| | Movimiento Bolivariano Revolucionario |
| MEP | People's Electoral Movement |
| | Movimiento Electoral del Pueblo |
| MERCOSUR | Southern Cone Common Market |
| | Mercado del Cono Sur |
| MIR | Movement of the Revolutionary Left |
| | Movimiento de Izquierda Revolucionaria |
| NAFTA | North America Free Trade Agreement |
| NGO | nongovernmental organization |

| | |
|---|---|
| NIC | newly industrialized country |
| OAPEC | Organization of Arab Petroleum Exporting Countries |
| OAS | Organization of American States |
| OCEI | Central Office for Statistics |
| | Oficina Central de Estadística e Informática |
| OECD | Organization for Economic Cooperation and Development |
| OPEC | Organization of Petroleum Exporting Countries |
| PCV | Communist Party of Venezuela |
| | Partido Comunista de Venezuela |
| PDVSA | The Venezuelan Oil Company, Inc. |
| | Petróleos de Venezuela, S.A. |
| PROCA | Program for the Caribbean |
| | Programa para el Caribe |
| PROMEXPORT | Export Promotion Office |
| | Oficina de Promoción de Exportaciones |
| PROVEA | Venezuelan Program for Education and Action in Human Rights |
| | Programa Venezolana de Educación-Acción en Derechos Humanos |
| RECADI | National Preferential Exchange Office |
| | Régimen de Caribio de Dinero |
| RED | Democratic Answer |
| | Respuesta en Democracia |
| SELA | Latin American Economic System |
| | Sistema Economico Latinoamericano |
| SIDOR | Orinoco Steel Works, Inc. |
| | Siderúrgica del Orinoco, S.A. |
| UNCTAD | United Nations Conference on Trade and Development |
| URD | Democratic Republican Union |
| | Unión Republicana Democrática |
| VPS | Venezuelan private sector |

# EDITORS AND CONTRIBUTORS

Felipe Agüero
Professor of Political Science
Ohio State University

Norman A. Bailey
President
Norman A. Bailey Associates
Washington, D.C.

Gary Bland
Senior Program Associate
Latin American Program
The Woodrow Wilson Center

Winfield J. Burggraaff
Professor of Political Science
University of Missouri

Jonathan Coles
Chairman of the Board of Directors
Mavesa, S.A.
Caracas, Venezuela

Brian F. Crisp
Professor of Political Science
Wake Forest University

Johanna Mendelson Forman
Director
Democracy Projects
The American University

Antonio Francés
Director of Research
Institute for the Advanced Study of Administration (IESA)
Caracas, Venezuela

Louis W. Goodman
Dean
School of International Service
The American University

Ricardo Hausmann
Chief Economist
Inter-American Development Bank

Janet Kelly
Dean
Institute for the Advanced Study of Administration (IESA)
Caracas, Venezuela

Miriam Kornblith
Professor of Political Science
Central University of Venezuela

Daniel H. Levine
Professor of Political Science
University of Michigan

John D. Martz
Professor of Political Science
Pennsylvania State University

Richard L. Millett
Professor of History
Southern Illinois University at Edwardsville

Moisés Naím
Senior Associate
Carnegie Endowment for International Peace

Juan Carlos Navarro
Researcher
Institute for the Advanced Study of Administration (IESA)
Caracas, Venezuela

Rogelio Pérez Perdomo
International Institute for the Sociology of Law
Caracas, Venezuela

Andrés Serbín
Director
Venezuelan Institute for Social and Political Studies (INVESP)
Caracas, Venezuela

Andrew Templeton
Datos, C.A.
Caracas, Venezuela

Joseph S. Tulchin
Director
Latin American Program
The Woodrow Wilson Center

# Lessons of the
# Venezuelan Experience

# Introduction: The Decline of Venezuelan Exceptionalism

For decades, Venezuela was an exceptional country in Latin America. If the norm in the region was political instability, Venezuela was a rock. In the years since a broad civilian coalition ousted the venal dictator Marcos Pérez Jiménez in 1958, president succeeded president in strict adherence to the Venezuelan constitution. If the norm elsewhere was armed forces that seized control of the government because of their impatience with civilian government inefficiency, corruption, insensitivity, or its seeming vulnerability to subversion, the military in Venezuela was a model of professionalism, even in the face of Cuban-backed armed insurgency in the 1960s. If the norm in other Latin American nations was unstable polarization between left- and right-wing political parties, cooperation between Venezuela's two leading parties, Acción Democrática (AD) and the Christian Democratic COPEI (Committee for Political Organization and Independent Election), created a stability lubricated by oil revenue that was sometimes characterized as *partidocracia* and other times as an "oil-igarchy." If the norm in the region was politicians insensitive to the needs of the population, Venezuelan leaders, by contrast, were socially responsible and progressive, funding social programs with money the state earned from the export of the nation's principal natural resource, petroleum.

That exceptionalism had won for Venezuela a privileged place in the international system. United States presidents singled out Venezuela to speak for the region and to serve as a link between the United States and the rest of the hemisphere.[1] Leaders of both major political parties, Social Democrats in Acción Democrática and COPEI's Christian Democrats, enjoyed enormous prestige within their respective international party organizations. Venezuela's democracy, together with its willing export of strategically vital quantities of petroleum, enabled the nation to enjoy a position of prestige in the international system far greater than warranted by the size of its population or its economy. The nation's exceptionalism extended to its per capita income, which at U.S.$3,041 (1980) was one of the highest in the region and distributed in one of the region's most equitable patterns.[2]

So exceptional was Venezuela, such a model of socially conscious democracy, that the nation was paid scant attention. To foreign journalists, social scientists, and politicians, Venezuela seemed predictable and, hence, of little interest. As an ally in the cold war, it was reliable without being crucial.[3] As an export-based economy with strategic economic activities in the hands of the state, it never set off a fever of foreign investment.[4] Even the nationalization of petroleum production in the hands of foreign corporations did not excite much international reaction.[5] Venezuela never seemed to attract much attention in the international media, either positive or negative. There were no coups, no earthquakes, no exotic carnivals, few picturesque indigenous peoples. Having made the transition from military to civilian rule, Venezuela was not a bureaucratic-authoritarian state, the hot social science topic in the 1960s and 1970s.[6] With its oil and its relatively equitable distribution of national income, Venezuela was not a model of distorted, dependent development, the analytic focus of students of the region in the 1970s.[7] Even historians and anthropologists seemed to avoid Venezuela.[8] No pre-Columbian civilization of note had occupied its territory; it had been an administrative backwater in the Spanish empire; it never had received massive waves of European immigrants; and it had not industrialized its economy to a remarkable degree.

In scholarly terms, Venezuela had the least interesting combination of characteristics—exceptional and unexciting without being a likely model for others. It was too exceptional to include in multicountry comparative studies of political or economic development, and it offered insufficient attraction as a single case to lure many students.[9] Its domestic academic community became increasingly isolated, both as a consequence of the institutional weakness of local universities and research centers and because public budgets continued to provide the opportunity to live a relatively unchallenged academic life. Those who studied Venezuela in other countries were a worthy but dwindling group who had an increasingly hard time finding interlocutors in the country.[10] Until well into the 1980s, chronically overvalued exchange rates also made field work in Venezuela more expensive than anywhere else in the region. A few months of field research in Venezuela were as expensive as a year in Argentina or Chile. The same lack of interest characterized public policy analysts and journalists.

# THE COLLAPSE OF VENEZUELAN EXCEPTIONALISM

For students of democracy the case of Venezuela was a closed book. After thirty-four years of elected civilian rule, few analysts thought that the military would interrupt the status quo. With a strong party system, a global economy, and a high standard of living, Venezuela appeared, at least to those viewing it from afar, to be gaining in democratic consolidation rather than being on the edge of an abyss. Even to longtime Venezuela watchers, no one could have predicted that the events of February 4, 1992, would unravel the region's second longest running democracy. But unravel it did.

As President Carlos Andrés Pérez sought to regain control of rebellious troops in the early morning hours of February 4, 1992, civilian support for democracy remained high, though confidence in the elected government was at an all-time low in opinion polls. Although troops loyal to the president were able to quash the uprising of the middle-ranking officers, led by Lt. Col. Hugo Chávez and his followers (the Bolivarianos), many citizens were sympathetic to the issues raised by this fractious military band. At the top of the list for both the rebellious officers and the public was their perception of corruption among public officials in government.

The economic "shock therapy" President Pérez introduced shortly after taking office in February 1989 had a dramatic impact on the middle class and the poor. The efforts of the Pérez government to privatize industry and reduce government involvement in the market created the basis for enormous growth in the Venezuelan economy. By February 1992, however, the benefits of this new economic policy had not yet trickled down to the average Venezuelan. As citizens watched their purchasing power decline, the gap between rich and poor widened, while the elites (businesspeople, politicians, journalists, and public officials) continued to maintain their luxurious existence. The perception of corruption in government became a chronic theme in the popular press.

It is tempting to say that the failed military coup of February 1992 suddenly made Venezuela exciting. But that would be grossly misleading and would suggest that only sensation-seekers should focus on Venezuela. The two military uprisings of 1992 revealed for all to see that the country suffered many serious problems and its "model" political system was miserably dysfunctional. The complex political process that forced President Pérez out of power on charges of corruption in 1993 also signaled that a much deeper institutional crisis had been brewing silently for a long time. Pérez's predicament revealed as well that Venezuela suffered from the political, economic, and social problems common to most Latin American countries. Venezuela became interesting as the political process by which it was governed unraveled. With this unraveling, with its efforts to reform the economy, its attempt to make the political parties more responsive to the citizenry, and the campaign to eliminate government corruption, Venezuela appeared to offer valuable lessons to other countries attempting to consolidate democratic government as well as to students of the region.

## THE SEEDS OF THE COLLAPSE

During the 1980s Venezuela gradually and increasingly became a typical Latin American country. While virtually all of the nations in the region passed through a transition from authoritarian to civilian democratic rule, Venezuela's democracy stagnated and deteriorated to the point where it appeared as vulnerable and unconsolidated as any other nation's. The debt crisis of the 1980s, followed by the painful economic adjustment program launched by the newly elected Pérez administration in 1989, brought to the surface the many flaws in the country's economy and exacerbated the profound institutional weaknesses that had been blurred or minimized by the illusion of a smoothly operating political system. Income distribution, once so laudably equal by Latin American standards, became progressively unequal, while per capita income, once so enviably high, slowly fell in comparison with the rest of Latin America. The national political leadership's dramatic incapacity to respond to the attempted coups, to the growing institutional decay, or to any of the deep-seated problems laid bare by such events precipitated a broad systemic crisis, the solution to which was not immediately evident.

In many ways, and not all of them positive or encouraging, the Venezuelan case today speaks to the rest of Latin America as it never has before. As the nations of the region consolidate their democracies amid social crises associated with economic restructuring and a deliberate and conscious insertion into the post–cold war global market, they might do well to study the Venezuelan case in detail to avoid some of the mistakes made by Venezuelans in allowing their political system to erode.

The central lesson of the comparison between Venezuela and the rest of Latin America is that democracy and development require continuous hard work to reconcile, even under the best of economic, social, and political circumstances. From the ouster of Marcos Pérez

Jiménez in 1958 until the coup attempts of 1992, Venezuelan elites seemed able to buffer with oil many of the problems that crippled democracies elsewhere; they later discovered that these buffers were not as strong as they looked.

The experiences of Venezuela suggest that certain premises about democratic transitions require review—in particular the mechanisms through which these political shifts occur. For example, the use of a formal or informal pact between leading political and military actors, frequently used to initiate the transition to civilian government, may have limited use in the consolidation of democratic rule.[11] Unlike the classic social contract, the keystone of modern democratic government, agreements like Venezuela's Pact of Punto Fijo (1958) do not provide the necessary means to ensure full political participation, the flexibility to incorporate new political actors, or healthy civil-military relations once civilian control is consolidated.[12]

Venezuela can be characterized as what Robert A. Dahl has called "polyarchy" and what Samuel P. Huntington has called a "second wave" example of democratization.[13] Venezuela's democracy extended citizenship to all adults, and the rights of citizenship included the power to vote out of office the highest government officials. Moreover, the transition to democracy in 1958 took place not through violence, but via an explicit pact that was negotiated among the key parties.[14] It was precisely the return of civilian control and the military's willingness to become subordinate to civilian authority that allowed this change to occur. That this military subordination was not complete was best demonstrated by the coup attempts of 1992 and 1993, begging analysis as to why elements of the military no longer chose to respect civilian control.

It is safe to say, as has been argued elsewhere, that the glue that kept Venezuela's military and political elites together—the high level of patronage and politicization of promotion—was a source of the 1992 upheavals in the military.[15] Another major factor was discontent among the armed forces with civilian leadership, which was at an all-time high. The officers who led the coup attempt were precisely those junior enough and sufficiently outside the patronage loop to feel the squeeze of the economic reforms instituted by President Carlos Andrés Pérez in 1989. The same junior officers found it distasteful to perform police actions against civilians who were similarly affected by the economic shock therapy. In the end, however, the long-running cohesiveness of civilian political elites and the highest-ranking military officials prevented a more disastrous outcome: a military takeover.

Whether the conditions exist for the consolidation of democratic politics in Venezuela is a subject of much speculation. Although it is easy to make the case for Venezuelan constitutionalism, and a case for the procedural components of Venezuelan democracy, it is more difficult to believe that any state can provide legitimate democratic government in the face of marked social inequalities and corporatist institutions (such as the Venezuelan military) that polarize rather than consolidate societal interests.[16] The state, a system operating on a social pact between military and political elites, indeed may not have had a social contract with the Venezuelan people.

The elections of December 1993 may become the spark for a "third transformation" or "third wave" of democratization. That is, unlike the pact that returned Venezuela to civilian rule in 1958, the process of consolidation may have begun through the more subtle processes of compromise, elections, and nonviolence.[17] The next challenge to Venezuela is the creation of "full citizenship" in a society that has experienced the formal procedures of democratic governance without incorporating the majority of its population into the process. One of the ironies of this challenge involves the political parties that have dominated the democratic history of Venezuela. While their sclerotic dominance has hindered the development of a genuine civil society, the parties may be key to Venezuela's third transformation. As groups outside the direct control of the state, both the reformed traditional political parties and the dynamic new parties can strengthen conditions for enduring democratic governance in a system with broader, ever-evolving citizen participation.

In any democracy, deepening economic crises that sharpen existing social inequalities may also provide a backdrop for abrupt political change.[18] This may have been the situation in Venezuela and, but for the solidarity between military and political elites, the political system may have broken down. At issue, however, is whether this alliance will continue, given the weakening of the political parties and the generational divisions among the economic elite, where the elder statespersons who support a return to statist economic policies are being challenged by young technocrats who want to proceed with free-market reforms.

The collapse of the political system and the failure of the country's leadership—business, labor, intellectual, and political—to respond to new domestic and international changes involve important lessons for building healthy democracies. Political institutions do not collapse or implode spontaneously, just as the Soviet Union did not implode without being subjected to excruciating external pressure. The political institutions of Venezuela, long corroded from within, collapsed under the pressure of a broadly based though inchoate popular drive toward modernity. It was as if, suddenly, people across the political and social spectrums observing the changes in the former Soviet Union, Eastern Europe, and elsewhere in Latin America said, "Basta! Enough! No more inefficiency, no more backwardness, no more corruption." Venezuelans were demanding their right to enjoy the peace, the predictability, the opportunity, and the creature comforts of the modern world; they wanted to be an integral part of that world, and that meant insisting on a government that was responsible to the electorate.

Many Venezuelans even had the chance briefly to experience first-hand what it meant to have higher living standards, thanks to the oil boom of the mid-1970s. In 1977, Venezuelan income per capita was boosted to an all-time high, many citizens joined the middle class, and more than ever were able to travel overseas. For most Venezuelans, this was their first time abroad and many could never do it again after living standards began to deteriorate. But all were left with strong images of life in developed countries. When Venezuelans complain about telephones, public transportation, or health care, they have as a reference not only the dismal condition of these services in Venezuela but also the standard they had experienced personally overseas. The expectations created by the high oil revenues and the experience of the mid-1970s created a massive demand for government actions aimed at satisfying these rising expectations. No leaders dared to explain that realizing such expectations might take a long time and perhaps even some painful policy corrections.

The social frictions arising from the dysfunctions and defects of the political system were lubricated by successive governments willing to sacrifice economic balance on the altar of political stability. Elites profited enormously from the distortions that misguided government intervention created. Thus, after the excesses of the first Pérez administration (1974–79), the governments of Luis Herrera Campíns (1979–84) and Jaime Lusinchi (1984–89) continued to maintain, and even deepen, an economic system based on massive subsidies, extensive government controls, artificial employment, and highly distorting protection. This approach caused major structural damage to the economy. It eliminated almost all traces of efficiency or competitiveness and rendered the distribution of income and wealth increasingly inequitable. It also fed the "illusion of harmony" under which much of the institutional decay, economic stagnation, and social regression took place. The illusion of harmony was based on increasingly larger public-sector budgets that avoided conflict at all costs. The behavior of different economic sectors, organized social groups, regions, or institutional actors was "stabilized" through a public-sector budget that relied on oil and foreign debt.[19]

The nation's political party system was particularly rigid in the face of change. All of Venezuela's elected presidents in the thirty-six-year period from 1958 to 1994 came from a generation of politicians who had been in exile together during the government of the dictator Marcos Pérez Jiménez. The nation's political party system failed massively, neglecting "organizing the masses and recruiting political leaders . . . [to] protect democracy against the toxins it secretes within itself in the course of its development."[20]

The country therefore did not develop mechanisms to resolve the tensions. Rather, policymakers ignored trade-offs. For example, no thought was given to the possibility that new lines for the Caracas subway system might mean fewer hospital beds for Maracaibo or that higher wages for university professors meant lower subsidies for Guárico's sorghum growers. The system was simply based on the popular maxim *"Hay pa' todo"* (there is enough for everything)—all claims, needs, and aspirations could be accommodated without wasting time in sorting out trade-offs and setting priorities among mutually exclusive funding actions.[21] In this way, difficult decisions for politicians and budgetary frustrations for any group (or even individual) with the capacity to rock the boat and seriously threaten social harmony were postponed and swept under the rug. For many years, politicians were spared the need to learn how to reconcile political priorities and economic imperatives.

Meanwhile, political entrepreneurs from all walks of life quickly learned that by loosely organizing a "social sector," and by submitting their collective claim on the national budget couched in terms of a group demand and with the implicit threat of social protests in case of disappointment, their share of oil money was practically guaranteed. The bulk of the population, without voice and without the capacity to organize their direct access to public funds, was left only with the benefits of artificially low prices and artificial jobs. The illusion of harmony was expensive to maintain, and eventually it became unaffordable. By the beginning of the 1980s oil income had become insufficient to finance all the claims on the national budget. The only other source of finance, international indebtedness, had dried up in the wake of Mexico's 1982 default on its huge foreign debt, which halted the flow of foreign funds to Latin America and left a legacy of crushing debt-service burdens in Venezuela.

The policies bred by the illusion of harmony left a political legacy that underlay much of the instability that Venezuela began to experience at the end of the 1980s: a society unprepared to resolve conflicts through means other than throwing money at them; a judicial system in shambles as a consequence of both the general devastation suffered by state institutions and its historic irrelevance; political leadership without the experience to sort out priorities and mobilize support for unpopular causes; and a civil society incapable of organized voluntary action other than to extract rents from the state. The result was that, as the 1990s began, organized social groups competing for scarce resources lacked the leaders, the structure, and the patience to endure a process in which their claims on the national budget were no longer guaranteed.[22]

## INTERNATIONAL PRESSURES FOR CHANGE

The end of the cold war and the triumph of liberal capitalism made it hard for most nations to deny the pressure to achieve modernity. But in Latin America the handwriting was on the wall even before the Berlin Wall came tumbling down. In the Western Hemisphere, U.S. hegemony, in concert with the neoclassical orthodoxy of the international financial institutions, meant that emergence from the debt crisis would push Venezuela and other nations in Latin America toward a more liberal, open economy and call on them to compete for economic survival in a global marketplace. Adding to the pressure on Venezuelan decision makers was the fact that some Latin American elites were already discovering the need for structural reform. The positive experiences of Chile and Spain—not to mention the East Asian newly industrializing countries (NICs)—and the frustrations with economic shocks in Brazil and Argentina made clear the types of policies required for Venezuela. Competition in the global market means increasing efficiency and a willingness to play by the new rules of the world system. Under U.S. hegemony, those rules included democratic politics and transparency in international relations, both commercial and political.

With the end of the cold war, the new question is whether Venezuela's political instability, indicated by the two coup attempts in 1992, will become the premise for a political and economic retreat by the United States and other members of the Organization of American States (OAS). The keystone of post–cold war U.S. and OAS realpolitik is that democracy is the ticket to international respectability and a prerequisite for favorable terms of international trade. In their Declaration of Santiago, affirmed in June 1991, the members of the OAS agreed to refuse political recognition and to erect a trade embargo against any country whose democratically elected leaders are overthrown by force. That is, no government deemed undemocratic will be allowed to become a full partner in the international economic and political system. For the United States, Most Favored Nation status in international trade can be granted only if a nation is certified by the U.S. president as having a satisfactory human rights record—a core element of democracy. In short, the external environment suggests that a return to nationalist and protectionist policies in Venezuela will be difficult, especially if such policies are accompanied by cronyism and corruption as they were in the past.

## THE RESPONSE OF THE VENEZUELAN
## STATE AND LESSONS TO BE LEARNED

In this domestic and international context, the Venezuelan political system simply was an anachronism. It lacked both the agility and the flexibility to deal with the problems of the day. Carlos Andrés Pérez, on returning to power in 1989, was sufficiently aware that the environment had changed to shift his economic policy to an austerity program under the tutelage of a cabinet of relatively young, foreign-trained, politically inexperienced technocrats.[23] His predecessor, Jaime Lusinchi, had sensed all was not well politically and had sponsored the creation of a bipartisan commission for the reform of the state, the Presidential Commission for the Reform of the State (COPRE), which labored hard and well for years. Pérez continued the program, and some of its works were shrewd, reasonable studies pointing to many of the nation's most serious political problems—the judiciary, the bureaucracy, the local organizations of the political parties, the communications media, and others.[24] Pérez was a major catalyst of decentralization and revitalized COPRE's weak efforts to reduce the concentration of state power. These efforts, however, were overcome by the turn of events.

How will the unraveling of democratic government culminate in Venezuela? Are the victories of new political parties in the December 1992 municipal elections and the December 1993 legislative elections the harbinger of a more or a less tyrannical party system in Venezuela? Will the impeachment of Carlos Andrés Pérez result in greater accountability of Venezuelan politicians? Will the Venezuelan party system become more open and representative as a result of the 1993 elections, in which new political parties achieved major gains despite the presidential victory of former COPEI leader Rafael Caldera? Will the serious economic reforms already under way provide for those citizens most adversely affected by the free-market economy? Will the Venezuelan armed forces resist the temptation to meddle in politics, despite the nation's economic and political problems? These are questions that will be answered by the choices Venezuelan citizens and their political leaders make in the years to come.

Certain lessons become particularly apparent as we examine the events of the early 1990s. Indeed, the case of Venezuela carries with it the possible signals that might trigger other such erosions of democratic transitions, but it also carries the hope that citizens are beginning to respond to situations where political parties and political leaders have failed. Citizen participation in all areas of political decision making may ultimately yield institutions that respond to the real public interest rather than the interests of party elites. The following are some lessons that can be derived from the case of Venezuela.

*Lesson One: Public confidence in civilian leadership is dependent on honest government and the public perception of accountability.* Allegations of corruption at the highest level of Pérez's government constantly undermined public confidence already weakened by years—including the first Pérez administration—of blatant and shameless cronyism. The difficult austerity program adopted by Pérez in 1989 as part of the effort to reform Venezuela's economic system required sacrifices from all citizens. With the implementation of the new policies, though corruption probably declined after 1989 (as both John Martz and Rogelio Pérez Perdomo argue here), the public perception of an elected government of corrupt leaders lingered. New political parties that focus on this theme may be more successful in pushing the issue of anticorruption to the forefront of political debate. Similarly, new citizens' groups that stress transparency in government also have had some success in beginning the deliberative process that makes reform possible. In particular, citizens organized around the December 1992 municipal elections to oversee the process. Stressing the need to combat fraud in voter choice, these new groups will continue to play an important monitoring function in future elections in a way Venezuelan leaders have never before experienced. Such efforts are not limited to Venezuela. In Argentina, for example, reform factions of the two major parties have raised the banner of transparency as a means of distinguishing themselves in the voters' minds from older leaders, without losing the backing that the party label might provide.

There is a growing popular revolt in Latin America against politicians who steal. In Venezuela, even as former President Pérez denounced the military rebels as "fascists," people on the streets cheered the rebellion as a strike against politicians who had robbed large sums of the nation's oil wealth. Similarly, honest government became a leitmotif for the Peruvian government of Alberto Fujimori, who used the notion as a rationale for closing down Congress and the courts in April 1992. The positive reaction to Fujimori's *autogolpe* (self-coup) showed that the traditional institutions had alienated a large segment of the population and discredited the democratic process through their corruption and incompetence. The downfall of President Fernando Collor in Brazil on charges of personal enrichment and the overwhelming support for his impeachment are another example of the importance of the public perception of clean government in winning popular support for democratic government. Finally, the early 1993 revolt against corrupt politicians in Guatemala saw President Jorge Serrano unsuccessfully attempting to follow Fujimori and shut down government institutions under the banner of the fight against corruption. The popularity of Serrano's successor, Ramiro de León Carpio, soared with his effort to force the resignation of corrupt members of the legislature. The real lesson of all of these examples is that Latin Americans may be willing to forego some of their democratic gains in return for the implementation of more austere solutions to rampant corruption, or in other words, military uprisings to cleanse the political process.[25]

*Lesson Two: In the process of economic and political reform, it is essential to communicate effectively with the public and to avoid raising expectations to unrealistic heights.* The Venezuelan experience dramatically illustrates the importance that expectations play in the process of reform. As described by Ricardo Hausmann, the Pérez government surprised the public with a reform program that ran counter to what people had come to expect from Pérez and to what they had been accustomed to for years. The reaction was violent and the government responded by promising too much, too soon. In arrogant fashion, the government failed to devote sufficient attention to the need to communicate effectively with the population and to design new messages, new forms of communication, and new ways of interacting with the public. New economic policies may or may not require new institutions, but they certainly require new political tactics and behavior. This was brought home clearly when the sharply declining levels of government popularity proved immune to the good news of Venezuela's having one of the world's highest growth rates or its extraordinary stock market performance and unprecedented achievements in foreign investment and export growth. Perhaps improved public services, a lower probability of being mugged in the street, or even a more consistent effort at reducing the moral indignation that was spreading throughout the country might have brought more stability than did sound macroeconomic indexes.

In this regard the government of Carlos Menem of Argentina serves as a good example, because it appears to have paid more attention to public perceptions and the results have been favorable. Since inflation was considered the principal obstacle to macroeconomic stability and inflationary expectations the most difficult problem for the government to solve, Argentine economic minister Domingo Cavallo decided to demonstrate the government's resolve by making the exchange rate and the restriction on the government's power to print money a matter of law. Even at the cost of considerable policy flexibility down the road, Cavallo argued that he could not begin his ambitious privatization program or attract foreign investment unless he confronted inflation. At the same time, he launched a public relations blitz in Argentina and the United States on the beginning of a new era in Argentina. Fiscal discipline was taken as public proof of the government's seriousness of purpose.

*Lesson Three: Given excessive access to and reliance on the wealth of the state, political parties can become informally privatized and lose their capacity to aggregate and articulate public preferences.* Much of Venezuela's political instability in the 1990s can be traced to the political parties' ceasing to provide an anchor for society when they became informally privatized. This process of political-party privatization was a result of the oil-financed, state-centered approach that began in the 1940s and deepened in the 1960s. As John Martz writes, the parties came to position themselves almost exclusively in the role of brokers between society and the state. With the increase in the scope of the state and with government involvement in all details of political and especially economic life, the Venezuelan brokers—political parties—moved from wholesale activity (influencing policy matters) to retail activity (influencing specific decisions or transactions). Given the loose control the parties had over their members, members found it easy, and then natural, to pursue brokerage functions on behalf of their private interests, as opposed to company, or party, interests. During the Lusinchi administration, for instance, it was well known that interest rates could not be increased even if the need to do so was critical because most members of AD's *cogollo* (the small group at the apex of the political parties that effectively controlled much of the country's political and economic life) had borrowed heavily from state banks and made a good business out of helping others gain access to the limited supply of underpriced loans.

As a result, ethics and other moral incentives used to recruit, promote, and otherwise manage a political party disappeared and the leadership was left with only material incentives as instruments of cohesion, persuasion, or control over the membership. These material incentives were drawn from the state and were possible largely as a result of budgetary laxity and interventionist policies. When the money dried up and economic reform moved the state from the center of economic life, removing the government's ability to support the brokerage activities of party members, the scheme collapsed and nothing was available to replace it. The government lost the support of its own party largely because the party lost the support of its membership, which now had to rely solely on economic incentives to operate. Members of Congress ceased to respond to the instructions of party elders, the leadership, or the *cogollos,* and any semblance of cohesion and party discipline disappeared. The previous scheme had also inhibited the emergence of civic traditions and social organization of the type long associated with stable democracies.

In short, as Daniel Levine and Brian Crisp make clear, when political parties exist on an excessive diet of "pork" for too long, they tend to become privatized de facto, relying too heavily on material incentives to recruit, retain, and manage members and abandoning other indispensable functions. They lose the capacity to utilize ideology and moral suasion to carry out traditional party functions, and they lose the capacity to be credible policy interlocutors when policies need to be analyzed and debated for the common good.

*Lesson Four: Decentralization and accountability—creating a sense of citizenship among the populace—are keys to democratic consolidation.* The growing support for smaller political parties in opposition to AD and COPEI was evident in the gubernatorial and mayoral races of December 1992. With those elections, it became clear that the strength of the two major parties could be preserved only if new political actors were allowed to become part of these two political machines. Electoral democracy can be sustained only if people believe they have legitimate choices. While Venezuelans continue to maintain steadfast support for the principles of democracy, the December 1992 vote reflected deep skepticism for elected officials and electoral institutions. To reverse this attitude, elected officials need to respond with improved government performance. The two major parties will need restructuring and grass-roots rebuilding efforts to regain public confidence. As Juan Carlos Navarro points out in his chapter, the new political actors in Venezuela will include neighborhood groups, watchdog organizations, and other nonparty actors who will grow stronger as political parties search for a way to reach out to new interests in Venezuelan society.

The consolidation of democracy in Latin America requires improved links between political parties and civil society. Decentralization without accountability does not take hold. In Chile, the country by far the most advanced in the process of democratic consolidation, the state has pushed hard to achieve meaningful decentralization of political power, including the power to tax, and has engaged in elaborate public discussions with local and regional political authorities. The major political parties were forced to respond to these reforms by developing their party organizations at the grass roots and by clearly demonstrating that they are relevant and appropriate for the new era. In Argentina, efforts by the Menem government to review elements of historic federalism by restoring functions to the provinces proved to be more complicated than anticipated and led to a series of adversarial encounters between the federal government and several provinces on matters of fiscal authority and judicial jurisdiction. In Mexico, the gradual allocation of responsibility and power to local political groups has contributed to the erosion of support once enjoyed by the Partido Revolucionario Democrático, the principal party of opposition to the government.

Decentralization and the separation of powers are not simple steps in the consolidation of democracy. They develop over time through constant public discussion. Dramatic change has occurred in Venezuela, where the *ley del sufragio,* or suffrage law, is moving the country to a more decentralized, representative democratic system. The creation of single members' districts, as opposed to voting for party slates, is a first step toward a more federal system and increased accountability. Likewise, the loss by AD and COPEI of gubernatorial seats to Causa R and the Movimiento al Socialismo (MAS) in the December 1992 elections indicates a growing desire on the part of Venezuelans to identify with local political leaders and institutions rather than with national entities.

*Lesson Five: The consolidation of democracy requires competitive, private, and unfettered media that responsibly serve the public interest.* Venezuela provides interesting insights into a phenomenon that is becoming increasingly salient throughout the region—the increasing political role of the media.[26] The shrinking of the state, the collapse of most public institutions, the elimination of national economic controls, and other factors that gave the government influence over the media have made businesspeople-cum-politicians-cum-media tycoons a major political force in the country. In Venezuela, as Andrew Templeton suggests, the media tycoons have replaced the *cogollos.* The growing importance of communications technology worldwide promises to strengthen this trend. A ravaged judicial system, a booming and reasonable demand to denounce and punish corruption, the lack of credibility of most institutions, and numerous elections that characterize a political system in the midst of decentralization and democratization give unprecedented and largely unchecked power to the mass media and those who control them.

Abuse of the right of freedom of the press inevitably contributes to public disorder and undermines efforts to consolidate a more open democratic political system. Although part of the solution to Venezuela's need for effective communication can be found in a more responsible approach by the media, other institutions must also play a part: professionalization of the media must become a goal of the media industry and the broader political system. Improved professional education and industry self-regulation can improve media performance. Perhaps more important will be the strengthening of the civil and political institutions that transmit information to and receive information from the mass media.

*Lesson Six: The social consequences of economic reform are politically significant and must be mediated through the political system and civil society.* The social consequences of economic restructuring must be understood as falling into two distinct categories with very different political repercussions. One effect is the increase in poverty, which Janet Kelly argues demands an effective response, even from a stripped-down, weakened state. The state cannot appear to be insensitive to the plight of the poorest of the poor. Poverty alleviation is an indispensable component of the program of a government committed to the substance of democracy, no matter how wedded it might be to privatization and restructuring. And, as Juan Carlos Navarro suggests, the alleviation of poverty can be facilitated most effectively at the local level through nongovernmental organizations or through the local and regional elements of the political parties. It is extremely hard to conduct effective distribution from the center of a political system, especially when a political party or the executive power of a federal government is weighted down with the tradition of its own corruption and inefficiency. The commitment to poverty relief became one of the most significant issues within the government of Patricio Aylwin in Chile. Before socialists and other progressives would agree to maintain for the 1994 elections the broad center-to-left alliance of political parties that won the presidency in 1990, the leading Christian Democratic candidates were required to commit themselves publicly to a concern for poverty.

The second category of social consequences has to do with the phenomenon of relative deprivation. As Andrew Templeton's chapter indicates, the Venezuelan case reminds us of how important it is to deal with people, even people who are fairly well off, who feel they are being deprived of the status and well-being that they once had or expected to have. Those who suffer such relative deprivation are the most vulnerable to appeals from antidemocratic political forces. The consolidation of democracy, especially during a period of economic restructuring, requires special attention to members of the middle class who feel themselves slipping in socioeconomic terms. These are people who normally participate in the political process. They must be given ample opportunity to articulate their views and their grievances through the political institutions of the consolidating democracy. Even in the United States during the presidential campaign of 1992, supporters of Bill Clinton rallied behind the slogan, "It's the economy, stupid." This was not the appeal of the poorest, but of those white-collar and other middle-class people who felt that they had suffered the worst effects of the long recession under the Reagan and Bush administrations. Whether they had or not is less important than their sense of having suffered and their need to express their grievance.

*Lesson Seven: The role of the military in the political system must be clarified and the institution must be able to express its institutional needs and interests through the constitutional process. To that end, a constant open dialogue must be maintained among the military, civil-political authority, and other sectors of civil society.* Ironically, we can see in retrospect that in Venezuela, the mission of the armed forces was as poorly articulated as it had been in Chile or Argentina, where the military was still retreating from its control over the state. There was serious confusion in the Venezuelan government as to the appropriate mission of the military and, as Felipe Agüero points out, serious problems resulting from political party influence in the armed forces. Although the Pérez government assumed the military's primary role was the defense of the territorial integrity of the nation, no one took that role seriously enough to discuss it regularly with the military hierarchy. Nor was there any effort to discuss the role of the military in public forums.

Even more serious, as Richard Millett and Winfield Burggraaff document, during the Carlos Andrés Pérez government there was virtually an abdication of responsibility by the civilian authorities of the management of the military. The Venezuelan military, now that it also includes the National Guard, contains seventy-one thousand members. Its size is troubling in a society where external threats do not merit so large a force structure. The military must not be a cushion for the unemployed who are displaced by the free-market reforms implemented by the state.

The level of civilian expertise in military matters, military education, the proper definition of the mission of the armed forces, and the role of the armed forces in the nation's security in subregional, regional, and global organizations are subjects of intense importance, especially in vulnerable democracies. As Agüero suggests, effective integration of the military into a consolidating democracy requires making the armed forces part of the normal conduct of democracy and assuring that civilian leaders take responsibility for the management of the institution. As democratic political conduct becomes more transparent and more accountable, so too the management of the military must become more transparent and accountable. To make that possible, the military must be made to feel that they are part of the constitutional process, not an adversarial estate held outside the political system.

## VOLUME SUMMARY

This book is organized in four sections. Part 1 discusses the major players in Venezuelan political life—political parties, the general public, the military, and new political forces—and the turmoil they have been experiencing in recent years. In chapter 1, John Martz examines the evolution and present status of the political party system in the context of political crisis. Given the more than three decades of stable and competitive elections, he explains, the events since 1989—riots, instability, coup attempts—are remarkable. But the failings of the party system, including democratic centralism, bureaucratization, and the complacent, corrupting leadership of entrenched elites, are undeniable. Moreover, the parties themselves are undergoing a process of deterioration. Martz concludes that sharp and tangible change in government performance is imperative if Venezuela's political difficulties are to be surmounted.

In chapter 2, Richard Millett and Winfield Burggraaff assess the events surrounding the two coup attempts of 1992. They describe the motivations of the Bolivariano rebels—both the factors most often mentioned by other observers and those the authors believe were probably the most influential. Significantly, despite thirty-four years of democratic rule, the Venezuelan armed forces retained the attitudes and mindsets of traditional Latin American militaries. Millett and Burggraaff explain that in addition to the systemic problems, the February 1992 uprising was facilitated by the tendency of most civilian and military leaders "to take the armed forces for granted, to assume that a coup was impossible." These authors conclude that the loss of credibility of civilian leadership more than any change in the military produced the failure of the country's civil-military relations.

Andrew Templeton discusses in chapter 3 the evolution of Venezuelan opinion. The primary basis for his study is a collection of opinion surveys conducted over the past twenty years. "Why was it," he asks, "that by early 1992 the gap between popular perceptions of the way Venezuela was and of the way Venezuelans felt it should have been had widened to such an alarming extent?" Templeton reports that the public most often cited economic discontent and dissatisfaction with corrupt and inefficient government as the cause for the February 1992 coup attempt. Survey results, Templeton concludes, point to long-standing public discontent on economic issues, dissatisfaction with the inefficiency of public administration, and disillusion with the capacity of existing institutions to resolve the nation's problems. Interestingly, at the end of 1992 nearly one-quarter of the Venezuelan population preferred a military candidate as the next president—but 80 percent were inclined toward a democratic system.

The emergence of new political actors is the subject of chapter 4, in which Juan Carlos Navarro develops a framework for understanding the roots, nature, and eventual future impact of these new players. The characteristics of these actors are varied: one organization seeks to increase the voice of the masses, another is concerned with professionalizing municipal management, and a business group calls for a market-oriented development strategy. Navarro also points out that the technocrats who played a prominent role in President Pérez's early economic reforms have political ambitions but have yet to form a political organization. These new actors may not fully mature politically for twenty years, and many of them share a belief in a limited party role and market-oriented economics. Their emergence or the pressures they generate against traditional actors, Navarro concludes, could provide the basis for momentous change in the political system.

In chapter 5, Felipe Agüero provides the first of two analyses of civil-military relations. According to Agüero, contrary to theories of democracy, Venezuela demonstrates that democratic government may nearly break down due to polarization—not among elites, but between mid-level officers and the political and military elites. Venezuela also shows what happens if civilian control fails to adjust to changing circumstances. Agüero reaches his conclusions through a review of three decades of civil-military relations under democratic rule, during which time relations moved from affirming democratic, civilian government to military institutional enhancement to a breakdown of discipline, ultimately setting the stage for an attempt to overthrow the elected government.

Part 2 of the book discusses the development of two major sectors of Venezuelan political and economic life, beginning with chapter 6 on the private sector. Moisés Naím and Antonio Francés address the impact on the private sector of the country's sudden shift to a market-oriented economy. Naím and Francés first provide an overview of the private sector, its traditional characteristics and political role, and then discuss its current status. "Venezuelan private firms will have to undergo an almost complete revamping of their traditional ways of doing business" as a result of the reforms, the authors note. Such change will take time, because the forces that are pushing firms forward will be partially offset by the inertia of the past. According to Naím and Francés, although it is too early to be definitive regarding the results of the Great Turnaround, it has injected a new dynamism into the private sector that will have to be controlled by the development of an effective regulatory framework.

In chapter 7, Jonathan Coles analyzes Venezuela's experience with agricultural reform. He provides a short discussion of past agricultural policy, considers the institutional actors traditionally involved, and examines the reforms implemented by President Pérez and the reaction to them. After a large drop in 1989, agricultural production recovered, despite the macroeconomic situation, bad weather, and political turmoil. Ironically, the February 1992 coup attempt served as a springboard to greater agricultural reform, allowing it to expand to a general restructuring of agrarian reform agencies. Coles argues that the traditional networks had been weakened by political dissension within AD and by the general dissatisfaction with politicians. Yet no sector was harder hit by the reform than agriculture, because it has been the most backward. Although change by shock treatment is "never the best way," Coles notes, it was necessary to force the adjustment to reality.

Part 3 focuses on various elements of the Venezuelan state, its history, recent development, failures, reform, and crises. Chapter 8, written by Daniel Levine and Brian Crisp, addresses the questions of state legitimacy, governability, and reform. Over the past twenty years Venezuela, like the rest of Latin America, has experienced an explosive growth of associational life, and the problems Venezuela has encountered in the 1990s all involve the relationship among this new "civil society," politics, and the state. Specifically, Levine and Crisp note, "the empowerment derived from civil society has only rarely been translated into enduring political organizations (not to mention power)." This popular movement has lost its political voice and lacks allies and clear channels of national representation. Strengthening Venezuelan democracy requires molding these new energies into a viable democratic project—that is, restoring both legitimacy and governability.

Ricardo Hausmann analyzes in chapter 9 Venezuela's resort to "quitting populism cold turkey," or to turning suddenly away from a long experience with an essentially populist economic policy. Faced with a host of severe macroeconomic imbalances, newly elected President Pérez radically shifted course in 1989. Hausmann addresses two central questions that he believes require consideration: What made Venezuela change course before the situation became totally uncontrollable and, since the results proved unpredictable, what can countries realistically expect from such macroeconomic reform packages? Hausmann finds that three important dynamics explain the politics of the economic adjustment: political forces appear to react with a lag, as evidenced by the February 1992 coup attempt; some politicians, such as former President Rafael Caldera, cater to the political forces expressed in such opposition; and finally, the lack of tax reform is at the root of fiscal and balance of payments problems.

In chapter 10, Janet Kelly assesses Venezuela's effort to develop an adequate social policy since 1958. She analyzes policy successes and failures, especially the impact of the reorientation of social policy with the Great Turnaround of 1989. The record shows that as long as oil income covered the cost, broadly based "shotgun strategies" to benefit the many were coupled with poor delivery that failed to respond to demands for improvement. The dismal results produced widespread doubts about the legitimacy of the political system. According to Kelly, the radical change of 1989 linked social policy to the market-oriented economic transformation. While Venezuelans would pay market prices, the poorest sectors, especially the basic needs of schoolchildren, were targeted for assistance. Lasting and effective change in social policy is not yet evident, and broad sectors of the population remain dubious. Ultimately, she argues, "greater equity will demand greater efficiency."

Corruption and the public perception of the problem are at the center of Venezuela's political crisis. In chapter 11, Rogelio Pérez Perdomo addresses this critical issue. "Corruption," he writes, "is regarded as one of the most serious threats to the functioning of the Venezuelan state and one of the principal destabilizing factors of the political system." Official corruption is attributable not to an increase in corruption as such, he adds, but to recent changes in the political system and the perception of the economic situation. Average citizens accept the myth that Venezuela is rich, so they reason that corruption must be to blame for economic austerity and declining public services. Also, the media bombard the public with new scandals and the mutual accusations of politicians, but no one of importance has been brought to justice. Pérez Perdomo's chapter provides an analysis of historical influences as well as contemporary factors contributing to corruption.

In chapter 12, Miriam Kornblith discusses the progress and role of constitutional reform in the midst of political crisis. In mid-1989, Venezuela launched the first thoroughgoing reform of the 1961 Constitution. Three years later, Kornblith argues, in the wake of the February

4, 1992, coup attempt, constitutional reform was at the center of the national debate—a major force for the stability of Venezuelan democracy. By the end of that debate, however, the constitutional issue was lost in the controversy surrounding the ongoing political crisis. Even so, Kornblith concludes, the debate served as an important institutional channel for the containment of political tension. Discarding the reform effort would further discredit democratic institutions, frustrate expectations of change, and weaken the present constitution.

Part 4 focuses on the international arena, specifically addressing Venezuela's foreign policy, the oil industry, and Venezuela's relations with the United States. In chapter 13, Andrés Serbín focuses on the transition in Venezuelan foreign policy arising from the changed domestic, political, and economic environment and the new international context. Oil and democracy will continue to be the hallmarks of the country's international identity—provided that constitutional government survives—since they are part of the national political culture. Venezuela's ability to promote that positive image internationally, however, is being lost due to domestic problems and the slump in the oil market. Serbín adds that Venezuela's international approach will be less consistent because of the need to reorient the economy, and that the events of 1992 have already redefined the president's role in international affairs and the high profile the country has maintained in the past.

Chapter 14, by Norman Bailey, examines the Venezuela–United States relationship within the context of energy policy, that is, the oil sector. From 1973 onward, Bailey observes, the United States has strengthened its strategic dependence on imported oil from the Persian Gulf states through conterproductive tax and subsidization oil policies. Had U.S. consumers paid free-market prices for oil, U.S., Canadian, and Latin American producers would be prospering and producing taxable wealth that would help relieve fiscal shortfalls. The good news is that the Venezuelan state oil company is well-run; the bad news is that the company is taxed punitively, Venezuela's gasoline prices are far too low, and the country remains part of the Organization of Petroleum Exporting Countries (OPEC). The two countries, Bailey concludes, must move to a close collaboration—he proposes a North American energy community—that will have more influence on the hemisphere than any other single factor.

Despite the best of efforts, time does not wait for a book to go to print, even an enlightening one on the lessons of the Venezuelan experience. Important events have occurred in Venezuela in recent months, from the time the manuscript first went to the copyeditor until the point at which final changes could be made. We therefore conclude this volume with an epilogue, the objectives of which are to bring the reader as up to date as possible on recent events and to enhance understanding of the issues raised in these pages by broadening the context for their discussion.

## THE FUTURE

One cannot conclude the introduction to a study of Venezuela without briefly noting that Venezuela's political system is likely to suffer from tremendous instability at least until the end of the century. Continuing turbulence will likely be fueled by the lack of consensus on economic policy, high expectations, persistent inequalities, weak (surprisingly enough) political parties, a rapacious media, a divided military, pampered elites, and a state that will be hard to rehabilitate—all of which are discussed in the following chapters. Meanwhile, the government is going to be constantly, and perhaps literally, under fire. At worst, Venezuela's democracy will continue to crumble or will fall in one swoop to another military uprising. Under such circumstances, the Clinton administration, the Organization of American States, and the rest of the international community would face a test of momentous proportions: helping restore democracy without further polarizing the nation. At best, Venezuela will be able to contain popular pressure for change as it continues to modernize its institutions and reform the economy, and thus succeed in preserving Latin America's second oldest democracy. It would be a terrible irony that, having long been exceptional for its democratic stability, Venezuela would end the century becoming exceptional again, this time for its political and economic instability.

## NOTES

1. See Robert Bond, ed., *Contemporary Venezuela and Its Role in International Affairs* (New York: New York University Press, 1977), and Sheldon Liss, *Diplomacy and Dependency* (Salisbury, N.C.: Documentary Publications, 1978).
2. Gross domestic product (GDP) per capita (1984 dollars): Inter-American Development Bank, *Economic and Social Progress in Latin America* (Washington, D.C.: Inter-American Development Bank, 1986).
3. In contrast to civilian indifference to Venezuela's armed forces, the Venezuelan military was active in inter-American military diplomacy, especially with respect to arms exchange and sales with the United States.

4. Foreign direct investment (FDI) in Venezuela was largely concentrated in oil and iron ore. When private companies in these sectors were nationalized, the importance of foreign capital became surprisingly small given the country's size and resources. The ratio of foreign capital to GDP for Venezuela in 1982 was 10 percent lower than the average for Latin America; see John Dunning and John Cantwell, *IRM Directory of Statistics of International Investment and Production* (New York: New York University Press, 1987). Only 3 percent of all manufacturing plants were foreign-owned in 1976 and that proportion did not increase during the 1980s. See World Bank Report no. 9028-VE, *Venezuela: Industrial Sector Report*, March 1991. In 1982, U.S. investment accounted for two-thirds of Venezuela's stock of FDI, yet it was only 5 percent of U.S. investment in Latin America; see Moisés Naím, "La empresa privada en Venezuela: Que pasa cuando se crece en medio de la abundancia y la confusión?" in Moisés Naím and Ramón Piñango, eds., *El caso Venezuela: Una ilusión de armonía* 4th ed. (Caracas: Ediciones IESA, 1988), 270.

5. See Franklin Tugwell, *The Politics of Oil in Venezuela* (Stanford: Stanford University Press, 1975); Terry L. Karl, *The Paradox of Plenty: Oil Booms and Petro-States* (Berkeley: University of California Press, 1991); and Gustavo Coronel, *The Nationalization of the Venezuelan Oil Industry: From Technocratic Success to Political Failure* (Lexington, Mass.: Lexington Books, 1993).

6. See Guillermo O'Donnell, *Modernization and Bureaucratic-Authoritarianism: Studies in South American Politics* (Berkeley: University of California Press, 1973).

7. For examples of seminal works analyzing dependent development, see Osvaldo Sunkel, "National Development Policy and External Dependence in Latin America," *Journal of Development Studies* 6, no. 1 (1969): 23–48; André Gunder Frank, *Capitalism and Underdevelopment in Latin America* (New York: Monthly Review Press, 1967); and Fernando Henrique Cardoso and Enzo Faletto, *Dependency and Development in Latin America* (Berkeley: University of California Press, 1979).

8. Where they did focus on Venezuela, as in Napoleon Chagnon's studies of the Yanamano, an aggressive primitive tribe located in the Venezuelan Amazon, the work never was linked with Venezuelan politics.

9. For example, there was no chapter on Venezuela included in two influential compendiums on politics in Latin America published in the 1970s: Juan Linz and Alfred Stepan, eds., *The Breakdown of Democratic Regimes* (Baltimore: Johns Hopkins University Press, 1978), and David Collier, *The New Authoritarianism in Latin America* (Princeton: Princeton University Press, 1979). Venezuela is included, however, in Guillermo O'Donnell, Philippe C. Schmitter, and Laurence Whitehead, eds., *Transitions from Authoritarian Rule: Latin America* (Baltimore: Johns Hopkins University Press, 1986), and in Larry Diamond, Juan J. Linz, and Seymour Martin Lipset, eds., *Democracy in Developing Countries: Latin America* (Boulder: Lynne Rienner, 1989).

10. The best scholarship on Venezuela in this period can be found in John D. Martz and David J. Meyers, eds., *Venezuela: The Democratic Experience* (New York: Praeger, 1977).

11. This point is discussed in Terry L. Karl, "Petroleum and Political Pacts in Transition to Democracy in Venezuela," *Latin American Research Review* 22, no. 1 (1986): 63–94, and idem, "Dilemmas of Democratization in Latin America," *Comparative Politics* 23, no. 1 (1990): 1–21.

12. The Pact of Punto Fijo is discussed in Felipe Agüero, "The Military and Democracy in Venezuela," and the general political inadequacy of civil-military pacts is discussed in Gabriel Aguilera Peralta, "The Armed Forces, Democracy and Transitions in Central America," both of which are in Louis W. Goodman, Johanna S. R. Mendelson, and Juan Rial, eds., *The Military and Democracy: The Future of Civil-Military Relations in Latin America* (Lexington, Mass.: Lexington Books, 1990), 23–38, 257–75.

13. See Robert A. Dahl, *Democracy and Its Critics* (New Haven: Yale University Press, 1989), and Samuel P. Huntington, *The Third Wave: Democratization in the Late Twentieth Century* (Norman: University of Oklahoma Press, 1991).

14. See Terry Lynn Karl, "Petroleum and Political Pacts: The Transition to Democracy in Venezuela," in O'Donnell, Schmitter, and Whitehead, *Transitions from Authoritarian Rule*, 196–219.

15. See, for example, Michael Burton, Richard Gunther, and John Higley, "Introduction: Elite Transformation and Democratic Regimes," in John Higley and Richard Gunther, eds., *Elites and Democratic Consolidation in Latin America and Southern Europe* (Cambridge: Cambridge University Press, 1992), 1–37; Daniel H. Levine, "Venezuela since 1958: The Consolidation of Democratic Politics," in Linz and Stepan, *The Breakdown of Democratic Regimes*, 82–109; and Enrique A. Baloyra, "Conclusion: Toward a Framework for the Study of Democratic Consolidation," in Enrique A. Baloyra, ed., *Comparing New Democracies: Transition and Consolidation in Mediterranean Europe and the Southern Cone* (Boulder: Westview Press, 1987), 297–302.

16. Adrian Leftwich, "Governance, Democracy and Development in the Third World," *Third World Quarterly* 14 (1993): 605–24.

17. See Dahl, *Democracy and Its Critics*, 311, and Huntington, *The Third Wave*, 165.

18. L. Sirowy and A. Inkeles, "The Effects of Democracy on Economic Growth and Inequality: A Review," *Studies in Comparative International Development* 25, no. 1 (1990): 126–57, and C. Tilly, "Does Modernization Breed Revolution?" *Comparative Politics* 5 (1973): 425–47.

19. "The Illusion of Harmony" is the subtitle of an influential book published in Venezuela in the early 1980s assessing the country's situation. The book concluded that Venezuela's extreme changes were not accompanied by the typical conflicts that tended to surface in other countries, and that this lack of conflict was largely illusory; see Naím and Piñango, *El caso Venezuela*.

20. Maurice Duverger, *Les partis politiques* (Paris: Armand Colin, 1951; New York: John Wiley and Sons, 1954), 425.

21. See Naím and Piñango, *El caso Venezuela*, 547.

22. Joseph S. Tulchin with Gary Bland, eds., *Venezuela in the Wake of Radical Reform* (Boulder: Lynne Rienner, 1993).

23. Moisés Naím, *Paper Tigers and Minotaurs: The Politics of Venezuela's Economic Reforms* (Washington, D.C.: Carnegie Endowment for International Peace and Brookings Institution, 1993).

24. COPRE, *La Reforma del Estado* (Caracas: Comisión Presidencial para la Reforma del Estado, 1988).

25. See, for example, James Brooke, "A Radical Idea Sweeps Latin America: Honest Government," *New York Times*, August 30, 1992, 5.

26. For a discussion of the role of the electronic media in the transition to democracy, see Thomas E. Skidmore, ed., *Television and Democracy in Latin America* (Baltimore: Johns Hopkins University Press, 1993).

# I
# The Players

# 1

# Political Parties and the Democratic Crisis

*John D. Martz*

Scribes have recorded the 1950s in Latin America as a period when authoritarianism held sway in the majority of nations. It was only toward the close of the decade that it became possible to write of a "twilight of tyrants," one which seemingly presaged the emergence of genuine democracies.[1] In Venezuela, ten years of brutal dictatorship ended in January 1958 with the flight of Gen. Marcos Pérez Jiménez. Within the year, competitive national elections initiated the nation's modern experience with democracy. Few observers would have predicted that the system would remain intact for the next third of a century, or that Venezuela would emerge as a thriving and vigorous champion of democratic government. Yet that is precisely what happened, and the political parties were central to this evolution.

Given this political backdrop, the convulsive drama that has unfolded since 1989 leaves the observer incredulous. A few short weeks after the internationally bedazzling inauguration of the popular Carlos Andrés Pérez for a second, nonsuccessive presidency,[2] protest demonstrations and unorganized mob violence wracked Caracas. The final toll, even in the most conservative estimates, ran to three hundred dead and more than one thousand injured. Although the government preferred to treat the outburst as an aberration, the upheaval laid bare the complaints of a public unaccustomed to the economic decline of recent years. The inadequate response by both the government and the parties contributed to the even more startling and unexpected military uprising in February 1992, which sought not only the ouster of the government but also the purging via public execution of the nation's top political leadership. Still another armed rebellion by a group of disillusioned army personnel in November 1992 further underlined regime instability. What was the role of the political parties in this progressive decaying of the political system? How did the leadership fail to sustain the participatory commitment of earlier years? And what does this tell us in general about political parties and the institutionalization of democracy in Latin America?

Certainly the failures of the parties were only a part of the picture. These destabilizing events, largely unanticipated at the outset, reflected prolonged economic decline, unchecked corruption, and concomitant social unrest, all of which alienated ordinary Venezuelans. Yet the deterioration of the parties was central to national unrest. From the inception of the democratic system it could be argued that "Venezuelan parties provide adequate channels for discontent; response to public demand is ordinarily perceptible."[3] In 1976, Enrique A. Baloyra joined me in a two-volume publication that was premised largely on the dominant influence and power of the parties.[4] The progressive increase in party elitism, however, enshrined in the exclusivistic practice of democratic centralism, gave cause for greater concern as the 1980s ran their course. Terms such as *petrification* and *malaise* crept into the vernacular.[5] It was apparent that the parties were decreasingly responsive to the public, and even the putative movement toward *apertura* (political opening) and reform gave little cause for optimism.[6]

## DEMOCRACY AND THE PARTY SYSTEM: THE PARTICIPATORY VISION

*The Early Years of Multiparty Factionalism*

At the outset of the Venezuelan democratic experience there were four parties: Acción Democrática (AD), founded in 1941; the Unión Republicana Democrática (URD) and Committee for Political Organization and Independent Election (COPEI), both formed in 1946; and the Partido Comunista de Venezuela (PCV), initiated in 1931. All but the last of these negotiated the Pact of Punto Fijo in 1958, which pledged a mutual commitment to democracy and to a common set of principles.[7] This obligated the signatories to a long-term policy assuring a responsible democratic process. The political truce was designed to diminish partisanship and avoid violence. The economic interests of the masses were to be incorporated through the mechanism of the parties, thereby promoting participatory activism while further enhancing the role of the parties. Rómulo Betancourt of Acción Democrática, victor in the 1958 elections, initiated the Punto Fijo model by incorporating both *copeyanos* (members of the COPEI party) and *urredistas* (members of the URD party) into his government. Jóvito Villalba pulled out the URD early on, but COPEI remained as loyal junior partner to the AD during a period of intransigent *fidelista* insurgency. Within the first five years of democracy, the AD had suffered two schisms, Villalba had driven leaders of the URD's younger generation out of the party, and new personalistic parties had appeared on the scene.

By 1968 the list of presidential candidates had grown longer and the number of party legislative slates had also increased. The system had fragmented, and proliferation reflected traditional *caudillismo* rather than legitimate doctrinal orientations and identifiable electoral constituencies. The single most disruptive occurrence was the third division of Acción Democrática, which tore it down the middle. This rift was accompanied by rival candidacies from the newly formed Movimiento Electoral del Pueblo (MEP) and the AD old guard, thereby opening the door to the narrow victory by COPEI's Rafael Caldera with only 29 percent of the vote. If not for the division, AD would have maintained its unbeaten electoral record while polling from 40 to 50 percent of the vote, and the history of the Venezuelan parties might well have been very different. As it was, Venezuelan democracy was strengthened by its first surrender of power by an elected government to a successor chosen from the opposition. In the process COPEI achieved legitimacy as a genuine popular alternative, while AD learned to function as leader of the democratic opposition. Furthermore, with the effective collapse of Venezuela's revolutionary marxist movement, electoral legitimacy was extended to the Communists and to such other leftist groups as the Movimiento al Socialismo (MAS) and the Movimiento de Izquierda Revolucionaria (MIR), each of which would run its own candidates by 1973. The entire system was opened to more extensive grass-roots involvement. The participatory vision of Venezuela's founding party leaders had led to a freedom of political action previously alien to national history. At the same time, it remained to be seen whether the country's highly fragmented party system could support the effective functioning of a strong, centralized presidential regime.

*Biparty Hegemony*

The failure of small parties on both the Right and the Left to form electoral coalitions produced a plethora of parties and candidacies in 1973. However, the public was readily persuaded not to waste its votes on secondary contenders. As a result, COPEI and AD dominated the electorate; since 1973 the two parties customarily polled from 80 to 90 percent of the valid vote, while maintaining a pattern of hegemonic turnover. The occupancy of Miraflores Palace, the seat of the president, shifted from COPEI to AD in 1973, back to COPEI in 1978, and once again to AD in 1983. Only with the 1988 victory of Carlos Andrés Pérez did the opposition fail to unseat the incumbent party. The spirit of Punto Fijo was gradually transformed into a comfortable partnership between the two parties.

The wealth and power of COPEI and AD effectively shut out all lesser rivals. Internal disputes were settled through compromise and bargaining. Party elites concentrated on maintaining a stability protective of the status quo, and the earlier emphasis on participation and attention to the grass roots gradually diminished. Ideological and doctrinal preoccupations also declined. Periodic calls for a modernization of party ideology did little to renew values, principles, and programs. The differences between COPEI and AD were blurred: the former (from its origins on the Right) and the latter (from its early leftist leanings) moved toward a broad center where electoral differences were more matters of personality or party loyalty than of meaningful and distinctive choices.

The fact of two-party domination after 1973 unquestionably provided solidity to the party system and suggested a further consolidation of the democratic process. The parties, with direct ties to labor, education, and peasant organizations, combined these alliances with linkages to business and finance as a means of assuring their centrality to politics and governance in Venezuela. With these liaisons, however, emerged a fragmentation or waning of earlier participatory values—envisioned by the founders of the system in both idealistic and pragmatic terms as basic to the future of the nation—which was symptomatic of the growing abyss between the pueblo and its leadership. Party elitism allowed a diminution of attention to grass-roots sentiment, accompanied by an inability at both the party and the governmental levels to anticipate popular demands and respond accordingly. Party loyalties began to falter, the leadership grew self-satisfied in defense of the status quo, and the capacity for governance came into question increasingly as the well-being of the democratic system pursued a path that threatened to end in decay.

## The Military Connection

The complacency that failed to recognize the shortcomings of the democratic system was further nourished by the successful incorporation of the armed forces as defenders of the political order after 1958. The founders of the new regime, eminently sensitive to military sentiment after having spent a decade of persecution at the hands of the dictatorship, labored long and hard over the reorganization and revitalization of the institution. President Betancourt masterfully socialized the military into an activist role on behalf of constitutionality and systemic legitimacy. His personal presidential touch was skillfully applied, and subsequent chiefs of state carefully courted the commanders of the services. The parties shared the conviction that the armed forces had a positive role to play in national affairs. Consequently, the independence of the military was assured, even though senior officers were often unofficially identified as partisans of either AD or COPEI.

The armed insurgency by *fidelista* revolutionaries in the early 1960s provided the military with a clear objective, and one consonant with the goals of democratization. Once this challenge had been rebuffed, attention was directed toward civic action and nation-building projects, although by the 1980s there were few specific objectives beyond the basic obligation of defending the nation's sovereignty and territorial integrity. A degree of politicization also crept into the armed forces, for the annual approval of senior promotions required congressional approval. Although the purpose of this process had been to strengthen civilian control, in practice it meant that ties with the parties, if informal rather than official, exercised some influence at higher levels. The rotation of senior officers every year, while broadening and invigorating the top leadership, also made it difficult to build more than superficial loyalty to any one minister of defense, chief of the general staff, or service commander. Thus although the parties had been successful in defining and building a military role that rested on allegiance to civilian authority, they could not automatically assume unthinking obedience from the armed forces. Just as the weaknesses of the parties were largely ignored, so it was that grievances and complaints from the military were also put aside as unworthy of serious attention.

## INTERNAL PARTY CHARACTERISTICS: EMERGENT ELITISM

### The Structures of Democratic Centralism

Organizationally, the emergence of modern, mass-based parties in Venezuela was accompanied by detailed and carefully articulated structures. As introduced and first implemented by AD, these were intended to maximize civic participation and to guarantee a constant flow of information and opinion from the bottom up. Betancourt, whose concepts of organizational architecture had taken shape even before the official founding of AD in September 1941, believed that party offices and activities should reach the furthermost corners of the republic. If the party were properly attuned to the masses, its activities should be unending, rather than limited merely to periodic exercises in electoral *struc+ure*

democracy. Discussion of local issues, sports and social activities, printing and distribution of political literature, membership recruitment—
all were intended to stimulate participatory democracy within the party,
as well as carry over to the nation at large. For AD, before and after its
1948–1958 decade in political exile, the basic organizational structure
was aimed at encouraging both civic participation and an efficient and
responsive functioning of the party itself.

AD

Ultimate authority within AD was vested in the national party convention, while the Comité Ejecutivo Nacional (CEN), or National Executive Committee, was assigned responsibility for implementation of convention decisions and for daily party operations. Membership in the
CEN was extended to the heads of functional secretariats such as labor,
peasantry, youth, and education; other members included the party
president and two vice presidents, secretary general, secretary of organization, and political secretaries (without portfolio). In addition, a
similar if less extensive structure existed at state and local levels. AD's
early successes were not lost on COPEI, which developed similar structures in moving beyond its original status as a regionally based party
with little electoral strength beyond the three Andean states. By the
time of Caldera's successful presidential bid in 1968, COPEI had extended its network significantly. While there were some organizational
differences from AD, COPEI also subscribed to the basic concept of a
carefully elaborated machine that would stimulate and strengthen popular participation. Parties that disregarded such requirements of modern mass movements fell by the wayside.

The successful parties, then, learned the necessity of effective organization. They also shared a belief in the importance of understanding
and heeding public opinion while supporting the political participation
of the rank and file. Both in theory and in practice, internal democracy
was recognized as mandatory if a party were to contribute constructively
to governance and to systemic political democracy. With the passing of
time, however, the Venezuelan parties displayed a growing proclivity toward elitist decision making and toward a bureaucratized democratic
centralism. This was evidenced by the process of candidate selection for
both the presidency and Congress.

## Controlling Candidate Selection

Few activities are more important, and potentially more sensitive, than
the choice of presidential candidates. An initial institutionalization of
the process occurred early in the democratic era, and grass-roots sentiment exerted a powerful influence. A prime example was 1963, when

President Betancourt believed that the fragility of the system dictated a coalition candidate supported by both AD and COPEI. Yet delegates to the AD national convention preferred a true *adeco* (a member of the AD party), thus producing the nomination and subsequent election of Raúl Leoni. There were few such differences in COPEI, where party founder Caldera was the popular choice in successive elections until he prevailed in 1968. Competition to succeed him produced a struggle five years later, but Lorenzo Fernández was the choice of both the convention and Caldera over Luis Herrera Campíns. The latter accepted his loss and returned victoriously five years later. Not until 1988 was there serious internal difficulty for the *copeyanos.*

For Acción Democrática the process of selecting candidates has been more irregular and even disruptive, although there has generally been a blend of elitist control and mass sentiment. The divisive 1967–68 confrontation was a classic illustration, when two leaders of the party's founding generation sought the candidacy. AD President Luis B. Prieto enjoyed great popular support, while Secretary General Gonzalo Barrios controlled the party machinery. The attempt at a party primary ended in violence and controversy. Despite his popularity Prieto was denied the nomination, provoking his defection and founding of the MEP. The AD rift was fundamental to Caldera's victory. Five years later, former President Betancourt was constitutionally eligible for another term but rejected this option; persuading Barrios not to try again, he orchestrated the passing of the torch to Carlos Andrés Pérez and a new generation of leaders.

Since that time the *adeco* rank and file has continued to be influential, although at the same time party elites have sought to control the process and avoid any renewal of internecine feuding. Luis Piñerua Ordaz was nominated in 1978 despite the unofficial opposition of Pérez; in 1983 Jaime Lusinchi prevailed, although only after a contested primary. In 1988 former President Pérez sought renomination AD against the determined opposition of President Lusinchi and the AD party leadership. The Pérez charisma was pitted against the power brokers, who activated the *maquinaria* (machinery) of party and government on behalf of Octavio Lepage, a longtime party stalwart. Fearful of uncontrolled internal strife, party leaders and Pérez's representatives negotiated a quasielectoral college whose membership numbered in the thousands. They sought to curb the exuberance of *carlosandresista* supporters while avoiding undue interference by party elites. The two-to-one margin for Pérez paved the way for a united party effort in general elections.[8]

On the whole, the choice of presidential candidates has reflected sen-

Elitist Control

timent among the party membership. Elitist control has proven far more decisive, however, in the selection of congressional candidates. Democratic centralism has operated without challenge, relying on the electoral system established at the beginning of the democratic era: proportional representation and voting by lists, which permits party leaders to monopolize the process. The CEN names candidates as well as dictates their place on the state list. Party discipline is rigorously invoked, and the authority of the leadership underlines the eminently elitist functioning of democratic centralism in the present system.[9] Moreover, the introduction of separate municipal elections in 1978 left the power of party elites untouched. In COPEI, for example, party statutes specify that the central committee has the authority to name one-third of the candidates on any given list. The more recent electoral law establishing separate races for state governors has been tested only twice—in 1989 and 1992—but the limited experience has not suggested any significant reduction in the continuing domination by party elites.

### Bureaucratization and Immobilism

Over the years the party bureaucracies have continued to grow. The introduction of new blood into the ranks of leadership has not been accompanied by a comparable number of retirements; political veterans tend to stay in harness. Meanwhile, party duties expand and bureaucratic niches proliferate. In the senior leadership alone, numbers have swollen. For example, in 1963 there were twenty-two members of the AD's Comité Ejecutivo Nacional; a quarter-century later there were some three dozen. Political secretaries (secretaries without portfolio) have increased, while the functional bureaus have also grown. The latter customarily have their own headquarters and staff, vying with one another for prestige, power, and financial support inside the organization.

Bureaucratization has also encouraged the evolution of individual fiefdoms representing a wide variety of particularized interests. Among the most powerful are those from the national labor movement, Confederación de Trabajadores de Venezuela (CTV).[10] The peasant movement, Federación Campesina de Venezuela (FCV), is another such example, if less influential than the CTV. There is also a host of other specialized groupings; both COPEI and AD, then, are multiclass parties incorporating a wide variety of constituencies and interests.

Theoretically these liaisons could be intended to assure close ties with the public and a keen sensitivity to public opinion—such was the hope of Betancourt and the founding generation of Acción Democrática. Progressive bureaucratization, buttressed by the sharing of power with COPEI, however, has resulted in an organizational hardening of the arteries. The leadership has spent much of its time and energy in the struggle for primacy within the party. The *cogollito*, or inner circle, is constantly awash with the brokering of power through informal understandings. The elites continually seek to maximize control over their own special constituencies in order to enhance their bargaining positions.                                                    *COPEI*

For COPEI, the trends have been less pronounced but nonetheless broadly similar to those in AD. Traditionally COPEI has had greater centralization, given the personal role of Caldera. The original leadership that accompanied Caldera was highly talented and over time contributed to the molding of a mass-based party with a responsive organization. In addition, its second generation emerged after a rich apprenticeship under the guidance of Caldera and his associates. COPEI avoided the internal feuding that was rampant within AD and that cost the latter rising young leaders who departed the party in the *mirista* (a member of the MIR party), *arsista* (a member of the Causa R party), and *mepista* (a member of the MEP party) divisions. The *copeyano* organization was somewhat less broad than its rivals, for the Social Christians have lacked the domination of the labor and peasant movements that are part of the AD tradition.

COPEI's leadership has also moved away from the grass roots over time, however, even as its leadership has been more tightly knit than that of AD. This was sharply dramatized when Caldera's longtime protégé, Eduardo Fernández, won the secretary generalship and asserted organizational primacy on behalf of Caldera's bid for a second presidential term in 1983. When Fernández then became the 1988 party nominee despite Caldera's own plans, his rigorous hold on the Social Christian machinery became apparent. Fernández's organizational stranglehold frustrated the stature and personal prestige of the former president, and allowed Fernández to retain control of the party even after his 1988 electoral defeat.

Such internal competition has little to do with doctrinal or ideological questions and is an unanticipated structural consequence of the Pact of Punto Fijo. The parties concentrated attention on the operation of their *maquinaria*. The loss of prestige by party elites was inevitable and became associated in the eyes of the public with systemic bureaucratization and the corruption of the state. As a prominent Venezuelan analyst noted, by the start of the 1990s the parties were preoccupied with preservation of the regime, whatever the shortcomings of performance; such was the "predominantly institutional orientation" that had evolved.[11]

# THE MYOPIA OF TRADITIONALISM AND RELUCTANT REFORMISM

## Systemic Adjustment

During the years of regime consolidation, Venezuelans took pride in their evolving democracy. This was manifest in 1964 when, for the first time in history, a popularly elected president completed his constitutional term and delivered power to another popularly elected president (Betancourt to Leoni). Five years later came the first democratic transferral of power from government to opposition (Leoni to Caldera). Popular support also deepened as the economy progressed and biparty hegemony produced a diminution of disorderly and unproductive multipartism. As early as the 1970s, however, public discontent began to surface. Imperceptibly at first, public opinion began to register disappointment over the performance of the system. To be sure, there was strong opposition to military rule, and the appeals of the Left were widely rejected; however, politicians were viewed with relative skepticism, as was true of the parties.

As political elites gradually grew aware of imperfections in the constitution of 1961, however, attention was directed toward a relaxation of local and regional elections, which were broken away from the national vote. According to existing arrangements, only once every five years did the citizen go to the voting booths. He or she would cast two ballots— the large for the presidential choice and the small for the predetermined party lists of senators, deputies, and officials at lower levels. In August 1978, selection of *concejales* (town councillors) was rescheduled for a date six months after national elections. This permitted greater attention to the local races, but party authority was protected by the process of candidate selection through the list system. In addition, state governors continued to be presidential appointees, which meant, in effect, that presidents chose on the basis of practical politics rather than state-based needs and demands.

## The Shaping of Apertura

Both COPEI and Acción Democrática began to recognize signs of public discontent, especially concerning the decline of the economy. For the Social Christians, this had been suggested by the resounding 1983 defeat of Caldera despite the esteem in which he was still held by most Venezuelans. AD, once again in power, sought to strengthen its position and press its advantage over the opposition. In December 1984, less than a year after his inauguration, Lusinchi established a blue-ribbon presidential commission for the reform of the state, the Comisión

Presidencial para la Reforma del Estado (COPRE). It was empowered to develop political and economic reforms, including direct elections of state governors, revised provisions for municipal administration, a variety of judicial reforms, and the financing of the parties.[12] With greater civic participation and broad systemic democratization at the core of its mandate, COPRE moved slowly but seriously toward a detailed set of recommendations. On October 10, 1988, a new organic law governing the municipalities was adopted. As subsequently modified on June 15 of the following year, elections for *concejales* were changed to permit the introduction of open lists at the local level.

COPRE had already issued a report in December 1988, following the election but prior to the inauguration of Pérez. The president-elect had also spoken out in strong if general terms about *apertura* during his campaign. The commission was urged to flesh out details missing from the original *reforma del estado* and to undertake a publicity campaign to attract popular support. COPRE President Carlos Blanco, who enjoyed ministerial status, summarized the projected reforms as comprising six fundamental objectives: political reforms, decentralization, administrative modernization, modernization of the legal system, modernization of public policies, and the development of civil society.[13]

COPRE's labors were to bear little fruit in several areas, but one concrete result was the definitive establishment of direct elections at the state and local levels. Government initiative, with the backing of the parties, led to congressional action to legitimize this reform. On December 3, 1989, state and local offices were contested for the first time in Venezuelan history. Municipal councillors were elected in 269 localities, while the newly created office of mayor appeared on the ballot, as did gubernatorial seats. Although the parties were important in the naming of candidates, the elections themselves were based on individual aspirants rather than party lists. Coming just a year after Pérez's reelection and ten months after the February rioting, Acción Democrática lost nearly half of the contested governorships and many of the local races as well.

Despite the historic character of the voting and the continuing requirement that all citizens vote, the Consejo Supremo Electoral reported an abstention rate of 53 percent. Many of the projected revisions, especially as elaborated under the label of "political reforms," required revisions of internal party rules and regulations. Such matters as candidate selection, the renewal of party leaders, campaign finances, and a general democratization of internal party operations were all dependent on the realization of *adeco* and *copeyano* elites that they and the national political system were each imperiled by inaction. So rigidly encrusted was this leadership, however, that only the most dire expressions of popular protest were likely to shake the myopia of traditionalism.

# WARNING SIGNALS IGNORED: DEMOCRACY AT THE BRINK

## Mistaken Messages and the 1988 Campaign

The level of public discontent with Venezuelan parties and politicians did not prove integral to the 1988 campaign, owing in no small part to the expectations aroused by the return of Carlos Andrés Pérez. The former president did not promise a repetition of his first term, when the petrobolivares had flowed. Although he declared that the situation was different, that times would not improve overnight, and that sacrifice would be necessary, public perceptions inevitably harked back to the good old days of the 1970s. Furthermore, Pérez often turned his campaign rallies into celebrations of personality rather than program.[14] His solid victory constituted a vote of confidence in his personal capacity to turn the country around in swift and dramatic fashion. This had not been his specific campaign message, but circumstances assured high expectations. A poll commissioned by the Pérez team conducted in late January of 1989 showed that voters expected an improvement within six months, and nearly one-third were confident that conditions would improve within a year.

The economic situation confronting the new government was far graver than had been expected. President Lusinchi had badly mismanaged the economy, including the payment of some U.S.$5.6 billion to service an unnecessarily disproportionate foreign debt. An import policy featuring subsidized exchange rates for dollars had enriched Lusinchi's friends while further shrinking the treasury. During his final months in office Lusinchi, anxious to assure his lasting popularity, engaged in financial extravagances and deficit spending that was more than generous. Resentful of Pérez as well, he had withheld information about economic and fiscal commitments from his successor. Consequently, Pérez and his advisers were unprepared for the magnitude of the problems they faced on taking office. The nation's reserves were largely depleted, the foreign debt was approaching U.S.$35 billion, the inflation rate was nearly 100 percent, and the cash flow was insufficient to meet existing obligations.

## Economic Policy and Public Protest

Instead of a measured tightening of controls, which had been Pérez's original plan, emergency measures were required. The government was forced to seek assistance from the International Monetary Fund (IMF) in the form of a U.S.$4.3 billion credit, which also meant immediate and stringent economic austerity. A new economic plan was announced by Pérez in mid-February 1989, consisting of the following provisions: a major devaluation of the bolivar, substantial increases in gasoline prices and transportation fares, and the removal of subsidies for most food items.[15] The president then characteristically left it to his ministers and chief economic advisers to fill in the details. The process did not prove felicitous; the most immediate difficulty came with the unparalleled public demonstrations that broke out a week later and produced a startlingly unanticipated challenge to the democratic system.

As time passed, both the government and party elites came to regard the February 1989 outburst as an aberration. The AD *cogollito* was preoccupied with strengthening its influence with the administration while jockeying for position prior to the next elections. COPEI expressed concern, but in relatively mild terms. Pérez, his self-confidence unshaken and his policy convictions unambiguous, proceeded with business as usual. Much of his time was devoted to foreign affairs, as he played to the hilt his role as a senior statesman of Latin America in particular and the developing world in general. His chief economic advisers—young and technically expert but politically inexperienced— pushed ahead enthusiastically with the president's program, while he himself ignored the politics of the situation. Thus, although the administration was well-staffed with trained personnel fully capable of devising a policy of economic modernization, it was less than sensitive to the immediate human needs of the poor.

The president himself, supremely confident of his own political instincts, was unwilling to hear dissonant voices. In due course he even ordered the cessation of all polling for the government—this from a man who had invested lavishly in both Venezuelan and North American pollsters and media experts for two years prior to his election. These factors all helped to lull Pérez into a comfortable complaisance, as renewed murmurs of public discontent were ignored in the face of an apparent upswing in the economy. By the close of 1991, most macroeconomic indicators were improving. Foreign reserves had been replenished while the inflation rate, although still something of a sore spot, had diminished to 40 percent. These and similar data were cited by the government as indicators of successful economic policies. Few nations in Latin America appeared to be recovering so impressively from the debt-ridden recession and stagnation of recent years, and the Pérez administration was not shy in extolling the virtues of its policies. Forgotten in the wave of official self-congratulation, however, was the continuing microeconomic deprivation of the poor. The breach between rich and poor widened, unemployment and underemployment were growing, and fully one-half the population lived below the official poverty level. During the closing months of 1991, the frequency of public protests was on the rise, although still regarded as a mere annoyance by the government. All of this was to change with the wrenching events of an attempted military coup that greeted Pérez after his return from a trip abroad on the evening of February 3, 1992.

*Crisis and Response*

The events of the attempted *golpe* need not be recounted in detail. Suffice it to recall the operational blunders and miscalculations of the conspirators, Pérez's narrow escape from assassination, his urgent pleas from a television studio the *golpistas* had failed to secure, and the loyal response of the armed forces under the direction of Gen. Fernando Ochoa Antich, the minister of defense.

With the state of military opinion and the strength of the armed forces' allegiance to the democratic system called critically into question, the immediate response from the two major parties was swift and unequivocal. Acción Democrática, whose secretary general, Luis Alfaro Ucero, had been with Pérez for much of the night, cast aside its sniping at the president to close ranks. COPEI also backed the government; within hours Eduardo Fernández had gone personally to Pérez to assure Social Christian support. With the democratic system hanging by a thread, COPEI recognized that it was scarcely the time for partisan politics. From the Left, which had been largely co-opted into the mainstream some years earlier, there were now sharp criticisms of the government and suggestions that the plotters were justified in seeking a change. More important, Rafael Caldera rose in Congress as a senator-for-life to unleash a searing attack on Pérez and the government. Denouncing the corruption of Venezuelan parties, he charged the government with a total loss of contact with the populace. It was a theme to which he would return repeatedly in coming months.[16]

Pérez's response was directed at the symptoms rather than the basic causes of malaise and discontent. As General Ochoa labored to identify the conspirators and reassert institutional authority within the military, the president played for time while searching for a new political consensus.

Public declarations by Pérez pledged a variety of economic reforms, although the rhetoric was more general than specific. The president also spoke of the need for a new political unity of will and action, suggesting a possible coalition government incorporating COPEI and minor parties as well. A special commission, the Consejo Consultivo

Presidencial, was created to advise Pérez during the crisis; its membership included prominent independents as well as a few party representatives. The blue-ribbon commission proved inconsequential and was soon discarded, but Pérez did negotiate an understanding whereby Fernández accepted the incorporation of two COPEI stalwarts into the cabinet.[17] At the same time, however, COPEI firmly rejected the notion of an electoral alliance with AD. As Fernández's campaign chief Gustavo Tarre Briceño put it, COPEI's ministerial participation was intended to support democracy. For the longer run, however, he regarded the *copeyano* option in 1993 as the best means of defending democracy.

Weeks passed, few policy changes were produced, and COPEI became increasingly uneasy over the potential political fallout resulting from its ties with the government. President Pérez planned to attend the Earth Summit in Rio de Janeiro in mid-June, but critics scoffed at his claims that the country had returned to normality. They saw his trip as inappropriate; both COPEI and MAS declared their intention of voting against congressional authorization for the trip. The conflict came to a head when Pérez submitted his official request to the Senate early in June. Twice the vote ended in a 23–23 tie, with *adeco* senators following party discipline and the opposition voting to deny authorization for the trip. A third tie vote would have meant rejection of the request, but on June 10 a pro-COPEI independent was pressured into changing his vote, thus providing the president with a 24–22 margin. The victory was Pyrrhic: COPEI promptly withdrew from the four-month-old coalition, further street violence erupted, and Pérez himself canceled the trip to Rio. FEDECAMARAS, the nation's major business and commercial organization, issued a document stating that the political parties were no longer representative of true Venezuelan popular will. It charged that in the four months since the attempted *golpe*, "the country does not perceive any of the necessary amendments and rectifications which were promised."[18] Amid the general hubbub, in which many doubted that the government would survive the night, Pérez played a master stroke, naming Ochoa Antich minister of foreign affairs and replacing him as defense minister with Gen. Iván Jiménez Sánchez, previously the chief of the general staff.

This move served several purposes. For one, it further solidified the president's ties with the armed forces. With Ochoa as chancellor, military fears that Pérez might "deliver" slivers of Venezuelan territory to Colombia in the process of negotiating the long-standing border dispute were assuaged. The appointment could also be seen as rewarding loyalty, since Ochoa from the night of February 4, 1992, had been Pérez's single most important source of support. Most important of all,

Ochoa was regarded as patriotic and incorruptible. His stature had grown through his willingness to criticize party elites for errors of commission and omission. In a statement to the press on June 7, for example, he had declared that "political leaders lost all credibility and moral authority" having failed to effect the "profound changes" demanded by the people.[19] Ochoa's appointment was an inspired act by Pérez that helped to buy further time for his presidency. Yet the subsequent reaction once again spoke to partisan interests and political advantage rather than to measures genuinely intended to ameliorate socioeconomic problems.

On June 17 former president Luis Herrera Campíns of COPEI called for the formation of a "national accord" that would incorporate all important social and political sectors in combating corruption, reforming finances and taxes, and improving the functioning of public services. As a means of reinvigorating the spirit of Punto Fijo, such an agreement would be "the best way of overcoming present difficulties and creating a new atmosphere."[20] Pérez himself had meantime told his party's CEN that any change in the constitutional mandate—a proposal that was gaining extensive press attention—would produce his own immediate resignation. Nonetheless, the Asociación Pro-Venezuela, an organization of businesspeople generally more liberal than FEDECAMARAS, was also calling for a national accord that, if unsuccessful, would lead toward the desirability of a presidential resignation. Even the church weighed in with a public pronouncement lamenting past inattention to the public and demanding swift government remedies.

Late June and early July found the government still beset by public protests in Caracas and elsewhere. Yet the president preferred such actions as restructuring his cabinet, with eleven ministers replaced at the end of June. In his Independence Day message on July 5, Pérez declared the military threat to have disappeared. Promising to fulfill all his previous political and economic promises before the 1993 general elections, he identified Venezuela's single most immediate problem as inflation, "a great enemy" that would necessarily "convert the fight against inflation into a national cause."[21]

Congress considered a wide range of constitutional reforms. Some had been voiced earlier as leading toward systemic *apertura,* but others were flagrantly opportunistic in nature. Opponents of President Pérez—whose voluntary resignation had never been a realistic possibility—suggested the option of shortening his term through constitutional means. While other measures were discussed in a variety of congressional committees, attention was focused on the question of the presidential mandate. On July 7 COPEI voted in favor of a referendum on a proposed one-year shortening of Pérez's term. Fernández described this as a one-time measure rather than a clause in the revised constitution. He saw it, however, as a necessary response to the national emergency. Assuming passage of the measure, national elections would be moved up a year to December 1993.

The timing would have been problematic, since congressional debates would run through August, leaving scant months for the referendum and campaign prior to national elections. Yet this could have been positive for COPEI, since its campaign structure was in place and the Fernández candidacy was a foregone conclusion. In Acción Democrática, it was believed that at least a year was necessary to prepare for an election. The very task of choosing from a number of precandidates would be demanding and divisive. Thus, while COPEI could envisage an early departure of Pérez as improving its chance of a prompt return to power, AD was equally partisan in its opposition. The composition of congressional forces made the *copeyano* strategy uncertain at best. Although the 95 AD deputies were a minority in the 201-member lower house, Acción Democrática could block measures in the Senate so long as party discipline held.

Opposition was further voiced in an unusual nationwide telecast on July 9, in which five diverse public figures reiterated the demand that Pérez resign.[22] Former President Caldera, who had earlier been the first to call for the president's immediate departure, derided the claim that normality existed in Venezuela. He was joined by the four others in the appeal to the president; the program met with mixed public reaction, while Pérez of course remained unmoved. The question of normality was denounced in a document from the Episcopal Conference, which proclaimed that the political and social crisis had actually been "aggravated." For the Venezuelan church, neither a new constitution nor a referendum would suffice. "Effective participation of the pueblo" was fundamental if meaningful progress were to be achieved. Until then, the unequal distribution of income and the rule of the privileged were the order of the day. Congressmen were attacked as being spokesmen for the private interests of the parties, which in turn were "not considered authentic representatives of the people."[23]

Congressional reactions continued to justify charges that neither the government nor the parties were attending to basic problems. The typical response was to lay the blame at other doorsteps. The administration pursued this approach when it resorted to censorship by suspending the video and song entitled "Por estas calles."[24] The work of the Venezuelan Yordano De Marzo, the song had already been performed for months both in Venezuela and abroad; its attack on the nation's political leadership as corrupt now brought down official wrath. Another diversion came in July 1992 with an unsubstantiated claim by the minister of interior relations that there had been antigovernment complicity between the small leftist party Causa R and the octogenarian writer and intellectual Arturo Uslar Pietri. Minister Luis Piñerua Ordaz vaguely spoke in confusing language of "the union of those two mentalities and the obscure ends that they pursue."[25]

The crisis continued unresolved, but the likelihood of further disruptions was generally minimized. This expectation was brutally shattered by a new, different, and more bloody uprising against the government over the weekend of November 27. A number of air force officers were involved, but the army remained loyal to the government in crushing the rebels. Contrary to the hopes of the conspirators, there was no popular support for their movement. By the thirtieth all vestiges of armed opposition had been eliminated. Numerous episodes of cold-blooded killings by the rebels before their defeat produced wide public condemnation. President Pérez's determined refusal to buckle under pressure, even as the palace was being bombed, also aroused grudging admiration. In the wake of the violence, then, the legitimacy of the administration and the constitution had been momentarily strengthened. The likelihood of yet another *golpe* against the president was slender at best.

Pérez had fought with the political shrewdness born of a long public career, propelled by a powerful instinct for survival. He had managed to retain office and defend constitutionality, but largely through political sleight of hand and toughness rather than policy responses to the socioeconomic realities that underlay the protest and disorder. His reactions were those of a preeminently political animal, drawing on insights and resources consistent with those of the party leadership from which he had emerged. None of this changed the fact that Venezuelan democracy was still at risk. The inadequacy of policy reforms proposed by the government was paralleled by the reactions of the major parties, whose leadership shared the rigidified mindset that had developed over the two preceding decades.

## THE PARTIES TODAY: FROM EXUBERANCE TO EXHAUSTION?

### The Design for Democratic Decomposition

In the wake of the unsuccessful *golpe,* state and municipal elections dealt a further blow to the government and Acción Democrática. In the contest for city mayors, COPEI won 125 as compared to 116 for AD,

19 for MAS, and 10 (including Caracas) for Causa R. Nationwide, COPEI polled 42 percent to 36 percent for AD. Of the twenty-two state governorships, the opposition won twelve and AD eight.[26] Furthermore, in the states of Sucre and Barinas the AD-controlled state legislatures declared their candidates victorious in hotly disputed races that the opposition also claimed (the MAS in Sucre and COPEI in Barinas). Angry arguments before the Consejo Supremo Electoral (CSE) led COPEI in early 1993 to wash its hands of the entire matter. The dispute was forwarded to the Corte Supremo de Justicia (Supreme Court), which refused to accept jurisdiction.

These details were important as indicators of continuing decomposition of the entire system. By March 1993 the two governorships remained unresolved and there was seemingly no institutional means of concluding the matter. The competence and legitimacy of the CSE to oversee the December national elections were also called into question. President Pérez was reshuffling his cabinet, and both major political parties projected presidential primaries despite the perils of further disintegration or outright fragmentation. Several widely publicized cases of alleged corruption—one even centering on Cecilia Matos, the president's mistress—captured the public's attention while underlining public perceptions of corruption. Indeed, public opinion polls continued to report corruption as a major source of discontent with and alienation from Venezuela's political leadership.

Political corruption has also flowed out of entrenched party elites.[27] The issue assumed major proportions during the first Pérez administration, when the unprecedented rise in oil prices produced a bonanza that Venezuela was incapable of absorbing. Money was plentiful, thus waste and sloppiness accompanied outright dishonesty and fraud. Pérez himself was later subjected to congressional investigation and, after a highly charged inquiry, was formally reprimanded by Congress for irresponsibility in overseeing influential subordinates. At the inaugural ceremonies for his successor, Pérez was charged by Luis Herrera Campíns with having "mortgaged" the country through financial excesses. Yet it was Herrera himself who succumbed to another boom in oil prices. Several high officials in his government were charged with corruption but fled the country before arrest orders could be served. When Herrera was succeeded by Lusinchi, the problem became even more public.

A lax administrator at best, Lusinchi relied heavily on his longtime private secretary, Blanca Ibáñez. Politically ambitious and skillful, she amassed a fortune recently calculated at more than U.S.$200 million. Lusinchi engaged in a long and messy effort to secure a divorce from his wife, but she angrily blocked any such action until he had left office.

In the meantime Pérez and the *cogollito* collaborated to frustrate Ibáñez's bid for a Senate seat. She and Lusinchi moved to Florida and were subsequently married. Charges of corruption still swirl about both of them, as well as around Lusinchi's former minister of interior relations, José Angel Ciliberto, a prominent *adeco*. Whatever the outcome of these and other charges now being pursued, they have served to persuade the public that official graft and corruption remain rampant and that no politician can be trusted.

An additional complication—largely organizational in nature—is the relationship between the president of the republic and his party. Rómulo Betancourt set the formal pattern when he requested and received from AD an official release from party discipline. This practice has endured, but the dynamics of the relationship are more complicated. In the first place, the previous position of a president vis-à-vis his party colleagues is critical. Caldera obviously enjoyed great prestige and influence with his party while occupying Miraflores. The situation was different with Herrera and progressively deteriorated as his unpopularity encouraged a distancing on the part of Caldera and other leaders of COPEI. For Acción Democrática, the experience with Pérez is instructive. Although he had been a party loyalist and organization man par excellence before his 1973 election, Pérez proved a stubbornly independent president. He brought into government many who were not party members, and particular reliance was placed on wealthy members of the private sector, including those popularly known as "Los Doce Apostoles." He often treated the weekly meetings with the Comité Ejecutivo Nacional as a forum in which he merely informed the party of his thinking.

During his second presidency Pérez again brought nonparty members into important government positions, most notably the young *técnicos* already mentioned. The party resented many of these appointments, but Pérez once again demonstrated his disinterest in receiving advice from the party. Only with the 1992 crisis did he turn to AD for a greater degree of collaboration. His ardent plea to an expanded group of leaders in mid-July (the Comité Político Nacional, or CPN) on behalf of projected tax reforms and a value-added tax was in sharp contrast to his customary method of operation. Furthermore, the party decision to reject his request for senatorial permission to attend the summit meeting of Iberian chiefs of state in Madrid was unprecedented. While Pérez's failure to gain the support and approval of the party was a sharp rebuke to his leadership, at the same time it underlined AD's willingness under extreme circumstances to insist on its own perception of political conditions.

*Reviving the Participatory Model*

There is no doubting the process of decay that the Venezuelan parties have experienced; neither is there any question that the entire system is facing its most intimidating challenges in three decades. The parties' evident weaknesses have been underlined by years of economic drift and a decline in living standards, which have been widely perceived as deteriorating even further during Pérez's second term. Public attitudes toward the parties and the democratic regime are powerfully suscepti- ble to existing socioeconomic conditions. Were the characteristics and perceptions of government performance to be viewed in a positive light, many of the parties' shortcomings would be overlooked or, at the least, accepted without great public protest.

For a revival of true party democracy, a variety of measures will be necessary. There is no single royal road to a certain future. Organiza- tional and structural reforms alone will not suffice—progress must go beyond the parties and reach the level of government performance. The flow of information and interaction between president and party must be steady. In addition, more than formalistic adjustments are nec- essary. Party leaders must recognize their errors and be willing to make amends, even when difficult or embarrassing. They must subject their partisan skills and pragmatic self-interests to acceptance of a renewed faith in the ideals of participatory democracy. In the absence of a clear doctrinal message and an unqualified commitment to the principles that motivated the founders of the Venezuelan democratic experience, the parties will find themselves increasingly isolated from the people, and the systemic political crisis will become only more profound.

## NOTES

1. Tad Szulc, *Twilight of the Tyrants* (New York: Henry Holt, 1959).
2. Invited guests included such European leaders of the Socialist International as Willy Brandt; developing world luminaries, including Julius Nyerere; and the vast majority of Latin American heads of state, among them Fidel Castro and Daniel Ortega.
3. John D. Martz, "Political Parties in Colombia and Venezuela: Contrasts in Substance and Style," *Western Political Quarterly* 18, no. 2 (June 1965): 333.
4. John D. Martz and Enrique A. Baloyra, *Electoral Mobilization and Public Opinion: The 1973 Venezuelan Campaign* (Chapel Hill: University of North Carolina Press, 1976); also Enrique A. Baloyra and John D. Martz, *Political Attitudes in Venezuela: Societal Cleavages and Political Opinion* (Austin: University of Texas Press, 1979).
5. For example, see John D. Martz, "Peligros del la petrificacaión: El sistemo de partidos venezolanos y la década de los ochenta," in Enrique A. Baloyra and Rafael López Pin- tor, eds., *Iberoamérica en los años 80: Perspectivas de cambio social y político* (Madrid: Centro de Investigaciones Sociológicas, Instituto de Cooperación Iberoamericana, 1982),

149–87; also John D. Martz, "The Malaise of Venezuelan Political Parties: Is Democracy Endangered?" in Donald L. Herman, ed., *Democracy in Latin America: Colombia and Venezuela* (New York: Praeger, 1988), 155–75.

6. John D. Martz, "Party Elites and Leadership in Colombia and Venezuela," *Journal of Latin American Studies* 24, no. 1 (1992): 87–121.

7. Detailed treatments are found in Daniel H. Levine, *Conflict and Political Change in Venezuela* (Princeton: Princeton University Press, 1973), and John D. Martz, *Acción Democrática: Evolution of a Modern Political Party in Venezuela* (Princeton: Princeton University Press, 1966). Many authors have followed these pioneering studies as the basis for further research on the spirit of Punto Fijo and its impact on the political system.

8. AD has employed so-called primaries and electoral colleges as a means of restricting participation and avoiding uncontrolled factionalism. Its conventions are limited to party members. COPEI, in contrast, customarily organizes "national" conventions at which prominent independents are incorporated into the process. This, it is claimed, allows selection of a truly national candidate with broad-based support from outside the party itself.

9. Although local leaders draw up preliminary lists, the national executive committees ultimately put together the official lists forwarded to the CSE. This elitist list-preparing process makes it possible to move candidates from their home territory, to insert prominent independents in strategic slots, and to protect the positions of a party's sacred cows.

10. In addition to the party's secretary of labor, one of the two AD vice presidents is also a ranking figure in the labor movement. It is even possible for the party secretary general to come from the CTV.

11. Juan Carlos Rey, *El papel de los partidos políticos en la instauración y el mantenimiento de la democracia venezolana* (Caracas: IFES/Centro de Asesoriá y Promoción Electoral, 1990), 37.

12. For a thorough discussion, see Margarita López Maya, Luis Gómez Calcaño, and Thaís Maingón, *De Punto Fijo al pacto social: Desarrollo y hegemonía en Venezuela (1958–1985)* (Caracas: Fondo Editorial Acta Científica Venezolana, 1989).

13. Comisión Presidencial para la Reforma del Estado, *La reforma del estado* (Caracas: COPRE, 1988). Also see Juan Carlos Rey, *El futuro de la democracia en Venezuela* (Caracas: Colección IDEA, 1989).

14. For those who observed Pérez in both 1973 and 1988, the personalistic appeal was still evident. He would arrive for rallies, repeat his familiar gesture of greeting, praise the community in which he found himself, and launch into generalized rhetoric that barely touched on policies while promising a revival of leadership and a renewal of the national spirit.

15. *Diario de Caracas,* February 16, 1989, 1.

16. For the full text, see Rafael Caldera, *Caldera: Dos discursos* (Caracas: Editorial Arte, 1992).

17. Onetime energy minister Humberto Calderón Berti was named to the foreign ministry, while José Ignacio Moreno León became head of the Investment Fund of Venezuela, also a cabinet-level position.

18. *El Universal,* June 11, 1992, 1.

19. *El Nacional,* June 7, 1992, 1.

20. Ibid, June 18, 1992, 1.

21. Ibid, July 6, 1992, 1.

22. Caldera was accompanied by Arturo Uslar Pietri, Luis Raúl Matos Azocar (a bitterly anti-Pérez *adeco* who soon departed the party), retired General Alberto Müller Rojas, and Ciro Añez, a prominent businessman.

23. Entitled "¿Donde está tu hermano?" the document appeared in Caracas newspapers on July 12, 1992.

24. The lyrics lamented, in part: "Por estas calles la compasión ya no aparece, y la piedad hace rato que se fue de viaje cuando se iba la perseguía la policia, oye conciencia mejor y escondes con la paciencia."

25. *El Nacional,* July 15, 1992.
26. In December 1989, Acción Democrática had won eleven of twenty contested governorships. Since then two federal territories have become states, increasing the total to twenty-two.
27. For a best-selling analysis of corruption, see Ruth Capriles Méndez, *Diccionario de la corrupción en Venezuela* vol. 3 (Caracas: Consorcio de Ediciones Capriles, 1959–92).

# 2

# More than Failed Coups: The Crisis in Venezuelan Civil-Military Relations

*Winfield J. Burggraaff and Richard L. Millett*

"Aside from the grenade attack on the house of former President Lusinchi, the attack on Deputy Antonio Ríos and the attack against a Navy lieutenant in Ciudad Bolívar on the evening of 28 September, everything is absolutely normal."[1] This September 29, 1992, observation by Defense Minister Gen. Iván Jiménez Sánchez underscores the turmoil in 1992 and into 1993 in Venezuela. Once widely viewed as a bastion of economic growth, democratic politics, and stable civil-military relations in South America, it is now a nation plagued by social and political strife and facing an uncertain future. Much of this uncertainty has been caused by unanticipated disturbances in the realm of civil-military relations.

For the last quarter-century Venezuela was routinely described by knowledgeable observers as the most stable democracy in South America; its only rival for that title in Latin America has been Costa Rica. During a thirty-year period that saw extremist challenges to the democratic system at home and successful military coups and oppressive authoritarian regimes in most neighboring countries, Venezuela appeared to be consolidating a civilian constitutional rule based on a strong political party system, regular free and fair elections, party alternation in power, and fundamental civil liberties. Although Venezuela faced, to a certain extent, the social and economic problems that most developing world countries face, strong civilian political leadership and the blessing of a thriving and lucrative oil export industry were viewed as two key ingredients in establishing and maintaining a relatively smoothly functioning democratic system.

Another essential ingredient in this democratic recipe was the national armed forces' acceptance of, and support for, democratic rule. Without the support of the military, democratic consolidation would have been impossible. In most Latin American nations during the

1970s and early 1980s, the military either directly dominated the political process or else shared power in an uneasy partnership with civilians who were always acutely aware of the need to respect military autonomy, ignore abuses of power by officers, and clear fundamental policy decisions with the high command before attempting to implement them. There was no tradition of military subordination to civil power, no effective mechanisms for exercising civilian oversight over military activities and budget, and at times little if any civilian input into basic policy decisions involving national security. Venezuela stood out as a surprising exception to these patterns, a situation that produced admiration and praise from foreign observers and promoted national pride among both civilians and the military.

In recent years, however, there have been more and more signs pointing toward the deterioration of the democratic system and worsening civil-military relations. Several of these signs were, to say the least, startling. The first was the February 1989 violent demonstrations, riots, and looting in Caracas and other urban areas over sudden government-decreed cost increases in fuel, transportation, and other basic necessities. The ensuing riots left hundreds dead. The next sign was the abortive coup by middle-level army officers in February 1992 that came frighteningly close to capturing or assassinating President Carlos Andrés Pérez and to seizing key Venezuelan cities. The even more violent uprisings of November 1992 seemed to many observers to indicate that Venezuela's democratic institutions were threatened with collapse and that civil-military relations in that nation were among the least stable in the hemisphere. The May 1993 removal of President Pérez and his constitutional replacement without overt military interference restored some confidence in the political system, but left basic questions of civil-military relations largely unanswered.

This chapter analyzes the roots and causes of the February 4 and November 27, 1992, coup attempts by looking at factors such as the controversial neoliberalism and internationalism associated closely with Pérez's second administration, worsening socioeconomic conditions, and generalized disgust with governmental mismanagement and corruption. The primary focus will be on the deepening frustrations and fissures within the military establishment over a variety of perceived intrainstitutional and extrainstitutional problems.

## THE ESTABLISHMENT OF DEMOCRACY AND THE TAMING OF THE MILITARY

The broad outlines of the post-1958 democratization of Venezuela are familiar to historians and social scientists with a working knowledge of the country. What is considered remarkable is that a nation that had military rulers for fifty-five of the first fifty-eight years of this century could embrace and sustain a civilian democratic political system.[2] A number of factors are responsible. First, the government of the armed forces that seized power in 1948 was rapidly transformed into the personalistic dictatorship of Gen. Marcos Pérez Jiménez (1952–58). The military lost position and status vis-à-vis the nonmilitary security forces of the regime, especially the large and powerful Seguridad Nacional. Pérez Jiménez increasingly relied on these security forces to shore up an administration notorious for corruption and brutality. By the end of 1957, both civilian and military groups openly challenged the dictatorship. The church, outlawed political parties, labor and business groups, and dissident elements within the armed forces rose up. The climactic event was the January 23, 1958, civil-military insurrection that drove Pérez Jiménez into exile and established a civilian-military junta.[3]

In an attempt to establish an enduring democratic system the three major political parties signed the Pact of Punto Fijo (1958), in which they pledged to respect the results of the 1958 elections and forge a government of national unity—in effect agreeing that the preservation of a democratic system took precedence over the fortunes of a single party. They also agreed to enact a "minimum program" of socioeconomic reform. The spirit of Punto Fijo became the cornerstone of the new democratic structure, especially under the astute leadership of Rómulo Betancourt (1959–64). Under the new constitution (1961) the military was to be obedient, subordinate to civilian authority, and apolitical. Since they were still associated with ten years of ruthless and corrupt dictatorship, the armed forces were more inclined to accept their new, subordinate role rather than risk getting burned again. This is evident in the vigorous response of the bulk of the officer corps to armed uprisings of right- and left-wing extremists, including military elements, between 1958 and 1962. In the next few years the largely conservative, anti-Communist military consolidated its loyalty to the democratic state through its successful counterinsurgency warfare against Castro-inspired rural guerrillas and urban terrorists. In addition, Betancourt and his successors went out of their way to provide the armed institution with increasing resources, higher salaries and benefits, and increased opportunities for advanced training at home and abroad.[4] They also lavished praise on military personnel for their new spirit of professionalism, patriotism, discipline, and sacrifice.

By the 1970s it appeared to both domestic and outside observers that the once politically dominant Venezuelan military had been tamed. Coups or even military threats or excessive demands were seen as things of the past. Nevertheless, behind the image of the apolitical military and harmonious civil-military relations there were and are potential problems and tensions.

One frequently cited officer complaint concerns one of the mechanisms of civilian control over the military—the system of promotions for high-ranking officers. By law, congressional approval is necessary for all promotions to colonel and general. Although the Senate rarely interferes with the defense minister's recommendations, there is a widespread feeling that politics is taken into account rather than the preferred criteria of professional merit and competence. In fact, in order to advance to the most senior ranks the majority of officers associate themselves with either of the two establishment parties, Acción Democrática (AD) or COPEI. As a result, there have been numerous accusations of political favoritism, for example allegations that junior officers are at times promoted over more senior officers for reasons of politics.[5] The military rebels of February 4, 1992, the self-proclaimed Bolivarianos, cited such alleged abuses in the promotion system as one of their grievances. Resentment over the promotion system and the belief that they had been passed over for political reasons also apparently played a large role in motivating many of the leaders of the November 27 uprising.[6]

Another area of military concern involves the proper strategic role of the armed forces and the means to carry out their professional responsibilities. After the antiguerrilla campaigns ended in the mid-1960s, the Venezuelan military gradually moved in the direction of developmentalism and a modified national security doctrine. This resulted in a broader role for the military in frontier and border areas and in government agencies and companies.[7] While military roles were expanding, the command and control system failed to keep pace, however. As a result, there has been mounting frustration over the failure of the legal and structural arrangements governing the military to provide a unified military command that would be empowered to act swiftly and decisively in a national emergency.[8]

A third area that has produced military discontent is the increasing use of the army and the National Guard (Fuerzas Armadas de Cooperación [FAC]) in quelling antigovernment disturbances and urban violence. The incorporation of the guard into the formal military establishment in the late 1980s made this issue even more acute. These forces were repeatedly called on to quell civil protests and disturbances during the administrations of Jaime Lusinchi (1984–89) and Carlos Andrés Pérez (1989–93). There are complaints that the National Guard is brought in to restore order for civilians whose failed policies and misgovernment brought on the disturbances in the first place. The guard also feels that it is being brought in to serve in essentially a repressive function for which it is not properly trained and which has the potential to tarnish its public image.[9]

## THE DEEPENING CRISIS IN THE CIVIL SECTOR: THE DETERIORATION OF THE POLITICAL MODEL

By the early 1980s Venezuela's democratic system, long the envy of so many of the country's neighbors, was losing its luster. Although such elements as regular free elections, high voter turnout, and freedom of expression were still present in the system, it was now almost universally believed that politics was controlled by entrenched, interlocking elites and that the two establishment parties, AD and COPEI, had gained a virtual monopoly on power. Democratic institutions had lost their early dynamism and politics had lost touch with the average person. Politicians were increasingly perceived as parasites on the body politic, lacking any incentive to reform a system that had provided them wealth, status, and power. In Georgie Ann Geyer's words, "Here was a country that everyone thought was a working democracy when it was really a combination of elections with a corrupt elitist system of the old Spanish style, where small groups ran everything"; Venezuela "long papered over its institutional failures with its hundreds of billions of dollars of oil wealth and the pretense of populism."[10]

Meanwhile, the bureaucracy grew beyond all reasonable bounds. In 1990, 150,000 new government jobs were added to the payroll even though no one knew how many state employees there were already.[11] Yet despite the huge bureaucracy and oil revenues, no public service, be it education, health, housing, or transportation, was functioning in a way that was minimally adequate. Moreover, virtually everyone was convinced that vast corruption was being practiced at the highest levels of the civilian and military bureaucracies.

## WORSENING ECONOMIC AND SOCIAL CONDITIONS

While public confidence in government was declining, Venezuela was undergoing a concurrent economic crisis, which began in 1982 with an unanticipated and dramatic fall in world oil prices and peaked about 1988 or 1989. In 1988 inflation rose to 36 percent and in 1989 to 81 percent, levels unheard of in Venezuela. The country suffered balance of payments deficits, a sharp devaluation of the bolivar, and high unemployment. In early 1989 President Pérez, a recent convert to neoliberalism, began to implement an IMF-sanctioned economic restructuring plan that eliminated most price and exchange controls, freed up interest rates, reduced government subsidies, and sold off government enterprises. The shock was almost immediate; 1989, a year in which the GDP contracted by 8 percent, "marked the worst recession in Venezuela's modern history."[12]

Predictably, *Venezuela Saudita* was becoming *Venezuela empobrecida.* From 1980 to 1992 the average Venezuelan, in real terms, lost over half of his or her purchasing power. From the late 1970s to the early 1990s individual daily caloric intake dropped from 2,651 to 1,350.[13] The portion of the population below the poverty line grew to 64 percent.[14] The ranks of the poor increased from 7.8 million in 1987 to 9 million in 1989.[15] In 1992 half the population earned the equivalent of around U.S.$100 a month, which allowed them only "one square meal a day."[16] More and more, Venezuelans were asking themselves: where had the billions of petrodollars gone?

Given the increasingly gloomy social conditions, it was inevitable that public protests would materialize, first under Lusinchi and later under Pérez. Students and workers launched antigovernment street demonstrations and work stoppages with increasing frequency.[17] As these often unruly protests mounted, police and security forces, along with the National Guard, were called in to maintain order. Confrontations between security personnel and demonstrators resulted in violent clashes, repressive measures, and growing human rights abuse allegations. But the still largely complacent political hierarchy appeared unmoved until the events of February 27 and 28, 1989.

## THE FEBRUARY 1989 RIOTS AND THEIR AFTERMATH

The February 1989 riots that hit Caracas and several other cities underlined both the strengths and the weaknesses of the Venezuelan model of civil-military relations. After two days of mounting disturbances, when it became obvious that conditions were beyond the control of the Metropolitan Police, President Pérez suspended constitutional guarantees, imposed a curfew, and ordered the military into Caracas. Within twelve hours nearly ten thousand soldiers, most drawn from outside the capital, were patrolling the streets of the city. Those citizens needing to be out after curfew had to apply to the defense ministry for permits.[18]

Although charges of military abuses of human rights surfaced following the riots, the armed forces appear to have carried out their mission with relative speed and efficiency.[19] The president declared that the armed forces had given "extraordinary proof of their loyalty to the country and their organization and discipline."[20] Much of the public seemed to share this view. An April 1989 poll gave the defense minister an 80 percent approval rating, and an August 1990 poll showed the military with the highest approval rating (64.6 percent) of any national institution.[21]

In the long run, the riots clearly had a negative impact on civil-military relations. Partly this was due to the further discrediting of civilian leadership and the additional economic strains that these events produced. Criticism of the Pérez administration mounted steadily during and after the riots, and the president's popularity and prestige began a steady decline. Public attention was increasingly focused on the issue of corruption, public and private.[22] This proved especially damaging to the image of AD, but it led to growing public cynicism regarding both major parties and their leaders.

The February 1989 riots also proved to be the beginning rather than the end of a prolonged period of public disturbances throughout the nation. In April 1989 disturbances in Maracaibo led to military forces being moved into that city. Throughout 1989 scattered incidents took place in numerous other cities, most notably in Mérida, where there was an ongoing series of confrontations between police and students. In February 1990 widespread demonstrations to protest government economic policies produced numerous clashes with police and National Guard units. From May through August, student and labor protests over increased gasoline prices provoked similar confrontations.[23]

As civil unrest continued, the military's involvement became increasingly controversial. For some of the high command, who had felt less than fully prepared for the February 1989 riots, a primary task was to improve the armed forces' ability to respond to such situations. One solution was to increase military ties with and control over the police. In June 1989, despite strong police protests, an army general was appointed to head the Metropolitan Police (PM). Earlier, responding to a police strike, the military had taken over PM offices in Caracas and in part of the state of Miranda.[24] In addition, National Guard units increasingly were engaged in duties previously left to the police; by late 1990, six hundred guardsmen were regularly employed in patrolling the streets of the capital.[25]

The high command was not hesitant to make public its increased commitment to policing functions. In February 1990 Defense Minister

Gen. Filmo López Uzcategui told a congressional committee, "We cannot remain in our garrisons. We must control these outbreaks of disorder and violence. We cannot wait for the disturbances to escalate into looting and burning important parts of cities before reacting." In June, when the rise in gasoline prices provoked widespread disturbances, he again declared publicly that the military was "ready to repel riots."[26] The general's remarks were underscored by the military's openly having held joint exercises on dealing with civil disturbances the previous month. At that time Gen. Juan Bastardo Velásquez, commander of the joint chiefs of staff, had declared that such exercises would be an annual event, designed to help the military improve "its effectiveness in reestablishing public order."[27]

The increasing tendency to use the military in internal police roles provoked growing concern among important civilian and military sectors. As early as June 1989, the president of Venezuela's Chamber of Deputies, José Rodríguez Iturbide, was expressing his concern over the use of military force to control civil disturbances. He expressed fears that mixing police and military personnel would produce conflict and confusion and suggested the need for new legislation to regulate relations between the police and the armed forces.[28] Despite significant support for his position, little was done. The Presidential Commission for the Reform of the State (COPRE) drafted proposed reforms of police statutes, devoting considerable attention to the role of the National Guard, but, through its 1991 sessions, Congress failed to act on these proposals.[29]

Civilian concerns were most evident in coup rumors, which began during the February 1989 riots and continued intermittently during the next three years. By June 1990 even such prominent figures as Oswaldo Álvarez Paz, governor of Zulia and a leader of COPEI, were declaring publicly that "all the seeds of a coup have been planted."[30] Two months later the *New York Times* ran a story discussing the coup rumors.[31] Both government and military leaders issued repeated strong denials of such reports, but the increasing frequency of such statements on their parts may have simply fueled the rumor mills.[32]

Among the military, the growing involvement in police-type functions was not accepted nearly as well by mid-level and junior officers as it apparently was by the high command. This was especially true among army officers, many of whom increasingly complained that their mission was to defend the nation, not to defend corrupt politicians from the population.[33] This attitude grew as civil disturbances continued throughout the early 1990s and was a factor in the February 1992 coup attempt.

## MILITARY DISCONTENT UNDER
## THE PÉREZ ADMINISTRATION

Although, as previously noted, deterioration in Venezuelan civil-military relations had been increasing for several years, the situation was made significantly worse by deliberate policies of the Pérez administration. Economic conditions for military personnel, especially at the lower officer and enlisted levels, had been deteriorating for some time.[34] The crisis brought on by the government's economic restructuring plan made this situation suddenly grow much worse. By some estimates, military officers' purchasing power fell by up to 90 percent.[35] Junior officers often could not afford housing, especially in Caracas, and had to share dwellings with family or in-laws. In addition, subsidies and other military benefits were reduced, compounding the financial burden. Discontent spread rapidly, especially among middle- and lower-level officers as these groups found their purchasing power evaporating. Lieutenants argued that they could not live on a net monthly pay of the equivalent of only U.S.$230 a month.[36] At the same time, due to the overall budget crisis, the defense budget was steadily shrinking. What money remained was becoming inadequate even to supply personnel with uniforms, boots, and daily food rations, much less to provide adequate maintenance and replacement of major equipment items such as aircraft and tanks.[37] Altogether, this situation made it easy for the Bolivarianos to gain support among all ranks except for the senior command.

Military discontent was not limited to specific grievances. As Gene Bigler has pointed out, evidence from throughout Latin America demonstrates that the military is responsive to public opinion. In Venezuela this response is directly linked to the military's perception of how well the democratic system is performing at any given point in time.[38] In the late 1980s and early 1990s the armed forces became increasingly concerned as support not only for President Pérez but for the whole democratic system seemed to wane. A key factor in creating this situation was corruption. So pervasive had concerns over this issue become that when Gen. Carlos Peñaloza Zambrano retired as army commander in June 1991, he directly addressed the issue, charging that pervasive corruption threatened Venezuelan democracy. "The state's leadership," he concluded ominously, "is too important to leave it only to politicians."[39] Probably the least surprising aspect of the coup attempt the following February was that its leader cited corruption in high military and political circles as a major justification for the rebels' actions.[40]

Month by month, the military became increasingly upset by widening civil disorder and the apparent breakdown of authority. For many officers the nation seemed to be on the edge of "social anarchy."[41] These fears, the perceived paralysis of civil leadership, and growing fissures within the military institution itself provided the volatile atmosphere that preceded the violent uprising of February 4, 1992.

International as well as domestic issues fueled military discontent under the Pérez administration. The president's heavy involvement in foreign affairs made him vulnerable to criticism for neglecting pressing domestic issues. While the armed forces focused increasingly on the deterioration of the democratic system, the alarming rise in criminal and political violence, an economically polarized citizenry, and what they perceived as growing threats to the security of the nation's frontiers, the peripatetic president seemed to be constantly abroad. Pérez made bold pronouncements on international and multilateral issues and constantly sought to exert leadership in global and regional forums. But he seemed unable or unwilling to provide the same level of leadership when confronting domestic problems. More and more officers came to believe that the president would sacrifice domestic interests to institutions such as the IMF and the World Bank in order to enhance his own international image. More important, his efforts to promote regional settlements were, at times, perceived by the military as undercutting national interests, especially as these related to territorial disputes and control over frontier areas. Several such issues were active during the Pérez administration. The long-lasting boundary issue with Guyana and conflicts with Colombia and with Trinidad and Tobago over maritime rights in the Gulf of Venezuela had dragged on for decades. The other concerns—the increasing encroachments of Brazilian gold miners on Venezuelan territory and narcotics and guerrilla activity along the Colombian border—were newer and involved dealings with nongovernmental groups.[42]

Of all these disputes, the maritime boundary issue with Colombia aroused the most emotions. In the fall of 1989 Venezuela signed a series of treaties first with Trinidad and then with Colombia concerning maritime rights. The Colombian treaties, which allowed that nation's free navigation in the gulf and on Lake Maracaibo, drew especially sharp criticism, with a large group of retired military officers openly condemning the pacts as a violation of national sovereignty.[43] Frustrated nationalist officers were upset at the president's apparent unwillingness to press Colombia for a solution to the long-standing territorial dispute in the Gulf of Venezuela; strong pressure, they believed, would force an outcome favorable to Venezuela, and failure to exert such pressure was seen as weakness or worse.[44] This issue continued to simmer, with Defense Minister Gen. Fernando Ochoa Antich criticizing the Colombian government's stand on the gulf issue at the end of January 1992, less than a week before the attempted coup.[45]

The president's use of the military in international ventures also aroused increasing criticism within some sectors of the armed forces. During the Pérez administration Venezuelan troops served in peacekeeping missions in Namibia, the Western Sahara, Nicaragua, and El Salvador. A few officers were even dispatched to Haiti and, in late 1991, there were strong rumors that Venezuelan troops would be part of a multilateral intervention force in that nation designed to force the return of President Jean-Bertrand Aristide to power. While the military had not been enthusiastic about the earlier ventures, this was the first to arouse strong opposition. The plan was quickly and publicly abandoned, but the entire episode contributed to the growing gap between the administration and many mid-level officers.[46]

Increasing military involvement in antinarcotics operations added to civil-military tensions and also produced problems with the United States. Rumors surfaced that the United States intended to establish military bases in Venezuela and that U.S. military aid to Colombia was intended to strengthen that nation for a conflict with Venezuela.[47] More fundamental was the natural reluctance or even anger among many officers faced with the prospect of involvement in narcotics conflicts, which they saw as the product of other nations' production and consumption. The ties between this issue and border clashes with Colombian guerrillas further complicated the issue.

## THE 1992 COUP ATTEMPTS

Despite rising grievances by both the military and civilians, mounting rumors of coups, and predictions by leading figures that an attempted coup was possible, the February 4, 1992, uprising took most Venezuelans and most foreign observers by surprise. Political Risk Services (International Business Corporation-USA) published its annual report on Venezuela in February and gave only a 5 percent chance of a military coup. Even that possibility was ascribed to a movement of the high command, not led by a group of junior officers.[48] For most Venezuelans, despite the rumors, coup attempts were still viewed as a past heritage from which the nation had escaped. In the words of one Venezuelan, "Had you asked me what the odds were for a coup d'etat in this country, I would have said they're 100 to 1."[49] Military intelligence had long had information on plots within the military. Coup leader Lt. Col. Hugo Chávez Frías had earlier been transferred out of Caracas because of such reports, but was also promoted and put in command of a key troop unit.[50] Further reports of such plots surfaced just hours before the uprising, causing Defense Minister General Ochoa Antich to meet the president personally on the night of February 3 when he returned to Caracas from Switzerland.[51] Nevertheless, the leaders remained untouched and the final preparations for the uprising proceeded unimpeded. General Ochoa Antich later admitted, "We received information, but we devalued it. . . . We just never could believe it."[52]

In one sense, the February coup attempt was the work of a very small minority of officers. Only five lieutenant colonels and no higher-ranking officers were directly involved in the Movimiento Bolivariano Revolucionario-200 (MBR-200), less than 10 percent of army units and virtually no air force or navy-marine units took part, and the entire effort collapsed within a few hours.[53] The small number involved, however, does not necessarily reflect the movement's potential support. Conspiratorial efforts, by definition, need to limit the number aware of and involved in their efforts. Also, since the movement was directed against the military hierarchy as well as the civilian leadership, the exclusion of general officers and colonels is hardly surprising.

Although in many ways the uprising seemed to follow a traditional Latin American pattern, there were some unusual, even unique elements. One was the active participation of sergeants, many of whom seemed to share the ideas of the coup leaders and not simply to have followed orders blindly. In the aftermath of the coup, 230 career sergeants were dishonorably discharged from the military. The high command also held a virtually unprecedented meeting with the sergeants, at which they voiced complaints over conditions and a host of what they claimed were broken promises. Later, some sergeants met with the press and issued their own manifesto, declaring, "We Bolivarians, especially those of us who are career soldiers, are neither leftist nor rightist. Our goal is a national one. We have no political affiliation whatsoever. Our intention of 4F was not to impose a dictatorship, but to change the so-called democratic system, which has been suffering distortion for about 20 years and which is snuffing out our sovereignty, our economy, our society. . . . What happened on February 4 was only a sneeze heralding a coming cold."[54]

The officers who led MBR-200 have repeatedly claimed, in the words of Lieutenant Colonel Chávez, that they "did not want to destroy democracy," but "quite the contrary, we struggled to defend it."[55] Lt. Col. Francisco Arias Cárdenas later expanded on this theme, declaring that, had they succeeded, "a broad-based constituent assembly would be called together and established without the pseudodemocratic political parties, to create the participative, democratic state that all of us Venezuelans need."[56] The leaders seemed to view themselves as the guarantors of true democracy, supporting the bulk of the population against a corrupt ruling class that "continues to cling to its privileges" and appears "incapable of understanding the evolution of the Venezuelan political process."[57] The use of such populist, antielite rhetoric is a recurring theme in almost all the postcoup interviews with those involved in the uprising.

The MBR-200 leaders, especially Chávez, refer repeatedly to the ideals of Simón Bolívar, his mentor, Simón Rodríguez, and other figures of early Venezuelan history to justify their actions. A former U.S. military attaché describes both the officers and the sergeants of the Venezuelan military as "steeped in the romanticism of the wars of liberation" and "imbued with the teachings of Simón Bolívar, el Libertador, and of the pantheon of revolutionary heroes."[58] This almost nostalgic harking back to the independence era for goals and ideals may symbolize an attempt to reject the uncomfortable and complex realities of modern international economic and political realities and a desire to find simple solutions that will restore the nation's past glory.

The actual program of the coup leaders remains somewhat unclear. They vigorously deny charges that they wanted to kill the president and/or establish a military dictatorship. Their original goals included calls to have public trials and possibly executions of those involved in corruption, dissolving the existing government and electing a constituent assembly, reversing government austerity measures and initiating emergency programs for the poor, and defending national sovereignty, a theme widely understood to mean taking hard-line positions on border disputes such as those with Colombia.[59] Later accounts indicated a plan to appoint a junta of notables, including former President Rafael Caldera and author Arturo Uslar Pietri, to run the nation until elections could be held.[60] Although these generalizations give some insights into the movement's motivations and goals, the underlying causes were much more complex.

The grievances held by those who led and supported MBR-200 can be divided into several broad categories. These include all the previously discussed factors, which had undermined the existing pattern of civil-military relations and helped create a situation in which many officers would be sufficiently unhappy to accept, if not actively support, a move against the government. But, while prominently mentioned at first, complaints over pay, housing, and a perceived decline in the prestige of the armed forces probably were secondary factors. As noted, the real pay of officers and enlisted men had fallen badly due to continuing inflation, promised government housing subsidies had failed to materialize, and declining oil prices threatened even further cuts.[61] The administration evidently took these grievances seriously since, after the February uprising, it moved quickly to alleviate them. Officers' pay was increased 30 percent shortly after the uprising, more money was put into military social welfare programs, and a subsidized housing program for officers was accelerated.[62] While such actions may have made some officers less likely to support a coup, these efforts neither mollified the imprisoned leaders of the February attempt nor in any way dissuaded those who later attempted to topple the government in November.

Complaints over politicized promotions were a frequently cited grievance and had become a subject of increased public debate in the period following the coup. Many officers openly resented what they saw as political rather than professional criteria dominating the selections for higher ranks.[63] Yet it must be noted that this was not a personal motive for the February plotters, as they had not been passed over for promotion. Neither did they cite any specific cases of political favoritism in promotions that they felt had damaged the armed forces or the nation. This was not the case in November, when officers who felt discriminated against for political reasons were involved in leading the uprising. In both cases these concerns weakened loyalties to the high command, making junior officers much more willing to conspire against their superiors.

Unhappiness over Carlos Andrés Pérez's approach to foreign policy, especially with regard to Colombia, was a factor in the February attempt. There was also resentment at a perceived knuckling under to foreign economic interests, notably those represented by the IMF. Lieutenant Colonel Francisco Arias, often portrayed as the movement's intellectual leader, admitted that the possibility of going to Haiti helped precipitate the timing of the coup, though he said the rebels opposed that "not because we were afraid to fight," but because "we opposed the idea out of Latin American consciousness."[64] External matters were probably also a secondary cause, however, being seen as further evidence of the general weakness and corruption of a detested administration.

The suffering of much of the population—attributed by the coup leaders to the policies of the Pérez administration—was frequently cited as a motivating factor. Lieutenant Colonel Arias said that "the wretchedness, the extreme poverty, the malnutrition from which the people were suffering" was a prime motivator. He condemned the administration's "frivolous and perverse attitude toward our people," charging that "the only emotion these gentlemen feel is contempt for the national pain."[65] Like complaints over pay, promotions, and evolving missions, concerns about deteriorating social conditions seem to have created a climate in which traditional loyalties were undermined, but not necessarily one in which many officers would conceive of a coup as the logical remedy for their complaints.

The leadership and nature of the February uprising appears to have been most influenced by concerns over the increasing use of the military in police roles, especially to put down protests over economic and political conditions and by growing anger over corruption. Lieutenant Colonel Chávez cited the military's involvement in putting down the February 1989 riots as a cause and charged that the military was being "transformed into a praetorian guard to protect a government that serves the interests of a small group of individuals."[66] Lieutenant Colonel Arias, in a broadcast during the uprising, condemned as "traitors those who are preparing us to repress and kill students."[67] Later he cited Bolívar as saying, "Damned be the soldier who turns his gun against the people," adding that "internal contradictions developed because the Army plans had begun to involve training us to control civil disturbances and demonstrations and to search universities."[68] For the Bolivarianos, their conversion to police was both a betrayal of their mission and a threat to their honor. By supporting or endorsing such missions, the high command discredited itself.

Most frequently cited by participants, neutral observers, and even critics of both uprisings as a prime motivating factor was the endemic corruption, both civilian and military, throughout the nation. Concerns over other issues could conceivably have been resolved through negotiations, but for the Bolivarianos corruption could be dealt with only by a generalized purge of those currently in power. Related to this issue was the widely accepted belief that the government and the two dominant political parties were too involved in the process, too incompetent, too indifferent to deal with the situation. Before beginning the uprising, Chávez wrote his mother that he was willing to risk his life in order to rid the nation of corruption. Later, to justify the coup, he cited Article 250 of the constitution, which he claimed "provides for the correction of violations of the Constitution specifically where . . . corruption is concerned. This vice that The Liberator attacked so often became the norm and still is the norm for this government."[69]

Other observers echoed these concerns. A former U.S. military attaché in Venezuela wrote that for officers the spreading corruption scandals "had one of two effects: for those easily corrupted they encouraged corruption within the ranks, for those who accepted their indoctrination as guarantors of democracy, they fostered a growing contempt for the political leadership."[70]

As important as the specific issues that motivated the uprisings are the factors that led those involved to believe their efforts would evoke strong public support and/or that the government would be unable to respond effectively. Among the most important of these was the *desprestigio*, the near total loss of prestige and credibility by the Pérez administration and the ruling parties. A poll taken shortly before the uprising showed 81 percent of Venezuelans having "little or no trust" in the Pérez government.[71] An earlier poll in 1990 had shown the ruling Acción Democrática as having fallen to third place among political parties with just 12.3 percent popular support. This same poll showed Venezuelans almost equally divided among those who considered the civilian governments of the previous thirty-two years as good, only fair, or bad. At the same time, however, 64 percent continued to express faith in the democratic system and 70.5 percent opposed a coup.[72] A 1992 poll showed 82 percent of Venezuelans wanting a reform of political parties, 7 percent wanting parties abolished, and only 4 percent wanting them left as they were.[73]

Corruption, combined with deteriorating economic conditions and aggravated by neoliberal austerity policies, severely undermined regime credibility. By the start of 1992, 80 percent of Venezuelans were living at or below the poverty level. Real wages fell sharply in 1989, 1990, and 1991.[74] A Roman Catholic priest working in the *ranchos* of Caracas stated that "the people feel that a successful coup could not have made anything worse and may have even made things better."[75] Members of the middle class, who believed that the country should be a mini–Saudi Arabia with oil-fueled prosperity, saw their quality of life deteriorate steadily over the past decade, converting them into what the *Economist* described as "Mr Pérez's most potent enemy."[76] This growing public disillusionment with the political system undoubtedly encouraged those involved in both the February and the November uprisings to believe that their efforts would meet with widespread public support.

The February uprising was facilitated by the tendency of most leaders, civilian as well as military, to take the armed forces for granted and to assume that a coup was impossible. This, in turn, made the leaders insensitive to military grievances and ready to undertake projects—such as the potential intervention in Haiti or the increasing use of the military in police roles—without considering how the bulk of the officer corps would react.

The inability of those officers at the top to appreciate adequately the depth and nature of the concerns and anger of their subordinates reflected the widening gap between the high command and mid-level officers. The yearly turnover of defense ministers and their rotation among the three services (even after its incorporation into the armed forces the National Guard was excluded from this arrangement) were conceived as a method of strengthening civilian control and preventing the rise of a dominant military leader. But this format also had the effect of greatly weakening ties between the rank and file and the high command. No officer served as defense minister long enough to gain the authority or loyalty of those below him, which is typical of most Latin American armed forces. The politicizing of the promotion process brought further aggravation. In addition, the involvement of military officials in the tide of corruption scandals caused them to lose much of their moral authority and prestige. In postcoup statements, Lieutenant Colonel Chávez declared that "the military high command had lost prestige with the officers," and Lieutenant Colonel Arias claimed that many officers were "beginning to oppose obeying the orders of immoral officers."[77] Even Defense Minister Ochoa Antich admitted that the relationship between higher- and mid-level officers had been weakened; he told a congressional commission that previously "command was supported by two elements, moral authority and affection," but added that these had "disappeared and now the junior officers feel that their chiefs are czars who treat them like slaves."[78]

In many ways, despite over three decades of civilian rule, the Venezuelan armed forces retained the attitudes and mindsets of traditional Latin American militaries. Junior officers and enlisted men tended to obey the orders of their immediate superiors without question, even when these involved disobedience to higher civilian authorities. Officers also tended to give their highest loyalty to the *patria* (homeland) rather than to the current administration or even the constitution.

Venezuelan officers also tend to see a clear division between the *poder político* (political power) and the *poder militar* (military power). This is facilitated by the implicit pact in force since the 1960s, which tended to leave military affairs to the military and civil affairs to the politicians, with little if any crossover between the two. It is worth noting that this line had begun to break down in the early 1990s; in response to numerous scandals involving military purchases and to growing austerity pressures, Congress and the executive branch have increasingly involved themselves in the military budget process. The postcoup appointment of General Ochoa Antich as foreign minister and of another general as head of the antinarcotics effort represented a further breach in this traditional wall of separation.[79]

The distinction between the *poder político* and the *poder militar*, combined with the growing gap between senior and mid-level officers, produced a new phenomenon. Some mid-level officers began to feel that they had more in common with the suffering mass of the population than they did with either civilian or military leaders. The idea that there was a third force, a *poder social*, with which they could and should identify, emerged.[80] This facilitated their belief that they were attacking not only on behalf of, but in concert with the needs and aspirations of, the bulk of the population.

Two final, general factors need to be considered. First, complaints about conditions are found in all armies at all times. That much of the military was acutely concerned over declining pay and benefits is hardly surprising. What was striking about the attitudes of many Venezuelan officers in early 1992, however, was the depth of these feelings and the spreading assumption that under the present system things would only get worse. Second, the very vagueness of the aims and ideology of those who led both coup attempts facilitated the organizing of the uprising. The leaders were much clearer about what they opposed than about what their alternatives were and how these would be implemented. In this regard, they were simply following a path well worn by generations of civilian politicians.

Although the Pérez administration and the military high command took some steps after the February uprising to deal with officers' grievances over pay, benefits, and missions, they did little if anything to restore public confidence in their economic and social policies, to deal with the issue of corruption, and to give either disgruntled officers or disillusioned civilians reason to expect that these basic issues would improve under the existing political framework. The result was the November 27 uprising, dominated by elements from the air force but including representatives of all the services. Despite efforts to incorporate civilian elements, especially on the far Left, into this attempt, the uprising failed. The rebels were hampered by poor coordination and badly overestimated the degree of public support for their efforts. The government was somewhat better prepared this time and the rebels never came close to capturing the president. If anything, the bloody nature of the November uprising, its ties to left-wing political groups, and the perceived personal motivations of some of the leadership made the bulk of the population even more hesitant to support a coup as a solution to the deteriorating political situation.[81]

The stated motives of the leaders of the November uprising were at least as vague as those enunciated the previous February. The government was castigated for its corruption, for producing "economic and social chaos," and for ignoring efforts to create a national dialogue. The only new element cited was the misuse of funds for military equipment and the resultant decline in the military's ability to carry out its missions. Aside from removing those currently in power and replacing them with an unspecified civil-military junta, the November *golpistas* offered no concrete solutions to the nation's problems.[82]

## CONCLUSIONS

Venezuelan civil-military relations remain in a state of chronic uncertainty and apprehension. The gap between the high command and the bulk of the officer corps has not been closed, and the *desprestigio* of the civilian government remains great, although the removal of Carlos Andrés Pérez has restored some faith in the process. In May 1992 a poll showed 63 percent of Venezuelans viewing the political situation as less stable than a month earlier and 69 percent either pessimistic or uncertain about the nation's future.[83] A later poll of Caracas residents gave Lieutenant Colonel Chávez first place among potential aspirants for the presidency in the next elections, with the margin varying from 10 percent when he was pitted against Rafael Caldera to 40 percent against Luis Piñerua Ordaz of AD.[84] An early 1993 poll showed similar results, with 30.6 percent supporting Caldera, 13.6 percent supporting Causa R's Andrés Velásquez, and 8.6 percent supporting Chávez; potential AD and COPEI candidates trailed well behind.[85]

According to a report attributed to the ministry of defense, through early May 1992 there had been 1,376 public demonstrations against the Pérez administration and its policies, 451 of which occurred in the months following the abortive February coup.[86] Civil disorders have continued since then, but the government has been much more reluctant to use the army to control them. On a somewhat lighter note, Chávez impersonators were among the most popular figures in 1992 carnival celebrations.[87] Popular enthusiasm for Chávez has declined, however, since the bloody November uprising.

The Pérez government and its successor have tried to deal with some of the causes of both military and civil discontent. Austerity measures have been softened, constitutional reforms have been proposed, and military pay and benefits have increased. The foreign ministry has taken a tougher public stand on the maritime dispute with Colombia, and the president curbed his foreign travels and no longer talked about military involvement in international operations.[88] Gestures have been made at dealing with corruption, including the sudden extradition of figures allegedly involved in international narcotics traffic. The dramatic decision to remove Pérez from office and to try him for alleged theft of public funds has given the population reason to hope for an end to official immunity and made any further coup attempts, at least in the near future, highly unlikely. But long-range confidence in the government's will and/or ability to deal with the corruption issue remains low, as demonstrated by resignations of public officials who feel frustrated and obstructed in their efforts to deal with this issue.[89] The caretaker administration that has replaced Pérez will probably be unable to make any fundamental change in this situation, and restoring public confidence will be a major challenge for the next administration. Only by successfully confronting this issue can that administration, whatever its leadership may be, hope to defuse tensions and restore effective civilian control over the armed forces.                    LESSONS

Several lessons can be drawn from the situation of civil-military relations in Venezuela. First, establishing effective civilian controls over armed forces and eliminating military intervention in politics requires more than changes in military attitudes and actions. Effective checks on civilian abuses of power must exist. If high civilian officials are viewed as having immunity and impunity, then it would be unreasonable at the least to expect the military to give up its privileges. Furthermore, when society as a whole begins to lose its respect for civilian government and institutions, the military's subservience to such groups will be affected. Writing before the February 1992 uprising, Rita Giacalone and Rexene Hanes de Acevedo observed:

> In Venezuela it seems rather safe to state that if the government is unable to convince popular sectors that it can improve present conditions in the short or medium term, if the parties lose their ability to channel demands into the system, and if violent demonstrations recur with some frequency, the probability of a military coup increases. Exacerbated popular demands would augment the need to employ the armed forces as an agent of repression. . . . It would also renew and deepen internal divisions between some groups opposed to engaging in repressive activities to protect politicians . . . and others interested in imposing order.[90]

The involvement of the military in police-type functions, especially when these included the control and repression of antigovernment demonstrations, exacerbated the problems of civil-military relations.

Such involvement virtually always serves to dirty up the military rather than to clean up the police. It is resented by both civilians and the military, and although it often appears to offer authorities a "quick fix" to a vexing problem, it fails to address and even diverts attention from the basic weaknesses of police and judicial systems. These factors should be kept in mind by anyone urging increased military involvement in antinarcotics operations.

The system of military education has failed to instill an adequate understanding of either the nature of democracy or the role of the military in a democratic system. The emphasis on idealism, sacrifice, and national pride may ill prepare officers for dealing with the real world of corruption, ambition, and political manipulation. Understanding of democracy was often simplistic at best. Lt. Col. Jesús Ernesto Urdaneta Hernández, one of the leaders of MBR-200, demonstrated this when he declared, "This democracy, as we have found, has been misunderstood by the leaders we have, who control it. . . .We firmly believe that a true democracy is a perfect system, which essentially attempts to achieve the good of the people, no matter what their origin or rank. . . . We have lived in a democracy and that enables us to analyze and work to correct it. I believe that is our responsibility."[91] Another coup leader, Lt. Col. Jesús Miguel Ortiz Contreras, defined democracy as "a system of changing elected officials in which the people elect those who are to represent them without behind-the-scenes manipulation."[92] Similar ideas have been expressed by more senior, retired officers. After the coup, former Army Comdr. Gen. Carlos Santiago Ramírez declared that the uprising represented "a step toward reclaiming national dignity in the face of a corrupt and negative democracy."[93] Retired Brig. Gen. Herminio Fuenmayor Pereira went even further when, after discussing the abuses of the Venezuelan political situation, he said, "The conclusion becomes obvious: if democracy is bringing us to a debacle, what good is democracy. Democracy has failed."[94] Such views, when combined with an education that exalts the armed forces' role as defenders and guarantors of democracy, can encourage rather than discourage events such as those of February 4 and November 27.

Venezuela has gone further than most Latin American nations in encouraging officers to attend public universities and allowing civilians to participate in higher military education, both at home and abroad. But these contacts may not have produced as much mutual understanding or communication as was hoped. There seems to have been little real comprehension by either group of the dynamics or basic mindsets of the other. Indeed, the study of political science by lieutenant colonels Chávez and Arias may have contributed to their belief that they had the right, indeed the duty, to intervene in the political process.[95]

Civilians often seem to have little better understanding of democracy than do elements of the military. Focusing on their economic situation and their anger with government corruption and inefficiency, they, too, look for simple solutions. Journalist José Vicente Rangel summed up this situation: "You must first realize that people do not link the *golpe* with a dictatorship. . . . They interpret it as a way out. Those same people in the polls, 90% of them favor democracy—at the same time, 90% say they are supporters of Comandante Chávez and the military. They simply do not see the connection between the military and a dictatorship."[96]

It is clear that the deterioration and loss of credibility by the civilian leadership, more than any change in the military institution, produced the failure of the Venezuelan model of civil-military relations. As early as December 1989, AD leader Hector Alonso López admitted, "As leaders we have lost touch with the people's situation."[97] He could have added that the government had also lost touch with the bulk of the officer corps. Postcoup statements by Arturo Uslar Pietri and Rafael Caldera, two of the most respected individuals in Venezuela, went even further. Uslar Pietri observed, "This action was not an isolated episode. It would be stupid to think that it was an ambitious and crazy adventure by a group wanting to seize power. . . . Those in the military feel the same distress that other Venezuelans are experiencing. The current democracy is not commensurate with the country's maturity."[98] At almost the same time, Caldera declared, "The coup is reprehensible and deplorable in every way, but it would be naive to think that this is just a matter of the adventures of a few ambitious individuals, who acted precipitously on their own, without realizing what they were getting into. There is an ambience, a groundswell, a perilous situation in the country, and if that situation is not confronted, many very serious problems lie ahead for us."[99]

Caldera's words aptly summarize the current dilemma in civil-military relations. Few members of either the military or civil society want violence and/or a dictatorship; almost all support at least the concept of elected, democratic government. But inability to agree on the forms of such a government, conflicts over definitions of democracy and responsibilities for both civil and military leaders, and the abuses and arrogance of power place this consensus in jeopardy. In the short run, a successful coup seems unlikely. In the long run, however, if the basic problems that produced and facilitated the February 4 and November 27, 1992, uprisings remain uncorrected, then the warning contained in the sergeants' manifesto—that "what happened on 4 February was only a sneeze heralding a coming cold"—may prove to be all too prophetic.[100]

# NOTES

1. Foreign Broadcast Information Service, *Daily Report: Latin America* (hereafter cited as FBIS), September 30, 1992, 55.
2. For information on pre-1959 civil-military relations see, for example, Robert L. Gilmore, *Caudillism and Militarism in Venezuela, 1810–1910* (Athens, Ohio: Ohio University Press, 1964); Winfield J. Burggraaff, *The Venezuelan Armed Forces in Politics, 1935–1959* (Columbia: University of Missouri Press, 1972); and Angel Ziems, *El gomecismo y la formación del ejército nacional* (Caracas: Editorial Ateneo de Caracas, 1979).
3. The fall of Pérez Jiménez and the transition to civilian rule are studied in Philip B. Taylor, Jr., *The Venezuelan Golpe de Estado of 1958: The Fall of Marcos Pérez Jiménez* (Washington, D.C.: 1968); José Umana Bernal, ed., *Testimonio de la revolución en Venezuela* (Caracas: 1958); and Joseph J. Doyle, "Venezuela 1958: Transition from Dictatorship to Democracy," Ph.D. dissertation, George Washington University, 1967.
4. Felipe Agüero, "The Military and Democracy in Venezuela," in Louis W. Goodman, Johanna S. R. Mendelson, and Juan Rial, eds., *The Military and Democracy: The Future of Civil-Military Relations in Latin America* (Lexington, Mass.: Lexington Books, 1990), 265, 272, and Rita Giacalone and Rexene Hanes de Acevedo, "The Military in a Subsidized Democracy: The Case of Venezuela," in Constantine Danopoulos, ed., *From Military to Civilian Rule* (London: Routledge, 1992), 146.
5. Gene E. Bigler, "The Armed Forces and Patterns of Civil-Military Relations," in John D. Martz and David J. Myers, eds., *Venezuela: The Democratic Experience* (New York: Praeger, 1977), 125; Paul W. Zagorski, *Democracy vs. National Security: Civil-Military Relations in Latin America* (Boulder: 1992), 79; and Daniel C. Hellinger, *Venezuela: Tarnished Democracy* (Boulder: Westview Press, 1991), 165.
6. Confidential interviews in Venezuela, March 1993.
7. Augusto Varas, "Military Autonomy and Democracy in Latin America," in Augusto Varas, ed., *Democracy under Siege: New Military Power in Latin America* (New York: Greenwood Press, 1989), 10.
8. See Jacobo Yépez Daza, "El realismo militar venezolano," in Moisés Naím and Ramón Piñango, eds., *El caso Venezuela: Una ilusión de armonía* (Caracas: Ediciones IESA, 1988), 339–43.
9. Confidential interviews with Venezuelan officers, September 1991 to September 1992.
10. Georgie Ann Geyer, "Democracy Betrayed," *World Monitor* vol. 5 (September 1992): 49.
11. *Wall Street Journal*, February 7, 1992, A15, and Geyer, "Democracy Betrayed," 49.
12. Philippe Erard, "Perspectives for Venezuela in the 90's: Investment Outlook," National Council for Investment Promotion (CONAPRI), Venezuela, Miami congressional workshop, January 1992, 3. See also Luis P. España and Marino J. Gonzalez, "Empobrecimiento y política social," *Seminario Interdiocesano de Caracas* (SIC) 56, no. 522 (March 1990): 63–78.
13. Geyer, "Democracy Betrayed," 46.
14. *Latin American Weekly Report* (hereafter cited as *LWR*), January 9, 1992, 10.
15. Andean Commission of Jurists, *Andean Newsletter* (Lima), June 12, 1989, 8.
16. *Wall Street Journal*, February 7, 1992, A15.
17. For information on the new social phenomenon of spontaneous street demonstra

tions known as *pobladas*, see *Andean Newsletter*, January 16, 1989, 7.
18. FBIS: March 1, 1989, 35; March 2, 1989, 59; and March 3, 1989, 52.
19. For examples of such charges see *Andean Newsletter*, April 10, 1989, 5–6.
20. FBIS, March 3, 1989, 52.
21. Giacalone and Hanes de Acevedo, "The Military in a Subsidized Democracy," 151.
22. By 1991 the issue had become something of a national obsession, a fact illustrated by the popularity of a three-volume *Diccionario de la corrupción en Venezuela* by Ruth Capriles Méndez (Caracas: Consorcio de Ediciones Capriles, 1959–92).
23. FBIS: April 10, 1989, 45; July 14, 1989, 64; October 31, 1989, 69; February 16, 1990, 68; July 26, 1990, 44; July 31, 1990, 44; and August 30, 1990, 57. *Andean Newsletter*: March 12, 1990, 6, and June 13, 1990, 6.
24. FBIS, June 12, 1989, 42.
25. *Miami Herald*, November 12, 1990, 11A.
26. FBIS: February 23, 1990, 56, and June 8, 1990, 42.
27. Ibid., May 31, 1990, 42–43.
28. *El Universal* (Caracas), June 18, 1989, 17.
29. FBIS, September 25, 1991, 44–45.
30. Ibid., June 8, 1990, 41.
31. *New York Times*, August 10, 1990, 3A.
32. See, for example, FBIS: March 21, 1989, 57, and August 14, 1990, 27.
33. Confidential interviews with Venezuelan officers, September 1991 to September 1992. See also Heinz R. Sonntag and Thaís Maingón, *Venezuela 4-F 1992: Un análisis sociopolítico* (Caracas: Editorial Nueva Sociedad, 1992), 67, 77.
34. Hellinger, *Venezuela: Tarnished Democracy*, 164.
35. Confidential interviews in Caracas, March 1993.
36. FBIS, December 13, 1991, 56–57.
37. Yépez Daza, p "El realismo militar venezolano," 347.
38. Bigler, "The Armed Forces," 129–30.
39. FBIS, June 24, 1991, 43.
40. *LWR*, February 20, 1992, 5, and *Christian Science Monitor*, February 7, 1992, 20.
41. Hellinger, *Venezuela: Tarnished Democracy*, 166. See also *Andean Newsletter*, June 13, 1990, 6–7, and FBIS, December 13, 1991, 56.
42. Hugo G. Posey, "In the Spirit of Bolívar: The Challenge to Democracy in Venezuela," *North-South* vol. 2 (June-July 1992): 12–13.
43. FBIS, October 26, 1990, 56. There have even been rumors that the president has Colombian ancestors.
44. See, for example, *Andean Newsletter*, November 9, 1989, 10; and *LWR*, February 20, 1992, 5.
45. FBIS, February 3, 1992, 43.
46. Ibid.: March 16, 1990, 73; August 29, 1991, 30; October 4, 1991, 45; and October 7, 1991, 57. Confidential interviews with Venezuelan and U.S. officers, August and September, 1992.
47. FBIS: October 17, 1989, 66, and October 21, 1991, 45.
48. Political Risk Services, *Venezuela: A Political and Economic Forecast*, February 1, 1992, C2.
49. *Wall Street Journal*, February 5, 1992, A6.
50. *El Universal*, February 20, 1992, 16. Interview with Andrés Serbín, September 1992. A biographical sketch of Chávez is found in Oldman Botello, *El golpe en Aragua: Crónica del 4-F en Maracay* (Villa de Cura, Venezuela: Editorial Miranda, 1992), 43–45.
51. *LWR*, February 20, 1992, 4.
52. Geyer, "Democracy Betrayed," 48.
53. For descriptions of the coup attempt, see FBIS: February 4, 1992, 37–44, and February 5, 1992, 27–37; *Latin American Regional Reports: Andean Group Report*, March 5, 1992, 1–3; *LWR*, February 20, 1992, 4–5; and *New York Times*, February 6, 1992, A3.
54. FBIS, May 26, 1992, 58–60.
55. Ibid., March 27, 1992, 28.

56. Ibid., July 27, 1992, 61.
57. Ibid., September 22, 1992, 41, and Posey, "In the Spirit of Bolívar," 12.
58. Posey, "In the Spirit of Bolívar," 12.
59. *Latin American Regional Reports: Andean Group Report,* March 5, 1992, 2.
60. *LWR,* August 27, 1992, 10.
61. *Economist,* February 8, 1992, 35; *Christian Science Monitor,* February 11, 1992, 4; *El Nacional,* April 6, 1992, 4D; and FBIS, October 29, 1991, 44–45.
62. *Economist,* February 22, 1992, 36; *Christian Science Monitor,* February 11, 1992, 4; and FBIS: April 2, 1992, 36–37; May 21, 1992, 29; and August 25, 1992, 39.
63. FBIS: February 19, 1992, 41, and July 7, 1992, 57–58; *LWR,* June 18, 1992, 3; Posey, "In the Spirit of Bolívar," 12; *El Nacional:* April 7, 1992, 6D, and April 24, 1992, 1D; *El Universal:* May 19, 1992, 14, and May 21, 1992, 12; and confidential interviews with Venezuelan officers, July to September 1992.
64. FBIS, May 6, 1992, 53.
65. Ibid., June 29, 1992, 41.
66. Ibid., 42. Interview with Steve Ellner, Universidad del Oriente, Barcelona, Venezuela, September 1992.
67. *New York Times,* February 7, 1992, A3.
68. FBIS, June 29, 1992, 41. Lieutenant Colonel Arias earlier charged that "some intend to turn our Armies into police forces and some of our leaders agree . . . because they must say yes in order to be promoted"; FBIS, February 28, 1992, 44.
69. *El Nacional,* February 6, 1992, 2D, and FBIS, June 29, 1992, 42.
70. Posey, "In the Spirit of Bolívar," 12.
71. *New York Times,* February 6, 1992, A3.
72. FBIS, August 21, 1990, 54.
73. "Venezuelan Opinion," *Hemisphere* vol.3 (Summer 1992): 27.
74. *Christian Science Monitor,* April 4, 1992, 3, and *Economist,* February 8, 1992, 35.
75. *Christian Science Monitor,* February 11, 1992, 4.
76. *Economist,* March 28, 1992, 43. Interviews with Andrés Serbín and Steve Ellner, September 1992.
77. FBIS: March 26 and 27, 1992, 28, and May 6, 1992, 53.
78. *LWR,* March 12, 1992, 5.
79. Ibid., August 6, 1992, 4.
80. Confidential interviews with Venezuelan officers, July to September 1992.
81. *Miami Herald,* December 5, 1992, 1A. For a brief analysis of the uprising, see Arturo Sosa A., "El 27 de noviembre de 1992," *SIC* vol. 56, no. 551 (January–February 1993): 37–46.
82. William Ojeda, *Las verdades del 27-N* (Caracas: Vadell Hermanos Editores, 1993), 44–50.
83. *El Nacional,* May 18, 1992, 2D.
84. FBIS, August 5, 1992, 44.
85. *LWR,* February 4, 1993, 49.
86. Ibid., June 11, 1992, 5.
87. FBIS, March 3, 1992, 30.
88. *Latin American Regional Reports: Andean Group Report,* April 9, 1992, 4–5.
89. Ibid., 1; *Miami Herald,* September 24, 1992, 16A; and FBIS, April 2, 1992, 41–44.
90. Giacalone and Hanes de Acevedo, "The Military in a Subsidized Democracy," 153.
91. FBIS, April 9, 1992, 43–44.
92. Ibid., 42.
93. *El Nacional,* February 27, 1992, 1D.
94. FBIS, April 20, 1992, 54.
95. Ibid.: July 27, 1992, 60, and September 21, 1992, 42.
96. Geyer, "Democracy Betrayed," 49.
97. FBIS, December 6, 1989, 36.
98. Ibid., March 6, 1992, 56. See also Arturo Uslar Pietri, *Golpe de Estado en Venezuela* (Bogotá: Grupo Editorial Norma, 1992), 157–62.
99. FBIS, March 6, 1992, 56.
100. Ibid., May 26, 1992, 60.

# 3

# The Evolution of Popular Opinion

## *Andrew Templeton*

Although military coups in their initial stages are by nature covert undertakings, popular opinion is involved in a double role. In the first place, the military is unlikely to attempt to overthrow a regime that enjoys tangible popular support. In the second place, and more important, the populace is more likely to support or tolerate alternative institutional arrangements—such as a military regime—if confidence in its elected leaders and satisfaction with the prevailing circumstances and existing institutions are low.

This chapter addresses the second of these issues within the context of Venezuela's two military uprisings of 1992. The theoretical underpinning of this analysis is the gap between the way popular opinion perceives the existing situation to be and how people think things *should be*.[1] The substantive material is derived from opinion surveys conducted over the past twenty years and in particular from the results of a longitudinal study based on national representative samples that has been conducted several times a year since 1968. method

### THE FEBRUARY COUP

A month after the attempted military coup of February 1992, a representative sample of 2,000 adult Venezuelans was asked why the coup had occurred. Ninety percent of respondents gave answers to this open-ended question, providing twenty-five classifiable replies.[2]

The answers reflect two broad areas of discontent. First are the issues of personal economic dissatisfaction, largely centering around the problem of inflation. Second are the perceptions of government inefficiency and administrative corruption. Obviously, these two concerns cannot be completely separated for analysis; certainly the first can be a result of the second and, in many cases, as can be seen from the duplication of replies, respondents mentioned both in answer to the survey question. It is important, moreover, to note that almost without exception the replies were criticisms of the existing regime; a mere 3 percent of respondents alleged that the ambitions of the military could have been a cause of the attempt. This may help to explain the apparent contradiction, commented on later, of popular opinion both tolerating the attempt and preferring a civilian government.

The replies suggest an explanation for the considerable popular sympathy the rebels of the February coup enjoyed, on the one hand, and the virtual lack of popular support for the government, on the other. These attitudes and the popular reaction to the coup attempt stand in sharp contrast to the responses of the late 1950s and early 1960s to similar situations, which, though not measured in opinion studies, were evident in popular behavior and have been succinctly catalogued by John Martz.[3]

Why was it that by early 1992 the gap between popular perceptions of the way Venezuela was and the way Venezuelans felt it should have been had widened to such an alarming extent? The two main areas of concern were economic discontent and bad government, but each of these covered subareas that require examination. Economic discontent, for example, is not only a reflection of the hardship caused by the economic "restructuring" of the Pérez government, but also a function of distributional conflicts rooted in the colonial era. Bad government covers ineptitude as well as corruption. Moreover, bad government refers not only to the existing regime, but also to previous governments, giving rise to the issue of public attitudes toward the political parties and other institutions of Venezuelan democracy. Finally, implicitly if not explicitly, the issues of popular attitudes toward the military and its role in national life, and of public perceptions of the concept of democracy as a form of government, require consideration.

Before attempting such analyses, two further points are germane to the discussion. First, in the realm of theory, a gap between the way things are and the way they ought to be is inevitable. The danger occurs when the gap widens beyond usual and tolerable limits. Perhaps the best recent example for U.S. readers is the 1992 Los Angeles rioting, sparked by the wide gap between the expected and the actual verdict in the Rodney King court case. Second, it must be realized that the survey research conducted in the twenty years or so before the crisis of 1992 was not designed as a specific backdrop to the events of that year; on the contrary, only on rare occasions was the issue of an alternative to democratic institutions considered worthy of inclusion in opinion surveys. Consequently, the longitudinal data in some areas are at best sketchy.[4]

## ECONOMIC DISCONTENT

The most complete survey information available relates to economic discontent, which is measured in the longitudinal study in a variety of ways. Respondents are asked to compare their personal economic situation with that of a year ago. They are then asked to give their expectations of that situation at a point six months into the future. Survey participants are next asked questions relating to their ability to purchase consumer durables and regarding their perceptions on the problems of inflation and unemployment. The detailed figures for the series are given in appendixes 3.2 to 3.5. Nevertheless, without unduly burdening the text, certain key figures are pertinent to the argument and are provided in the main chapter text.

A basic measurement of economic dissatisfaction is the extent to which people feel that they are worse off than in the past. Table 3.1 illustrates these perceptions for certain key periods since 1980.

One can surmise that the populace will endure being worse off than in the past if it feels optimistic about the future. Table 3.2 gives the responses on how Venezuelans were feeling about the future for each of the same periods.

Given the findings illustrated in tables 3.1 and 3.2, there is evidence of economic discontent for at least a decade before the attempted coups of 1992. Since 1980, at least one-third of the population has always considered itself to be worse off than the year before and never more than 25 percent felt that they would be better off in the near future. In addition, examining the data following the bolivar devaluation of February 1983 and the looting riots of 1989, one sees sharp drops in the levels of economic satisfaction and confidence. Finally, a comparison of the first survey following the February coup attempt and the last

Table 3.1
ECONOMIC SITUATION COMPARED WITH A YEAR AGO

|  | Selected Quarters | | | | | | | |
|---|---|---|---|---|---|---|---|---|
|  | 1980-1 (%) | 1981-4 (%) | 1983-2 (%) | 1988-4 (%) | 1989-3 (%) | 1991-4 (%) | 1992-1 (%) | 1992-3 (%) |
| Better off | 18 | 25 | 7 | 26 | 6 | 20 | 17 | 18 |
| Neither better nor worse | 36 | 40 | 31 | 38 | 24 | 26 | 26 | 22 |
| Worse off | 45 | 35 | 61 | 35 | 68 | 52 | 57 | 58 |
| N = | 3,000 | 3,000 | 3,000 | 2,000 | 2,000 | 2,000 | 2,000 | 2,000 |

*Source:* PN.
*Note:* Percentages total less than 100 due to rounding and/or "don't know" responses.

Table 3.2
ECONOMIC EXPECTATIONS FOR THE NEXT SIX MONTHS

| | Selected Periods (Approximate Quarters) | | | | | | | |
|---|---|---|---|---|---|---|---|---|
| | 1980-1 (%) | 1981-4 (%) | 1983-2 (%) | 1988-4 (%) | 1989-3 (%) | 1991-4 (%) | 1992-2 (%) | 1992-3 (%) |
| Better off | 22 | 25 | 14 | 20 | 13 | 14 | 13 | 13 |
| Neither better nor worse | 24 | 32 | 28 | 27 | 23 | 28 | 28 | 28 |
| Worse off | 38 | 31 | 39 | 35 | 56 | 52 | 51 | 53 |
| Don't know | 16 | 13 | 19 | 18 | 9 | 6 | 9 | 6 |
| *N* = | 3,000 | 3,000 | 3,000 | 2,000 | 2,000 | 2,000 | 2,000 | 2,000 |

*Source:* PN.

survey preceding the November attempt suggests that despite government efforts, the sentiment of the population was virtually unchanged.

Thus, at the end of 1991, more than half of the population thought that it was worse off than the year before and a similar proportion of citizens expected their economic situation to deteriorate. The point here, of course, is the sharp increase in these negative indexes at the beginning of the Pérez government and the concomitant program of economic "restructuring" compared with the levels of earlier years—a widening of the gap from unsatisfactory to intolerable levels.

## INFLATION

The principal component of economic discontent in 1992 was inflation. This was not always the case in Venezuela. Throughout most of the 1980s, unemployment was considered by those surveyed to be a greater problem than inflation. In 1985, for example, 71 percent of the respondents mentioned unemployment as the most important concern, as opposed to the 28 percent who noted inflation. By the end of the decade, however, perceptions had changed: in the second quarter of 1989, following the looting riots, 51 percent mentioned unemployment and 45 percent mentioned inflation. Table 3.3 demonstrates the importance of the problem of inflation from 1990 through 1992.

The increasing salience of the issue of inflation in the past few years cannot be overemphasized. In the first place, it was and is a real issue. Prices increased by 320 percent in the three years preceding the first coup attempt, after having risen by 250 percent during the Lusinchi administration (1984–89)—and this in a country that experienced extremely low levels of inflation from the 1930s through the early 1970s.[5]

Table 3.3
WHAT IS THE MOST IMPORTANT PROBLEM
WITH THE ECONOMY?

| | Selected Periods (Approximate Quarters) | | | |
| --- | --- | --- | --- | --- |
| | 1990-2 (%) | 1991-2 (%) | 1992-2 (%) | 1992-3 (%) |
| Inflation | 67 | 72 | 76 | 77 |
| Unemployment | 33 | 28 | 24 | 23 |
| $N=$ | 2,000 | 2,000 | 2,000 | 2,000 |

*Source:* PN.

Second, it seems that the populist nature of most Venezuelan governments in the past has tended to make them more concerned with unemployment than inflation. Nowhere was this more evident than in the measures taken during the first Pérez administration (1974–79), when Venezuela was faced for the first time since World War II with severe inflationary pressures.

Contrary to expectations surrounding economic "restructuring," Venezuela has not experienced increasing unemployment since 1989; rather, official figures show unemployment declining. Similarly, despite high positive interest rates, the Caracas Stock Exchange index rose 1,000 percent in the first three years of the second Pérez government. As far as popular discontent is concerned, whereas unemployment affects primarily those who lose their jobs and whereas rising markets benefit a limited number of stockholders, inflation harms almost everyone—particularly salary and wage earners who traditionally have been the main supporters of the democratic regime.[6]

## SATISFACTION WITH GOVERNMENT

It is a common tenet of electoral theory that inflation and unemployment levels are fundamental in determining the level of popular support for governments. Indeed, Seymour Martin Lipset has advanced the hypothesis that if the "misery index" is high enough, that is, if the sum of the rates of inflation and unemployment is over 10 percent, then the reigning government can be expected to lose the succeeding elections.[7] Although Margaret Thatcher's career and the election results in Australia and Ireland have disproved this hypothesis several times, it has held for the Venezuelan elections of 1973, 1978, and 1983. As can be seen from table 3.4, in these three years the misery index correlates closely with the share of votes obtained by the government party. In

Table 3.4
MISERY INDEX AND ATTITUDE TOWARD GOVERNMENT
(1973–92)

| | Nov. 1973 (%) | Nov. 1978 (%) | Nov. 1983 (%) | Nov. 1988 (%) | Nov. 1989 (%) | Nov. 1990 (%) | Nov. 1991 (%) | Mar. 1992 (%) | Aug. 1992 (%) |
|---|---|---|---|---|---|---|---|---|---|
| Misery index | 17 | 16 | 28 | 33 | 80 | 43 | 38 | 40 | 41 |
| Favorable attitude to government | 37 | 36 | 16 | 37 | 14 | 22 | 19 | 14 | 13 |
| Vote for government party in Dec. elections | 34 | 37 | 29 | 42 | N/A | N/A | N/A | N/A | N/A |
| *N* = | 2,500 | 3,000 | 3,000 | 2,000 | 2,000 | 2,000 | 2,000 | 2,000 | 2,000 |

*Source:* PN.
N/A = not available.

1973 and 1978, both figures correlate with another measure—that of the public's evaluation of the job the government is doing.

In the elections of 1983 and 1988, the two major party candidates, Rafael Caldera of COPEI and Carlos Andrés Pérez of AD, were able to disassociate themselves to a certain degree from their party representatives in government. Furthermore, they were able to persuade a significant proportion of electors of the value of personal qualities, compensating for the less favorable public perceptions of their respective parties.[8] Nevertheless, examining the survey series through August 1992, one can see that popular support for the government had reached dangerously low levels by November 1989 and did not recover before Pérez was forced from office in May 1993.

The measurement of public evaluations of the job the government is doing forms a bridge between the two major issues raised in the post-coup study previously mentioned. Clearly this measurement, which is used in one form or another in public opinion surveys in most countries,[9] is a reflection of a variety of factors coupled with the important question of economic satisfaction. Tracing the rise of public concerns like "bad government and corruption" to their highest levels, one must return to 1983 and the devaluation of the bolivar. The devaluation was the first of three catalytic events (the others being the riots of 1989 and the military uprisings of 1992) that since 1980 have influenced the evolution of popular opinion with respect to existing institutions and, perhaps more important, to the national ethos itself.

The last year in which Venezuelans generally were able to believe in the myth of their own prosperity was 1982. OPEC petroleum averaged

Table 3.5
FAVORABLE ATTITUDES TOWARD GOVERNMENT ACCORDING
TO SOCIOECONOMIC LEVEL

| | Socioeconomic Level | | | | |
|---|---|---|---|---|---|
| | A–B (%) | C (%) | D (%) | E (%) | N |
| 1972 | 27 | 34 | 27 | 21 | 2,500 |
| 1975 | 34 | 37 | 35 | 28 | 2,500 |
| 1983 | 27 | 20 | 16 | 11 | 3,000 |
| 1988 | 30 | 38 | 37 | 36 | 2,000 |
| 1989 | 22 | 18 | 15 | 10 | 2,000 |
| 1990 | 24 | 23 | 21 | 23 | 2,000 |
| 1991 | 16 | 13 | 15 | 25 | 2,000 |
| 1992 (March) | 24 | 12 | 12 | 16 | 2,000 |
| 1992 (August) | 16 | 9 | 9 | 18 | 2,000 |

*Source:* PN.
*Note:* (A–B) the rich and very rich, usually high social position for several generations; (C) professionals and white-collar workers, ranging economically from people of consider-able wealth to those of quite modest resources; (D) blue-collar working class in regular employment with social security and severance benefits; (E) marginal class, casual work-ers, single parents, and poor families. Over the period of the surveys discussed in this chapter, Datos, C.A., has estimated that the socioeconomic division has shifted (see note 38 herein).      C-| D

| | Percent of Shift over Time | |
|---|---|---|
| | 1970s (%) | 1980s (%) |
| A–B | 3 | 2 |
| C | 24 | 20 |
| D | 40 | 38 |
| E | 33 | 40 |

U.S.$32 per barrel (1982 prices), gross national product (GNP) per capita was close to 50 percent of the average of the Organization for Economic Cooperation and Development (OECD) countries, and prices had risen by less than 10 percent over the previous year. The im-pact of the 1983 devaluation was not only economic, as seen in tables 3.1 and 3.2, but also reflected in disillusion with institutions and to a certain extent with the nation itself. We can measure this political disil-lusion in several ways. The first is through the percentages reflecting fa-vorable attitudes toward the government referred to in table 3.4. In table 3.5, the data are presented for a period of twenty years and are di-vided according to the socioeconomic level of the respondents.[10]

While all segments of the population have become increasingly criti-cal of the government, the largest decline is seen in segments C and D,

Table 3.6
ANOTHER GOVERNMENT WOULD HAVE DONE A BETTER JOB

|  | (%) |
|---|---|
| 1978 | 28 |
| 1983 | 36 |
| 1986 | 19 |
| 1987 | 16 |
| 1988 | 15 |
| 1989 | 12 |
| 1990 | 13 |
| 1991 | 14 |
| 1992 (April) | 16 |
| 1992 (August) | 18 |

*Source:* PN.

which, apart from accounting for almost 60 percent of the population, have been shown to be the best informed politically, the most critical, and to have "higher levels of support for rules of democratic procedure."[11] A crucial element of the crisis of 1992 was the erosion of support for existing institutions, particularly the government and the traditional parties, within those segments of the population that were their strongest supporters in the early years of the post-1958 democracy.

Disillusion with the political parties in government is reflected in the answer to the question of whether a government different from the one in power would have done a better job of running the country. Table 3.6 shows the responses to this question from 1978 onward. Until the end of the Herrera government in 1983, about one-third of the population felt that another party would do a better job. By the middle of Lusinchi's term, only 16 percent of the respondents believed so, and in the wake of the disturbances of 1989, the percentage had fallen to 12 percent.

In 1978, of those who responded that another party would have done a better job, 75 percent mentioned COPEI, the main opposition party. In 1983, 89 percent mentioned AD, then in opposition. When asked in 1983 for which party they would vote if only COPEI or AD existed, 83 percent mentioned one or the other; only 10 percent said they would abstain or destroy their ballot form. When asked in the same (PN) survey who should govern Venezuela if the country were to experience a grave crisis, only 10 percent mentioned a military government; the remainder mentioned either traditional leaders or parties. By the middle 1980s, however, the lack of faith in institutions and in the country was beginning to manifest itself.

Table 3.7
CAUSES OF VENEZUELA'S LARGE FOREIGN DEBT (1984)

|  | (%) |
|---|---|
| External economic factors | 11 |
| Bad administration of nation's funds | 36 |
| Administrative corruption | 33 |
| Excessive consumption by all Venezuelans | 6 |
| Other replies; don't know | 14 |

*Source:* PN.
*N* = 3,000.

## THE BOLIVAR DEVALUATION

In November 1984, respondents were asked what had contributed most to create the country's large foreign debt. The answers (see table 3.7) eloquently make their point: the blame for the crisis of 1983 was placed squarely on the shoulders of the administrations that had been running the country.

Earlier, during the first months of the Lusinchi government, respondents were asked to assign levels of responsibility for the economic crisis confronting the country. Table 3.8 shows that the respondents assigned responsibility not only to the governments but also to businesspeople and to the population itself. Although most blame was placed on the Herrera government, the Lusinchi administration, in office for barely six months, did not escape, nor did the national ethos.

A curious side-effect of this questioning on the national direction is reflected in popular attitudes toward Venezuela's basic industry, petroleum. In the November 1984 study referred to earlier, respondents were asked to name the country's most important industry: 49 percent cited agriculture and 42 percent petroleum. A year later, in September 1985, the percentages had hardly changed, with 46 percent mentioning agriculture and 41 percent petroleum. At this time, petroleum accounted for 80 percent of Venezuela's export value and the country imported ten times more by value in agricultural produce than it exported.

The two years following the 1983 devaluation were characterized by a public debate on where Venezuela had gone wrong. Although the real issue was that petroleum revenues had not been used wisely, the debate increasingly revolved around a nostalgic return to the simpler, prepetroleum days, emphasizing in particular the neglect of agriculture and the need to import food staples that previously had been produced

Table 3.8
RESPONSIBILITY FOR ECONOMIC CRISIS (1984)

| | A Lot (%) | Some (%) | Little (%) | None (%) | Don't Know (%) |
|---|---|---|---|---|---|
| Present government | 48 | 18 | 14 | 13 | 7 |
| Previous government | 62 | 15 | 9 | 8 | 6 |
| Trade unions | 39 | 22 | 13 | 13 | 13 |
| Businesspeople | 49 | 23 | 11 | 8 | 10 |
| Egoism of Venezuelan people | 44 | 21 | 13 | 14 | 8 |
| World economic situation | 44 | 21 | 12 | 9 | 14 |
| International petrol. prices | 43 | 20 | 11 | 8 | 18 |

*Source:* PN.
*N* = 2,000.
*Note:* Percentages total more than 100 due to rounding.

locally and even exported. Over the course of this debate, the petroleum industry was blamed for causing the economic problems much in the same way that Japanese exports have been blamed for causing U.S. economic difficulties.

In this same 1985 survey, 53 percent of respondents agreed that the country was suffering a crisis of confidence, versus 29 percent who disagreed.[12] Agreement was strongest among white- and blue-collar workers (C and D socioeconomic groups). The open-ended replies as to the principal cause of the crisis of confidence were depressingly similar to the reasons given seven years later as to the causes of the first coup attempt: economic factors and bad government or corruption.

When the same respondents were asked to assign blame for the crisis to specific factors, they gave the replies summarized in table 3.9. Corruption, egoism, and the decline in moral values and leadership all reflect a popular concern that goes beyond a straight criticism of the performance of elected governments. This concern is further illustrated in public perceptions of the honesty of the leadership of various institutions, as shown in a September 1985 survey (table 3.10).

The very institutions—Congress, trade unions, public administration, and state enterprises—that were the cornerstones of the post–Pérez Jiménez democratic system were also held in lowest esteem. Only the universities and the armed forces escaped relatively unscathed.

## GOVERNMENT INEFFICIENCY

From the preceding data it is evident that by the end of 1985 there was considerable popular disillusion with public institutions and those who

Table 3.9
RESPONSIBILITY FOR CRISIS (1985)

| | Much (%) | Some (%) | Little (%) | None (%) |
|---|---|---|---|---|
| Corruption | 86 | 9 | 2 | 2 |
| Bad administration of natural resources | 74 | 17 | 5 | 3 |
| Decline of moral values | 50 | 26 | 12 | 7 |
| Egoism of Venezuelan people | 30 | 25 | 27 | 24 |
| World economic situation | 59 | 26 | 9 | 4 |
| Lack of leadership | 43 | 27 | 13 | 11 |

*Source:* PN.
*Note:* Percentages total more or less than 100 due to rounding.

Table 3.10
LITTLE OR NO CONFIDENCE IN HONESTY OF THOSE WHO
MANAGE VARIOUS INSTITUTIONS (1985)

| | (%) |
|---|---|
| Public administration | 67 |
| Trade unions | 64 |
| State enterprises | 60 |
| Congress | 57 |
| Banks | 54 |
| Police | 52 |
| Retail commerce | 52 |
| Private sector | 44 |
| Television | 43 |
| Press | 39 |
| Universities | 33 |
| Armed forces | 28 |

*Source:* PN.
*N* = 2,000.

ran them. The criticism centered around "government" as an all-embracing term and was concerned with ineptitude on one hand and venality on the other. Examples of ineptitude are legion; there is no need to dwell on them. Table 3.11, which indicates some of the problems the population had encountered during the month preceding the time of the survey, is as good a measure as any for Venezuela, a country in which, at least until the end of the 1980s, the government had expanded to such an extent as to assume responsibility not only for basic services but also for food supply.

These figures, together with those quoted earlier on inflation and unemployment, bring to mind V. S. Naipaul's comparison of Argen-

Table 3.11
PROPORTION OF POPULATION EXPERIENCING PROBLEMS
WITH BASIC SERVICES

|  | 1981 (%) | 1984 (%) | 1987 (%) | 1988 (%) | 1989 (%) |
|---|---|---|---|---|---|
| Power cuts | 52 | 39 | 39 | 37 | 35 |
| Water shortage | 54 | 55 | 41 | 46 | 39 |
| Robbery | 7 | 10 | 6 | 13 | 13 |
| Shortage of basic necessities | 45 | 73 | 56 | 69 | 76 |
| N = | 3,000 | 2,000 | 2,000 | 2,000 | 2,000 |

*Source:* PN.

tina's political life to a colony of ants or an African tribe: "Full of events, full of crises and deaths, but life is only cyclical and the year always ends as it begins."[13] Every president-elect since 1968 has promised to control inflation, increase employment, reduce crime, and improve public services. At the end of each presidency, the indexes for each problem have been as high or higher than they were at the start of the term.

## CORRUPTION

As was suggested earlier, popular opinion can probably accept harsh economic conditions if at the same time it is optimistic about the future. Similarly, it could be argued that the population is more likely to accept inefficiency in government if it is perceived as simple incapacity. Indeed, a wealth of anecdotal evidence from the 1960s demonstrates the comparisons being made at the time between the administrative abilities of the new democratic regime and those of the preceding dictatorship; popular calls for its overthrow on those grounds are absent. By the 1980s, however, the emphasis had shifted and the government was not only seen as inefficient, it was also believed to be corrupt.

Again, one must recall the impact of the 1983 devaluation and recognize that, despite the petroleum boom of the previous decade, Venezuela was a poor country. The preeminent question seemed to be, Where did the money go? This question, in fact, was one of COPEI's slogans during the 1978 elections, the first time that the issue had been seriously raised in an electoral contest.[14] Nevertheless, the COPEI leadership played down the existence of corruption and shifted its line of attack toward the issue of ineptitude. Corruption had first been raised as an issue after the coup of 1945, particularly by AD, with the establishment of the Tribunal of Civil and Administrative Responsibility and later in the 1960s as a means of discrediting the Pérez Jiménez regime.[15] The concept of administrative corruption was by no means absent from the popular consciousness, but it had not become a major issue of the political agenda of the government and opposition; this inattention might be related in part to the "people in glass houses" syndrome, but it can also be attributed to the national ethos itself.

Attitudes toward corruption are not the easiest to measure in quantitative terms, yet the results of two surveys conducted in 1985 and 1991 help shed light on the latter assertion concerning national ethos.[16] Respondents were asked to rate certain behaviors on a scale from "not at all bad" to "very bad." Various situations were posited, ranging from a traffic police officer asking for a bribe to a politician accepting favors from an industrialist. The surveys showed virtually no change in attitudes over the six-year timespan. In the 1991 survey, in only two scenarios did more than 30 percent of the respondents qualify the behavior as "very bad." Only 9 percent, for example, considered it very bad for a politician to accept the use of an industrialist's private aircraft; 36 percent stated that it was not at all bad; and 37 percent said that they would do it themselves. Forty percent saw nothing bad in a government official engaging in nepotism; only 25 percent considered it very bad for a government official to accept a gift of money from a businessperson bidding on a government contract. Given this tolerant attitude, why is it that by 1992 corruption had become a salient issue for popular opinion, as well as the principal justification given by the military for attempting the February coup?

Three main hypotheses can be considered. First, popular opinion evolves slowly on most issues, particularly if they are complex.[17] As explained earlier, the issue has existed certainly since 1945,[18] and after 1983 was increasingly mentioned by respondents in public opinion surveys. Second, corruption involving the provision of foreign exchange at rates far below market value (the RECADI, or National Preferential Exchange Office, scandal) from 1983 to 1989 was far more widespread than earlier scandals. Although prior to 1989 it was not (and for not very creditable reasons) widely diffused by the media, the scandal was sufficiently far-reaching to become common knowledge among large segments of the population: 69 percent claimed to have heard of it, 79 percent of whom believed it involved corruption. Following the abolition of RECADI in 1989, the media felt less threatened economically[19] and placed the corruption issue squarely (though not always fairly) on the national agenda, not only attacking the minor players but also reaching for those responsible at the top echelons.

Finally, and this point is more open to discussion, there has been an increasing awareness among the population of the wide disparities in income between the few and the many. This distributional conflict, coupled with general economic discontent and the exhortations of political leaders for further belt-tightening, led many to believe that the wealthy must have obtained their riches illicitly.

## DISTRIBUTIONAL CONFLICT

Although, as Janet Kelly illustrates in chapter 10 of this volume, the contrast between wealth and poverty is evident even to the most obtuse observer setting foot in Venezuela for the first time, the issue attracts surprisingly little attention from the intellectual community. The distributional conflict has obviously been ignored by neoliberal economists responsible for or sympathetic to the post-1989 economic restructuring, but it has also been largely neglected by those opposed to the present economic policies. As M. Panic has argued, "It is their neglect of social problems and political realities that makes the policy prescriptions of many economists, both 'monetarists' and 'Keynesians,' so impractical."[20] Although this comment appears particularly true of the post-1989 experience, it would be a mistake to assume that the distributional problem is of recent date or has ever been seriously addressed, even by populist administrations.

With regard to survey research, one can argue that despite the long existence of the distributional conflict, it has been slow to develop as a salient issue among popular opinion. Throughout the 1970s, while the longitudinal measures showed consistently higher levels of economic dissatisfaction and criticism of government performance among the least privileged segments of society, there is no evidence of a desire for retribution from them. For example, from a national representative sample conducted in 1973, Enrique Baloyra and John Martz concluded: "Neither were the lower classes more adamant about redistribution, nor were the upper less concerned with economic issues."[21] Table 3.12 summarizes the answers given by respondents of different socioeconomic levels when asked in 1974 whether a socialist revolution would be good or bad for Venezuela.

Distributional conflict can be contained in periods of economic growth, as Venezuela seems to have experienced in the twenty years prior to 1983. By 1977, however, signs of marked differences in perceptions of economic well-being already were becoming apparent among different socioeconomic levels. Table 3.13 outlines the responses given

Table 3.12

WOULD A SOCIALIST REVOLUTION BE GOOD OR BAD FOR
VENEZUELA? (1974)

| | Socioeconomic Level | | | |
| --- | --- | --- | --- | --- |
| | A–B (%) | C (%) | D (%) | E (%) |
| Good | 32 | 34 | 38 | 34 |
| Bad | 55 | 36 | 25 | 20 |
| Other reply/don't know | 13 | 30 | 37 | 47 |

*Source:* PC, October 1974.
*N* = 1,000.
*Note:* Percentages total more than 100 due to rounding.

when participants were asked to describe their personal economic situation in 1977, and table 3.14 gives the responses to a similar survey in June 1982.

In a September 1987 PN survey, respondents indicated that the wealthy had considerable advantages over the poor on a series of rated items. The greatest perceived advantage was in the receipt of good medical attention; advantages in housing and child education followed close behind.[22] The Venezuelan populace also appears to have long perceived the close relationship between having money or power and obtaining justice. In response to the question on whether the courts would protect their rights in a conflict with a powerful person, the proportion responding that they would be protected reached its nadir in an October 1991 survey. At that time, only 9 percent replied positively, the lowest proportion since this question was first asked fifteen years ago and a decline from 17 percent in 1986; negative responses were given by 77 percent.

Table 3.13

WHICH STATEMENT BEST DESCRIBES YOUR PERSONAL
ECONOMIC SITUATION?

| | | Socioeconomic Level | | | |
| --- | --- | --- | --- | --- | --- |
| | Total sample (%) | A–B (%) | C (%) | D (%) | E (%) |
| I have enough to live well | 5 | 24 | 9 | 6 | 1 |
| I have enough to live | 32 | 55 | 51 | 36 | 15 |
| I have barely enough to live | 44 | 15 | 32 | 46 | 52 |
| I do not have enough to live | 18 | 5 | 7 | 13 | 31 |

*Source:* PN, June 1977.
*N* = 3,000.

Table 3.14
WHICH STATEMENT BEST DESCRIBES YOUR PERSONAL
ECONOMIC SITUATION?

| | | Socioeconomic Level | | | |
|---|---|---|---|---|---|
| | Total sample (%) | A–B (%) | C (%) | D (%) | E (%) |
| Meet expenses without problem | 20 | 30 | 23 | 18 | 18 |
| More or less meet expenses | 44 | 54 | 58 | 52 | 40 |
| Barely meet expenses | 30 | 14 | 18 | 29 | 40 |

Source: PN.
N = 3,000.
Note: Percentages total less than 100 due to rounding and "don't know" responses.

✓  On the basis of their 1973 survey data, Baloyra and Martz concluded that "social classes do not seem to constitute important conflict groups . . . at least in a classical Marxist sense."[23] This does not mean, however, that there was no popular awareness of socioeconomic differences. In 1973, 57 percent of the sample described themselves as belonging to the middle class and 31 percent to the poor or low-income class.[24] Sixteen years later, respondents were asked to classify themselves on a scale of one to ten, ranging from lower class to upper class. Table 3.15 demonstrates how this self-assessment corresponds to the objective Datos, C.A., assessments of socioeconomic level.

The overall results were similar to those of the 1973 survey: 51 percent classified themselves as middle class and 39 percent as lower class. In this same survey, respondents were asked their opinions on the degree of conflict that existed among various segments of the population. Eighty-two percent responded that there were considerable conflicts of interest between rich and poor, and 64 percent responded that conflict existed between the upper and middle classes. Sixty-eight percent felt the differences in income between rich and poor were too large. Objec-

Table 3.15
ON A SCALE OF ONE TO TEN, HOW DO YOU RATE
YOURSELF BY CLASS?

| | | Socioeconomic Level | | | |
|---|---|---|---|---|---|
| | Total sample | A–B | C | D | E |
| Mean | 4.0 | 5.6 | 4.9 | 4.1 | 3.0 |

Source: PN, August 1989.
N = 2,000.

Table 3.16
REAL VERSUS ESTIMATED EARNINGS FOR SELECTED
OCCUPATIONS (1987)

| | Earnings Are (mean) (bolivars) | Estimated Earnings (mean) (bolivars) |
|---|---|---|
| Construction worker | 5,400.00 | 6,550.00 |
| Bus driver | 5,900.00 | 5,890.00 |
| Factory owner | 62,790.00 | 32,400.00 |
| Company manager | 23,370.00 | 16,590.00 |

*Source:* PN, August 1989.
$N = 2,000$.

tive evidence of these opinions is reflected in the responses given as to what they calculated earnings to be for a group of occupations and what they estimated earnings should be (see table 3.16).

Venezuelans appear to have accepted the existence of differences in earnings, but also to have felt that the actual differences were too large. The accelerated emergence of this characteristic, which became an important element in the 1992 crisis, can be seen in a follow-up survey in 1991.[25] Whereas in 1989 respondents estimated that the average earnings of a factory owner were twelve times those of a construction worker, in 1991 they were estimated to be fifty times greater. Further apparent evidence of social conflict arose in response to a question about the general strike (Did you favor or oppose it?) called by the trade unions in 1989: the lower classes approved of it much more than did the upper classes (table 3.17).

Table 3.17
DID YOU FAVOR OR OPPOSE THE 1989 GENERAL STRIKE?

| | In Favor (%) | Against (%) |
|---|---|---|
| Poor people | 58 | 16 |
| Housewives | 52 | 15 |
| Trade unionists | 60 | 7 |
| Middle class | 29 | 18 |
| Businessmen | 8 | 64 |
| Wealthy | 9 | 59 |

*Source:* PN, June 1989.
$N = 2,000$.

## POPULAR MALAISE

By the end of the decade, there was evidence from sample survey research alone of a level of popular malaise that should have seriously concerned Venezuela's political leaders. Alfredo Keller, in an acute analysis of the crisis, has examined the increasing impatience shown toward the government since 1968 by comparing the Datos, C.A., survey figures on favorable attitudes toward the government with the percentage of votes cast for the winning presidential candidate. Table 3.18 illustrates, as Keller points out, that the crisis of 1992 had a lengthy gestation.[26]

The malaise had reached crisis proportions very shortly after the accession of President Pérez. Three factors may be responsible for this result. First, during the last years of the Lusinchi administration, allegedly for electoral reasons and with a disastrous effect on the national treasury, the government primed the economy and the economic situation had improved relative to the previous year. This improvement brought in its wake increased levels of optimism and higher expectations. Second, expectations were further raised by the election of President Pérez, whose campaign reinforced the ingenuous belief among many Venezuelans that during his second presidency the country could return to the prosperity enjoyed during his first administration.[27] Third, when the new government was faced with the reality of the economic situation, Pérez, to the surprise of many Venezuelans, opted for a monetarist and free-market approach that brought about a sharp increase in prices. The ground was laid for discontent to turn a serious situation into a crisis.

Table 3.18
ELECTORAL RESULTS AND GOVERNMENT SUPPORT

| National Elections | Share of Votes[a] (%) | Support 8 Months after Election[b] (%) | Frustration Index[c] |
|---|---|---|---|
| 1968—Caldera | 29 | 30 | +1 |
| 1973—Pérez | 49 | 44 | −5 |
| 1978—Herrera | 47 | 32 | −15 |
| 1983—Lusinchi | 57 | 32 | −25 |
| 1988—Pérez | 53 | 22 | −31 |

[a]Source: Consejo Supremo Electoral, Venezuela.
[b]Source: Datos, C.A. (PN).
[c]Keller's index, or the difference between share of votes and favorable attitudes toward government eight months after taking power.

Table 3.19
NEGATIVE ATTITUDES TOWARD GOVERNMENT

| | Total sample (%) | Socioeconomic Level | | | |
|---|---|---|---|---|---|
| | | A–B (%) | C (%) | D (%) | E (%) |
| April 1989 | 39 | 31 | 37 | 40 | 41 |
| June 1989 | 48 | 29 | 39 | 45 | 61 |

*Source:* PN.
N = 2,000.

Table 3.20
PERSONAL FEARS ABOUT THE ECONOMY (APRIL 1989)

| | (%) |
|---|---|
| Inflation/removal of price controls | 73 |
| Unemployment | 28 |
| Lack of personal security | 21 |
| Shortages | 20 |
| Economic crisis | 15 |
| Coup d'état, repetition of February disturbances | 15 |

*Source:* PN.
N = 2,000.

# THE CRISIS OF 1989   RIOTS

Like the devaluation of 1983, the riots of February 1989 had a profound effect on popular opinion, particularly among the poorer segments of the population. A measure of negative attitudes toward the government in the two surveys following the riots indicates the importance of the socioeconomic circumstances (table 3.19).

In the April 1989 survey, respondents were asked to state in their own words their principal fears and anxieties, first for themselves and second for the country. As can be seen in table 3.20, their personal fears centered around the economic problems confronting them. Table 3.21 shows that as far as the country was concerned, though economic fears remained important, emphasis appeared to shift toward a concern for the fragility of institutions. Table 3.22 breaks down the answers to four items in table 3.21 according to the socioeconomic level of the respondent.

Given the coup attempts of 1992, these results suggest that the working class was either more prescient or more politically realistic than the elite. It may also indicate the apparent lack of concern of the nation's

Table 3.21
## FEARS ABOUT THE NEAR FUTURE OF THE NATION

|  | (%) |
|---|---|
| Rumors of a coup | 29 |
| Inflation, removal of price controls | 25 |
| Unemployment | 15 |
| Civil war | 13 |
| Repetition of February disturbances | 12 |
| Elimination of democracy | 11 |
| Curfew | 3 |
| Revolution | 2 |
| Conflict | 2 |

*Source:* PN.
*N* = 2,000.

Table 3.22
## NATIONAL FEARS, BY SOCIOECONOMIC LEVEL

|  | Socioeconomic Level | | | |
|---|---|---|---|---|
|  | A–B (%) | C (%) | D (%) | E (%) |
| Rumors of a coup | 14 | 24 | 32 | 27 |
| Civil war | 7 | 10 | 11 | 18 |
| Repetition of February disturbances | 5 | 12 | 13 | 11 |
| Elimination of democracy | 5 | 14 | 11 | 8 |

leaders—first because they themselves belong to the elite class. Second, Venezuela's leaders' opinions are largely molded through interaction with the elite, and third, leading government figures, including the president himself, were, for different reasons, isolated from the feedback at the grass roots that is normally provided by a party organization.[28]

## APPROACHING THE CRISIS OF 1992

Throughout 1990 and 1991, popular support for the government continued at a very low level, never reaching more than 25 percent of the population. By the end of 1991, all the sentiment indexes were below those of 1988 and had in fact fallen since the beginning of the year, despite an increase in economic growth of over 9 percent. In the last survey of 1991, three months before the first military uprising, respondents were asked how they generally felt the country was doing; answers were weighted heavily toward mediocre to bad (table 3.23).

Table 3.23
HOW DO YOU FEEL VENEZUELA IS FARING? (NOVEMBER 1991)

| | (%) |
|---|---|
| Very well | — |
| Well | 2 |
| More or less well | 29 |
| Not very well | 28 |
| Badly | 23 |
| Very badly | 16 |
| No answer | 1 |

*Source:* PN.
*N* = 2,000.
*Note:* Percentage totals more than 100 due to rounding.

Even more alarming were the replies as to how confident the respondents were that in four to five years the country would be prosperous. Once again, the contrast in opinion between the upper and lower socioeconomic levels is striking (table 3.24).

## THE POLITICAL PARTIES

The high level of popular rejection of the traditional political parties had also become apparent by the end of 1991. Table 3.25 summarizes which parties respondents would like and not like to see win the next presidency. Although every party had its supporters and opponents, the ratio of rejection to acceptance of the two traditional parties, AD and COPEI, was eight to three. The highest level of support for an indepen-

Table 3.24
HOW CONFIDENT ARE YOU THAT IN ABOUT 5 YEARS
VENEZUELA WILL BE PROSPEROUS? (NOVEMBER 1991)

| | | Socioeconomic Level | | | |
|---|---|---|---|---|---|
| | Total sample (%) | A–B (%) | C (%) | D (%) | E (%) |
| Very confident | 8 | 9 | 8 | 8 | 9 |
| Quite confident | 7 | 14 | 6 | 7 | 7 |
| Somewhat confident | 19 | 26 | 24 | 19 | 16 |
| Not very confident | 39 | 40 | 39 | 39 | 38 |
| Not at all confident | 23 | 9 | 21 | 23 | 25 |
| Don't know | 4 | 2 | 2 | 3 | 5 |

*Source:* PN.
*N* = 2,000.

Table 3.25
WHICH PARTIES WOULD YOU LIKE AND NOT LIKE TO WIN
THE NEXT PRESIDENCY? (1991)

|  | Would Like (%) | Would Not Like (%) |
|---|---|---|
| AD | 14 | 43 |
| COPEI | 12 | 35 |
| MAS | 8 | 25 |
| Communist | 4 | 40 |
| Independent military | 18 | 24 |
| Independent business | 8 | 15 |
| Independent academic | 12 | 11 |
| None of these | 9 | 3 |
| Don't know | 16 | 16 |

*Source:* PN.
*N* = 2,000.

dent military president came from the C and D socioeconomic levels. Thus, only three years after the presidential election in which AD and COPEI together garnered 90 percent of the vote, only 26 percent of the voting population supported them when asked for this survey. In the last survey before the elections of 1988, 65 percent of the respondents stated they supported a political party, with 90 percent of them backing either AD or COPEI; 28 percent of the sample claimed to be registered party supporters.[29] This two-party dominance of the Venezuelan political arena was not, of course, new. Both AD and COPEI had played major roles in Venezuelan politics since 1958, and in the four presidential elections from 1973 to 1988 the two combined had never received less than 80 percent of the votes cast.

## THE MILITARY AND DEMOCRACY

As Carlos Andrés Pérez once stated, "Latin American militarism should not be blamed on the military. It is due to our political movements that have not been able to understand our respective countries and have created vacuums. These vacuums have then been filled by the only organized institution that exists in the Latin American countries."[30] Certainly the evidence suggests that by the end of 1991, Venezuelan popular opinion perceived that a power vacuum existed—a perception that must have been shared by many military officers.

The role of the military in Latin America has provided ample material for an academic subdiscipline of its own, engaging scholars for the past thirty years or more.[31] Yet not until the current crisis did the issue of military rule greatly concern Venezuelan survey researchers. This does not mean that the military alternative did not exist in the public consciousness; Venezuela's political experience until the early 1960s and the example of its continental neighbors ensured that this was not the case. Rather, the lack of attention paid to the issue by survey researchers suggests that up through the 1980s, the establishment was convinced that the key political concern was the electoral prospects of the two major parties. This was not an unreasonable view, as almost all survey research throughout the 1970s and 1980s indicated a strong popular preference for what was loosely defined as democracy and which for the majority of Venezuelans was associated—unlike a dictatorship—with freedom of expression.[32]

Although democracy was preferred, military rule was not unthinkable. In the 1973 Baloyra and Martz survey, participants responded to questions on the role the armed forces should play in national life; more than a third agreed that the military should support popular will when the regime does not correspond to popular aspirations (table 3.26).

In the same survey, 51 percent of the respondents agreed that there were occasions in which military coups were justified; 32 percent disagreed.[33] Two years earlier in 1971, respondents were asked who would be a better president of Venezuela, and more than one-third preferred a military man (table 3.27). Surveys in 1972 and 1980 produced almost identical results.

Finally, as seen earlier, the military has consistently received higher levels of popular respect than any other national institution. One could argue that, although dormant, the Pérez Jiménez thesis that only the military possessed sufficient technical capacity and administrative honesty to manage the country[34] was by no means completely rejected by popular opinion.

Table 3.26

WHAT ROLE SHOULD THE ARMED FORCES PLAY
IN NATIONAL LIFE? (1973)

| The military | (%) |
|---|---|
| should support popular will when the regime does not correspond to popular aspirations | 35 |
| should always respect institutional government | 31 |
| should act only when the constitution is not being obeyed | 18 |
| should intervene in politics whenever it deems necessary | 12 |
| no answer | 4 |

$N = 1,513.$

Table 3.27
## WHO WOULD BE A BETTER PRESIDENT OF VENEZUELA? (1971)

|  | (%) |
|---|---|
| A political leader | 20 |
| An independent civilian | 34 |
| A military man | 35 |
| Don't know | 12 |

Source: PN.
N = 2,500.

## WHERE DO WE STAND NOW?

The survey results discussed here provide strong evidence of long-standing popular discontent on economic issues, dissatisfaction with the efficiency and probity of public administration, disillusion with the capacity of existing institutions to resolve the nation's problems, and increasing conviction that these institutions are not only inefficient but also corrupt. In addition, they indicate that the discontent and disillusion is most critical among those segments of the population that gave support to the democratic regime in its early years and that appear to have benefited least from it. The issues discussed here have certainly not been the exclusive province of survey research. Many of them were likely evident to even the casual observer and, with the exception of the distributional conflict, have been repeatedly discussed by respected intellectuals in the national media.

At the end of 1992, Venezuela stood with both feet firmly planted in mid-air. Democratic institutions had survived two violent coup attempts and the municipal and state elections that were held the week following the second coup. Survey research findings showed support for the Pérez government at an all-time low, economic discontent higher than at the end of 1991, and confidence in the future unchanged from previous years. The two major parties remained discredited, and almost one-fourth of the population stated they would prefer a military candidate as the next president. At the same time, however, the surveys indicated that over 80 percent of the population was inclined toward a democratic system of government, and that most citizens rejected the coup attempt of November 27, 1992 (see tables 3.28 to 3.30).

## STATISM OR RESTRUCTURING

Finally, where popular opinion stands today on the issue of economic restructuring—which many believe was central to the events of 1989

## Table 3.28
## ATTITUDES TOWARD GOVERNMENT AND COUNTRY
## (AUGUST 1992)

|  | (%)<br>Favorable | (%)<br>Unfavorable |
|---|---|---|
| Attitude toward government | 13 | 63 |
|  | Better Off | Worse Off |
| Compared with last year | 18 | 58 |
| Next 6 months | 13 | 53 |
|  | Confident | Not Confident |
| Country will be prosperous in 4 to 5 years | 20 | 59 |
|  | Would Like | Would Not Like |
| Next president |  |  |
| AD | 10 | 51 |
| COPEI | 15 | 35 |
| Military | 23 | 21 |

*Source:* PN, August 1992.
$N$ = 2,000.

## Table 3.29
## DO YOU PREFER THE PRESENT SYSTEM OR A
## MILITARY GOVERNMENT? (MARCH 1992)

|  | (%) |
|---|---|
| Would choose present system of government | 63 |
| Would choose a military government | 26 |
| Neither/no answer | 11 |
| Those who did not choose present system ($N$ = 736) | (%) |
| A military government | 32 |
| The present system reformed | 56 |
| Neither/no answer | 12 |

*Source:* PN, March 1992.
$N$ = 2,000.

## Table 3.30
## RESPONSES TO THE COUP OF NOVEMBER 27, 1992

|  | (%) |
|---|---|
| Strongly in favor | 9 |
| Somewhat in favor | 13 |
| Against | 76 |
| No answer | 2 |

*Source:* DT, December 2–4, 1992.
$N$ = 654.

Table 3.31
## WHAT ASPECTS OF ECONOMIC REFORM ARE YOU IN FAVOR OF? (MARCH 1992)

|  | Total sample (%) | Socioeconomic Level | | | |
|---|---|---|---|---|---|
|  |  | A–B (%) | C (%) | D (%) | E (%) |
| Price control | 53 | 18 | 38 | 52 | 65 |
| Exchange control | 59 | 27 | 61 | 60 | 59 |
| Control of foreign investment | 64 | 51 | 57 | 66 | 65 |
| Maintenance of subsidies | 70 | 24 | 61 | 72 | 75 |
| Import control | 59 | 30 | 54 | 59 | 62 |
| State ownership | 61 | 21 | 48 | 60 | 72 |

*Source:* PN.
*N* = 2,000.

and 1992—requires examination. Once again, the survey research findings on this issue indicate that popular sentiment evolves slowly on complex issues. In March 1992, respondents were asked to position themselves on a scale ranging from a pro- to an antimarket economy approach (table 3.31). Despite the criticisms of "government" amply illustrated earlier in this chapter, the survey data suggest that the economic model of the 1960s to the 1980s remains favorably viewed by a majority of the population. Economic "restructuring," at least in its initial stages, is simply a euphemism for lower living standards. After thirty years of a paternalistic, misguided development model, which reached its peak with the implementation of the subsidies and controls of 1983 to 1988, it was at best naive for the Pérez government to expect popular opinion to accept the changes as rapidly as they were made.

In 1971, respondents were asked to rank the most important jobs of a national government; the most important task, across all socioeconomic levels, was to provide work for all citizens (table 3.32). In the same year, a large-scale study was conducted using a representative sample of 5,000 respondents, with the objective of measuring popular sympathy for the private sector and attitudes toward "statism"—or state-centered government. The survey participants overwhelmingly preferred the latter, and the responses suggested that, at least in 1971, the Venezuelan private sector (not the foreign oil companies) was irrelevant to popular opinion. For example, 66 percent believed that statism would lead to lower prices; 80 percent felt that a large state would provide better education; 67 percent noted that it would mean a better future for young people; and 66 percent responded that it would provide a more equitable distribution of wealth.[35] By the end of the decade, 94

Table 3.32
HOW WOULD YOU RANK THE TASKS OF A NATIONAL
GOVERNMENT? (1971)

|  | | Socioeconomic Level | | | |
| --- | --- | --- | --- | --- | --- |
|  | Total (%) | A–B (%) | C (%) | D (%) | E (%) |
| Guarantee liberty | 5 | 9 | 8 | 6 | 2 |
| Equality for all | 4 | 9 | 7 | 4 | 3 |
| Work for all | 38 | 28 | 31 | 38 | 43 |
| Personal security | 9 | 20 | 14 | 9 | 5 |
| Possibilities of progress | 14 | 22 | 24 | 15 | 8 |
| Care for poor | 29 | 11 | 15 | 26 | 39 |

*Source:* PN, October 1971.
*N* = 2,500.
*Note:* Percentages total less than 100 due to rounding and "don't know" responses.

percent of the respondents stated that government should control prices, 69 percent supported fixed minimum wages, and 58 percent felt that government should control imports.[36]

## LESSONS AND CONCLUSIONS

Among the principal causes of incompetence in any enterprise is the "tendency to reject or ignore information which is unpalatable or which conflicts with preconceptions."[37] Survey results have shown that since the early 1980s, increasing popular discontent has led to an erosion of support for the existing institutional system, making it unlikely that it can survive without substantial modifications. Fundamental to this discontent is the performance of the economy, leading the majority of the population to question the efficiency and probity of the government, on the one hand, and the distributional structure of Venezuela's society, on the other hand. While the political establishment has ignored or rejected the first issue, the capitalist establishment has equally ignored the second.

The lessons for Venezuela and probably for other developing world countries involved in economic restructuring appear to be fairly clear and not too complex. First, if the political establishment is unable to secure sufficient consensus or impose sufficient authority when abandoning a paternalistic economic model, the outcome will be an intensification of distributional conflicts and a questioning of the legitimacy of institutional structures. Second, it follows that consensus is difficult, if not impossible, to obtain in a society that practices universal suffrage but exhibits disparities in wealth and income that are as broad as they are in Venezuela.[38] Universal suffrage involves, implicitly if not explicitly, not only a fair share of the vote, but also a fairer share of the cake.[39] Although distributional conflicts can be contained during periods of growth, as witnessed in Venezuela from 1960 to 1980, the expectation gap[40] generated during periods of growth will, when followed by a period of stagnation or decline (Venezuela in the 1980s), lead to an acute popular awareness of social cleavage.

The most important characteristic of a liberal government is the negative quality of not being totalitarian.[41] The experience of dictatorial alternatives in Venezuela and neighboring countries was probably as strong a force as any in preventing popular discontent with the Pérez government from being translated into widespread, overt support for the military coups. Nevertheless, to end this chapter as it began, it is Hume the empiricist, rather than Leoni the neoliberal, who provides the most appropriate text for our experience and the best lesson for our future.

# APPENDIX 3.1

*Economic Situation Compared with Previous Year (by Quarter)*

| Year | Better Off (%) | Worse Off (%) | Year | Better Off (%) | Worse Off (%) |
|------|------|------|------|------|------|
| 1975 | 21 | 47 | 1986-2 | 16 | 51 |
| 1976 | 31 | 30 | 1986-3 | 18 | 50 |
| 1977 | 29 | 29 | 1986-4 | 18 | 51 |
| 1978 | 33 | 23 | 1987-1 | 19 | 49 |
| 1979 | 20 | 25 | 1987-2 | 14 | 56 |
| 1980 | 14 | 57 | 1987-3 | 18 | 52 |
| 1981 | 18 | 49 | 1987-4 | 23 | 41 |
| 1982 | 18 | 41 | 1988-1 | 26 | 35 |
| 1983-1 | 11 | 57 | 1988-2 | 25 | 36 |
| 1983-2 | 7 | 61 | 1988-3 | 23 | 41 |
| 1983-3 | 8 | 60 | 1988-4 | 23 | 42 |
| 1983-4 | 13 | 43 | 1989-2 | 12 | 62 |
| 1984-1 | 9 | 48 | 1989-3 | 6 | 68 |
| 1984-2 | 9 | 52 | 1989-4 | 7 | 73 |
| 1984-3 | 7 | 60 | 1990-1 | 14 | 59 |
| 1984-4 | 7 | 62 | 1990-2 | 8 | 66 |
| 1985-1 | 15 | 42 | 1990-3 | 11 | 63 |
| 1985-2 | 11 | 61 | 1991-1 | 22 | 48 |
| 1985-3 | 11 | 58 | 1991-2 | 18 | 54 |
| 1985-4 | 10 | 56 | 1991-3 | 20 | 52 |
| 1986-1 | 17 | 47 | 1991-4 | 20 | 52 |
|  |  |  | 1992-1 | 17 | 57 |
|  |  |  | 1992-3 | 18 | 58 |

*Note:* Survey was not conducted or question was not asked for periods where data is missing. This table does not include "neither better nor worse" responses or "don't know" responses.

# APPENDIX 3.2

*Expected Economic Situation in Next Six Months (by Approximate Quarters)*

| Year | Better Off (%) | Worse Off (%) | Year | Better Off (%) | Worse Off (%) |
|------|------|------|------|------|------|
| 1974 | 33 | 28 | 1986-2 | 20 | 43 |
| 1975 | 30 | 28 | 1986-3 | 21 | 40 |
| 1976 | 33 | 24 | 1986-4 | 21 | 44 |
| 1977 | 22 | 32 | 1987-1 | 24 | 37 |
| 1978 | 27 | 23 | 1987-2 | 15 | 49 |
| 1979 | 16 | 48 | 1987-3 | 14 | 48 |
| 1980 | 22 | 38 | 1987-4 | 22 | 32 |
| 1981 | 25 | 31 | 1988-1 | 31 | 23 |
| 1982 | 24 | 27 | 1988-2 | 21 | 29 |
| 1983-1 | 15 | 47 | 1988-3 | 18 | 34 |
| 1983-2 | 14 | 39 | 1988-4 | 20 | 35 |
| 1983-3 | 21 | 27 | 1989-2 | 14 | 52 |
| 1983-4 | 38 | 14 | 1989-3 | 13 | 56 |
| 1984-1 | 23 | 38 | 1989-4 | 10 | 61 |
| 1984-2 | 29 | 30 | 1990-1 | 21 | 43 |
| 1984-3 | 19 | 45 | 1990-2 | 11 | 59 |
| 1984-4 | 23 | 41 | 1990-3 | 17 | 50 |
| 1985-1 | 31 | 25 | 1991-1 | 23 | 39 |
| 1985-2 | 23 | 43 | 1991-2 | 14 | 54 |
| 1985-3 | 21 | 41 | 1991-3 | 14 | 52 |
| 1985-4 | 23 | 41 | 1991-4 | 14 | 52 |
| 1986-1 | 25 | 33 | 1992-1 | 13 | 51 |
| | | | 1992-2 | 13 | 51 |
| | | | 1992-3 | 13 | 53 |

*Note:* Survey was not conducted or question was not asked for periods where data is missing. This table does not include "neither better nor worse" responses or "don't know" responses.

# APPENDIX 3.3

*A Good Time to Buy (by Approximate Quarters)*

| Year | Consumer Durables (%) | Automobiles (%) | Year | Consumer Durables (%) | Automobiles (%) |
|------|------|------|------|------|------|
| 1982-4 | 20 | 11 | 1987-2 | 15 | 7 |
| 1983-1 | 15 | 11 | 1987-3 | 14 | 7 |
| 1983-2 | 11 | 7 | 1987-4 | 18 | 10 |
| 1983-3 | 11 | 8 | 1988-1 | 26 | 14 |
| 1983-4 | 13 | 8 | 1988-2 | 23 | 12 |
| 1984-1 | 8 | 5 | 1988-3 | 27 | 17 |
| 1984-2 | 7 | 4 | 1988-4 | 27 | 17 |
| 1984-3 | 6 | 4 | 1989-2 | 10 | 3 |
| 1984-4 | 10 | 6 | 1989-3 | 8 | 4 |
| 1985-1 | 12 | 8 | 1989-4 | 11 | 6 |
| 1985-2 | 12 | 7 | 1990-1 | 19 | 7 |
| 1985-3 | 10 | 6 | 1990-2 | 14 | 6 |
| 1985-4 | 13 | 7 | 1990-3 | 16 | 6 |
| 1986-1 | 14 | 9 | 1991-1 | 24 | 11 |
| 1986-2 | 11 | 7 | 1991-2 | 18 | 10 |
| 1986-3 | 14 | 10 | 1991-3 | 19 | 9 |
| 1986-4 | 19 | 14 | 1992-1 | 16 | 10 |
| 1987-1 | 17 | 6 | | | |

*Note:* Survey was not conducted for periods where data is missing.

## APPENDIX 3.4

*Unemployed, Looking for Work (by Quarter)*

| Year | Unemployed (%) | Looking for Work (%) | Year | Unemployed (%) | Looking for Work (%) |
|------|------|------|------|------|------|
| 1978 | 4 | N/A | 1986-4 | 13 | 17 |
| 1979 | 5 | N/A | 1987-1 | 10 | 15 |
| 1980 | 7 | 10 | 1987-2 | 13 | 17 |
| 1981 | 7 | 10 | 1987-3 | 11 | 13 |
| 1982 | 10 | 2 | 1987-4 | 12 | 13 |
| 1983-1 | 10 | N/A | 1988-1 | 10 | 14 |
| 1983-2 | 13 | 16 | 1988-2 | 8 | 12 |
| 1983-3 | 11 | 13 | 1988-3 | 8 | 12 |
| 1983-4 | 14 | 17 | 1988-4 | 7 | 12 |
| 1984-1 | 14 | 20 | 1989-1 | 11 | 17 |
| 1984-2 | 15 | 18 | 1989-2 | 9 | 14 |
| 1984-3 | 14 | 20 | 1989-3 | 11 | 18 |
| 1984-4 | 13 | 16 | 1989-4 | 11 | 17 |
| 1985-1 | 17 | 20 | 1990-1 | 10 | 17 |
| 1985-2 | 13 | 16 | 1990-2 | 12 | 18 |
| 1985-3 | 14 | 17 | 1990-3 | 11 | 17 |
| 1985-4 | 13 | 17 | 1991-1 | 13 | 19 |
| 1986-1 | 13 | 17 | 1991-2 | 11 | 17 |
| 1986-2 | 12 | 18 | 1991-3 | 10 | 14 |
| 1986-3 | 13 | 16 | 1992-1 | 9 | 14 |

N/A = not available.
*Note:* Survey was not conducted for periods where data is missing.

# APPENDIX 3.5

*Most Important Problem Facing Venezuela (by Quarter)*

| Year | Unemployment (%) | Inflation (%) |
|------|------------------|---------------|
| 1984-1 | 63 | 34 |
| 1984-2 | 69 | 29 |
| 1984-3 | 68 | 31 |
| 1984-4 | 68 | 30 |
| 1985-1 | 68 | 30 |
| 1985-3 | 71 | 28 |
| 1986-1 | 71 | 27 |
| 1986-2 | 70 | 29 |
| 1986-3 | 68 | 29 |
| 1986-4 | 65 | 33 |
| 1987-1 | 63 | 34 |
| 1987-2 | 61 | 36 |
| 1987-3 | 61 | 36 |
| 1987-4 | 58 | 40 |
| 1988-1 | 60 | 39 |
| 1988-2 | 57 | 42 |
| 1988-3 | 50 | 44 |
| 1988-4 | 48 | 45 |
| 1989-1 | 53 | 45 |
| 1989-2 | 51 | 45 |
| 1990-2 | 67 | 33 |
| 1990-3 | 62 | 38 |
| 1991-2 | 72 | 28 |
| 1992-2 | 76 | 24 |
| 1992-3 | 77 | 23 |

*Note:* Question was not asked for periods where data is missing.

# NOTES

1. Leo Crespi, 1969 conference AAPOR (American Association for Public Opinion Research); quoted in Elizabeth Noelle-Neumann, *The Spiral of Silence* (Chicago: University of Chicago Press, 1984), 112.
2. In this and subsequent surveys and tables the following abbreviations will be used to identify the source: PN, Datos national opinion survey face-to-face in-home interviews; PC, Datos major city opinion survey face-to-face in-home interviews; OD, other Datos in-home face-to-face surveys; DT, Datos telephone interview surveys. The data presented in this chapter are derived primarily from the Datos, C.A., longitudinal study of public opinion known as the Pulso Nacional (PN). This survey, which has been conducted since 1968, is based on face-to-face in-home interviews with representative samples of voting-age Venezuelans. The design is that of a stratified probability sample with probabilities proportionate to size, and it covers the whole country (with the exception of the Federal Territory of Amazonas and the offshore island federal dependencies). On average, fifty interviewers are used in each survey and a minimum of 30 percent of each interviewer's work is verified in the field by the Datos, C.A., field supervisors. See PN (Pulso Nacional) survey, Datos, C.A. March 1992 ($N = 2,000$).
3. John Martz, "Guerrilla Warfare and Violence," *Secolas Annales* 1 (1970): 141–65.
4. Data sets of the complete Datos longitudinal opinion study are available for scholars at the Roper Center, University of Connecticut, Storrs, and at the Universidad Simón Bolívar, Caracas.
5. Price index, Caracas metropolitan area, Banco Central de Venezuela (BCV), 1984 = 100.

| January | 1950 | 21.9 |
|---|---|---|
| | 1960 | 26.3 |
| | 1970 | 29.2 |
| | 1980 | 61.2 |
| | 1985 | 108.5 |
| | 1986 | 199.3 |
| | 1987 | 134.6 |
| | 1988 | 186.1 |
| | 1989 | 253.9 |
| | 1990 | 465.2 |
| | 1991 | 634.7 |
| December | 1991 | 812.7 |

6. See Martz, "Guerrilla Warfare." Also see Enrique A. Baloyra and John D. Martz, *Political Attitudes in Venezuela* (Austin: University of Texas Press, 1979), 46–58.
7. WAPOR (World Association for Political Opinion Research) conference, Barcelona, 1985. See also Samuel Brittan, "Inflation and Democracy," in Hirsh and Goldthorpe, eds., *The Political Economy of Inflation* (Cambridge, Mass.: Harvard University Press, 1978), 161–85.
8. See Andrew Templeton, "Candidates Still Count," paper delivered at the AAPOR/WAPOR conference, St. Petersburg, Fla., 1986.
9. See Robert Worcester, ed., *Political Opinion Polling* (New York: St. Martin's Press, 1983).
10. Datos, C.A., follows normal survey research practice by attempting to classify respondents according to various socioeconomic characteristics. Eleven variables are used, such as education, profession, possession of consumer durables, schooling of children, domestic service, and so on. The two important items that explain most of the variance are, as would be expected, the residential zone and the type of dwelling. Income, for various well-known reasons, is not a particularly useful tool. For additional details, see Andrew Templeton, *A Third World Experiment in Opinion Leader Identifica-*

*tion* (Amsterdam: European Society for Opinion and Marketing Research, 1986). See also Baloyra and Martz, *Political Attitudes in Venezuela*, and note 38 herein.

11. Baloyra and Martz, *Political Attitudes in Venezuela*. Also see Templeton, *A Third World Experiment in Opinion Leader Identification.*
12. PN, October 1985, *N* = 2,000.
13. V. S. Naipaul, *The Return of Eva Perón* (New York: Knopf, 1980), 101.
14. In the 1968 campaign COPEI raised the issue of corruption in the basic industries of Guyana but in a very minor way.
15. See Rómulo Betancourt, *Política y petróleo* (Caracas: Monte Avila Editores, 1986), 270–72.
16. PN, October 1985 and October 1991, *N* = 2,000.
17. See Daniel Yankelovich, *Fortune*, October 5, 1992, 102–4.
18. After the death of dictator Juan Vicente Gómez in 1935, his successors confiscated his property and that of his closest relatives; see Rogelio Pérez Perdomo, "Corruption and Political Crisis," chap. 14 herein.
19. Ibid.
20. M. Paníc, "The Inevitable Inflation," *Lloyds Bank Review* (July 1976): 1–15.
21. Baloyra and Martz, *Political Attitudes in Venezuela*, 14.
22. PN, September 1987, *N* = 2,000.
23. Baloyra and Martz, *Political Attitudes in Venezuela*, 14.
24. Ibid., 224.
25. PN, September 1991, *N* = 2,000.
26. Alfredo Keller, "Indicadores sociales y electorales," paper presented to the annual assembly of ADLAF (German Association for Research on Latin America), Bonn, 1992. Note: Keller uses proportion of votes cast, whereas in table 3.4 I use proportion of total electorate.
27. Keller (ibid.) agrees with this analysis.
28. It could be argued that the leaders of the traditional parties had also lost grass-roots contact; see, for example, the rise of Causa R.
29. PN, November 1988, *N* = 2,000.
30. President Pérez press conference, Mexico, 1975, quoted in Carlos Rangel, *The Latin Americans* (New York: Harcourt, Brace, Jovanovich, 1977), 234. See also Ramon Díaz Sánchez, *Venezuela Independiente* (Caracas: Eugenío Mendoza Foundation, 1962), 296, and Enrique Baloyra, *Golpes and Democratic Norms in Venezuela* (Chapel Hill: University of North Carolina Press, 1979).
31. For example, see Edwin Lieuwen, *Arms and Politics in Latin America* (New York: Frederick A. Praeger, 1960); Eric Nordlinger, *Soldiers in Politics: Military Coups and Governments* (Englewood Cliffs, N.J.: Prentice Hall, 1977); Abraham F. Lowenthal and J. Samuel Fitch, *Armies and Politics in Latin America* (New York: Holmes and Meier, 1986); and Louis W. Goodman, Johanna S. R. Mendelson, and Juan Rial, eds., *The Military and Democracy* (Lexington, Mass.: Lexington Books, 1990).
32. See PN, 1978, *N* = 3,000.
33. Baylora and Martz, *Political Attitudes in Venezuela*, 227.
34. See Ramon Díaz Sánchez, *Venezuela Independiente* (Caracas: Eugenío Mendoza Foundation, 1962), 295–96.
35. OD, Estudio Appel Datos, C.A., 1971, *N* = 5,000.
36. PN, November 1979, *N* = 3,000.
37. Norman F. Dixon, *On the Psychology of Military Incompetence* (London: Jonathan Cape, Ltd., 1976), 152.
38. FUNDACREDESA (Center for Studies on the Growth and Development of the Venezuelan Population Foundation) estimates that 80 percent of Venezuelans live in poverty, while 8 percent possess "all the economic power and enjoy the greatest social and cultural benefits." These estimates do not differ widely from those of Datos, C.A. See *El Nacional*, February 19, 1993, and the chapter by Janet Kelly herein. The increase in size of the marginal class in Venezuela over the past twenty years has been a seriously neglected problem; the debate centers almost entirely around the current

economic problems. As with the other issues discussed in this chapter, rising poverty is a problem of long gestation; beginning with differential birth rates in the 1960s while death rates were universally falling, it was seriously aggravated by the large-scale immigration of marginal citizens from neighboring Andean countries during the boom years of 1973 to 1980. Datos, C.A., estimates that at present rates, 50 percent of the population will be classified as socially, economically, and culturally marginal by the beginning of the next century. This is, of course, an issue for another study, but students of the problem would be wise not to ignore Charles Kindleberger's advice: if there are enough "free riders," the bus of public goods never leaves the garage; see Charles Kindleberger, "Responsibility in Economic Life," in *The Market on Trial,* Christopher Johnson, ed. (London: Pinter Publishers, 1989), 75–85.

39. Thomas Humphrey Marshall, *Citizenship and Social Class* (Cambridge: Cambridge University Press, 1950).

40. "The gap between the standards of living and the status people have and those they would like to have," Paníc, "The Inevitable Inflation," 5.

41. Karl Bracher, *The Age of Ideologies: A History of Political Thought in the Twentieth Century* (New York: St. Martin's Press, 1984), 166, quoting George H. Sabine, *A History of Political Theory.* Consider also Winston Churchill's oft-quoted aphorism: "Of all . . . democracy is least bad." Bracher also makes interesting comments on Latin American democracy problems (*The Age of Ideologies,* 271–75).

# 4

# Venezuela's New Political Actors

## Juan Carlos Navarro

Venezuelans like to describe their political environment these days using the expression "very fluid" or "very dynamic." In this particular, popular opinion is absolutely right. The last decade has brought a new breed of political actors and organizations that—having different goals, channels of expression, and degrees of consolidation—constitute a new set of forces that is becoming increasingly vocal and influential in Venezuelan politics. What they have in common is that they have all developed outside the political parties and in particular outside Acción Democrática (AD) and COPEI, even if some have engaged or will engage in the near future in electoral participation through new parties or electoral movements. In addition, their identities have been built to a considerable extent on criticism of the role, behavior, and leadership of the established parties, a remarkable phenomenon in a political system well known for the pervasive influence that parties have in all conceivable areas of public policy, government, and even social and economic organization.

The aim of this chapter is to develop a framework in which these new and decisive recent developments of Venezuelan politics can be adequately understood in terms of their sources, nature, and eventual future impact. More precisely, I try to provide a preliminary answer to the following questions: Who are the new political actors? What are their defining characteristics? What kind of relationships have these new actors developed with established or traditional political forces? And what is likely to be their evolution? Given that much of the information presented here has received only limited scholarly attention, emphasis is placed on description and classification.

The four initial sections present both definitions and descriptions of several of the new political actors, whose significance constitutes the main focus of the chapter. The fifth section explores in additional detail the most recent developments unleashed by the failed military coup of February 1992, as far as the new political actors are concerned, and the final section contains some hypotheses concerning the probable impact of the new actors and their future relations with the traditional Venezuelan political actors.

## FIGHTING FOR "VOICE" IN THE VOTING PROCESSES

Reporting findings from a 1973 national sample survey, Enrique Baloyra stated:

> Data on the sense of political efficacy indicate that it is confined to voting in elections (64.7 percent), and that citizens feel largely inefficacious in all other areas of political activity. Solid majorities believe that government officials do not take them into account (73.9 percent), that citizens lack the ability to influence government policy (65.9 percent), and that the complexities of politics are beyond their comprehension (70.3 percent). These feelings do not necessarily measure "backwardness" or "underdevelopment," for they may very well reflect the reality of Venezuelan politics, in which the masses lack effective channels to influence government.[1]

A distinctive characteristic of several of the political actors classified for the purposes of this chapter as "new" is that they represent a social response to the state of affairs described by Baloyra. They see themselves largely as spearheading a new current of political participation that was not supposed to exist under the original rules of the game established at the beginning of the democratic period more than three decades ago. Some of them constitute attempts to open or encourage nonconventional participation in the political sphere, while others are trying to reform and expand the voting rules and institutions so that these are more conducive to enhanced representation, responsiveness, and citizen participation. All of them want, in short, to improve the "voice" option within the Venezuelan political system.[2]

A good instance of the first kind of movement is RED (the acronym of Respuesta en Democracia, and the Spanish word for network). RED is a group of young professionals, several with relationships dating back to their student union days. After the failed coup in February 1992, RED decided to organize itself as a group dedicated to exploring and promoting new forms of social and political participation within the Venezuelan democratic system. More and better channels of participation, opposition to hierarchical organizational structures in politics, and the creation of new ways of exercising social and political leader-

RED

ship are the main components of the vision of politics that this group is trying to promote.[3] According to some of their leaders,

> One of the problems that we are trying to solve has to do with the professionalization of politicians. This is a problem that all democracies in the world have. When there is no organization that counteracts the power they have, professional politicians tend to become isolated from the people they are supposed to be representing. In Venezuela, this problem is particularly important given that there is no tradition here of political participation using ways other than political parties. . . .
>
> As a society, we have to undertake a learning process, which includes a different way of doing things. Prevailing political structures correspond to a country far simpler, less populated and with not so many concentrated problems. Perhaps such structures fulfilled their role successfully at the moment they were created. In fact, they were so successful that there were 30 years of stability. Yet, our society is today more complex.[4]

By late 1992 RED members had created an electronic network intended to facilitate communications among emergent social and political groups through a bulletin board system. They also were the original proponents of a meeting of new political actors that took place in July 1992 in Caracas, in which different groups presented and exchanged information concerning what they were trying to achieve: from electoral campaigns to provision of social services, from diffusion of the principles of classic liberalism to public opinion campaigns favoring some policies or legislative reforms, and in which the degree of commitment and consensus was very high. RED is planning several other initiatives, such as a monitoring system of the performance of public servants and political representatives, to be applied experimentally to members of Congress, and a sort of fair open to the public in which all new social and political initiatives will show their projects and achievements to the general public.

The notion of a network as the structural model of political organization has gained popularity among several of the newest political actors, far beyond the boundaries of RED. Elías Santana, a prominent community leader active in several of the initiatives here described, writes:

> Given that we already possess an internal culture of working as a network, perhaps the option should be to create a network of networks. A system that deals with every organization with the same care and attention that they provide to their associates, guarantee-

ing information, consultation, participation channels, opportunities for meeting each other and the possibility to act in coordination.

A network of networks has the advantage of not being a federation of groups, having a board of directors that represents everyone or that concentrates the leaders or every group up to the point in which the inner dynamics of all of them get hurt on behalf of a superior interest. The network makes the action of every sector easier and stronger, multiplying its efforts on society and on the public opinion environment. It becomes a force that can be seen as a whole or in part, but not so solid as to generate friction or to receive impacts.[5]

On the other hand, several other movements are trying to act as "public interest lobbies," dedicated to producing what we could call "positive political externalities," promoting legislative reforms that in their view would result in better representation, fairness in voting processes, or plainly a better government. Some of them not only emphasize public opinion campaigns aimed at Congress, the executive, or the judicial system, but also encourage citizen participation in public affairs and generate attitudes conducive to good citizenship.

A case in point is Queremos Elegir, an organization born in 1991 that has as its main goal to promote the simple majority–single member voting system as the preferred tool for limiting the hold that party machines have on Venezuelan politics. Members like to emphasize the difference they see between "voting" and "choosing," the latter implying the fullest and richest exercise of political rights, as opposed to a passive attitude toward elections. Responding to the well-known criticism directed at simple majority systems, in terms of their presumed failure in securing minorities' representation, one of the leaders of Queremos Elegir points out:

> They [the political parties] almost exclusively have the monopoly in nominations, so that the elected official's commitment to the voter gets distorted. In the closed list system, candidates are selected by the party's top leadership [*cogollos*]. Hence, given that the selected ones are indebted to those that made the selection, the winners are loyal to the parties' top leadership. This is a very concrete logic. In a case like this, the voters are actually the political parties, and the electoral population merely endorses.[6]

In the aftermath of the coup attempt of February 1992, under suspended constitutional guarantees and at a time when public opinion polls showed considerable public support for the coup leaders, Queremos Elegir, with support from other groups, organized a rally in Caracas using the slogan, "Neither corruptocracy nor dictatorship, we want true democracy." The rally took the authorities by surprise and was the strongest public demonstration in support of democracy since February 4.

Apart from its continuing pressure in favor of the simple majority system, Queremos Elegir is undertaking other projects. One that is worth mentioning—launched as a joint effort with the Escuela de Vecinos[7]—involves training electoral "auditors" who will participate as fair witnesses at the polls, preventing the "minority vote redistribution" for the benefit of large parties.

Neither RED nor Queremos Elegir intends to compete in elections as an organization, and this frees them from the strongest pressures that political participation imposes on those that do enter the electoral arena. Like several organizations with similar goals, these two believe they can make a difference in Venezuelan politics without necessarily becoming political parties or electoral groups. Their strategy assumes that they can either persuade or push those in power toward making the right decisions, and also that they can count on the active and relatively sophisticated polity of contemporary Venezuela to feed and support their effort.

Whether these groups are right or wrong is too early to say, but a couple of preliminary judgments can be made concerning their activities. First, they have already had an impact: the electoral system has been modified since the late 1980s to introduce the simple majority system at the municipal level and to a limited degree at the national level, a reform that cannot be totally credited to the activities of the groups of the type described here—COPRE[8] has no doubt played an important role, and so have the few leaders of established parties that are sympathetic to the reforms—but that was certainly influenced by them. Second, these groups seem to be in touch with public opinion, since every political survey shows strong criticism of political parties, their behavior and internal structure, and solid support of better representation. In addition, these new political actors have been attracting media coverage, thus increasing their voice in Venezuelan politics.

The type of organization just described has been made possible in the context of the very active "civil society" that has developed in Venezuela in the last couple of decades at every social level. Neighborhood associations, grass-roots movements, and diverse nongovernmental organizations are currently providing the leadership, social experience, and managerial capabilities needed to develop successful political initiatives, even if they have missions other than political activism.[9]

## FIGHTING FOR "EXIT": IS A NEW KIND OF POLITICAL PARTY POSSIBLE?

The search for enhanced "voice" is, however, only one of the ways that new political actors are trying to influence politics in Venezuela. "Exit"—understood not as an antidemocratic movement but as the search for groups (other than traditional political parties) that are willing and able to compete in elections—is also a route that has been and continues to be explored.

There has been no shortage of challengers to AD's and COPEI's electoral dominance in contemporary Venezuelan history. Seven presidential candidates competed in 1963, six in 1968, twelve in 1973, ten in 1978, twelve in 1983, and twenty-three in 1988. These figures can be misleading, however, given that AD and COPEI have become players in monopolistic competition since 1973,[10] accumulating jointly at least 85 percent of the presidential vote and 75 percent of the legislative vote in national elections.[11]

Instead, the political actors referred to in this section are trying to be nonconventional challengers, in the sense that they want to build political organizations that have appeared at a time when the Venezuelan public, or at least a sizable and vocal part of it, has developed a profound aversion to political perspectives that are typical of the nation's large and small political parties. Consequently, they constitute attempts to develop political organizations that have both electoral efficacy and cultural adequacy in relation to what their leaders think are the new political preferences of Venezuelan citizens.

What are the characteristics of the political parties that citizens reject? It is relatively easy to write a list:[12]

(1) Corruption: Venezuelans tend to think that corruption is the source of many of the problems the country is facing, and they perceive political parties as essentially tolerant if not active promoters of corruption.

(2) Invasiveness: political parties played an essential role in setting up social and political institutions in Venezuela—unions, professional associations, and so on—and they by themselves constituted the main avenue of participation and social influence. Yet they resist relinquishing that role when several new options

resent
parallelism

have appeared, such as neighborhood associations and a diverse set of nongovernmental organizations. In practice, the consistent reaction of political parties to these new models of political participation has been to control, sometimes setting up "parallel" associations controlled by party officials, or trying from time to time a takeover of the association's directorate, so that the group will serve party goals. The new social organizations resent this behavior, the result being that one of their defining characteristics is to consider political parties an opposing force, hostile to their views and goals as to political representation and social activism.

(3) Lack of internal democracy and organizational rigidity: the parties are seen as controlled by a small group of "apparatchiks" absolutely committed to the preservation of their authority and influence on Venezuelan politics, with no regard for their fellow party members or the public in general. They have virtual authority to impose candidates against the majority's wishes and to exert control over substantial resources.

(4) Critical shortage of "statesmanship": the party leadership (that is, the members of parties' national boards and members of Parliament) is generally perceived as a set of experienced power brokers who are not able to articulate an inspiring and coherent vision of the direction of Venezuelan society.

(5) Excess of influence in day-to-day public decision making and private activities: one of the paradoxes of Venezuelan politics is that, after winning the presidency, the political party consistently proceeds to free the elected president of party discipline, which usually means the president launches a program that has little to do with party ideological orientation, and at the same time the party expects a good share of influence not only in appointments and pork-barrel politics but in all kinds of particular decisions that constitute the everyday life of modern government. It is typical to find a Venezuelan newspaper reporting on how the national board of the party in government has decided that a particular public policy will or will not be implemented.[13]

(6) Outright dependence on clientelism as a form of political affiliation: political parties are seen as a combination of "clubs of contractors" and "shameless populists" who win elections and attract activists exclusively by granting them access—sometimes improper if not openly illegal—to government contracts, welfare payments, and favors. It is widely believed in Venezuela that a good share of public sector inefficiency is due to the dominance

of this type of practice (and, hence, of party politics) in the way public bureaucracies are managed.

This abundance of undesirable characteristics generally attached to existent political parties provides a solid platform for an organized group to campaign against. The problem is that to campaign on such a platform, one has to create a political organization that will appear to the public at first as just "another political party," playing by the rules and regulations that are responsible for the actual structure and behavior of established parties. Thus a new group looking for support must build a political base in a unique or nontraditional way right from the start, hoping to be recognized as a political actor proposing a nonclientalistic relationship, or it must reach the public using the precise message and leadership the public is supposed to be waiting for, thereby generating credibility. Either of these approaches, or a combination of both, requires considerable skill and resources, both in face-to-face contact with voters and in mass communication.

One political organization that is trying to solve this puzzle is Decisión Ciudadana (Citizen's Decision), a voter group working in Baruta, one of the most populated and affluent municipalities in Caracas. It defines itself as a group of concerned citizens proposing new models of municipal management and government that are more professional and more participatory than the formats of existing parties. The group is trying to build its electoral strength at the local level, emphasizing personal contact and community involvement of the leaders. Yet Decisión Ciudadana has faced some criticism of having become "another political party" by several nongovernmental organizations and citizen associations. In response, one of the promotional materials distributed in 1991 by the group reads: "It is very important to make it clear that, given that this group includes social leaders coming from different organizations—such as neighborhood associations, environmental groups, professional and business groups, sporting, regional and cultural associations—these organizations should be involved under no circumstance as parts of our project . . . they should preserve their roles of sectorial or spatial representation and not become involved in any specific political project."

Decisión Ciudadana's founder and candidate for mayor, Angel Enrique Zambrano, narrowly lost in the local election of 1989 and won in 1992, defeating an incumbent from COPEI. Decisión Ciudadana has established footholds in several other jurisdictions, knowing that its criticism of the workings of traditional political forces goes far beyond Baruta, but for the time being, it has chosen to concentrate its scarce

1989 New Electoral
laws

resources in that municipality. It hopes to show that a local government
can be managed in an alternate way, creating a "demonstration effect"
that would eventually enable the organization to be launched at the national level. Decisión Ciudadana's strategy has been made possible only
as a result of new electoral laws that, starting in 1989, allowed for direct
election of governors and mayors for the first time in Venezuelan history.[14]

Another political organization that is relevant in this respect is Factor
Democrático (FD). In contrast to Decisión Ciudadana, FD chose to
compete at the national level from its inception instead of concentrating its efforts on a single jurisdiction. It started in 1988 as a handful of
professors and businesspeople who gathered to debate national problems and held two common tenets: the inability of established party
elites to lead the country (and the need to replace them democratically) and the rejection of the development model centered around
pervasive state intervention in a closed economy. The founding document of FD reads:

> This country's agenda is clear. Many Venezuelans have been talk-
> ing about it, pointing to one or the other of the goals that are in-
> cluded in such an agenda: a participative civil society; a state
> strengthened in its law enforcement, social assistance, educational
> advancement and technology promotion capabilities; a market
> economy; an active and open intellectual climate; a new way of be-
> coming organized in politics, able to compete with the parties we
> know and with other forms of organization. . . . Making this pro-
> gram a reality requires a new leadership and a new way of practic-
> ing politics. In this, there can be no confusion. The political
> leaders we know cannot implement what has been hereby pro-
> posed, because their habits and interests prevent them from
> doing so.[15]

The group centered around one of its founders, Diego Bautista Urbaneja, and by the end of 1991 had decided to become a political organization aiming to compete in national elections, a decision reinforced
by the experience of the first three years of Carlos Andrés Pérez's administration, in which a group of committed reformers made a difference but soon faced a stalemate due to lack of party support.[16] The
failed coup in February precipitated the launching of FD in a public
event in Caracas on June 25. As of early 1993, FD was arousing enthusiasm among the substantial group sharing deep dissatisfaction with established parties, and it was concentrating its effort on the process of
building and consolidating an effective organization. It remains more a

promise than an accomplished fact, however, and its impact on Venezuelan politics remains to be seen. The strengths of these alternative political organizations are their closeness to public opinion about political parties and the high quality of their human resources. Their weaknesses are the lack of financial means to achieve widespread influence, the "credibility gap" they have to face as soon as they identify themselves as political organizations, and, perhaps, their weak influence beyond the urban middle classes. It is difficult to say whether the platform these organizations are developing will be able to reach beyond highly motivated and activist professionals and managers: on the one hand, it can be no coincidence that the founders of these groups are drawn almost exclusively from these social categories, yet on the other hand so were AD's and COPEI's original activists, which did not prevent those parties from gaining widespread support among all social strata. These new organizations are betting on the fact that the average level of political education of the Venezuelan citizen has improved over the last three decades in such a way that not only the elite but the majority of Venezuelans are able to understand their message and are willing to support it.

## THE NEW CLASS POLITICS AMONG UNION AND BUSINESS LEADERSHIP

The general dissatisfaction with parties has run parallel to a process of maturation and regrouping among unions and business organizations. In both social categories new ways of thinking and acting politically have been developing and have had an impact on Venezuelan politics, in spite of the visibility and strength that traditional workers' federations and business associations retain. A good example is Roraima, a group of businesspeople who gathered in 1982 and produced a document containing a well-structured plea for radical change in the economic orientation of the country. The document was widely circulated among top-level politicians and given to President Jaime Lusinchi. Among Roraima's points were:

> The current reality of Venezuela is the one of a democratic regime with many achievements in the political sphere . . . but, we have to recognize that its economic and social results are disheartening. . . .
>     Ten years ago oil prices in the international markets reached levels near petroleum's objective value, which opened to Venezuela the expectation of a future of unprecedented growth and prosper-

ity. Today, by the end of the most promising decade in Venezuelan history, these expectations are nothing but a painful memory.[17]

The document goes on to propose a new development strategy based on market-oriented policies, blaming the state-centered approach adopted in the 1960s for the main economic ills of the country. Disappointed by the lack of resonance it found both in the political leadership and in traditional business associations, Roraima turned to the political system as the main focus of its attention. In 1987, the group produced another document, this time a comprehensive review of the failures and weaknesses of the democratic regime, written from a perspective committed to democracy.[18] Again, the study was distributed to all significant political and social actors. It contains a comprehensive agenda for reforming political institutions (including reforms of the electoral and judicial system), strengthening citizen participation and neighborhood associations, limiting the power of the executive, and reducing the control political parties have on public decision making.

Such an agenda looks similar to those that are being put forward by the other new alternative political groups. Roraima, however, has chosen to concentrate on presentation and diffusion of the agenda to other political actors as its favored channel of influence. The policy changes implemented by the economic advisers of Carlos Andrés Pérez—against the will of AD—were basically consistent with the ones proposed by Roraima several years before, but the fact remains that such changes had no solid political base in an established party, so they proved to be as short-lived as the influence of the economic advisers. Now, after the failed coup and several serious attempts by AD to derail the economic policy, Roraima is trying to put itself in motion again, with consequences that are not yet apparent.

On the labor side, deep transformations have taken place during the last decade, the most important of which is no doubt the Nuevo Sindicalismo. This movement had its roots in the rebellion of workers in several unions against the dominance of traditional, party-affiliated unions, in particular those belonging to mainstream unionism under AD's control, the Confederación de Trabajadores de Venezuela (CTV). Even though it is a diverse social movement rather than a unified organization, there are two major branches of the Nuevo Sindicalismo. One of them has grown within and is directly dependent on Causa R; the other branch is independent of Causa R—being composed of activists who in some cases have relationships with several political organizations but remain independent—and is less "socialist" in its political views.

Causa R is currently a national political party[19] but was born as the result of union struggles in Guyana during the seventies. As the organization gains prominence in national politics while arousing enthusiasm among workers across the country as a credible union-level option, it is an open question how the group will avoid the down side of combining class representation with party politics—one of the traits of AD's controlled unionism that is radically challenged by the Nuevo Sindicalismo.[20]

Although the Nuevo Sindicalismo is still far from dominant in Venezuela, it has already won elections in several key unions, such as the steel and aluminum workers in Guyana, oil unions in the Zulia region, and the Metro company in Caracas, to mention a few. In fact, its importance would be far larger within CTV if the confederacy practiced internal democracy to a larger extent.

What these groups all have in common is a vision of representation of workers' interests that rejects submission to party politics, stresses union democracy, and combines a fierce defense of workers' rights with an emphasis on individual responsibility and work ethic. Where a traditional union leader would take a worker's complaint to the managers, the "new unionism" leader would take the complaining worker along to the meeting with the managers so that the leader can be better informed, simultaneously creating a process in which the individual worker must be willing to sustain his or her claim in person.

These developments have not passed unnoticed among Venezuelan businesspeople, managers, and government officials, who often find themselves negotiating with "official" union leaders who have little or no legitimacy or influence in day-to-day union activities. In 1992, when the government was discussing the privatization plan for an important public enterprise, representatives met with top CTV leaders (who were also AD's national leaders and members of Congress) and persuaded them to cooperate, only to discover afterward that they had no leverage regarding the behavior of the concerned enterprise union, democratically dominated by Nuevo Sindicalismo activists. In another instance, a private firm well known for its concern with labor's welfare and involvement in the functioning of the plant needed to discuss key issues with union representatives, yet had difficulty identifying the right person to contact because the "official" union representative was unable to gather more than 10 percent of the workers for a meeting; the majority of workers supported a parallel union led by Nuevos Sindicalistas. In general, the prevailing opinion among managers and owners is that, even if the new style of union activism is harder to manipulate using under the table agreements with union leaders, it is also much more sophisticated and inclined to cooperate in restructuring processes, introducing "total quality" managerial practices, and developing innovations in the production process.

Some of these developments in the field of workers' organization are not limited to urban workers. A group of initiatives to develop peasant organizations outside AD's control and without the blessing of the traditional Federación Campesina de Venezuela (Peasant Federation of Venezuela) are already in place in several areas of the country.

## THE "NEW CLASS" IN VENEZUELAN POLITICS: TECHNOCRATS

One of the important developments of the last three years in Venezuelan politics is the forceful emergence of a small group of highly qualified professionals (mainly economists educated at the best U.S. schools and with no stated party affiliation) who gained unprecedented influence over Carlos Andrés Pérez's government policies. They were the authors of the structural adjustment package put in place by the new administration, were blamed for its unpopular effects, and were widely condemned by left-wing forces and by the same leaders of AD who were supposed to be providing political support for the administration. The market-oriented reforms launched by these groups were comprehensive and rested on presidential power as their sole base of support. They resembled the reforms Roraima had been proposing for almost a decade and represented a profound departure from the economic model developed during the past thirty years in Venezuela.[21]

These technocrats were seen by party leadership as complete outsiders with an opposing view of government's role in society. As a result, political support for their reformist policies was never strong and undermined the overall coherence of the government at the cabinet level, since AD insisted on having party leaders in key posts to balance the effect technocrats were having on top-level government decisions.

In addition, the poor design of the political strategy needed to govern the transition to a market economy further undermined the reform process. Even if presidential commitment has been strong, the political crisis unleashed by the February coup attempt put the technocrats on the defensive; several were forced to leave the government and those who remained worked at avoiding a major setback of the reform process rather than moving it forward.

The fate of members of this group in Venezuelan politics is unclear. Even though they emerged from academia, it is undeniable that several entertain political ambitions. No established political party seems inclined to create room for them, however, in part due to their current lack of popularity, but mainly because mainstream party leadership, both in AD and in COPEI, remains alien to market-oriented policies.[22] It seems that there are only two avenues open to technocrats: either they create a new political organization, which might mean joining one of the new political actors, or they try a hostile takeover of one of the major parties. Neither approach is easy, given their relative lack of political experience. It is hard to imagine, however, that a group that has been so influential in recent times should vanish completely from the scene.

## OTHER POLITICAL FORCES IN THE MIDST OF POLITICAL CRISIS

The coup attempt at the beginning of 1992 had two effects as far as new political actors are concerned. First, it created excellent conditions for them to emerge from the shadows, accelerating the pace and commitment of several and creating conditions for others to become public. Second, it reopened a forgotten dimension of Venezuelan politics, the struggle between democracy and authoritarian rule that filled the first century and a half of Venezuelan history. It is indeed a paradox that just when so many new developments in Venezuelan politics are growing—trying to move the political system toward "more and better democracy," to use Roraima's words—a serious nondemocratic challenge reappears, benefiting in turn from the lack of confidence citizens have in established political forces.

Although the coup failed, it created an unprecedented political crisis that risks the destruction of democracy itself. The main components of the crisis are the lack of legitimacy of established political parties, deep divisions among the military, the rebirth of leftist urban guerrillas, and a low level of development of new political actors. In a moment of widespread confusion these new actors have been able to attract some public attention but have not been forceful or decisive.

In the rarified political environment created by the coup attempt, however, at least two actors of a different nature from those mentioned so far have entered the public scene: one is the armed forces and the other armed subversive groups. It is too early to say whether these groups will become permanent players or are merely temporary outbursts of irrationality.

The military is not at this point a unified actor because, according to several observers, it is divided between top-level commands and middle-to low-level commands, professionals and politicians, Bolivarianos and democrats. Although this chapter is not the place to develop a detailed analysis of this complex phenomenon, it is worth noting that such divisions have resulted so far in an inability to coalesce around universally respected leadership, a basic requirement of a more forceful intervention in the crisis resolution and eventually of a coup d'état. The coup attempt of November 27, 1992, can be understood as a confirmation rather than a refutation of this point, given the role that lack of good coordination, of mutual trust, and of ideological coherence seems to have played in its failure.

Little is known about the substantive proposals or policy orientations of the different divisions of the armed forces, with the exception of a strong nationalism and some degree of opposition to market-oriented reforms, particularly the privatization process; another factor preventing military intervention could be the absence of a well-defined view of how to contend with the severe social and economic problems that Venezuela is facing. Nevertheless, the military has become an important player in Venezuelan politics, and one of the proofs of this assertion is that all of the other political actors have now planned to establish contacts with members of the armed forces.

As for armed subversive groups, little is known, with the following exceptions: they have attempted at least one political assassination (the failed attempt on AD's union leader, Antonio Ríos) in a country where such acts have been absent since the attempt on President Rómulo Betancourt in the early sixties, and they have been able to recruit among high school and university students since February 1992. A connection between these far-left organizations and some sectors within the military has been the subject of speculation but is still to be established conclusively, particularly given that much of the modern culture of the Venezuelan armed forces was built fighting against these same guerrilla groups three decades ago. The fact remains, however, that several leaders of these organizations participated actively in the coalition behind the coup attempt in November.

## NEW DIMENSIONS OF VENEZUELAN POLITICS

In summary, there are plenty of new political actors in the Venezuelan polity, but for the most part they are not fully developed as movements and organizations, and they lack the strength to challenge established political actors. A lineal projection of the present, assuming "politics as usual" as the baseline, implies that it may take from ten to twenty years for many of these actors to become mature and, assuming they make it, to become dominant in any respect—elections, public opinion, or social organization. The same projection suggests that established political actors—mainly political parties and semicorporatist institutions of class representation such as CTV, FCV, or FEDECAMARAS—are here to stay for the long term.

Two components of recent developments would allow for a different scenario. First is the question of whether we are witnessing a major realignment in Venezuelan politics, similar to the one that occurred at the beginning of this century when the traditional Liberal and Conservative parties vanished and gave way to a completely different kind of political organization represented by AD and COPEI, which were better suited to the new social structure. Second is the impact of an eventual scenario of authoritarian rule on the new actors. I will discuss these briefly in turn.

Much has been said in recent political commentary in Venezuela about the "exhaustion" of Punto Fijo, the foundational pact of the contemporary political system.[23] The main components of that pact can be readily conceptualized in terms of a certain mode of development and a certain political structure. The mode of development was basically the CEPAL (Comisión Económica para América Latina y el Caribe) model, fashionable during the 1960s, based on import substitution policies and strong and pervasive state intervention in the economy. In Venezuela this model acquired some idiosyncratic traits due to the oil-exporting nature of the economy; it became essentially an agreement to finance the public sector, with contributions coming from the oil industry, while avoiding taxing other economic agents and activities. The political structure was a party-centered democracy combined with a complex system of semicorporatist interest representation.[24]

After more than three decades, these two components have entered a profound crisis, the economic model as a result of both feasibility considerations (declining oil income, massive loss in public sector managerial and intervention capabilities) and global trends (pressures to globalize, general movement toward market-oriented economic arrangements, free trade), and the political structure as a result of processes that are far more difficult to see clearly and have not been the subject of detailed study thus far.[25] The political equilibrium has been broken, creating the potential for a major political realignment.

This condition is not sufficient for political realignment, but an argument can be made that it coincides with other major favorable circumstances: a significant change in sociodemographic characteristics of the population—including a rising average educational level, the consolidation of urbanization, and the coming of age of a professional and managerial middle class—and, above all, the inability of major established political organizations to adapt themselves to the new circumstances of Venezuelan society. Perhaps the most important question is why such a resourceful and powerful organization as AD—or COPEI—has not been able to generate at least the seed of a credible and modern new leadership from within, as so many Venezuelan citizens are persuaded it has not. Why is there currently no young, legitimate labor leadership in AD? Why are there no "technocrats," who were trained under the sponsorship of the parties? Why have political parties been considered one of the main opposing forces by Venezuelan nongovernmental organizations and new social organizations? Why is it that being an "independent" (that is, not identified with any political party) has become the political label proudly preferred by ever more Venezuelan voters? The answers to these questions concern complex processes that probably have their roots in the internal struggles and divisions suffered by major parties in the sixties, but the facts they allude to show an acute contrast with the experience of other dominant political organizations in Latin America—the Mexican Institutional Revolutionary Party (PRI) being a case in point—that dominant, large, and rigid as they have been, were able to initiate long-term renewal processes of the party leadership and structure.

One of the consequences of the political situation is that wide sectors of Venezuelan society do not feel well represented in the current political structure. All the new political actors share a deep dissatisfaction with the way established parties deal with citizens and oppose clientelism, the lack of party democracy, and the party invasion of many spheres of social activity. Many, if not all, differ from parties in the way they see the role of the state in society and the feasibility and desirability of traditional populist[26] and antimarket biases in public policy.

Figure 4.1 shows a simplified schematic definition of the main political actors. The two main clusters of political actors are the established parties, in the area where an interventionist approach to economic policy and a party-centered view of the political system dominate, and the new actors, clustered where the opposite ends of the categories converge.[27] Causa R represents an outlyer, evolving as a political actor with a strong quasisocialist state-centered approach combined with a fresh view of the role of parties in the political system. If these dimensions describe the most important preferences of Venezuelan citizens of today,[28] the Venezuelan political system might be in for a momentous change, either through the forceful emergence of new actors or by irresistible pressures on traditional actors that would eventually radically

**Figure 4.1**
**Venezuelan political actors in a two-dimensional space**

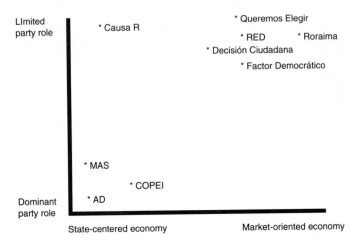

change their ideological orientation and political practice. Even if many of the new political actors turn out to be weak and ephemeral as organized forces, they will have contributed substantially to either of these possible outcomes by providing new channels of political socialization for a new generation of leaders.

Authoritarian rule would obviously disrupt the kind of political evolution we have been sketching, making it far more difficult for the new actors to organize themselves and to concentrate on the deep problems of the Venezuelan polity. Nevertheless, if the highly speculative scenario that has just been presented is at least partially valid, authoritarian rule would be only a complicated detour on the journey to a similar point, a delay in the process of reaching the long-term adjustment of the political system and in the profound changes that are taking place in the polity, assuming repression is not so consistently applied that it would put an end to the democratic potential now so abundant in Venezuelan society.

I would like to give thanks to Janet Kelly and Ramón Piñango for their criticism of an early draft of this chapter, to Moisés Naím for the initial suggestion to write about the new political actors in Venezuela, and to the Woodrow Wilson Center. The editors, particularly Louis W. Goodman, contributed substantially to improve the final version. I also thank the many political activists working within new political organizations of different kinds in Venezuela, to whom I am personally indebted for the experiences and the information that made this chapter possible.

# NOTES

1. Enrique A. Baloyra, "Attitudes toward the Democratic Regime," in John D. Martz and David J. Myers, eds., *Venezuela: The Democratic Experience* (New York: Praeger, 1977), 51.
2. I have used the terms *voice* and *exit* as the organizing categories of the first part of this chapter. They are taken from Albert Hirschman's well-known work in which *voice* refers to a social response to crisis that involves the use of criticism within an organization, as opposed to abandonment in search of new organizations that may eventually fulfill the same social function (the "exit" option). As will become clearer as my argument develops, by *exit* I do not refer to the authoritarian option—which has recently appeared in the Venezuelan political scene—but rather to the attempt to create political organizations different from the dominant political parties. See Albert Hirschman, *Exit, Voice and Loyalty* (Cambridge, Mass.: Harvard University Press, 1970).
3. Respuesta en Democracia, "¿Qué somos? ¿Qué queremos? ¿Cómo lograrlo?" (RED, Caracas, 1992, mimeographed).
4. *Economía Hoy,* July 31, 1992, 5.
5. Elias Santana, *Una RED para la conspiración transparente* (Caracas: Respuesta en Democracia, 1992), 7.
6. *Economía Hoy,* August 5, 1992, 5.
7. The Escuela de Vecinos de Venezuela provides training and support for community groups and neighborhood associations, favoring community organization and participation. It was founded in 1980 by Elías Santana and several other experienced activists in the neighborhood associations movement that appeared with force in the most important Venezuelan cities during the seventies. Currently the school runs both a radio and a television program centered in local initiatives; it has absolutely no party affiliation.
8. COPRE, the Presidential Commission for the Reform of the State, was established in 1984 by President Jaime Lusinchi as a governmental agency charged with both technical and advocacy roles in the process of changing the structure of the Venezuelan government. Even if a careful evaluation of its achievements has yet to be made, one can fairly say that the change in electoral laws, making possible direct elections for governors and mayors as well as the drive toward decentralization, can be credited largely to the work of COPRE. To date, COPRE remains the most compelling example of the willingness of the established political leadership to undertake reforms. See Comisión Presidencial para la Reforma del Estado, "La abstención electoral de 1989" (COPRE, Caracas, 1990, mimeographed).
9. For a more detailed account of the activities of "civil society" in Venezuela, see chapter 8 by Daniel H. Levine and Brian F. Crisp in this volume.
10. See J. C. Rey, "El futuro de la democracia en Venezuela," in José A. Silva Michelena, ed., *Venezuela hacia el 2000: Desafíos y opciones* (Caracas: Editorial Nueva Sociedad, 1987), 183–245.
11. See Miriam Kornblith and Daniel Levine, "Venezuela: The Life and Times of the Party System," in Scott Mainwaring and Timothy Scully, eds., *Building Democratic Institutions: Parties and Party Systems in Latin America* (Stanford: Stanford University Press, 1993). In at least two opportunities—1963 and 1968—one of the challengers was able to gather the strength to achieve a close third at the ballots. Several groups are working on the possibility of launching an "independent" presidential candidacy in the next national election, using the low popularity of major parties to break bipartisanship. Simple identification as "independent" excludes these initiatives from our list of new political actors, given that, in their peculiar way, "independents" are one of the most traditional expressions of the Venezuelan party-dominated political system, thus representing a traditional response to the political crisis.
12. This summary is intended as a list of how political parties tend to be perceived by the Venezuelan public, and it does not pretend to prove or demonstrate that parties do

have such characteristics. For a provocative attempt to contrast realities and opinions on this subject, see Michael Coppedge, "Partidocracia and Reform in Comparative Perspective," paper presented at the conference "Democracy under Stress: Politics and Markets in Venezuela," sponsored by the North-South Center in collaboration with the Instituto Venezolano de Estudios Sociales y Políticos (INVESP), November 11, 1992, Caracas. In any case, criticism and detachment with respect to political parties is one of the well-established facts of contemporary Venezuelan politics: according to a recent study by the Supreme Electoral Council (CSE)—the highest authority in Venezuelan elections—militants and sympathizers of political parties together constitute only 25.3 percent of the adult population, down from 38.4 percent in 1983 and 48.7 percent in 1973 (CSE, Estudio de Opinión Pública, 1991). Significantly, such a loss of prestige as that suffered by political parties has not been paralleled by a comparable loss in the legitimacy of democracy as a political system, even though some effect in that direction has appeared recently. According to Arístides Torres, from 1977 to 1988 the percentage of voters "not satisfied" with democracy stabilized around 15 percent, and those preferring a dictatorship were a stable minority of 10 percent during the same years. In fact, however, the share of the population declaring a preference for dictatorship jumped from 10 percent in 1980 to 17.7 percent in 1990: "The economic crisis and the negative evaluations of politicians and parties, which up until then (1989) had not undermined the confidence in the system, started to act, diminishing its legitimacy levels"; see Arístides Torres, "La evolución de las actitudes hacia el sistema político en Venezuela," in *COPRE Venezuela, democracia y futuro: Los partidos políticos en la década de los 90, reflexiones para un cambio necesario* (Caracas: COPRE, 1990), 178.

13. Andrés Stambouli, "La razón de partido como obstáculo al cambio" (Washington, D.C., 1991, mimeographed).

14. In this respect, Decisión Ciudadana was just one of many (around 600, according to recent reports by the CSE) electoral groups ready to participate in the municipal and state elections in December 1992, compared to the 157 groups that participated in the 1989 election (*El Diario de Caracas*, September 4, 1992, 8). At least at the local level, democratic participation and competition are booming in Venezuela, to the point that it can be argued that these alternative groups are having the single most important effect in renovating the leadership of established parties. The change in electoral laws has unleashed a powerful wave of political entrepreneurship that is not limited to new political organizations. If one wants to look at the future national leadership in Venezuela, one should pay attention to the newly elected governors and mayors.

15. Factor Democrático, *Hacia otra Venezuela* (Caracas: Factor Democrático, 1993), 4.

16. J. C. Navarro and R. Rigobón, "La economía política del ajuste estructural y de la reforma del sector público en Venezuela," *Coyuntura económica latinoamericana* 22, no. 3 (1992): 131–51.

17. Roraima, *Plan de acción: Proposición al país* (Caracas: Grupo Roraima, 1983), 6–7.

18. M. Granier and J. A. Gil, *Más y mejor democracia* (Caracas: Grupo Roraima, 1987).

19. Andrés Velásquez, Causa R's founder, was elected governor of the state of Bolívar in 1989, an election in which his popularity among workers of the steel and aluminum industries allowed him to defeat the powerful party machine of AD in that state. He won reelection in 1992, after three years in which he earned a good reputation as regional administrator. Another leader of the organization, Aristóbulo Istúriz, won in the same opportunity an upset against an incumbent from AD in the local mayoral election in the most important municipality, Libertador, which encompasses two-thirds of Caracas.

20. A public statement by César Gil, a union leader from AD, makes the tension explicit: "As members of the parliament we have a political message that is dictated by the party that brought us to represent it in the chambers, and we have another unionist message as CTV union leaders" (*El Nacional*, March 10, 1992, cited in R. Díaz, "El movimiento sindical venezolano ante la crisis" [Veneconomía: Seminario Presiden-

cial, Puerto La Cruz, 1992, mimeographed]). Will Causa R end up using its union strength as a tool in electoral politics, or will it maintain its commitment to independent class representation?

21. See Moisés Naím, "The Launching of Radical Policy Changes, 1989–1991," in Joseph S. Tulchin with Gary Bland, eds., *Venezuela in the Wake of Radical Reform* (Boulder: Lynne Rienner, 1993), 39–94, and Navarro and Rigobón, "La economía política."

22. If the analysis developed in this chapter is correct, there are potentially big payoffs waiting for any political enterpreneur able to articulate a promarket, antiparty message—which, incidentally, does not necessarily mean that the payoffs are bigger than those existing for a populist and more traditional message, as the current popularity of Rafael Caldera demonstrates. Preliminary indications show that some individual party leaders are starting to move in that direction. In COPEI, the secretary general and presidential nominee in the last elections, Eduardo Fernández, has been talking insistently of a "social market economy" as the defining orientation of his political program. Oswaldo Álvarez Paz, the Zulia state governor, has recently been far more explicit and consistent in this regard. In AD, Carmelo Lauría, a businessman turned professional politician and a party leader, has been moving his message in a similar direction lately. It goes without saying that the credibility gap faced by any new political organization is magnified for leading figures within traditional political parties, who in some cases have strong links to past policies and administrations; this is aggravated by the fact that the new groups have to rely on political organizations that feel no identification with the new message. Yet the fact remains that some are trying.

23. Terry Karl has seen the roots of such exhaustion in the original characteristics of that pact. More generally, "pacts may adversely affect state efficiency in the long run. Pact-making is generally based on agreements that carve up the state in a complicated spoils system, which in the end may deeply corrode efficacy and productivity. In the Venezuelan case, the roots of both these problems can be located in the stage of democratic transition"; see Terry L. Karl, "Petroleum and Political Pacts: The Transition to Democracy in Venezuela," *Latin American Research Review* 22, no. 1 (1987): 63–94.

24. See Rey, "El futuro de la democracia," and J. C. Navarro, "Pactos políticos y estilos decisionales: Tres teorías frente al pacto de Punto Fijo y el pacto social," *Politeia*, no. 12 (1988): 193–200.

25. For an important exception, see Rey, "El futuro de la democracia."

26. I use the Dornbusch and Edwards definition of populism as "an approach to *economics* that emphasizes growth and income redistribution and deemphasizes the risks of inflation and deficit finance, external constraints, and the reaction of economic agents to aggressive nonmarket policies"; see Rudiger Dornbusch and Sebastian Edwards, eds., *The Macroeconomics of Populism in Latin America* (Chicago: University of Chicago Press, 1991), 9.

27. Figure 4.1 shows more than just a theoretical affinity: a few weeks after the failed coup in February, leaders of several of these groups gathered to discuss the feasibility of launching a common effort aimed to both rescue democracy and guarantee the continuity of the new directions in economic policy, in spite of the strong criticism that many of the participants had concerning the general performance of Carlos Andrés Pérez's administration. Although the initiative did not go very far, business, labor, community, and academic leaders nevertheless were able to talk openly with mutual trust and agreement. There is, in fact, a considerable degree of overlap in membership among the new political groups.

28. In March 1992, 48 percent of the urban voting population answered "none" to the question, "Which is the party whose ideas concerning how this country should be governed do you agree the most with?" The response to the same question in 1984 was 24 percent (*Mercanálisis*, Estudio de Opinión Pública Urbana, March 1992).

# 5

# Debilitating Democracy: Political Elites and Military Rebels

*Felipe Agüero*

Despite numerous signs of discontent, the violent military uprisings of February and November 1992 came as a surprise. Since the early 1980s, Venezuelan elites and both foreign and local scholars had been noting the impact that deteriorating economic conditions were having on the standard of living of average Venezuelans and the discredit that mounting episodes of corruption bestowed on leading officials. Sensitive to these developments, and purportedly having to deal with occasional unrest in the ranks, military officers were said to be discontent. Different accounts of existing factions in the military invariably included one bent on intervention. Although these accounts seemed to substantiate earlier prognostications about the impact that the end of oil-led growth would have on the chances of intervention by the armed forces, governing elites always discarded them for what they were: rumors.

Almost three decades of continuous military subordination had made intervention inconceivable. In fact, since the uprisings in the navy toward the end of President Betancourt's administration, the armed forces had not taken any action against constitutional government. In the eyes of civilians, political intervention could come only from armed forces proclaiming hard-core national security doctrines, such as those in the Southern Cone. Yet, the startling outburst of machine-gun and artillery fire from the rebels' attack on Miraflores Palace in the early morning hours of February 4, 1992, suddenly closed the gap between rumors and deeds, a gap that had remained all too wide for an elite accustomed to military respect for civilian authority.

In the rest of Latin America, observers had also grown used to seeing Venezuela as one of few exceptions to the military-authoritarian wave that hit most countries to the south in the 1960s and 1970s. In those countries, the democratizing elites in transition from authoritarianism often took inspiration from the earlier successes of pact making and the consensual style of the Venezuelan leadership. It was thus discouraging to see a democratic regime generally regarded as consolidated on the verge of breakdown, especially at a time when nearly all of Latin America rejoiced in the promise of its new democratic governments.

What, then, led a group of officers in a military praised for its allegiance to democracy to attempt the overthrow of Venezuela's constitutional government? One answer has been that the rebel action expressed the anger of a population impoverished by the combination of economic crisis and what were perceived as faulty and unfair government policies. As a retired general put it: "If the people are unhappy, unmotivated, frustrated and angry, it is easy to infer that the 'armed' part of the people should be in this same state of discontent."[1] This view is not fully out of line with the one implicitly anticipated by accounts that foresaw military intervention as the result of an eventual arrest in the dynamism of oil-led economic growth.[2] The problem with this view, however, is that, by establishing a direct relationship between popular discontent and military response, political institutions and elites are exempted of any direct role or responsibility.

Here it will be argued, instead, that in societies with a complex set of institutions and a modern professional military, "popular anger" does not automatically reflect on the "armed part of the people." Institutions play the key mediating role in buffering changes in government performance from sudden reversals in legitimacy, and, in this particular case, in separating popular discontent from automatic military response. If, as occurred in Venezuela, widespread lack of popular enthusiasm with the state of the political system echoed in a similar propensity in large sectors of the military, then analysis should focus on the kind of institutional deterioration that made this possible.

This chapter will show that, although the rebels expressed solidarity with the plight of a discontented populace, their subversive action responded to a more complex set of factors involving the discredit of political institutions and the loss of legitimacy of both civilian and military elites. The rebel movement expressed the resentment of a large number of officers toward the closed "partyarchy" that dominated the political system and that brought harm to military professionalism. It was this perception of harm to the institutional and professional interests of the military that broadened officers' sensitivity to the grievances of civil society and that ultimately led to rebellion.

The account of the crises of 1992 would remain incomplete, however, if the *failures* of the coup attempts were not also accounted for.

After all, none of the rebel attempts succeeded, being crushed both times by actions from the military itself. Poor planning and execution of the coup attempts, in addition to the inability to attract the actual support of a larger number of officers, certainly played a role. I discuss the failure instead as a result of the rebels' inability to marshal the participation of the high command, which pointed to the fact that the rebels' attempt encountered an elite that, despite appearances of divisions, was fundamentally unified. This enduring legacy of the agreements that gave birth to Venezuelan democracy denied the rebels an important facilitator of regime breakdown.

Just as the Venezuelan transition of 1958 to 1959 was the source of inspiration for democratic elites in other countries in the 1980s, the crisis that exploded in 1992 ought to warn these elites about the perils involved in oligarchic party practices and negligent treatment of professional militaries. At a more theoretical level, the Venezuelan experience points to the diverse ways in which democratic persistence may be seriously jeopardized. Studies of democratic consolidation often insisted on the role of elite agreement just as much as studies of democratic breakdown highlighted the role of disunity and polarization among elites.[3] The recent Venezuelan experience, however, shows that democratic regimes might approach the point of near breakdown without going through a process of elite polarization. Even with the allegiance and loyalty of all elite sectors, in an institutionally sophisticated polity a democratic regime may approach near breakdown as a result of vertical polarization, in which nonelites and subaltern officers are pitted against government and party elites.

The Venezuelan experience also reveals that mechanisms for civilian control that were useful at the initial stages of democratization failed to adjust to changing circumstances, until they could no longer secure a proper balance between the level of autonomy demanded by professionalism and the subjection to civilian control demanded by democratic government. The confusion between genuine democratic allegiance by the top military leadership and the deleterious intrusion of party influences to which the armed forces were led to succumb ultimately harmed military professionalism and discipline. The Venezuelan experience shows that breach of discipline from within middle-level positions might develop in modern professional militaries in contexts other than revolutionary circumstances or blatant leadership failure in external conflict. This breach may also develop from a cumulative perception among the bulk of the officer corps that harm is being inflicted on professionalism by a distorted horizontal relationship between civilian elites and the top military leadership.

## THE ECONOMY, PUBLIC DISCONTENT, AND THE MILITARY

The rebels had planned to reverse neoliberal economic policies and to promote an emergency program to combat poverty.[4] These plans were a direct reaction to the market-oriented economic adjustment policies surprisingly unleashed by President Pérez at the start of his second administration, including price liberalization and deregulation; these reforms had contributed to the ignition of popular anger that resulted in the bloody riots of February 1989. In retrospect, the utilization of the army for the repression of the riots and subsequent popular demonstrations pushed many officers to develop more sympathy for the repressed than for the political leadership. The rebels' statements about their plans thus seemed to support the view that saw the rebel movement as a direct reflection of the anger and frustration of the people over the economic situation.

Indeed, since the decline in oil prices in the early 1980s, the economy had ceased to grow and found itself stuck with large unfinished projects from the previous decade, with artificially subsidized services and an expanding debt. Between 1981 and 1985, GNP underwent negative growth, then grew slightly the next three years, only to decline steeply (−8.3 percent) in 1989. As unemployment reached almost 10 percent that year, inflation reached its peak (80 percent) and real wages continued to decline, reaching a decrease of 45 percent for the whole decade.[5] During the following years the economy improved substantially, becoming the world's fastest growing economy in 1991 (9.2 percent GNP growth). Inflation and unemployment also declined, and real wages started to pick up. However, there was no immediate improvement in the provision of services for the dissatisfied majority or in their living conditions, nor did the economy turn the tide of the regressive income distribution of previous years.[6] Thus, by the time of the coup attempt of February 1992, popular discontent was still high and manifest.

Military personnel were not spared the effects of the economic downturn, and their living standards declined just as did those for their civilian counterparts.[7] This shared experience obviously contributed to the identification of many officers with the people's hostility toward ruling officials. The rebel group was not staging a corporatist grievance about the standard of living of military personnel, however, nor was it complaining about treatment of the budgetary needs of the military as an institution, because it was obvious that these had been fairly satisfied.[8] Since the inauguration of democracy, military spending had indeed fol-

Table 5.1
VENEZUELA: MILITARY BUDGET[a] AS A PERCENTAGE OF
NATIONAL BUDGET, 1958–89

| Year | Percentage | Year | Percentage |
|------|------------|------|------------|
| 1958 | 3.29 | 1974 | 3.04 |
| 1959 | 3.08 | 1975 | 3.57 |
| 1960 | 1.99 | 1976 | 5.51 |
| 1961 | 0.30 | 1977 | 4.89 |
| 1962 | 6.08 | 1978 | 5.83 |
| 1963 | 0.59 | 1979 | 5.73 |
| 1964 | 0.27 | 1980 | 4.89 |
| 1965 | 0.66 | 1981 | 4.05 |
| 1966 | 0.98 | 1982 | 6.82 |
| 1967 | 1.53 | 1983 | 6.25 |
| 1968 | 1.40 | 1984 | 8.98 |
| 1969 | 1.09 | 1985 | 6.38 |
| 1970 | 1.01 | 1986 | 5.83 |
| 1971 | 2.23 | 1987 | 5.02 |
| 1972 | 5.80 | 1988 | 5.46 |
| 1973 | 6.21 | 1989 | 6.81 |

*Source:* Beatriz di Totto Blanco, "Revisión del régimen jurídico aplicable a los gastos de defensa y seguridad del estado," research paper, Advanced Course on National Defense, Institute for the Advanced Study of the National Defense, ministry of defense, Venezuela, Caracas, May 1990, 45.
[a]Military budget here does not include allocations itemized as security and defense for the ministries of interior, foreign affairs, and justice.

lowed relatively stable and predictable patterns and it had never become a pressing cause of concern for the armed forces. Over time, the military budget tended to follow the same upward trend set by the national budget and, as table 5.1 shows, the military increased its share of the national budget in a stable manner twice in this period, in 1972 and 1982. Regarding the state of the economy, the rebel group was not principally concerned about the military's or its own standing as much as it was concerned with the effects of the economic situation on the population.

Nonetheless, the military movement that arose in February 1992 saw itself responding to a set of demands that went far beyond discontent with economic policies. It placed far greater emphasis on its opposition to "the barriers of bureaucracy, party rule, and corruption," and blamed "presidential tyranny" for what it saw as generalized national malaise. The following excerpt from a document released by the rebel leaders after the failed coup depicts well their criticism of the political process and the extent of the blame they placed on the parties' leadership and the executive branch of the government:

In Venezuela there exists no separation between the branches of government, because political parties, in a deliberate breach of their role as intermediaries between state and society, conspired to usurp popular sovereignty and to have the executive seize all powers of the state. Accordingly, the executive turned into tyranny and the exercise of popular sovereignty was led to become no more than a grotesque farce. . . .

With this purpose, the presidential candidate and the top party leadership meet before the elections deliberately to turn the electoral process into a procedural farce by deceiving the law. . . .

The crime is completed when the candidate and the party leadership conveniently choose party members for Congress, because selection is based on subservience of the future legislator to the will of the eventual president. This leads to a legislative power which is hostage to the executive power, which, in turn, appoints the members of the judiciary on the same basis, securing serviceable justices. The candidate to the presidency of Venezuela thus secures beforehand his real, absolute, and effective control of all powers of the state and with it the partisanship of the judiciary and the lack of representativeness of Congress. . . . This situation creates a tyranny as a result of the degeneration of political parties.[9]

The rebels resented partyarchy and its oligarchical consequences and offered themselves to protect democracy from the tyrannical usurpers. In so doing, they touched a raw nerve in the political system that had been bothering Venezuelan elites for some time and that showed in the visible signs of political institutions' decreasing legitimacy among an increasingly apathetic electorate.[10] Many of the issues so bluntly put forth by the rebels had in fact been the concern of sectors of the political elite, which had previously attempted officially to address them through the creation of a special commission, the Presidential Commission for the Reform of the State (COPRE), during President Lusinchi's administration. The goals of "democratizing democracy" that the proposed reforms entailed—via reforms of the judiciary, the political parties, and the electoral system—marked the awareness about the decline in the levels of legitimacy that ostensibly haunted the parties-controlled political regime inherited from the founding pacts and since reproduced through the so-called *pacto tácito*.[11]

The rebel military movement, targeting its grievances at the heart of partyarchy, shook the bad conscience of political elites. In the period immediately following the February coup attempt, the rebels' complaints resonated among elites who expressed guilt, pointed fingers,

and promised more reforms. Gen. Fernando Ochoa Antich, for instance, then minister of defense and critical player in quashing the rebellion, overtly criticized the political elite and the quality of its leadership and called for substantial economic, social, and political changes.[12]
Similarly, the Consultative Council, appointed by President Pérez following the defeat of the rebellion to appease remaining discontent,
urged sweeping reforms that also hit at the core of the institutions of
partyarchy and the practice of corruption that was tolerated.[13]

   The rebel movement thus reflected general disillusion with the state
of the political regime and expressed widespread popular discontent
that combined economic grievances with demands for participation
and anger against what was perceived as a closed, unaccountable, and
corrupt elite. Contrary to appearances of *caudillismo* that flowed from
the charismatic leadership of Lt. Col. Hugo Chávez, chief of the rebels,
this was not the case of a power-hungry, smart, and ambitious group of
officers, whom official circles portrayed as madmen. They were, instead, officers who had coalesced as a group several years back and who
mustered enormous sympathy among middle and junior officers as well
as retired officers.[14] Because the military movement expressed widespread popular dissatisfaction with the state of the economy and the
political system, it validated an accepted generalization about military
intervention in complex modernizing societies, namely, that it does not
take place in the absence of a prior perception of extended civilian support, based on the perceived loss of legitimacy of the major institutions
in the political system.[15] As critical institutions of democracy—the judiciary, political parties, the central bureaucracy—gradually lost credibility, the military could no longer find in them the legitimacy buffer from
which to resist exposure to the mounting waves of popular discontent,
especially at a time in which the military was more often brought to perform repressive tasks by the very elite whose leadership it now severely
criticized.

## STATE-MILITARY RELATIONS
## AND THE EROSION OF DEMOCRACY

Decreasing legitimacy of political institutions and military exposure to
public discontent generally precede military intervention. Although
necessary, these factors are, however, not sufficient. For the military
to intervene, the specific bridges that link the military to civilian authorities must be severely damaged. The military must perceive that
its specific interests as an institution suffer due to the deteriorated
leadership capacity of civilian officials. The perception of specific
damage in the military's corporate interests is ultimately what precipi-

tates the negative effect of the other ingredients and sparks military intervention.[16]

The ultimate test of a consolidated democracy is its ability to resist temporary, even if strong, waves of popular unrest and institutional weakening, for which military subordination to civilian officials is of the essence. The uprisings of 1992 showed that this subordination was not fully guaranteed and, therefore, that institutional weakening transpired not only in those areas in which the COPRE recommendations sought redress but also in the very core of the ability of state authorities to subject the military to their supremacy.

In fact, the level and tone of criticism from military circles to civilian authorities gradually escalated during the 1980s to levels that are unusual in democracies considered to be consolidated. Former Defense Minister General García Villasmil, for instance, warned that "unless the democratic system is improved, it would become necessary to expand the influence of the armed forces so that they can act as referees."[17] Much of the military's criticism grew out of dissatisfaction with the civilians' inability to properly handle military or defense affairs placed under their responsibility.[18] In a direct criticism of civilian capabilities, former Defense Minister Gen. Luis Enrique Rangel Burgoín stated: "It is inadmissible for us in the military that none of the members of Congress' Defense Committee . . . has served in the military or has had any training in defense and security. And yet they handle military and security legislation!"[19] Military critics traced this leadership vacuum back to the organizational reforms effected by President Betancourt in the early 1960s, which at the time were justified to ensure civilian control, but which over time had rendered a formal structure of control devoid of substantive capacity for guidance in military affairs. Political elites were criticized for giving precedence to political patronage over professional development and encouraging, as a result, military bureaucratism and distorted professionalism.[20]

The specific sources of the military's discontent should therefore be examined in the structure of civil-military relations that peculiarly evolved in the context of democratization in the late 1950s and early 1960s. The connections between failures in these structures, the declining legitimacy of political institutions, and the specific consequences of economic distress stand behind the military threat to democratic stability.

## THREE DECADES OF CIVIL-MILITARY RELATIONS UNDER DEMOCRACY

Civil-military relations in Venezuela since the inauguration of democracy have been much more complex and nuanced than would suggest a simple contrast with the kind of civil-military relations that evolved under changing political regimes in the rest of South America. This is largely the result of the pervasiveness of the military in Venezuela's previous political development, where military rule was the norm for most of the country's life as an independent nation.[21]

The military was a major agent of political change during most of this century and played a prominent role in the period preceding democratization. It was, for instance, instrumental in opening the way to the first, and failed, democratic experiment of the Trienio (the period from 1945 to 1948 during which democratic politics was attempted under AD leadership, before being overthrown by the military) in conjunction with Acción Democrática and then in forcefully ending the experiment in 1948. Later, in 1952, it led the way to Pérez Jiménez's dictatorship, supported him in the fraudulent plebiscite of 1957, only to oust him in 1958, this time in agreement with a democratic coalition of civilians, with whom it sponsored the foundational democratic elections of 1959. In this active political role, the military sided with one or another political faction and consequently suffered from the purges that followed and the subsequent rehabilitation of previously purged officers. Democracy's birth in Venezuela, as with every other preceding regime, was very much the result of actions undertaken by the military.[22]

How, then, and how much, was the military confined to the barracks after the inauguration of democracy? There is no question that—following the agreements of Punto Fijo between the major political forces that were then enshrined in the 1961 Constitution—the regime inaugurated with the elections of 1959 was a full-fledged democracy. The military did not retain the kind of prerogatives or clout that the militaries of other South American countries assured for themselves after the transitions from authoritarianism.[23] In Venezuela, the constitution unequivocally stated that "the National Armed Forces form a non-political, obedient and non-deliberative institution, organized by the State to secure national defense, the stability of democratic institutions and respect for the Constitution and Laws, the observance of which shall always be above any other obligation. The National Armed Forces shall be in the service of the Republic and in no case of that of any person or political partisanship."[24]

The inaugural years, however, were not free of tension. In the early 1960s, for instance, the administration of President Betancourt faced severe threats from military uprisings, of both right-wing and left-wing inspiration.[25] Substantive commitment from the military to the new democratic arrangement was not guaranteed, and President Betancourt certainly did not take it for granted. In order to ensure the subjection of the military to civilian control, major changes in military and defense organization were promoted during Betancourt's presidency, with lasting impact on the structure of civil-military relations.

*Affirming Democratic Norms and Civilian Control in the 1960s*

With the purpose of weakening military power, President Betancourt reaffirmed a decree passed by the junta of Adm. Wolfgang Larrazábal in 1958, which replaced the general staff (*estado mayor general*) with the newly created joint staff (*estado mayor conjunto*). Whereas the general staff had integrated the top command structure (*comandancias generales*) of each of the four service branches, the joint staff now had only advisory functions within the defense ministry. The *comandancias generales* were detached from the joint structures and granted institutional autonomy for most matters, maintaining only administrative coordination with the defense ministry. They separated, as did their academies and staff schools, and in the organizational chart, they became directly dependent on the president.[26]

Government officials sought in this way to enhance their power by eliminating the institutional sites for interservice military coordination and by having the president deal directly and separately with each one of the service branches. This measure was not liked in the army, but the other services reaped benefits by detaching themselves from joint structures previously dominated by the army. Starting with this reorganization, each service branch acted separately from the other, especially regarding budgetary matters and purchases, which were negotiated directly with the president. A system was created in which the armed services exchanged direct subordination to the president for substantial institutional autonomy in the handling of internal and budgetary matters.

Another critical element of control established during this time was mandatory retirement for officers after only thirty years of service, combined with the almost yearly rotation of upper-level officers in the top command positions. With quick turnover in the upper echelons there was no time for officers to develop political leadership potential while on active duty. In addition, the promotion of officers in the higher ranks—a prerogative of the president—was closely monitored by Congress, which had to give its consent. In this way, the largest political parties held considerable leverage in military promotions, eventually instilling in aspiring generals or admirals a sense of loyalty to the major parties in Congress.

Further, the failure of the insurrections staged from leftist and right-ist quarters during Betancourt's presidency provided the opportunity for purging hard-liners on both sides. In addition, the reincorporation into active duty of officers forced into retirement by the previous regime enlarged the number of active supporters of the new regime among the military.

The engagement in countersubversive warfare also was critical in forging solid democratic allegiance in the military. The turn to armed revolutionary strategy by sectors of the Left, sympathetic to Fidel Castro's orientations in Cuba, led them to initiate guerrilla activities first in the cities and then in the countryside. The connections established between these guerrilla groups and foreign support provided the government with the opportunity to turn the countersubversive struggle into an impeccable professional mission, such as the defense of national territorial integrity. In pursuing this mission the military forged a commitment to the defense of the recently inaugurated democracy, inextricably linking countersubversive warfare with the defense of democratic institutions.[27] Contrary to the experience of other armed forces that engaged in countersubversive activities elsewhere in South America, in Venezuela the military did not seek an expansion of its political role. In part, this was due to the strong presidential leadership under which this mission was conducted[28] and to the fact that the armed forces had not developed the kind of security doctrines that the military in Argentina and Brazil, for instance, utilized to support their claims for military role expansion.[29]

President Betancourt assumed an extraordinary role in cultivating relations with the military with the goal of advancing democratic allegiance. Aware of the precarious situation that followed the ouster of the dictatorship, and facing subversive armed struggle and occasional rebellions in the military, the president understood the urgency of assuring the military's loyalty. He engaged in intense camaraderie with military officers, visiting their quarters frequently and opening the Casa Militar, the military staff of the presidency, as a way for officers to expediently express their grievances and submit requests to the president. This unusual presidential exertion helped cement military loyalty during the precarious early years, and it also contributed to the institutionalization of a system that combined direct subjection of the military to the president with autonomy for the internal regulation of the service branches, with little coordination between them.[30] With the continuation of Betancourt's policies through the end of the decade, the military became firmly committed to the burgeoning democratic regime and well integrated in the newly created institutions.

*The 1970s: Military Institutional Enhancement*

No longer focused on counterinsurgency, the military started redefining doctrines and missions, based on a reassessment of Venezuela's
geopolitical context.[31] Along with the formulation of an outward-
looking defensive posture, in the context of a volatile regional scenario,
the military emphasized the development of "state presence" in less
populated areas close to the borders of neighboring countries.[32] Civic
action programs, originally conceived as part of the counterinsurgency
struggle, now included larger construction operations with a view to
promoting the integration of remote areas. The Organic Law on Defense and Security, which the military pursued and obtained in 1976,
defined all territories along the border as security zones of public interest and placed them under the supervision of the defense ministry. In
addition, the military began to have greater influence in policies toward neighboring countries by maintaining a strong presence in the
frontiers division of the foreign affairs ministry.

Strategic production facilities also were defined in the new organic
law as security zones of public interest placed under supervision of the
defense ministry. This move coincided with an increasing role in development tasks, which followed the expansion of industry, the public
sector, and bureaucracy. The new organic law, for instance, created
the National Defense and Security Council with working committees
on political, economic, social, military, and mobilization affairs, all coordinated by a military-chaired permanent secretariat, although with
weak linkages to the rest of the civil bureaucracy. Military officers participated in the boards of a number of state-owned firms and directly
managed and controlled firms producing munitions and light
weaponry and a number of agencies that benefited military personnel
in the areas of social security, welfare, insurance, tourism, investments,
and foodstuff.[33]

The 1976 organic law reflected an expansive view of military and security roles, and some observers even likened it to the national security
views prevailing in the Southern Cone.[34] The organic consequences of
a more encompassing military role in security and development were
never really brought to fruition, however, and military circles later attempted to moderate the interpretation of this law in a manner better
adapted to the conditions of Venezuelan democratic institutions.[35]

Supporting the expansion and shift of military participation and
roles was the remarkable strengthening of the military institution via
further modernization and professionalization. This was in turn supported by the increasing resources provided by the expanding oil-based

economy and the special efforts made in the defense area. The average yearly share of the military budget as a percent of the national budget increased from 1.5 in the 1960s to 4.4 in the 1970s (see table 5.1), which allowed for equipment modernization and increased benefits for members of the armed forces.[36]

A significant accomplishment regarding institutional strengthening in the 1970s was the improvement of military education and training. For instance, graduation requirements were made more demanding and admission to military academies became much more competitive. The military's educational system was expanded and diversified with the creation of the Institute for Advanced Studies in National Defense (IAEDN) in 1972, which brought together upper-level civilian and military officials, and the Armed Forces Polytechnical Institute in 1975, which provided the military with an independent source of higher education. These new institutional sites opened fresh avenues for civilian-military dialogue, otherwise restricted to the topmost positions in the military and the state.[37] The institutional developments of the 1970s thus left a strengthened and more capable military that was organizationally and functionally diversified and thriving in self-confidence.

### The 1980s: Crisis of Professionalism and Breakdown of Discipline

The central organization of defense laid down in the 1960s, combined with the modernization and strengthening that the military underwent in the 1970s, had resulted in an institutional hybrid by the start of the 1980s. This amalgam consisted of an organization that was distinct and strong, yet restrained by its own organizational deficiencies at the top; an organization that had ample room to conduct itself autonomously, yet was subjected to the personal control of the president and the influence of political party forces.

Proof of the military's institutional strength within the political system was the deference with which it was treated by other sectors, the unquestionable veto power it held in certain areas of policy,[38] and the ability to pursue its interests. It succeeded, for instance, in pushing for dearly held demands, such as the Organic Law on Defense and Security, the revision of regulations on the draft, the restitution of a unified academy, an increase in its share of the budget (6 percent in the 1980s), and the revision of the Organic Law of the Armed Forces, which, in 1983, extended the professional career from thirty to thirty-three years of service.

The military's autonomy, however, was recognized in the handling of budgetary, organizational, and other internal matters. The ministry of defense was run by military officers exclusively, as were a number of semiautonomous state agencies. The *comandancias generales* of each service and the joint staff decided on planning, missions, training, and weapons purchases with almost no outside supervision. Congress did not receive itemized budgets for its approval, and financial operations by the services were occasionally carried out even without the knowledge of the minister.[39]

Thus democratization since the 1960s had not entailed the disappearance of the military's historical domestic power. During this period the military's institutions had been strengthened, but so had civilian institutions such as state bureaucracy, political parties, and sectoral organizations.[40] The military exercised its strength and autonomy within the specific context of Venezuela's democratic structure. In the 1980s, however, interaction within this context had come to exacerbate a number of flaws in civil-military relations. Autonomy and the absence of outside controls in budgetary matters, for instance, provided fertile grounds for corruption, which ultimately harmed the institution. Many episodes of corruption in obscure deals and contracts were uncovered during the 1980s involving general officers who nonetheless were never taken to court.[41]

Furthermore, the organizational devices for presidential control that were institutionalized in the 1960s turned into sources of inefficiency. The divide-and-rule principle applied to the service branches at the start of democratization denied the military indispensable mechanisms for unified central planning and operations that have become standard in modern defense establishments. Presidential coordination at the top, devoid of organizational support, proved unable to supplant other mechanisms for coordination and resulted in major duplication and inefficiencies. Concerned military chiefs became increasingly vocal in the criticism of this aspect. Gen. Jacobo Yépez Daza, for instance, criticized in 1984 from his post as chief of the Operational Planning Group in the ministry of defense the poor legislation delineating responsibilities of top civilian and military authorities in the planning and conduct of defense affairs. The principle of unified command, he argued, does not operate when "power is in fact shared more or less subtly by the minister of defense and the services' chiefs of staff, and between them and the chiefs of intelligence and of the president's military household."[42]

These problems were aggravated by the strict application of limits to years of service, which further weakened military leadership and its ability to maintain policy continuity and long-term planning. As a result of strict enforcement of these limits, there could be, for instance, seven different ministers of defense during a five-year presidential term. Similar effects resulted from the policy of rotating upper-level officers after no more than one year in their posts. Critics saw these practices as outdated instruments to weaken military power. Further, these practices also revealed that civilian officials attended to the military only out of fear of intervention and with little regard for professional needs.[43]

A major source of problems stemmed from the distortions introduced by party influences in the military. Political parties, through their control of the executive and the exercise of congressional powers in the approval of upper-level promotions, were regarded over the years as an integral part of the civilian control structure. However, the penetration in the military of the partyarchy reigning in the political system reached the point of negatively affecting military professionalism. Merit and seniority in promotions and assignments often were bypassed in favor of party criteria and patronage. The expectations of officers aspiring to the higher grades were strongly affected by the pervasiveness of party influence, encouraging party subservience over professional excellence. Networks were informally created that resulted in better assignments or other benefits outside the regular bureaucratic and hierarchy lines. Incumbent presidents often forced the promotion of certain individuals or expanded the number of positions at will for political purposes. An early warning was uttered in the early 1980s by former Defense Minister Gen. Rangel Burgoín, who stated, "It is criminal to allow officers with limited qualifications or no merit to bypass the requisites established in the military system, by resorting to outside or hidden favors [using] former presidents, the church, political leaders, retired generals, their wives or other individuals in order to guarantee their promotion."[44]

Party influences also led, in the eyes of many officers, to the expansion of military bureaucracies away from professional concerns and to a perverse utilization of the armed forces in roles more in tune with party needs than national defense. In fact, the rebels criticized those "generals subservient to politicians" who facilitated the use of army forces for the "delivery of school supplies, presidential security, vaccination campaigns, tree planting, etc., tasks which ought to be performed by others and which carry us away from our essential purpose."[45]

In sum, toward the end of the 1980s more and more officers complained that they were not being treated as professionals. This resulted from the fact that, as a renowned Venezuelan social scientist put it, "the military has become a sector whose policies are defined more by criteria of distributions of quotas of power at the domestic level than by considerations of internal security and external defense."[46]

The very dynamics of party influence in the military, however, especially at the higher echelons of the military leadership, led to a collu- sion between military and civilian elites, which alienated the more ju- nior officers. Not only did the benefits of party influence, patronage, and corruption not reach down to the lower levels, but also they ap- peared more contemptible in the eyes of officers more recently ex- posed to the professional teachings of military academies and staff schools, untainted by the realities of actual civil-military interaction at the top. The antielite feeling—against "corrupt politicians and submis- sive generals"—that developed among junior officers expanded and precipitated when the growing perception of threats to military profes- sionalism met the increasing loss of legitimacy of political elites and the waves of public discontent visible toward the end of the 1980s.

The admission by the top military leadership of the vertical rift that had developed in the army did not come until after it exploded in 1992 in the uprisings of February and November. But it was then recognized as a major threat and attracted the attention of the leadership. The for- mer chief of the joint staff admitted, for instance, that "all of us in the leadership share responsibility for not having perceived with clarity the signs of dissatisfaction uttered by the collective"; the commanding gen- eral of the army similarly granted that "internal relations in the armed forces . . . have relied on hierarchies that have been more formal than real."[47]

The distortion of military professionalism was brought about by the combination of the problems that both the political system and the structure of civilian-military relations faced in the 1980s. The resent- ment of middle-level officers—especially well-placed to perceive the harmful effects of this situation on their institution—was exacerbated when, in addition, they saw themselves forced to participate in the re- pression of public discontent by the very elites they blamed for both the national and their own organization's crises.

## UNIFIED ELITES AND THE CRISIS OF DEMOCRACY

Despite powerful motives and capabilities, the 1992 coup attempts did not succeed. The factors contributing to this failure were numerous and diverse, not the least being President Pérez's luck in avoiding assas- sination during the February revolt. More fundamental, however, was the fact that the rebels found no support among any of the political elites and that no group of generals was willing to follow their lead. Generals and politicians opposed the rebels as a unified military and civilian elite. As retired Gen. Alberto Müller Rojas rightly observed after the February attempt, "There is so far no break in the symbiosis that has existed between military and political elites."[48]

As was shown earlier, the rebels did have support from large segments of society, however, and it was the expectation of this support that encouraged them to stage the coup attempt. This support came from spontaneous outbursts of popular outrage and did not express or follow any significant elite group. The elites maintained their democratic allegiance and, despite growing signs of dissent within their ranks since the mid-1980s, no "disloyal oppositions" developed in Venezuelan politics. That is, no organized group had been "knocking at the barracks" for the support of the armed forces and no elite segment had renounced legal means as the way to gain access to power.[49]

In other recent cases, such as Argentina under presidents Raúl Alfonsín and Carlos Menem and Spain in February 1981, military revolts failed when the rebels met with no support from among the elites.[50] Because the Venezuelan crisis of 1992 came after decades of stable democracy, however, it should not be compared with crises that took place in newly established democracies right after the transitions from authoritarianism, such as Argentina under Alfonsín or Spain under Adolfo Suárez.

The Venezuelan crisis should instead be contrasted more productively with cases in which democratic crisis and breakdown occurred after periods of relative stability, such as in Chile, Uruguay, and Brazil, and also in Argentina prior to the 1976 coup. In these cases, democratic breakdown was preceded by a complex process, at the core of which always stood severe elite disunity and polarization.[51] In each instance, deafening "knocks at the barracks" by civilian politicians enticed, or straightforwardly pushed, the military into successful interventions. In the last analysis, as Juan Linz has maintained, breakdown is the "result of processes initiated by the government's incapacity to solve problems for which disloyal oppositions offer themselves as a solution."[52] In Venezuela, however, an important part of the military felt compelled to revolt without any elite sector knocking at the barracks to request intervention, and without the pull of a power vacuum, since the absence of elite polarization prevented one from developing. Although disloyal oppositions play critical roles in regime breakdown in most cases, in Venezuela a situation of near breakdown was reached even in the absence of disloyal oppositions.

In fact, even during periods of heated conflict, Venezuelan politics still exhibited a "consensually unified elite,"[53] including the military elite. While this elite feature may be indispensable for the attainment of democratic consolidation (as Michael Burton, Richard Gunther, and

*[handwritten: vertical rather than horizontal polarization]*

John Higley have argued), the Venezuelan experience reveals that it is not sufficient to keep consolidated democracies from suffering severe institutional deterioration, to the point of near breakdown. Democratic regimes with unified elites may approach such a point as a result of vertical rather than horizontal polarization, in which, for instance, non-elites and subaltern officers in the armed forces are pitted against party and government elites.

Elite unification had been firmly established in Venezuela since the Pact of Punto Fijo, which opened the way to the overthrow of Marcos Pérez Jiménez and the consensual inauguration of democracy. The pact attained procedural agreements for the successor governments and set the way for a style of compromise and negotiated decisions on major issues involving the parties, the church, business, labor, and, in some aspects, the military. The agreement actually expanded to include the basic features of a development strategy in which the state played major regulatory roles in the expansion of the oil-based economy. Economic growth and the gradual configuration of a predominant two-party system engaged in centripetal competition also strengthened over time the consensual dimensions of the initial pact.[54]

An expanding network of state agencies and interest associations provided the site for intense elite interaction. Private organizations representing business, labor, and other sectoral interests found correlates in an increasing number of sectoral public agencies for interest intermediation, which gave way to a semicorporatist structure sometimes referred to as a populist conciliation system.[55] In it, under consensual development strategies and an expanding-sum economic game, private interests met state bureaucrats and technocrats in central government roles and in the over four hundred decentralized public entities and enterprises with state participation. From above, centralized party elites pervaded most networks with an interest in purposely promoting negotiation and compromise as a means for stability.[56]

It is true, however, that this consensual basis was shaken since the decline of economic growth and particularly since Black Friday in 1983, when stringent economic measures were announced that gave official recognition to the exhaustion of the development strategy that had so far prevailed.[57] The incoming government of Acción Democrática in 1983 proposed a new social pact to face the crisis, and its leading officials proclaimed that the dominant "elite reconciliation" system, which had been functional for the early democratization period, had turned into an obstacle for the promotion of badly needed political, social, and economic changes.[58] The proposed pact did not come to fruition, however, and since then and through the 1980s different postures were

*[handwritten: 1983 Black Friday]*

espoused about ways of facing the crisis. Views that favored trimming
the state and the bureaucracy, greater efficiency in state enterprises,
and privatization cut across the party divide and were pitted against
more traditionally populist and distributionist postures.[59] Debate also
centered on the reform of political institutions with a view to enhancing participation and decentralization, from which sprang the creation
of COPRE during President Lusinchi's administration. Consensus was
further debilitated, severely affecting intraparty relations, and in 1989
President Pérez chose to unleash a coherent package of liberal economic policies, criticized by others as dogmatically neoliberal.[60]

Despite signs of a weakened consensus, elites remained essentially
unified. Internal tensions and rivalries notwithstanding, all relevant
elites condemned the military uprisings and proclaimed their support
for the democratic regime, which was not tantamount to unconditional
support for President Pérez and his policies.[61] Although numerous sectors were demanding the president's resignation, a good testimony of
elite unity was the rejection by COPEI (the leading opposition party) of
a proposal submitted to the Senate to hold a referendum to reduce
President Pérez's term. COPEI's positions were emphatically reaffirmed
by its top leader, Eduardo Fernández: "The armed forces must obey
President Pérez. The majority of Venezuelans gave him their trust and a
mandate that can be revoked only at the ballot box and not through a
military coup or a civilian coup."[62] The formation by the president of a
short-lived Consultative Council consisting of notables from all sides,
and which made a number of consensual proposals, was also a sign of
elite unity, as were the proposals by business leaders to reinvigorate the
initiative of a national pact among government, parties, and the private
sector.[63] These levels of unity, which also included the top military leadership, made it extremely hard for any rebel attempt to succeed.

## CONCLUDING OBSERVATIONS

Unity is likely to suffer from the challenges that face political elites.
The turn to dramatic changes in development strategies and economic
policies, for instance, will affect the basis on which much of the elite
network and consensus operated in the past, and the split between neoliberal reformers and traditional populists is likely to sharpen. Major
decisions on pending political reforms also are likely to be divisive,
and the consequences of electoral reforms, perhaps bringing more rel-
evance to previously marginal parties, will introduce uncertainties yet
unknown to Venezuelan politics. Although all these developments may

lead unity to weaken, and with it the ability of the regime to resist new military threats if they were to emerge, the result does not necessarily have to be the formation of disloyal oppositions. Just as institutional deterioration was much of the elites' own doing, so may be institutional reform in ways that facilitate both relegitimation and conflict resolution.

The problems facing the elites extend beyond problems of unity. The discussion in this chapter shows that unity had, in fact, not been the problem and that despite it the regime nearly was brought to an end. Extreme elite disunity should not, obviously, be let to prosper, but the main challenge is one of opening up political institutions, making them more visibly responsive, and diminishing the exclusive role of party elites in crucial decisions across state and civil institutions. Re-establishing confidence in political institutions would allow the expression of opposition and grievances over social and economic issues that would not automatically turn into antiregime postures. Recrafting political institutions for democratic reequilibration, therefore, ought to diminish the emphasis on central elite control of participation and compromise, which explicitly characterized elite behavior during the early years of the democratic regime.[64]

The challenges facing Venezuelan politics in this regard are part of a more general crisis in the balance between the demands of governability (and its oligarchic deformations, including corruption) and those of responsiveness and participation, which also affect a number of older democracies in the advanced industrialized world. Recent crises and corruption episodes among the party elites in Spain, Italy, and Japan, for instance, testify to the fact that the problems facing Venezuela are not exclusive to developing world democracies and suggest that solutions ought likewise to be considered with wider, comparative schemes.[65] The problems inherent in unbalanced emphases on elite control as a device for stability should also come as a warning for newer democracies elsewhere in the region seeking consolidation.

If Venezuelan elites confront the challenges to their unity and successfully advance institutional reforms, many of which have already been initiated, they still have to take on the arduous task of reconstructing democratic allegiance among the bulk of the officer corps in the military. Even if the rebels' repeated failure to oust the government during the 1992 attempts makes it unlikely that there will be another try in the near future, the democratic commitment of the military cannot be taken for granted, at least not for a long time. And the democratic regime will not be safe unless this task is promptly and successfully tackled. This result will partly be a function of the success

*must*

with which political institutions regain legitimacy among the public; but it also will depend on the ability of civilian elites to create structures of state-military relations that do not interfere with professionalism. The recent military crisis should lead civilian elites, quite paradoxically, not to think of the military exclusively as a source of potential intervention, but to think of the members of the armed forces as professionals who deserve to be treated as such. This view should entail, among other things, thinking about reforms of the mechanisms for the assertion of civilian control. The mechanisms currently in place, which might have worked during the early stages of democratization, have obviously proved not to work.

The penetration of partyarchy corrupts professionalism and, in addition, creates enough resentment in the ranks to defeat the purposes of control. Quick turnover in the top positions and barriers to interservice coordination certainly weaken the military leadership, but they also weaken the organization's professional performance and should therefore not constitute the core of civilian control. In fact, advanced industrial democracies and the new southern European democracies have promoted exactly the opposite—that is, more joint organization and more stability in the ranks for long-term planning, as mechanisms through which civilian control and professional performance may be successfully obtained.[66]

Whatever schemes are devised, the scenario for state-military relations will be affected by the impact the processes of state modernization and political and economic reforms will have on military missions, size, and the mode and extent of insertion in state structures. At the same time, this scenario will be shaped by the military's own search for ways to accommodate the new context, which may well lead to higher levels of military autonomy.[67] Rethinking civilian control will be made more complex as this new scenario unfolds and will demand special efforts from civilian elites if both military subordination and professionalism are to be guaranteed.

I would like to thank generals José Antonio Olavarría, Pedro Remigio Rangel Rojas, Raúl Salazar Rodríguez, and Jacobo Yépez Daza, as well as Beatriz di Totto Blanco and Luis Beltrán Petrosini, for helping me clarify numerous aspects of the 1992 crisis, during a visit to Caracas in November 1992 to participate in a conference sponsored by the Venezuelan Institute for Social and Political Studies (INVESP) and the North-South Center of the University of Miami. They, of course, have no responsibility for the statements I make in this chapter.

# NOTES

1. "A Coup at What Cost?" *Latin America Monitor, Andean Group* 9, no. 2 (March 1992): 1.
2. Studies of Venezuelan politics in the 1970s and 1980s generally held the chances of continued democratic stability as dependent on the continuation of economic prosperity. It was argued, for instance, that discontinuity in the conditions that had supported a "subsidized democracy" should lead to a reassessment of the military's position and loyalty in the political system. See Rita Giacalone and Rexene Hanes de Acevedo, "The Military in a Subsidized Democracy: The Case of Venezuela," in Constantine P. Danopoulos, ed., *From Military to Civilian Rule* (London: Routledge, 1992), 127–57; John D. Martz and David J. Myers, "Venezuelan Democracy and the Future," in John D. Martz and David J. Myers, eds., *Venezuela: The Democratic Experience* (New York: Praeger, 1977), 359–91.
3. John Higley and Richard Gunther, eds., *Elites and Democratic Consolidation in Latin America and Southern Europe* (Cambridge: Cambridge University Press, 1992); Juan J. Linz, *Crisis, Breakdown, and Reequilibration* (Baltimore: Johns Hopkins University Press, 1978).
4. *Latin American Weekly Report*, February 20, 1992, 5.
5. Moisés Naím, "Paper Tigers and Minotaurs: The Politics of Venezuela's Economic Reforms" (Washington, D.C.: Carnegie Endowment for International Peace and Brookings Institution, 1993).
6. Net per capita income had been declining steadily since 1977, reaching its lowest point in 1989; see ibid. Labor's share of national income had declined from 51.5 percent in 1969 to 35.1 percent in 1990; see FUNDAFUTURO, *Cuando Venezuela perdió el rumbo: Un análisis de la economía venezolana entre 1945 y 1991* (Caracas: Ediciones Cavendes, 1992), 140. Throughout the 1980s the lowest 20 percent of the population received about 5 percent of the national income, while the highest 20 percent received about 48 percent of the national income; Janet Kelly, "The Question of Inefficiency and Inequality: Social Policy in Venezuela," manuscript, Institute for the Advanced Study of Administration (IESA), October 1992.
7. Married junior officers often were forced to share housing in order to afford the rent. See Naím, "Paper Tigers and Minotaurs"; Roberto Romanelli, "Ya no tienen acceso a la vivienda ni a la atención médica: Los militares retirados sufren los embates de la crisis," *El Universal*, December 20, 1991, 12; José R. Díaz, "Los militares quieren una mejor calidad de vida," *El Universal*, September 24, 1991, 19; and Winfield Burggraaff and Richard L. Millett, "More than a Failed Coup: The Crisis in Venezuelan Civil-Military Relations," paper presented to the conference "Lessons from the Venezuelan Experience" at the Woodrow Wilson International Center for Scholars, Washington, D.C., October 19–21, 1992, chap. 2 herein.
8. Alberto Müller Rojas, *Relaciones peligrosas: Militares, política y estado* (Caracas: Fondo Editorial Tropykos, Fondo Editorial APUCV/IPP, Fundación Gual y España, 1992), 24.
9. Document of the Movimiento Bolivariano Revolucionario-200 (MBR-200) of June 24, 1992, quoted in Angela Zago, *La rebelión de los angeles* (Caracas: Fuentes Editores, 1992), 141 (my translation).
10. Michael Coppedge, "Venezuela's Vulnerable Democracy," *Journal of Democracy* 3, no. 4 (October 1992): 32–44; Ricardo Combellas, "La democracia venezolana: Del reto de su instauración al reto de su consolidación," in Carlos Barba Solano, José Luis Barras Horcasitas, and Javier Hurtado, compilers, *Transiciones a la democracia en Europa y América Latina* (Mexico: Universidad de Guadalajara and Latin American Social Science Faculty [FLACSO], 1991); Luis Gómez Calcaño, "La vitrina rota: Interrogantes sobre la democracia venezolana," in Diego Cardona, coordinator, *Crisis y transición democrática en las paises andinos* (Bogotá: Centro de Estudios de la Realidad Columbiana, 1991).

11. See Ricardo Combellas, *La democratización de la democracia* (Caracas: IFEDEC, 1988), and idem, *Propuestas para reformas políticas inmediatas, Reformas inmediatas del poder judicial,* and *Propuestas para impulsar el proceso de descentralización territorial en Venezuela,* Discussion Paper No. 1 (1986), 5 (1987), and 9 (1987) (Caracas: Ediciones COPRE). Also see Allan R. Brewer-Carías, "La descentralización política en Venezuela: 1990, el inicio de una reforma," in Dieter Nohlen, ed., *Descentralización política y consolidación democrática: Europe-América del sur* (Caracas: Editorial Nueva Sociedad, 1991), 131–60.

12. Heinz Sonntag and Thaís Maingón, *Venezuela 4-F 1992: Un análisis sociopolítico* (Caracas: Editorial Nueva Sociedad, 1992), 38. In regard to the position of retired officers, Gen. Jacobo Yépez Daza, president of the Association of Retired Military Officers, appeared at the office of the attorney general to seek reassurance for the officers arrested following the defeat of the coup attempt (*Latin American Weekly Report,* February 20, 1992, 5) and linked the coup attempt to the government's "failure to fight corruption, provide security to people and their property, make public services more efficient, and offer order and fairness to all Venezuelan people"; *Latin America Monitor, Andean Group* 9, no. 2 (March 1992): 995.

13. See the final report of the Consultative Council in the appendix to FUNDAFUTURO, *Cuando Venezuela perdió el rumbo.*

14. The Movimiento Bolivariano Revolucionario-200 had been forming for the past dozen years at least, according to former Army Comdr. Gen. Carlos Peñaloza Zambrano; see Sonntag and Maingón, *Venezuela 4-F 1992,* 22. Official estimates set the figure of army personnel involved in the February conspiracy at about two thousand. The November conspiracy involved a couple of generals, an admiral, and a large number of air force personnel.

15. "It seems unlikely that military leaders would turn their arms against the government unless they felt that a significant segment of the society shared their lack of belief [in the legitimacy of the regime] and that others were at least indifferent to the conflicting claims for allegiance"; Linz, *Crisis, Breakdown, and Reequilibration,* 17. Also see Abraham F. Lowenthal, "Armies and Politics in Latin America," *World Politics* 27, no. 1 (October 1974): 107–30; J. Samuel Fitch, "Armies and Politics in Latin America: 1975–1985," in Abraham Lowenthal and J. Samuel Fitch, eds., *Armies and Politics in Latin America* (New York: Holmes and Meier, 1986), 26–55; and Eric Nordlinger, *Soldiers in Politics: Military Coups and Governments* (Englewood Cliffs, N.J.: Prentice-Hall, 1977). In Argentina, the group of officers that rebelled at different times—with no support from society—during Raúl Alfonsín's administration were seeking not to overthrow the government but to obtain guarantees on specific issues. See David Pion-Berlin, "Between Confrontation and Accommodation: Military and Government Policies in Democratic Argentina," *Journal of Latin America Studies* 23 (1991): 543–71, and Deborah Norden, "Democratic Consolidation and Military Professionalism: Argentina in the 1980s," *Journal of Inter-American Studies and World Affairs* 32, no. 3 (fall 1990): 151–76.

16. For a treatment of the Venezuelan case in the comparative context of Latin America, see Felipe Agüero, "Las fuerzas armadas y el debilitamiento de la democracia en Venezuela," paper presented at the international seminar "La democracia bajo presión: Política y mercado en Venezuela," Caracas, November 9–11, 1992.

17. Quoted in Luis Enrique Rangel Burgoin, *Nosotros los militares* (Caracas: Editorial Sol, 1983), 61.

18. In 1989 I noted that "the expanding gap between military goals and means, coupled with patronage practices and formal mechanisms of civilian control, has given rise to increasingly outspoken signs of military discontent. The military's criticism is broadly targeted against both the unwillingness or inability of civilians to provide substantive guidelines for the defense sector and military development and the harmful effects of party influences and patronage"; Felipe Agüero, "The Military and Democracy in Venezuela," in Louis W. Goodman, Johanna S. R. Mendelson, and Juan Rial, eds., *The Military and Democracy: The Future of Civil-Military Relations in Latin America* (Lexington, Mass.: Lexington Books, 1990), 268.

19. See Rangel Burgoin, *Nosotros los militares*, 105.
20. See Gen. Jacobo Yépez Daza, "El realismo militar venezolano," in Moisés Naím and Ramón Piñango, eds., *El caso Venezuela: Una ilusión de armonía* (Caracas: Ediciones IESA, 1988), 328–49, and Col. José Machillanda Pinto, *Poder político y poder militar en Venezuela, 1958–1986*, 2d ed. (Caracas: Ediciones Centauro, 1988).
21. Winfield Burggraaff, *The Venezuelan Armed Forces in Politics, 1935–1959* (Columbia: University of Missouri Press, 1972).
22. J. L. Salcedo-Bastardo, Luis Herrera Campíns, and Beníto Raúl Losada, *Tránsito de la dictadura a la democracia en Venezuela* (Barcelona, Venezuela: Ariel, 1978), and Judith Ewell, *Venezuela: A Century of Change* (Stanford: Stanford University Press, 1984).
23. See Felipe Agüero, "The Military and the Limits to Democratization in South America," in Scott Mainwaring, Guillermo O'Donnell, and J. Samuel Valenzuela, eds., *Issues in Democratic Consolidation: The New Latin American Democracies in Comparative Perspective* (Notre Dame, Ind.: University of Notre Dame Press, 1992), 153–98.
24. The Venezuelan Constitution in Albert P. Blaustein and Gisbert H. Flanz, eds., *Constitutions of the Countries of the World* (Dobbs Ferry, N.Y.: Oceana Publications, 1983).
25. For civil-military relations in this period and the subsequent administrations, see José Antonio Gil Yepes, "Political Articulation of the Military Sector in Venezuelan Democracy," in Martz and Myers, *Venezuela*, 148–82; Gene E. Bigler, various sections on Venezuela in Robert Wesson, ed., *The Latin American Military Institution* (New York: Praeger, 1986); Gene E. Bigler, "Professional Soldiers and Restrained Politics in Venezuela," in Robert Wesson, ed., *New Military Politics in Latin America* (New York: Praeger, 1982), 175–96; and Elsa Cardozo de Da Silva, "Militares y política: Propuestas para el estudio del caso venezolano," in Carlos Juan Moneta, compiler, *Civiles y militares: Fuerzas armadas y transición democrática* (Caracas: Editorial Sudamericana, 1990), 77–94.
26. See decree 288 in Eduardo C. Schaposnik, *Democratización de las fuerzas armadas venezolanas* (Caracas: Instituto de Investigaciones Sociales, 1985), 238–44.
27. One specific manifestation of this was, for instance, the military's role in supervising the electoral process under the general guidance of the Supreme Electoral Council; see María Pilar Villabona Blanco, "Política y elecciones en Venezuela," *Revista de estudios políticos* (Madrid), no. 53 (September–October 1986): 215–37.
28. In this regard, the Betancourt doctrine—which proposed denying recognition to governments born of military coups and aimed at isolating dictatorial governments, generally of a right-wing bent—played an important role. Venezuela applied the Betancourt doctrine by denying diplomatic recognition to the unconstitutional regimes established in El Salvador in 1960, in Peru and Argentina in 1962, in Haiti in 1963, and in Bolivia, Brazil, and Ecuador in 1964. In this way, the doctrine associated the defense of democracy with fighting not only leftist guerrillas but also right-wing military coups as well as conspiracies inspired abroad, such as the participation of dictator Rafael Trujillo of the Dominican Republic in the assassination attempts against President Betancourt; see Robert J. Alexander, *Rómulo Betancourt and the Transformation of Venezuela* (New Brunswick, N.J.: Transaction Books, 1982).
29. See David Pion-Berlin, "Latin American National Security Doctrines: Hard- and Softline Themes," *Armed Forces and Society* 15, no. 3 (spring 1989): 411–29.
30. Müller Rojas, *Relaciones peligrosas*, 156–57.
31. The defeat of the guerrillas gave way to the pacification policies of President Rafael Caldera in the early 1970s, which allowed the incorporation of former guerrillas into the political system.
32. Andrés Serbín, "Percepciones de amenaza y equipamiento militar en Venezuela," INVESP paper 010-010-1989, and Aníbal Romero, "La situación estratégica de Venezuela," *Ciencia política*, no. 4 (third trimester, 1986): 25–42.
33. Gil Yepes, "Political Articulation of the Military Sector," 169–70. Around the military's domestic role in development there developed contending views among civilians. See, for instance, José Vicente Rangel, "Problemas fundamentales de seguridad y defensa de Venezuela," in Aníbal Romero, ed., *Seguridad, defensa y democracia* (Caracas:

Editorial Equinoccio, 1980), 29–56; Luis Enrique Alcalá, "La doctrina de seguridad en Venezuela," in Romero, *Seguridad,* 141–51; and José Vicente Rangel et al., *Militares y política: Una polémica inconclusa* (Caracas: Ediciones Centauro, 1976).

34. Judith Ewell, "The Development of Venezuelan Geopolitical Analysis since World War II," *Journal of Interamerican Studies and World Affairs* 24, no. 3 (1982): 295–320, and Aníbal Romero, *La miseria del populismo: Mitos y realidades de la democracia en Venezuela,* 2d ed. (Caracas: Ediciones Centauro, 1987), 303–9.

35. See Giacalone and Hanes de Acevedo, "The Military," 146–47, and Müller Rojas, *Relaciones peligrosas,* 132–33.

36. According to Bigler ("Professional Soldiers"), salaries for military personnel increased 140 percent in real terms between 1960 and 1974. Retirement, health, and other social security benefits were reinforced with the passing of the Organic Law of Social Security in 1977. See also Robert Looney, *The Political Economy of Latin American Defense Expenditures* (Lexington, Mass.: Lexington Books, 1986), and Franklin Tugwell, "Petroleum Policy and the Political Process," in Martz and Myers, *Venezuela,* 237–54.

37. The extent of civilian-military interaction has been the subject of controversy among top military leaders. For instance, attendance of military officers in courses at civilian universities has been alternately promoted and discouraged by the military leadership. Some have viewed it as beneficial for the overall civic formation of the officers, whereas others have viewed it as a source of distraction from the main professional concerns or even as perniciously subjecting officers to the radical inclinations of university students.

38. For instance, in policies toward neighboring rival Colombia; see Gil Yepes, "Political Articulation of the Military Sector," 164.

39. Agüero, "The Military and Democracy in Venezuela"; Di Totto Blanco, "Revisión del régimen jurídico"; and Gil Yepes, "Political Articulation of the Military Sector," 55, 165, 267.

40. Daniel H. Levine, "Venezuelan Politics: Past and Future," in Robert D. Bond, ed., *Contemporary Venezuela and Its Role in International Affairs* (New York: New York University Press, 1977), 7–44.

41. Müller Rojas, *Relaciones peligrosas,* 70–71, and Hugo G. Possey, "In the Spirit of Bolívar: The Challenge to Democracy in Venezuela," *Hemisphere* (June-July 1992): 12.

42. Yépez Daza, "El realismo militar venezolano," 340. Strong emphasis on this point is also found in Machillanda Pinto, *Poder político y poder militar,* 179, and Müller Rojas, *Relaciones peligrosas,* 119.

43. Yépez Daza, "El realismo militar venezolano," 340. See also Vice Adm. Elías Daniels, *Militares y democracia* (Caracas: Ediciones Centauro, 1992), 62–63, and Müller Rojas, *Relaciones peligrosas,* 118–20.

44. Rangel Burgoin, *Nosotros los militares,* 61 (my translation). Additional critical references to these practices may be found, for instance, in Machillanda Pinto, *Poder político y poder militar,* and in Müller Rojas, *Relaciones peligrosas,* 23–24, 67–72, and 225–35.

45. Zago, *La rebelión de los angeles,* 149 (my translation).

46. Gil Yepes, "Political Articulation of the Military Sector," 177.

47. See, respectively, Elías Daniels, *Militares y democracia,* 167, and Pedro Remigio Rangel Rojas, commandant general of the army, "El papel de las fuerzas armadas: Renovación democrática, apertura económica y las nuevas relaciones cívico-militares," presentation in the conference "La democracia bajo presión: Política y mercado en Venezuela," Caracas, November 11, 1992.

48. Müller Rojas, *Relaciones peligrosas,* 342.

49. For the notion of "disloyal opposition" and its role in democratic breakdown, see Linz, *Crisis, Breakdown, and Reequilibration,* 27–38.

50. For Argentina, see Pion-Berlin, "Between Confrontation and Accommodation," and Norden, "Democratic Consolidation"; for Spain, see Felipe Agüero, "Regierung und

Streitkräfte in Spanien nach Franco," in Walther Bernecker and Josef Oehrlein, eds., *Spanien Heute,* (Hamburg: Vervuert Verlag, 1991).

51. See, for instance, Arturo Valenzuela, *The Breakdown of Democratic Regimes: Chile* (Baltimore: Johns Hopkins University Press, 1978); Alfred Stepan, "Political Leadership and Regime Breakdown: Brazil," in Juan J. Linz and Alfred Stepan, eds., *The Breakdown of Democratic Regimes: Latin America* (Baltimore: Johns Hopkins University Press, 1978), 110–37; and Guillermo O'Donnell, "Permanent Crisis and the Failure to Create a Democratic Regime: Argentina, 1955–66," in Linz and Stepan, *The Breakdown of Democratic Regimes,* 138–77.

52. Linz, *Crisis, Breakdown, and Reequilibration,* 50.

53. "Although [elites that are consensually unified] regularly and publicly oppose one another on ideological and policy questions, all important elite factions share an underlying consensus about rules of the game and the worth of existing political institutions"; Michael Burton, Richard Gunther, and John Higley, "Introduction: Elite Transformations and Democratic Regimes," in Higley and Gunther, *Elites and Democratic Consolidation,* 11. See also John A. Peeler, "Elite Settlements and Democratic Consolidation: Colombia, Costa Rica and Venezuela," in Higley and Gunther, *Elites and Democratic Consolidation,* 81–112.

54. Terry L. Karl, "Petroleum and Political Pacts: The Transition to Democracy in Venezuela," *Latin American Research Review* 22, no. 1 (1987): 63–94; Daniel H. Levine, "Venezuela since 1958: The Consolidation of Democratic Politics," in Linz and Stepan, *The Breakdown of Democratic Regimes,* 82–109; Daniel H. Levine, "Venezuela," in Myron Weiner and Ergun Özbudun, eds., *Competitive Elections in Developing Countries* (Durham, N.C.: Duke University Press, 1987), 248–82; and Daniel H. Levine, "Venezuela: The Nature, Sources, and Future Prospects of Democracy," in Larry Diamond, Juan J. Linz, and Seymour Martin Lipset, eds., *Democracy in Developing Countries: Latin America* (Boulder: Lynne Rienner, 1989), 247–89. Although the Left was not included in the initial deliberations leading to the Pact of Punto Fijo, it did participate in the making of the 1961 Constitution. The Left's exit to initiate armed struggle strengthened the unity of the regime's elite and helped solidify the democratic allegiance within the armed forces. The reincorpration of the Left in the political system in the 1970s further strengthened the initial consensual traits of Venezuela's political regime.

55. Juan Carlos Rey, "El futuro de la democracia en Venezuela," *Síntesis* (Madrid), no. 5 (May–August 1988): 181–82. Also see Jennifer McCoy, "Labor and the State in a Party-Mediated Democracy: Institutional Change in Venezuela," *Latin American Research Review* 24, no. 2 (1989): 35–67.

56. Focusing on elites in this context, Gil Yepes characterized them as essentially "divided elites." He was, however, addressing what he saw as the "organic statist" features of the political system and the functional arrangement of the elites within it in the form of "monopolistic compartments" that maintain intragroup solidarity and protection and lack mutual confidence. This does not contradict my assertion about Venezuelan elites as unified around essentially consensual views on the rules of the game and the worth of political institutions. See José Antonio Gil Yepes, *The Challenge of Venezuelan Democracy* (New Brunswick, N.J.: Transaction Books, 1981), 21, and idem, "Political Articulation of the Military Sector," 156. For a description of elite members in this network, see Diego Bautista Urbaneja, "El sistema político o cómo funciona la máquina de procesar decisiones," in Naím and Piñango, *El caso Venezuela,* 251; Rey, "El futuro de la democracia," 194; and Combellas, *La democratización de la democracia,* 112–13. For the number of state enterprises see Gil Yepes, *The Challenge,* 99.

57. Officially the VII Plan de la Nación for the period 1984–88 blamed the crisis on the exhaustion of the growth model; see Margarita López Maya, Luis Gómez Calcaño, and Thaís Maingón, *De Punto Fijo al pacto social: Desarrollo y hegemonía en Venezuela (1958–1985)* (Caracas: Fondo Editorial Acta Científica Venezolana, 1989), 59.

58. Ibid., 96.

59. Bautista Urbaneja, "El sistema político," 162.

60. See, for instance, Rafael Caldera, "Economía, confianza y sentido común," *El Nacional*, August 3, 1992. Also see Isabel Licha, *Tecno-burocracia y democracia en Venezuela: 1936–1984* (Caracas: Fondo Editorial Tropykos, 1990).

61. See, for instance, the views stated by former President Rafael Caldera during the joint session of Congress on February 4, 1992, in his *Caldera: Dos discursos* (Caracas: Editorial Arte, 1992). For a view from leftist quarters, see Enrique Ochoa Antich, *Los golpes de febrero: De la rebelión de los pobres al alzamiento de los militares* (Caracas: Fuentes Editores, 1992).

62. *El Nacional*, November 12, 1992, 1 and D1, and November 10, 1992, 1 and 12.

63. Although this proposal did not succeed, it expressed the coalescent behavior of elites. See Antonio Francés and Moisés Naím, "The Venezuelan Private Sector: From Courting the State to Courting the Market," paper presented at the conference "Lessons from the Venezuelan Experience," Woodrow Wilson International Center for Scholars, Washington, D.C., October 19–21, 1992, chapter 6 herein, and Sonntag and Maingón, *Venezuela 4-F 1992*, 59–60.

64. Terry Karl noted "the central dilemma of elite-ascendant processes" (such as the Venezuelan), in which "the very modes of transition that appear to enhance initial survivability by limiting unpredictability may preclude the future democratic self-transformation of the economy or polity further down the road"; see Terry Lynn Karl, "Dilemmas of Democratization in Latin America," *Comparative Politics* vol. 23, no. 1 (October 1990): 13.

65. Gianni Baget Bozzo, an Italian member of the European Parliament, recently described the problems facing Italian democracy in ways that could well have been written for Venezuela: "When a country goes through an economic crisis, in which empoverishment relative to previous levels makes itself felt, the lack of confidence in institutions leads but to violent behavior: the violent responses of institutions," *El País*, Madrid, December 25–26, 1992, 6.

66. See Felipe Agüero, "Democratic Consolidation and the Military in Southern Europe and South America," in Nikiforos Diamandouros, Richard Gunther, and Hans-Jürgen Puhle, eds., *The Politics of Democratic Consolidation in Southern Europe* (forthcoming 1994), and Martin Edmonds, ed., *Central Organizations of Defense* (Boulder: Westview Press, 1985).

67. The military had already advanced proposals for reforms of the constitution and the Organic Law of the Armed Forces, touching on critical issues such as career limits, promotion regulations, the creation of a joint high command, and other initiatives that would lead to enhanced autonomy. See the special issue of *Revista del ejército* on the 171st anniversary of the Carabobo battle, Caracas, June 28, 1992, 88–122.

## II

# Two Key Sectors

# 6

# The Venezuelan Private Sector: From Courting the State to Courting the Market

*Moisés Naím and*
*Antonio Francés*

Never before in history had the Venezuelan government placed so much faith and transferred so much responsibility to the private sector as it did through the policy reforms adopted in 1989. Such reforms meant that prices were freed, state companies privatized, imports and exports liberalized, foreign companies welcomed and encouraged to invest. The policy changes also implied the sweeping deregulation of entire economic sectors and, in some cases, even the reliance on private, nongovernmental organizations for the provision of social services. In fact, these changes made markets, entrepreneurship, and private investment the critical success factors of the government's new economic policy.

Such a challenge requires a private sector that must be quite different from what it has been previously. Furthermore, its relationship with the state must change as dramatically as the way in which it approaches markets or treats its clients.

The purpose of this chapter is to offer an overview of the Venezuelan private sector (VPS) by briefly describing its main attributes and then discussing the forces—political, economic, international, and so on— that shaped it into its present configuration. We also discuss the political role that the VPS has traditionally played, the consequences that the reforms of 1989 have had on Venezuelan private firms, and the way they have reacted to the new, radically different environment. We conclude by highlighting some of the most significant lessons that can be gleaned from the early VPS response to economic policy reforms aimed at putting the market nearer to the center of economic life.

## THE VENEZUELAN PRIVATE SECTOR AT A GLANCE

In the mid-1980s Venezuelan firms were characterized as young, highly diversified, only mildly competitive, profitable, highly indebted, domestic, family owned and managed, organizationally retarded, and not especially Venezuelan in the technology they used or the origins of their owners.[1] More than 80 percent of industrial firms in the country had been established after 1960 and only seven of the seventy largest private corporations existed before 1940. By 1950, only thirteen of the now more than thirty-five Venezuelan banks were already in operation.

Even if their size in most instances did not seem to justify it, private companies typically became highly diversified. Many factors determined this propensity to diversify, including the risks entailed in an extremely volatile business environment, the massive incentives the state provided for the creation of new businesses in different sectors, the lack of foreign and domestic competition, a small and closed domestic market, the lack of inducements and capacity for private firms to grow through exports, and the need to react to the diversification moves of rivals.

Obviously, a captive market without much competition and massive public subsidies allowed for attractive profit margins. Profitability was periodically jeopardized by the government's aggressive initiatives—mostly price controls—and by sudden macroeconomic crises. Nonetheless, over the years private firms developed sophisticated financial, operational, and political strategies that enabled them to hedge such risks.

One expression of such hedging was the extreme indebtedness that became commonplace among Venezuelan private firms until 1989. The government kept interest rates well below inflation while maintaining a fixed exchange rate and a lax monetary policy that made credit exceedingly easy to obtain. These incentives, plus tax laws that allowed for interest payments to be fully deductible and the volatility of the business environment, combined to make it almost necessary for businesses to minimize the amount of their own money they invested in their companies.

The possibility of financing growth and new ventures almost exclusively through more debt—thus reducing the need to locate new sources of private capital, find partners, or access the stock market—created a concentrated ownership structure.[2] Furthermore, the youth of the firms often meant that the founder was still at the helm and that managers were recruited mostly from the founder's family and friends.

Lack of competition, the prosperity brought about by the country's growth, and the government's use of its oil income to subsidize and sponsor private enterprise did not create many incentives for Venezuelan managers to run tightly efficient organizations. Rather than urging businesses to assess the impact of new technologies or products, the incentives were instead geared to motivate businesspeople to assess the most effective way to court ministers and politicians. After all, the signature of one of these bureaucrats on a public document could easily make or break a firm, while its clients often did not have many options other than to buy from it, regardless of price, quality, or service.

Late and fast-paced industrialization in the oil-boom years of the 1960s and 1970s meant a plethora of opportunities for a relatively small number of entrepreneurs. This imbalance contributed to biasing the priorities of most existing businesses toward their diversification. The incentives to diversify early and into a wide array of businesses, combined with the lack of inducements to compete through lower costs and better quality, created a pattern of highly diversified and not very efficient "mini-conglomerates."[3]

Ownership patterns in the private sector and its overall performance are more a function of the policy environment than of the business or market realities. For example, consumer industries, both durable and nondurable, are almost entirely owned by the private sector with few state-owned companies present in these markets. Private companies in this sector owed their existence and growth essentially to import substitution policies, particularly after 1960. After growing rapidly in the 1970s, most of these firms languished during the 1980s, resulting in further concentration and ineffectual export drives. At the end of that lost decade, the number of industrial establishments was exactly the same as it had been ten years before. This sobering observation acquires an even more dramatic meaning when placed in the context of the massive resources the state squandered promoting, subsidizing, and sponsoring "industrial development" through misguided policies. Such policies tried to compensate for the damaging effects of the controls and restrictions the same state imposed on the private sector. Instead, excessive controls on prices and market behavior and ill-designed subsidies to the costs of existing firms generated ever-growing levels of concentration, corruption, and stagnation.

In contrast to the consumer products sector, in the area of raw materials and intermediate industrial products, where many of the country's natural comparative advantages lie, there is a significant presence of state-owned enterprises. In petrochemicals, Pequiven (a subsidiary of the national oil company Petróleos de Venezuela S.A., or PDVSA) was successful in correcting a disastrous previous attempt by the state to operate in this sector. Although Pequiven is a relatively well-managed corporation, it has concentrated much of its activity in petrochemicals, thus effectively retarding its development. It has several joint ventures with foreign partners, and in the 1990s its internal resistance to allowing more private firms to enter the sector will be placed under great strain by the economic realities faced by PDVSA and the country as a whole. In metals, the steel- and aluminum-producing subsidiaries of Corporación Venezolana de Guyana have also monopolized the country's industrial development in this sector. The result has been an expensive and not very profitable industrial complex. The emerging trend in these industries has been to form strategic associations between the state, which owns and controls the natural resources, and foreign and domestic private enterprises. Downstream processing is increasingly transferred to the private sector. Mining has also been basically reserved for state enterprises, such as FERROMINERA for iron ore, BAUXIVEN for bauxite, and MINERVEN for gold. Again, all available data show that the complete dominance of the state in these sectors has retarded their development. The hypothetical costs associated with the development of these activities by the private sector cannot by any calculation compensate for the costs associated with the current state of affairs. Inefficiency, indebtedness, politicization of commercial decisions, and missed opportunities have been the norm.

In spite of legal barriers limiting foreign ownership, multinational corporations sometimes associated with local capital remained dominant in global industries such as automobiles (General Motors, Ford, Fiat, Renault, Toyota), appliances (General Electric, Philips), glass (Owens Illinois, Guardian), tobacco (Philip Morris, American Tobacco), soft drinks (Pepsi-Cola, Coca-Cola), consumer electronics (Sony, Philips, Matsushita), and detergents and personal hygiene (Procter and Gamble, Colgate-Palmolive). Multinational businesses hold a leading but not necessarily dominant position in pharmaceuticals, which is a fragmented sector, confectionery (Nabisco, Nestlé), canned and processed food (Kraft, Heinz, Del Monte), and milling (Ralston-Purina, Cargill). On the other hand, until the early 1990s beer, liquor, edible oil, textiles, apparel, footwear, leather, wood processing, and furniture were essentially dominated by locally owned companies. The same applied to intermediate goods such as cement, tiles, paint, and other construction materials as well as to the pulp and paper and graphic industries, where the leading role was played by Venezuelan firms even though foreign companies in some cases had a minority participation.

The VPS is undergoing massive changes as a result of the new policies adopted in 1989 and the new international realities. Table 6.1 presents a synthesis of these emerging changes. In essence they reflect the

Table 6.1
THE VENEZUELAN PRIVATE FIRM:
DOMINANT CHARACTERISTICS AND EMERGING TRAITS

| Main Traits until Late 1980s | Emerging Traits in 1990 |
| --- | --- |
| Profitability depends to a large extent on government decisions | Profitability more dependent on markets and competitiveness |
| Access to government protection and subsidies is main strategic focus | Access to international markets and technology is main strategic focus |
| Wide diversification | Restructuring and consolidation |
| Domestic orientation | Growing international scope |
| Highly leveraged, funding mainly through debt | Increased capitalization, funding through local and international open capital markets |
| Highly concentrated ownership | Higher propensity for joint ventures and public stock offerings |
| Family run | Increased separation of owners and managers |
| Emphasis on "know who" | Emphasis on "know how" |

need to cope with more competition, tighter financial markets, compressed profit margins, and the unavoidable requirement to become more competitive and international. These changes in strategy will also affect ownership patterns, organizational structures, and staffing criteria. Private conglomerates owned and managed largely by members of the same family group will increasingly be displaced by corporations run by salaried professional managers. This change is also bound to have significant political consequences, which we discuss later.

## A BRIEF HISTORY OF THE VENEZUELAN PRIVATE SECTOR

The opening of the Venezuelan economy after 1989 sought to reverse the dual features of increasing statism and protectionism developed throughout three decades of democratic regime and inward-looking economic policies. During this period, governments fostered the "controlled development" of the private sector, which meant protecting it from foreign competition and subsidizing it, while severely limiting its autonomy. The same governments pursued, simultaneously, aggressive policies of expansion of state-owned enterprises, especially in the so-called basic industries where the country had comparative advantages. This doctrine, stemming from a number of trends and sources, was common in Venezuela and throughout Latin America after World War II.

Import substitution was the preferred policy trend in all developing nations, as was state control of public and social services. Nationalizing oil and other basic industries responded to the aim of appropriating the rents produced by the exploitation of the country's exhaustible natural resources. Peculiar to the Venezuelan case, thanks to the oil revenues that accrued to the state, the development of the Venezuelan private sector depended on government patronage to an unusual extent. Second, the need to consolidate the young and constantly threatened democratic regime of the 1960s created significant incentives for governments in power to buy the support of the private sector with huge infusions of resources to support its activities. Third, Venezuela was a latecomer to the industrialization process and efforts were constantly made to recoup—through massive bouts of public spending—lost time and opportunities. Fourth, the activities of foreign enterprises were limited in Venezuela to an unusual degree during the last three decades; such traits, however, were relatively new. (Table 6.2 summarizes the development of the private sector in Venezuela.)

Venezuela was one of the most backward Spanish colonies and experienced one of the most ravaging and destructive wars of independence in the hemisphere. Nineteenth-century Venezuela was an undeveloped rural country, lacking even a unified national currency, let alone an integrated national economy. At the beginning of the twentieth century, the private sector consisted mainly of a number of feudalistic hacien-

## Table 6.2
## THE EVOLUTION OF THE VENEZUELAN PRIVATE SECTOR

|  | 1870 to 1920 | 1920 to 1960 | 1960 to 1990 |
|---|---|---|---|
| Role of foreign investment | *Pathbreaking* Railroads, mining, telephones, electricity, rubber, trading | *Dominant* Oil, banking, manufactured imports, television | *Overregulated* Selective IS manufacturing |
| Role of private domestic investment | *Incipient* agricultural trade (coffee, cocoa), banking | *Emerging* IS manufacturing, banking, commerce, mass communications | *In expansion* IS manufacturing, banking, retail, mass communications, services |
| Role of public investment in industry and utilities | *Negligible* | *Incipient (after 1950)* Telephones, steel, petrochemicals | *Dominant* Oil, mining, basic manufacturing (steel, aluminum, petrochemicals), electricity, telecommunications |

IS = import substitution.

das, where *peones* (laborers) were paid in tokens and often recruited by force into the local *caudillo's* private army. Many haciendas were granted by the long-ruling dictator Gen. Juan Vicente Gómez to his lieutenants, as a reward for services rendered during the many wars against the constellation of local warlords who periodically challenged the government. Small shopkeepers, traders, and craftspeople represented the remainder of the private enterprise.

Early in the nineteenth century the first international—mostly European—trading houses had been established. The export of coffee and cocoa and the import of manufactured goods constituted the bulk of their activities. Some were subsidiaries of British and German trading houses, but a few were Venezuelan companies established by resident immigrants. The most important of the latter were H. L. Boulton, established in the 1820s, which operated what was perhaps the first regular boat service from Caracas to New York, and Casa Blohm, established in the 1830s. Since 1820 the state initiated the promotion of business activities through the Junta de Comercio y Agricultura, following the Spanish tradition of state intervention.

During the government of President Antonio Guzmán Blanco, in the late 1800s, the first important wave of foreign investment in independent Venezuela took place. Guzmán undertook the rebuilding and modernization of the country, and foreign capital was perhaps his most important instrument. British capital helped build the first railroads (Caracas–La Guaira and Valencia–Puerto Cabello), and American and British capital developed gold mining and rubber in the Guyana region in the 1880s.[4] Electricity and telephones were introduced by local service companies controlled by American and British capital. Agriculture, developed in Los Andes and the central region and focused mainly on the production of coffee and cocoa for the international market, was booming in the 1890s. In 1855, 354 industrial establishments, essentially craft shops, existed in the province of Caracas, covering the central area of the country. Main activities were light manufacturing, including sugar, rum, tobacco, textiles, and footwear. After 1880 larger enterprises, employing up to sixty workers, began to appear in Caracas and Valencia.[5] Starting in 1825 with the establishment of Banco de Venezuela, banking flourished with the creation of the Companía de Credito in 1870, patterned after France's Credits Mobiliers. Banco de Caracas was created in 1876, Banco de Maracaibo in 1882, and Banco Comercial de Venezuela in 1884, all promoted by merchant interests in Caracas and Maracaibo.[6]

During the Guzmán years a pattern began to unfold. The VPS was divided in two. The first part included enterprises that were started privately, without official support, but that eventually became subject to governmental meddling, such as in trading and light manufacturing. The second consisted of enterprises promoted by the state, often through concessions. Mining and public services were typical examples of state-sponsored companies. It was not unusual to find high-ranking government officials as open or hidden partners in these enterprises, as well as an important presence of foreign capital. This lagged behind early industrialization in many other Latin American countries.[7]

After 1920, Venezuelan oil revenues started filling the traditionally empty coffers of the public treasury and were largely spent in repaying a long-standing public debt and building public works, roads in particular. From 1936 to 1960 the country's GDP experienced growth rates of nearly 8 percent per annum, and some scholars estimate they were even higher in the 1920s. During this period (again thanks to oil) Venezuela attracted the largest foreign investment of any country in Latin America. Direct investment by U.S. private firms rose from U.S.$20 million in 1919 to about 240 million in 1929. By 1926 crude oil had replaced coffee as the nation's main export. The oil industry employed less than 1 percent of the work force, and its main contribution to the domestic economy occurred through taxation, established at less than 25 percent until 1943.[8] Foreign banks attained a substantial presence in Venezuela prior to 1929. In 1920 deposits in foreign banks operating in the country were three times the volume of those in locally owned banks. The crash of 1929 changed this situation: deposits in foreign banks were more than halved, whereas those in local ones were only marginally reduced.

On the other hand, manufacturing establishments of any significance at the beginning of the century were limited to two breweries (in Caracas and Maracaibo), a match factory, and a textile mill in Valencia. Subsequently a paper mill was established (in 1905), as well as a cement plant (1907), a cigarette factory (1911), a vegetable oil plant (1912), a meat packer and a dairy (both in 1912). In 1913, 160 manufacturing enterprises were registered in an industrial directory, most of them craft shops. The capital invested in manufacturing was B 55 million, compared to 212 million in farming, 104 million in ranching, 170 million in transportation, and 302 million in commerce. Few enterprises employed more than a hundred workers.[9]

The early VPS also included a number of trading houses, three banks (Banco de Venezuela, Banco Caracas, and Banco de Maracaibo), a few local electricity and telephone companies, the railroads, and coffee plantations. General Gómez's practice of granting business privileges and concessions to members of his circle was maintained and became an established component of the country's business culture.[10]

Further industrial expansion during the 1920s concentrated in sugar, cigarettes, beverages, and textiles. In the early 1930s manufacturing expansion came to a temporary halt. According to the Industrial Census of 1936, manufacturing employed around thirty thousand persons and represented an invested capital of approximately B 200 million. Increased domestic demand, fostered by rising oil revenues, resulted in expanded imports of manufactured goods rather than the development of domestic manufacturing, and many domestic producers faced stagnation. During the Gómez years (1908–36), participation of foreign direct investment, which had been mostly concentrated in railroads, public services, mining, and international trade, dramatically increased with investment in banking and, chiefly, in oil production. Multinational businesses, however, procured their supplies abroad, adding little demand, in the short term, to Venezuelan producers of goods and services. The role of the state increased at the same time through the granting of concessions to carry out such activities.

After Gómez's death in 1936, the ministry of development began to promote private industrial enterprises through concessional credit, the waiver of import duties, and the like. The Treaty of Commercial Reciprocity, however, signed with the United States in 1939, reduced import duties for many items produced in Venezuela, reinforcing the trend to buy foreign goods and further hampering domestic industrial development.[11] World War II disrupted international trade and broke this trend. Manufacturing increased rapidly throughout the 1940s and 1950s, doubling output every seven years. The number of employees in manufacturing activities rose from 60,000 in 1941 to 111,000 in 1951 and 157,000 in 1961.[12] Between 1948 and 1958 large oil refineries were established by the multinational oil companies. In 1940 waivers of import duties on machinery and raw materials represented B 3 million, whereas two years later the figure reached a booming 20 million. In 1946 the Venezuelan Development Corporation (Corporación Venezolana de Fomento, or CVF), a public agency under the ministry of development, was established to promote participation in the development of the private sector through concessional credit, loan guarantees, and direct equity. This marked an important turning point in the relationship between the state and the VPS. The creation of the CVF institutionalized the access of the private sector to massive state subsidies. Until its dismantling in 1990, the CVF became the conduit through which sizable portions of the state's oil revenues were channeled to the

CVS dis 1990

private sector. It also became a powerful magnet for corruption and all variety of fraudulent schemes designed to finance politicians, union leaders, and businesspeople.

In 1949 the Central Bank of Venezuela was established and was granted the exclusive right to issue legal currency, a right that until then had been given to private commercial banks. During the 1950s, under Marcos Pérez Jiménez's military dictatorship, the trend toward the nationalization of "strategic" enterprises first emerged. In 1954 the government acquired the private telephone company, owned by British investors.

The commercial treaty with the United States was revised in 1952, import tariffs were raised for a number of products, and foreign investment in manufacturing soared, especially in consumer products and, of course, oil and iron. Domestic producers of beer, edible oil, cement, and other products also benefited from increased trade protection.

During the 1940s and 1950s more than two million Europeans immigrated to Venezuela. Many of them became entrepreneurs, enlarging the ranks of the VPS mostly in construction, apparel manufacturing, furniture making, and metalworking, as well as in retail, services, and farming.

Import substitution industrialization was adopted as an official policy by the newly elected democratic government in 1960, as expressed in its Four-Year Plan. Substantial tariff protection was granted to domestic industry, and credit at low, subsidized interest rates became readily available. Mostly unrecoverable public credits to the private sector reached astronomical magnitudes. A renewed phase of state-sponsored growth and diversification opened up for the VPS. In 1960 the Corporación Venezolana de Guyana (CVG) was established to develop natural resources in the southeast region, rich in minerals and hydroelectric potential. In 1962 Siderúrgica del Orinoco (SIDOR), a subsidiary of CVG, started operations, and ALCASA, an aluminum smelter, was established, also as a CVG subsidiary. CVG's creation dramatically increased the industrial role of the public sector. Private companies developed as suppliers and contractors, as well as processors of basic products, around CVG plants. A number of failed private companies, however, passed into the hands of the CVF after defaulting on their debts.

In the 1960s the financial sector diversified. In 1970 the Banking Law was reformed to limit foreign participation in Venezuelan private banks and foreign banking operations in the country. In 1971 the Christian Democrat Caldera administration renounced the bilateral commerce treaty with the United States and in 1973 joined the Andean Pact, enthusiastically embracing its Decision 24, the policy framework that severely restricted foreign investment. Caldera's administration also adopted the Andean Pact's policy of industrial programming by sector. Under this policy, government planners of the different member countries negotiated and eventually agreed which industries would be "allocated" to each of the countries, thus giving the country the exclusive rights for the "development" of that particular industry. This policy failed catastrophically and not only retarded significantly the industrial expansion of these countries but introduced severe distortions that harmed these economies for many years.

Large increases in oil prices during the 1970s provided the Venezuelan government with vast resources that, again, were partially funneled toward industrial development, in both the private and the public sectors. Extensive public works programs fostered the construction industry. Large investments were made in petrochemicals, aluminum, steel, and electricity, all sectors where private investment, local and foreign, was either not allowed or severely restricted.

The nationalization of the oil industry in 1975 dramatically increased the role of the state in the economy and reduced that of the private sector in general and foreign enterprise in particular. Nonetheless, private domestic businesses boomed. Companies owned by foreign investors, including retailing, television, and advertising, had to divest to Venezuelan private investors as a result of Decision 24. Jointly owned companies became common, including state capital, domestic private capital, and foreign capital in any possible combination. Foreign firms retrenched to technologically sophisticated industries such as glass, automobiles, cosmetics, and pharmaceuticals.

Several financial institutions were established in 1974 and 1975 by the public sector to assist private companies. Alongside the old CVF were established the Fondo de Crédito Industrial, Corpoindustria (for small- and medium-size industrial enterprises), Fondo de Crédito Agropecuario (for agriculture), and Fondo de Desarrollo Urbano.[13] The financial sector experienced a period of expansion and concentration, becoming dominated by seven large banking groups. A number of important banks defaulted or had to be bailed out and taken over by the state, including Banco Nacional de Descuento, Banco de Comercio, and Banco de los Trabajadores.

The late 1970s marked a peak for both governmental promotion of private enterprise and expansion of public enterprises. Commercial activities remained relatively backward: official policy deemed such activities a necessary ill at best, and downright parasitic at worst, denying them the support and resources for development it generously offered to manufacturing and agriculture.[14] Substantial concentration and vertical integration resulted, fostering inefficiency, lack of competition, and high profit margins and, closing the circle, reinforcing the negative view of commercial intermediation.

In the late 1970s and the 1980s, the debt crisis, international isolation, domestic stagnation, and severe impediments to the development of more competitive strategies, structures, and business attitudes made the private sector even more dependent on the state. A state that never before had to confront foreign exchange scarcities and severe budget constraints reacted by experimenting with all sorts of controls, restrictions, and misguided economic policies designed to avoid facing the harsh realities that had been brewing for years.

Successive governments tried to micromanage the economy through the control of every industrial project, every import order, or every price increase, mainly through the granting or withholding of official protection. Conversely, as we discuss in the next section, businesspeople and business associations developed a wide array of highly effective mechanisms to influence government officials and the politicians who appointed them.

## THE VENEZUELAN PRIVATE SECTOR AS A POLITICAL ACTOR

If we take politics to mean activities aimed at influencing the conduct of the state, the VPS has always been political. It was given birth by the state and was bred, nurtured, and not infrequently owned by individuals whose daily activities had more in common with those of politicians than those of entrepreneurs. This should come as no surprise for a country in which its two main economic eras—one based in agriculture and the other in oil—were dominated by decisions in which the state had almost complete dominance and in which markets and market behavior were seen as politically destabilizing, economically unreliable, or both.

Furthermore, the low level of institutionalization of the state apparatus, the deficiencies of the legal system, and the superficiality of the process through which public officials are held accountable for their decisions allowed government officials extraordinary latitude and discretion in their decision making. It was only natural that the sponsorship of a sector by the state often meant the *personal* sponsorship of the specific government official (or small group of government officials) with the power to allocate, more or less at their will, the support of the state. The systematic interaction occurred between a small number of individuals who controlled firms in privileged sectors and an equally small number of politicians and high-level bureaucrats who had the power to make or break these firms.

The influence that public officials, and the politicians on whom they depended, had over the fortunes of private firms was enormous. In addition to the special permits required to conduct a wide variety of normal business activities, such as opening a new plant, acquiring a foreign partner, or advertising promotional discounts, the government also controlled both the prices at which many goods and services were sold and the costs of most of the inputs companies needed. Often essentially similar companies in the same sector ended up paying different prices for the same imports, or having different import quotas of the same product assigned to them. Depending on their influence over the public officials who had the discretion to make these decisions, two companies could obtain government loans at different interest rates and with different terms and conditions. From 1983 to 1989, foreign exchange controls transferred to government officials the decisions of how much foreign currency a given company could buy and which of the existing exchange rates was applicable to each transaction.

Moreover, when private companies faced state-owned enterprises as competitors, suppliers, or clients, the profit opportunities arising from having a special, collaborative relationship with the managers of these public enterprises were also immense. Usually when a private company had to compete with a publicly owned enterprise, prices were fixed by the government at levels determined by the costs of the public enterprise. As a general rule, such costs were higher than those of the private firm, a fact that added handsomely to the profit margins of the private company. Even if such margins tended to be partially eroded by the long collection period of government debts, they generally still allowed for profits well beyond those that would emerge in private market transactions.

This structure of incentives, and the pattern of business and managerial behavior it engendered, tended to suppress most forms of market competition while encouraging aggressive oligopolistic behavior. As is normal in oligopolies, when firms depend more on the decisions of their few rivals than on the decisions of consumers without much choice, actions directed at competing firms also became a central element of any Venezuelan company's strategy for profit, growth, and survival. Such actions were either collusive—to agree on prices, market sharing, advertising, distribution channels, labor practices, and credit policies—or exclusionary. The latter approach included tactics directed at building barriers to the entry of new competitors as well as maneuvers aimed at eliminating existing rivals or at countering their attacks.

Over the years, periods of relative stability and collusion among rival firms were followed by fierce exclusionary battles, where all sorts of predatory commercial behavior and ruinous rivalry became common. Given the political nature of the private sector and the centrality of government intervention in the economy, whenever these oligopolistic wars broke out, the state was dragged into them. The interests of different government agencies or individuals within the government were often closely aligned with those of the warring private groups, thereby transferring the conflict to the public sector. In addition, the predatory behavior of the (usually large) corporate actors involved often forced the government to intervene. The anticompetitive business manner of private groups at war with one another generally had more to do with the state than with the market, more with politics than with prices.

Such a context of highly personalized, informal, ad hoc, and often illicit transactions between businesses and individuals working for the state significantly shaped and constrained the development of institutionalized forms of business representation. Although business federations, councils, and associations varied in influence through the years, their political significance has tended gradually to decline. As the discretionary power of public officials over business decisions increased, institutions created to formally represent business faced great difficulty in providing their individual members with more profitable government representation services than those they could muster on their own. Furthermore, the fragmented and oligopolistic structure of the business sector has made it difficult to articulate under a common institutional setting the interests of different sectors and even different companies. Pharmaceutical producers, car assemblers, and textile manufacturers, for example, are some of the extreme examples of sectors where companies in the same business could not maintain a single, unified organization to represent their interests vis-à-vis the state. In each of these sectors several rival business associations or chambers emerged as a consequence of the impossibility of reconciling the widely differing interests of their member companies.

As a result of these circumstances, the traditional institutional setting through which the private sector seeks to be represented *formally* in public policy debates and its capacity to influence or even participate effectively in the process of public policy formulation have weakened enormously. This, of course, does not mean that the interests, opinions, and perspectives of the private sector were excluded from the policymaking process. Business preferences were injected into the policy process by cabinet members and other public officials with ties to the business establishment and through extensive informal consultations that high-level policymakers and, especially, the president conducted with private sector friends and supporters.

The role of "free agents" or individual businesspeople, who through their personal access and influence could steer state action toward their own particular aims, also contributed toward eroding the importance of the formal institutional brokers. Paradoxically, even as practical influence over specific public decisions tended to be preempted by the free agents, the number and complexity of these institutional brokers, charged with formally representing business interests, increased.

FEDECAMARAS (Federación de Cámaras de Comercio y Producción) was founded in 1944 with the purpose of organizing and representing business interests to serve as the umbrella organization to which all chambers of commerce, business associations, and employers' groups are affiliated. FEDECAMARAS was recognized as the formal representative of the private sector in almost all laws that created institutions where the presence of labor and business was deemed necessary. This allowed FEDECAMARAS to appoint or nominate individuals for state councils, steering committees of public agencies, and even boards of directors of state-owned enterprises. Later, in 1971, a law was passed creating National Sectoral Councils for industry, trade, banking, and agriculture that would provide more specific representation for businesses in these sectors.

In the 1960s, to support democracy and the development of a domestic industrial base through import substitution, a group of business executives and some politicians founded a new business sector organization called Pro-Venezuela. It rapidly became almost totally dependent on the state for its budget and never achieved significant legitimacy as an organization representing business.

During the seventies and eighties a wide variety of specialized chambers and associations representing specific sectors and interests of the business community were created. These were associations of firms in divisions such as metalworking, plastics, or broadcasting, and even subsectors such as auto parts, dry cleaning services, or radio stations. Business firms also had incentives to organize along functional and regional groupings like the Venezuelan Association of Exporters (AVEX) or FEDEINDUSTRIA, the Federation of Small and Medium Enterprises, promoted by the government to compensate the influence that big business had in FEDECAMARAS. Binational business associations such as the Venezuelan-American Chamber of Commerce or the German-, Italian-, Colombian-, and Japanese-Venezuelan chambers catered to the interests of foreign companies and those of Venezuelan firms with trade and investment links to these countries. While government intervention created substantial incentives for individual firms to deal directly with the state, it also forced the state to promote the formalization of existing cartels. Such formalization became necessary to allow the bureaucracy to process with some semblance of order and fairness the myriad business decisions that had been taken over by the state. In 1986, for example, the government expanded even further its price-control system. Decree 1,717 transferred to the state pricing decisions for a large number of items, including toothpaste, the sand used at construction sites, a cup of coffee (with two different prices depending on whether it was consumed standing at the coffee counter or sitting at a table), and the foam used for manufacturing mattresses and coffins (also with two different prices depending on quality). To implement this scheme, the bureaucracy had to produce estimates of cost structures for all of the thousands of products with controlled prices and also decide on a "reasonable" profit margin for each one. Such an exercise obviously unleashed an uncontrollable set of individual negotiations that could not be handled by the overwhelmed bureaucracy. The government's reaction was to decide that all pricing negotiations must be formally conducted through the appropriate business association. Each of these chambers or business associations had to determine a cost structure collectively agreed on by all its member companies and enter into negotiations with the government to arrive at a price. This scenario suggests that, at the time, promoting competition was not a main priority for the government.

In any case, appointing the chambers as the official interlocutors of the government certainly did wonders for the interest that companies had in their sectoral associations. This approach strengthened, and in some instances even created, the Venezuelan chambers of cosmetic industries, of building materials, of luncheonettes and coffee houses, and of funeral services, to name a few examples. The same approach was taken with the government's allocation of foreign exchange, where, in theory, the quotas assigned to each company depended on the overall negotiations between the ministry of finance and the specific chamber. In addition, to obtain an import license from the government, the importer had to secure a written agreement for the import from the chamber where local producers—and quite often even some importers—of the goods were grouped.

Many individual companies with the appropriate contacts could bypass this scheme and gain direct access to the government to procure

*Chambers*

whatever decision, allocation, permit, or incentive they needed. None-theless, having the chambers and associations play some role provided a facade of formality and order that was useful in legitimizing the over-all policy framework. In fact, the membership of FEDECAMARAS grew from 168 chambers in 1970 to 282 in 1992. *But very bad*

The increase in the number of organizations representing different business sectors or activities masked a more important trend that has had grievous consequences for the private sector as a whole. The situation created a pattern of incentives where the owners and top managers, in whom the real decision-making power of a company rested, concentrated on direct and personalized dealings with politicians and high-level bureaucrats. Active participation in the institutional activities of the affiliated chamber was often delegated to middle-ranking managers—usually former government officials—who had little power or influence in the firm. Frequently a chamber hired the individual in the government with whom the association had to deal and appointed him or her the executive director of the chamber. *early 80s*

A significant example of this trend occurred in the early 1980s, when *example* a staff member of FEDECAMARAS (and a former government employee) succeeded in getting elected as its president with the vote of a large number of small chambers of the interior. This ended the tradition whereby the president of FEDECAMARAS had always been the chief executive officer of any of the larger private companies in the country. From then on, FEDECAMARAS has had difficulty in enlisting the active participation and support of the decision makers of the largest and most influential private corporations in the country. The political significance of FEDECAMARAS has diminished even further due to the conflicts of interest among the different sectors, regions, and activities that preclude FEDECAMARAS from arriving at consensual positions on most policy issues of national interest. *ATTEMPTS TO*

Two representative attempts at influencing public policy sponsored *INFLUENCE* by groups formed by the chief executive officers of the largest compa-*PUBLIC* nies of the country were both channeled through ad hoc associations *POLICY* that bypassed FEDECAMARAS and other existing private sector institutions. One, in the mid-1980s, was sponsored by a group that took the *1990* name of the office building in which the group met: Roraima. Roraima *Ex* hired a group of local and international consultants and in 1984 produced their Proposal to the Country. In it, the group essentially tried to persuade the country, and especially the newly elected government of President Jaime Lusinchi, to adopt the market-oriented economic policies that most other countries in the region and elsewhere were beginning to implement. That attempt did not succeed, and Roraima had to wait five years to see its recommendations find their way (largely through other sources) into the policies adopted by the Pérez administration. Another example occurred in 1992, when a different group of chief executives of some of the country's largest private corporations, worried by the deep deterioration of the political situation catalyzed by the failed military coup of that year, sought to find ways to curb the instability. They tried to promote a National Pact between the government, the two main political parties—Acción Democrática and COPEI—and the "private sector." A series of meetings with all the participants in the pact resulted in the first stages of drafting a general agreement. When the details of the initiative were leaked to the press, the president of FEDECAMARAS, a former employee of one of the private sector promoters of the pact, gave an irate press conference denouncing the initiative and stressing that no pact could be legitimate without the active participation and endorsement of FEDECAMARAS. For this and other reasons the initiative failed and no pact of this kind was ever signed during the Pérez administration.

Meanwhile, as we discuss in the next section, intense oligopolistic wars that ravaged the fortunes and reputations of individuals and companies participating in them continued with impunity.

## DISCOVERING COMPETITION: THE PRIVATE SECTOR'S REACTION TO THE 1989 REFORMS

The reforms of 1989 caught the country by surprise. No one had really expected that the newly elected president, Carlos Andrés Pérez, would embrace market-oriented policies to the extent and with the swiftness that he did. The private sector was no exception.[15]

Two main factors dominated business's initial reaction to the new policies. First was the need of most private firms to improvise rapidly business strategies to deal with unforeseen and unprecedented circumstances that were threatening their survival. While for years business had been demanding the adoption of market-based policies, most firms never really believed such an approach would ever be taken. As a result, private firms were woefully unprepared to deal with the consequences of these policies and the many traumatic adjustments that typically accompany their implementation.

In addition, the institutional arrangements through which the private sector interacted with the state in the past rapidly lost any effectiveness they may have had left. The formal network of business councils, chambers of commerce, and the assorted associations representing business had extreme difficulty in devising timely and adequate responses to the new situation. Most of these organizations suffered from the confusion and perplexity resulting from an environment that no longer needed the services in which they had specialized for most of their institutional existence. Bargaining with public bureaucrats for foreign exchange allocations, prices, and import or export quotas and even publicly denouncing the inadequacy of the government interventionist policies were no longer necessary. The possibilities for "free agents," specific businesspeople, or their representatives to extract special concessions for individual companies also decreased as a result of the loss of discretionary power of government officials.

In general, the influence of the private sector over the government was further constrained because the administration moved too fast in too many different policy areas to allow for any concerted action on the part of the private sector to steer policies toward the interests of a specific group or sector. That the policy options available at the time did not allow the government much freedom to maneuver also added to the relative independence with which the policies were formulated and implemented.

Moreover, the very nature of the policies, with their propensity to create a level playing field for all participants and eliminate special privileges for specific sectors, obviously helped to buffer government officials and their policies from the particular groups that fought to retain the privileges they had enjoyed for decades.[16]

The immediate consequences of the initial decisions taken by the Pérez administration created a threatening situation for most private firms. While all costs increased dramatically, demand dwindled to levels that had not been seen for years. In sectors such as consumer durables, sales plunged. After having had years in which two hundred thousand new cars were sold, the automotive sector saw in panic how, in 1989, it could not sell even forty thousand units. The 10 percent drop in GDP that the country experienced, combined with a devaluation of almost 200 percent, an inflation level that surpassed 80 percent, and a decline in real salaries of 20 percent, put the cash flows of most private companies under the most severe strain in their history.

Furthermore, most businesses were being choked by the massive inventories they accumulated in 1988 in anticipation of the devaluation that any administration inaugurated in 1989 had, inevitably, to impose. These inventories were financed locally at the subsidized and highly negative interest rate determined by the government. Once controls on the interest rate were eliminated by the new administration, the rate shot up 150 percent. Freeing the interest rate and allowing it to reach levels consistent with inflation ended a long era where gross financial distortions had been allowed to accumulate. Government policies had created all sorts of incentives for private companies to be undercapitalized and financially overextended, while their shareholders could amass funds that were normally deposited abroad in private accounts. After the reforms, real interest rates made it financially unbearable for the highly leveraged firms to carry large inventories.

For most private companies, however, the biggest threat during the initial years of the reforms arose from the government-imposed requirement to partially refinance the U.S.$6 billion in letters of credit associated with the massive imports businesses made in 1988. At that time, the government encouraged—and in some cases even required—that imports be financed by letters of credit for which it guaranteed the foreign exchange rate. Once the exchange rate was allowed to float and depreciate by more than 150 percent, the government was faced with the difficult task of explaining that using public funds to cover the foreign exchange losses stemming from the guarantees issued to importers by the previous administration would propel the fiscal deficit to levels that would generate a dangerous bout of hyperinflation. The decision was made to partially transfer these losses to the private companies that had incurred them, thus adding even more pressures to their already negative cash flows.[17]

Naturally, private sector exports soared to an all-time high. Private companies that had exported U.S.$649 million in 1988 exported more than U.S.$1.5 billion in 1989. Companies reexported inputs and, to a much lesser extent, machinery that they had imported a few months earlier. But the bulk of exports consisted of the manufactured goods for which companies could not find local buyers. Furthermore, an attractive exchange rate and a sizable and ill-conceived export subsidy created even more reasons for companies to aggressively seek ways to sell their local production abroad. Some even utilized the criminal skills honed in a decade of corruption-prone government intervention and claimed the export subsidy by falsifying records and bribing public officials to create exaggerated or nonexistent export sales. The other means by which private companies dealt with their cash-flow problems in 1989 was simple, effective, and, for most of them, unprecedented: shareholders repatriated some of the funds they had abroad. That year about U.S.$1 billion entered the country, a sizable portion of which went to support financially strapped firms.

Another major change that companies had to digest was the most comprehensive trade reform in the country's history. Almost all quantitative restrictions on imports administered through government permits were abolished and average tariffs dropped from 35 percent in 1988 to less than 10 percent in 1990.

One of the most surprising facets of the Venezuelan adjustment is that while private companies had to endure severe hardships in the initial years of the reforms, few filed for bankruptcy. Companies were restructured, capitalized, bought, sold, and merged, but rarely did they go out of business altogether.

The liberalization of foreign investment in early 1990 also had major repercussions for the local business sector. On the one hand, the fact that foreign firms could now freely invest and operate in the country even in sectors that had been off limits to foreigners created new and threatening competition for local firms. On the other hand, a free and more welcoming environment for foreign companies also opened many new opportunities for foreign firms. The foreigners' technology, marketing skills, and access to export markets could now be coupled with whatever resources and skills local companies might have to create profit from the many opportunities left untapped by years of isolation and economic decay.

The deregulation of foreign investment was extended to the stock market, where for the first time foreigners were allowed to own local securities. The Caracas Stock Exchange, the largest and most significant in the country, had been small, primitive, and dormant but became the center of feverish activity. As a result of its opening to foreign investors and of the fact that money management became one of the most profitable activities in the country during the first years of the reforms, demand for local securities soared. A large pool of funds was chasing a small number of securities, thus propelling their price to unheard of levels. In 1990, no other stock market in the world had a better performance in dollar terms. In 1991, the boom tended to level off—total returns grew by 34 percent in dollars—but it continued to show signs that clearly marked a break with the past. Closely held companies that only a few months before would not even consider the possibility of utilizing the stock market to raise capital or float their debt instruments could no longer afford to ignore such alternatives. Stock market activity was also spurred immensely by a series of takeovers, some of them hostile.[18]

The liberalization of foreign investment also made viable the privatization of a wide array of state-owned enterprises, such as hotels, airlines, telecommunications, power plants, and shipyards. Foreign investment increased dramatically in the initial years of the reforms, even in the face of the instability that characterized the country's political life during this period. In 1991, largely thanks to the privatization of 40 percent of the phone company, new direct foreign investment reached almost U.S.$2 billion. This figure stands in sharp contrast with the fact that the book value of *total* foreign direct investment registered in Venezuela at the end of 1990 was a paltry U.S.$3.6 billion.

Foreign investment in Venezuela in the 1990s and beyond is likely to become a more dynamic source of economic activity than in the past. Political and institutional instability, together with the stiff competition the country will face from other countries also seeking to attract foreign investment, may constrain the growth rate. Nevertheless, even allowing for an eventual deterioration of the political and institutional environment—and short of the unlikely emergence of a government radically opposed to private enterprise—foreign investment in Venezuela will probably increase in the future. If the political situation stabilizes and the reforms initiated in 1989 are fine-tuned and better grounded in the country, Venezuela could easily become one of the most powerful magnets for foreign investment in the region.

A similar argument applies to the export performance of the private sector, even though great caution should be exercised when interpreting the results of the initial years of the reform process in this respect. Private sector exports have been growing at a faster pace than in the past and it can be safely assumed that this trend is likely to continue unless a major political debacle forces a return to inward-looking statism. This higher growth of private sector exports relative to the past should not be too difficult to attain, given the astonishingly low levels that such exports exhibited before the reforms were implemented.

Some evidence of the export potential of the private sector can be gauged by considering current export levels in the context of factors that determine the export performance. It should be taken into consideration, for example, that the state has historically monopolized business activities in the sectors where the country enjoyed natural comparative advantages and that, hitherto, private sector exports have been essentially made by companies created to serve the small and protected domestic market. Furthermore, government policies that support export activity have been in place for only a few years and some of them—such as the exchange rate—have not been consistently aligned with this aim. Physical infrastructure geared toward a more internationally competitive private sector is inadequate, and the institutional support system that the state has to provide to exporters suffers the consequences of being part of a public sector ravaged by years of excesses, corruption, and incompetence. When all of these factors are taken into consideration, the growth of private sector exports shown in figure 6.1 becomes even more significant.

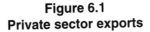

**Figure 6.1**
**Private sector exports**

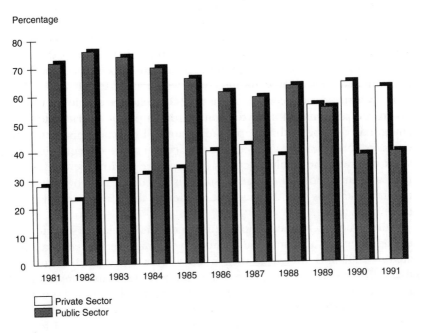

In general, reforms have revitalized the private sector. Private capital has been repatriated, new export-oriented companies have been created, foreign investment has increased, public companies have been privatized and are investing in expanding and modernizing their operations, closely held companies are widening their ownership through the stock market, inefficient companies are streamlining their operations, and financial markets are more active than ever. But perhaps the most important change is that private companies have more reasons to invest time and money to become more competitive and worry about how to better serve the needs of consumers, instead of being obsessed over the needs and desires of bureaucrats and politicians.

## THE LACK OF AN EFFECTIVE REGULATORY FRAMEWORK

Not all the results of the reforms were positive. Business concentration increased, and the extreme deficiencies of the regulatory framework for business have combined with the institutional weaknesses of public agencies in charge of enforcing such regulations to allow significant distortions to emerge. The portfolio of most banks is highly concentrated in loans to affiliated companies or to other private businesses owned by their shareholders and directors. Moreover, there is mounting evidence that, in many cases, the quality of such portfolios is extremely low and that the capitalization of most banks is grossly insufficient to cover the losses implicit in the mountain of bad loans they have accumulated with related parties. Bank supervision in Venezuela has been historically weak and the crisis in 1994 indicates that it has not escaped the propensity for corruption typical of public bureaucracies in charge of dealing with the private sector. The same applies to the Comisión Nacional de Valores (the agency in charge of regulating the stock market), the public agencies that enforce environmental protection laws, and those in charge of supervising compliance by radio and television stations with the rules established in the concessions given to them by the state.

Other public agencies, whose effectiveness is crucial for the healthy development of a strong and competitive private sector, were all created in 1992 and are still in their infancy. This is true for the agencies that enforce consumer protection and antitrust and antidumping laws. It is also the case for the public agencies responsible for the regulation of the utilities that have been or are in the process of being privatized. The state's ownership of the telephone company never called for the state to develop the independent regulatory capacity that it needs now, when the phone company is the largest private company in the country. With the privatization of the airlines, water, electricity, garbage collection, hospitals, public transportation, toll roads, and many other public services, the demands for regulatory services by the state will grow much faster than its capacity to provide them effectively. It is a safe bet, unfortunately, that this regulatory gap will be the source of many scandals, political attention, and public dissatisfaction.

Other unexpected results of the 1989 reforms were the many takeovers and oligopolistic wars that broke out among the different economic groups in the private sector. The competition introduced by the reforms altered the delicate equilibrium among rival groups that had been reached after years of intermittent wars followed by periods of collusion and market-sharing agreements. Whenever competition appeared, it seldom expressed itself through price competition or other forms of marketing tactics that had been inhibited by the interventionist policies of the government. Instead groups competed through efforts aimed at controlling the supply of raw materials and other inputs, financing, and distribution channels. Therefore, rivalries were essentially directed at gaining control of some strategically critical company that would in turn insure greater control, protection, or influence over the actions of other companies in the same markets.[19]

Once the policies restricting competition were lifted, most companies entered into an oligopolistic frenzy, trying to counter their rivals' advances either through the acquisition of existing companies or through expansion into new sectors. Such expansion was now possible given that the previous policies had essentially created high barriers to the entry of new competitors into sectors dominated by traditional firms. Other moves by large firms, however, turned nasty and became an additional source of the political instability that rocked the country.

Given the weaknesses and, for many practical purposes, the nonexistence of the judicial system in Venezuela, many conflicts tend to be fought in the media. Thus, in the past, many businesspeople discovered the value of "owning" journalists and writers with easy access to the opinion pages of newspapers. This allowed firms to participate in the elaborate media ploys that were used to influence government officials, repay political favors, attack competitors, or counter the attacks of business rivals. In recent years, however, large private companies have moved beyond the strategy of having close quasi-employment links with active journalists and media figures and have begun investing aggressively in newspapers, magazines, radio, and television stations. This trend has reached the point where almost no media company is independently owned. The few whose owners are not directly linked to one of the large private conglomerates have also been penetrated by these business interests, and it is not unusual to find their main journalists or even their directors serving as highly paid "consultants" of a specific conglomerate.

The implications of this pattern for the future evolution of democratic processes in Venezuela are obviously as worrysome as those it has for the evolution of a more competitive private sector. The ways these tendencies develop will be closely intertwined with the evolution of the political situation in the country. Only with more competition and a state with sufficient independence to promote such competition will the more negative consequences of these trends be avoided.

## CONCLUSIONS: WHAT HAVE WE LEARNED?

The major changes that have profoundly altered the business environment in Venezuela are too recent to have definitive judgment passed on their effects over the private sector. Nonetheless, several patterns are becoming obvious enough to be highlighted.

The first point is that the reforms have injected an unprecedented dynamism into the private sector. In general, private firms have survived without too much damage the simultaneous impacts of recession, devaluation, trade liberalization, high inflation, and political instability. The experience of the first few years in terms of investment, job creation, capital repatriation, exports, and productivity gains is still too difficult to assess with precision, but dramatic improvements are evident with respect to the past. This observation should be carefully interpreted, however, given the dismal performance of the past. It is also necessary to point out that the results fell short of the general, and largely unrealistic, expectations of public opinion as to the time the private sector needed to reach the investment, export, and employment levels that could provide the standard of living to which Venezuelans had been accustomed under populist policies. This gap between expectations and actual results is bound to have significant political consequences in the future unless expectations become more realistic.

The second general observation is that unless the government acts with speed and effectiveness in strengthening the regulatory agencies needed to support a healthy and competitive private sector, the future evolution of this sector will reflect the flaws and distortions resulting from the predatory behavior of unchecked oligopolies with access to massive financial resources and uncanny political ability. The country could very well follow a pattern of oligarchic development that would greatly limit its capacity to integrate effectively with the world economy and greatly hamper its economic performance.

Probably the most difficult challenge facing both the public and the private sectors in Venezuela, and in other comparable countries as well, is the development of the public support systems that private firms in other countries enjoy. In the past, whenever the public sector tried to help private companies develop, the result was disastrous. Massive public resources were poured into companies that were created only to take advantage of governmental giveaways or companies that had to operate in an environment that canceled whatever efforts they did to become more competitive. This pattern—in which the targeted efforts by an activist government to help private enterprises have a lethargic effect in their competitive drive while encouraging corruption, inefficiency, and waste—is not exclusive to Venezuela. The rest of Latin America, Africa, some parts of Asia (such India, Pakistan, and the Philippines), and even European countries such as Italy, the pre-Thatcher United Kingdom, and France have suffered the consequences of government policies aimed at directly supporting the expansion of specific sectors or even firms.

In other countries, however, the contrary seems to have occurred. If targeted industrial policies in Japan, Taiwan, South Korea, Thailand, and Malaysia have not been a crucial element in the successful international expansion of their private firms, at least their policies have not burdened them with massive foreign debts, inefficient companies, and stagnating economies. A different set of macroeconomic policies certainly provided an important impetus for the success of these countries. But the differences between the experiences of Venezuela and other Latin American nations and those of Southeast Asian countries could probably also be found by looking at their politics and at the institutional capacity of their state apparatuses. Only a state that is capable of collecting taxes with some efficiency, for example, or of making sure that all subsidies do not become perpetual can consider building elaborate schemes to support the international expansion of targeted sectors and firms. In the mid-1990s the Venezuelan state can do neither.

Yet Venezuela continues to be able to count on its massive natural resources, a privileged location, and the positive legacy of many years of large public investments in infrastructure and human capital. It also has a private sector with massive foreign holdings and a substantial capacity to adapt to new circumstances. If the difficult political transitions that the country is bound to experience in the nineties do not strangle private investment—especially foreign investment—and if, amid all of the social and political changes that will be taking place, macroeconomic policies continue to reflect a reasonable respect for the maintenance of basic equilibrium, the Venezuelan private sector may provide, against all odds, positive surprises.

## NOTES

1. Moisés Naím, "La empresa privada en Venezuela: ¿Que pasa cuando se crece en mediode la riqueza y la confusión?" in Moisés Naím and Ramón Piñango, eds., *El caso Venezuela: Una ilusión de armonía* 4th ed. (Caracas: Ediciones IESA, 1988), 154.
2. Although raising capital or debt from the stock market was not perceived as necessary or interesting for most private firms, a small group of businesses has over the years sought financing from the open market. The Caracas Stock Exchange was established in 1947 but remained relatively dormant until the late 1980s. In 1992, about 140 companies were registered, including many of the largest Venezuelan private sector corporations, and were handled by fifty-eight active brokers. On average, around three hundred transactions take place on a given day, reaching about B 430 million. Financial markets, however, remain comparatively narrow.
3. Naím and Ramón Piñango, *El caso Venezuela*, 28.

4. See María Elena Gonzales Deluca, *Negocios y política en tiempos de Guzmán Blanco* (Caracas: Universidad Central de Venezuela, 1991).

5. See Federico Brito Figueroa, *Historia económica y social de Venezuela* (Caracas: Ediciones de la Biblioteca, Universidad Central de Venezuela, 1978).

6. See Nikita Harwich Vallenilla, *Formación y crisis de un sistema financiero nacional: Banca y estado en Venezuela (1830–1940)* (Caracas: Fondo Editorial Buría y Fondo Editorial Antonio José de Sucre, 1986).

7. See W. Reiss, "Economic Groups in Brazil," Ph.D. dissertation, University of California, Berkeley, 1986. See also Economic Commission for Latin America and the Caribbean (ECLAC), *The Process of Industrial Development in Latin America* (New York: ECLAC, 1966).

8. See Weinne Karlsson, *Manufacturing in Venezuela*, Institute of Latin American Studies, Publications Series A Monographs, no. 2 (Stockholm: Almquist and Wiksell, 1975), 29.

9. Ibid., 60.

10. See Ruth Capriles Méndez, *Los negocios de Román Delgado Chalbaud* (Caracas: Biblioteca de la Academia Nacional de la Historia, no. 49, 1991).

11. See Clemy Machado de Acedo and Marisela Padrón, *La diplomacia de López Contreras y el tratado de reciprocidad comercial con Estados Unidos, 1936–1939* (Caracas: Ministerio de Relaciones Exteriores, 1987).

12. Karlsson, *Manufacturing in Venezuela*, 68.

13. Nikita Harwich Vallenilla, "Bancos," in *Diccionario de historia de Venezuela* (Caracas: Fundación Polar, 1988), 286–91.

14. According to ministry of development records, 9,940 industrial projects were approved between 1960 and 1989, 1,250 of them during the 1960s, 3,450 during the 1970s, and 5,240 in the 1980s.

15. Moisés Naím, *Paper Tigers and Minotaurs: The Politics of Venezuela's Economic Reforms* (Washington, D.C.: Carnegie Endowment for International Peace and Brookings Institution, 1993), 45–57.

16. The major exceptions the government granted the private sector were the extremely favorable conditions it gave to mass media companies (television and radio stations as well as newspapers), to small- and medium-sized enterprises affiliated with FEDEINDUSTRIA, and to the specific company CADA, a supermarket chain. These firms were allowed to swap debt for equity at deep discounts to cover the losses they (and almost all private firms) incurred due to the effects of the devaluation on their short-term commercial debts with foreign suppliers and banks that had been covered by letters of credit.

17. The Council of Industries (CONINDUSTRIA), the business association of manufacturing companies, sued the government without success, requesting that it honor the foreign exchange rates contained in the letters of credit issued in 1988.

18. The largest and most significant of these hostile takeovers was that of Banco de Venezuela by the Banco Consolidado and the Latinoamericana insurance and banking group. As usual, this commercial war between two of the country's largest private groups also spilled over into the state, dragging into the battle public servants, politicians, journalists, judges, the comptroller of the currency, and the local equivalents of the Securities and Exchange Commission and the Internal Revenue Service.

19. Naím, *Paper Tigers and Minotaurs*, 65.

# 7

# Reforming Agriculture

## *Jonathan Coles*

Governments have tended in recent years to intervene less in their economies, rely more on the market, and advance free trade. The agricultural sector, however, has generally escaped these liberalizing trends. Agricultural reform has been difficult to achieve in both developed and developing countries, and agricultural protectionism has threatened to paralyze progress toward freer world trade. The European Community's Common Agricultural Policy and Japan's rice policy have shown the strength of the political forces opposing agricultural reform in these highly developed economies.

In contrast, the Venezuelan economic adjustment program of the early 1990s was able to include radical agricultural policy reform. In less than three years, the government drastically reduced trade barriers and began restructuring a complex apparatus of government intervention and rent distribution built over more than fifty years of agricultural policies backed by petroleum income. This reform began almost two years into President Carlos Andrés Pérez's second term and surprisingly gained momentum under the adverse political conditions that enveloped the government after the first coup attempt in February 1992. Why was it possible to accomplish these changes in spite of resistance on all sides? Will the achievements of the reform serve as the foundation for further progress, or will they disappear in a return to the old policies?

This chapter is presented in three parts: the situation before the reform as it developed from the historical evolution of agricultural policies, the agricultural reform and its preliminary results, and lessons and recommendations.

## THE EVOLUTION OF AGRICULTURAL POLICY (1936–89)

Explicit agricultural policy began with the end of Gen. Juan Vicente Gómez's regime and the creation in 1936 of modern government institutions, including the ministry of agriculture. Two major periods are evident in the history of agricultural policy. Prior to 1968, governments attempted to compensate farmers for the harmful effects of petroleum wealth on rural sectors through investments in production and welfare improvement. From 1969 on, with many more voters now living in cities than in the rural areas, governments were increasingly concerned with compensating consumers for inflation. Managing the "food price dilemma"—the inherent conflict between the consumer's desire for low food prices and the farmer's desire for high prices—became the central goal of policy. 2 periods

### Sowing Petroleum (1936–68)

When General Juan Gómez died in 1935 after ruling for twenty-seven years, petroleum was beginning to revolutionize Venezuela's agricultural economy. Petroleum discovery and the end of a tyrannical political system gave the country the chance to make a quantum leap from a backward system to a modern democratic society. But these events also caused enormous difficulties. Managing the opportunities and the problems created by such change became the central problem of governments after Gómez. The phrase "sowing petroleum" (*sembrar el petróleo*) captured the country's general objective of converting new nonrenewable material wealth into sustainable economic and political development. "Sowing petroleum" also captured the desire to reconcile the conflicts between petroleum and agriculture.

Oil-producing areas offered much higher salaries and better working conditions than the semi-feudal hinterland. The growing supply of foreign exchange strengthened the currency, making imports relatively more attractive than exports; profits from coffee and cocoa exports declined after having long been the principal source of foreign exchange. As these export crops lost their economic predominance, Venezuelans migrated to the cities and the oil-producing areas. The new wealth from oil stimulated consumer demand for imported goods in the cities, while the growing contrast between urban and rural life bred resentment in rural areas and guilt among many who moved to the cities.

Prior to 1968, governments followed two clearly distinguishable strategies for sowing petroleum. From 1950 to 1959, the military government under Gen. Marcos Pérez Jiménez promoted immigration from postwar Europe and built rural roads and electricity distribution and irrigation systems. After winning the 1959 elections, the democratic coalition backing President Rómulo Betancourt distributed land and soft credit to native campesinos.

Pérez Jiménez's government selected the areas that offered most promise for modern agricultural production and promoted their development through the provision of large irrigation systems, roads, housing, and electricity. To obtain the personnel needed for this new type of farming, the government offered immigrants incentives to settle in these areas. Critics called this approach "superimposed agriculture" because it was based on changing the natural lay of the land and importing people who did not even speak the local language.

As in all tropical countries, controlling water in Venezuela was crucial for efficient agricultural production. Both the Lake Maracaibo basin to the east and the Orinoco River basin to the west carry rainwater and soil from the Andes mountains to the sea through the piedmont and the plains. Draining and saving excess rainwater for use in the dry season makes it possible to exploit the area's enormous productive potential.

Much of the impressive network of roads, dams, irrigation channels, and electricity that exists today was either constructed or designed in the Pérez Jiménez years, but it is scarcely utilized and in disrepair. Critics say the dictator's government relied too much on bricks and mortar, and not enough on the human and environmental aspects of development. Many of the irrigation projects have caused environmental problems and were too large to manage effectively.

When Pérez Jiménez fell in 1958 and the Social Democratic Acción Democrática (AD) won the 1959 elections, the coalition of major parties backing Rómulo Betancourt, who served as president for the next five years, was concerned with making native farmers, the campesinos, better producers and better citizens. Together with labor, the campesino movement became one of the most important groups in AD and one of the keys to the party's success in controlling the most remote areas of the country.

The Agrarian Reform Law of 1960 became the charter for agricultural development. The law reserved all unclaimed land for agrarian reform and established a system that conditioned the use and property of these lands to rules administered by the National Agrarian Institute (IAN), which was also charged with rural development and extension activities. Meanwhile, the Agrarian Bank (BAP) provided loans at a 3 percent rate of interest. The democratic government continued investing in public works, but it now restricted newly developed lands and irrigation projects to campesinos.

The government created a separate organization for agricultural research, including the National Fund for Agricultural Research (FONAIAP) and the National Council of Agricultural Research (CONIA). The agrarian reform law incorporated the most advanced thinking on rural development at the time, but adjudicating land disputes and distributing highly subsidized credit under political pressure proved to be a daunting task. The political appointees in the state delegations of IAN accumulated enormous discretionary power. "Definitive" land titles (which were also revocable) proved difficult for farmers to obtain because provisional titles gave government officials greater discretionary power. The good intentions written into the law were easily corrupted by party and personal interests.

With the decline of the marxist threat and the paralysis created by the politicized administration of the agrarian program, enthusiasm for the reform waned at the end of the 1960s. But the political culture it bred—an ideology of class conflict—would remain for many years. The state's role as mediator between landowners and landless campesinos was applied to the relationship between farmers and agroindustrial firms. The underlying assumption justifying government intervention was and remains that the state serves the general interest, whereas private parties are motivated by self-interest. The contrast between the traditional Jeffersonian values that dominated agrarian policymaking over these years and those implicit in the more "modern" approach could not be sharper, as is shown in table 7.1.

*Pleasing Producers and Consumers (1968–89)*

COPEI President Rafael Caldera's election in 1969 signaled the growing importance of consumers and the urban middle classes. From this

Table 7.1
CONTRASTING STYLES OF AGRARIAN VALUES IN VENEZUELA

| Traditional Agrarian Values | Modern Agrarian Values |
| --- | --- |
| Autarchic self-sufficiency | Active trading: exports and imports |
| Produce everything you eat | Export surpluses/import deficits |
| Import substitution | Seek positive balance of trade |
| Commerce is speculative | Trading generates wealth |
| Sectors are inherently in conflict | Sectors are mutually interdependent |
| Agriculture is social | Agriculture generates wealth |
| Government plans production | Producers make their own decisions |
| Government should defend weak farmers by fixing prices and controlling imports | Government should establish rules for all |
| Government manages the sector | Government should intervene selectively |

point on, agricultural policy shifted from protecting campesinos by stimulating production in rural areas to managing the impact on consumers of higher food prices.

State-owned marketing boards were common in a variety of countries at differing levels of development. Caldera's government responded to the call of the growing middle class of farmers for protection from their more powerful buyers' "unfair" prices by creating a state marketing agency, the Corporación de Mercadeo Agrícola (CMA). As continued political pressure pushed farm prices above world levels, the government "reserved" imports exclusively to CMA and sometimes "delegated" imports and exports to private firms.

In Carlos Andrés Pérez's first administration (1974–79), CMA became the principal source of indirect subsidies. Pérez also decided to forgive outstanding farm loans. The culture of nonpayment of loans, long established in the campesino sector, was now extended to all types of farmers. COPEI President Luis Herrera (1979–84), however, clipped CMA's wings and relied instead on import and consumer price controls.

Reflecting his party's control of the farmers', cattlemen's, and campesino associations, AD President Jaime Lusinchi (1984–89) pleased these organizations by ensuring high prices. He compensated the cost to consumers by controlling almost all food prices and imports and by giving processing firms conditioned access to import permits at subsidized exchange rates. Lusinchi also pleased friendly construction firms with "soft" contracts to build or repair rural roads and drainage and irrigation projects.

The high-price policy produced almost a doubling of land planted with corn and sorghum. It was dubbed the "agricultural miracle" until it became increasingly clear that this last addition of compensatory agricultural policies was financially unsustainable. Despite the country's diminishing petroleum income, however, the Lusinchi government maintained controls on food prices and was compelled to finance the preferential exchange rate subsidy with international reserves. Lusinchi thus left Pérez with a financial crisis as the latter began his second term in January 1989.

*The Institutional Cobweb in 1989: Realities and Actors*

When the reform program began in 1990, irresponsible politics had subverted the original development programs and created a dense cobweb of institutions—and only a few privileged "spiders" knew how to get around. The key programs in modern agricultural development, re-

## Figure 7.1
## Share of major categories (national production)

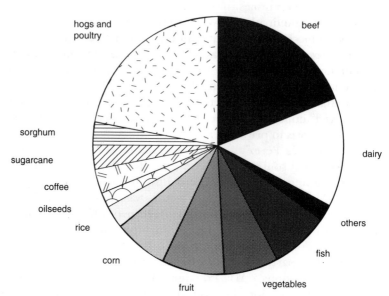

search, credit, road building, irrigation, and land administration were practically paralyzed. In 1990, agricultural sector production had dropped to less than 6 percent of the GDP. Agricultural exports accounted for less than 3 percent of total exports—one of the smallest percentages in the developing world. Less than 14 percent of the population remained rural, a demographic characteristic comparable to Germany or Japan but highly atypical of Latin America, whose average rural population is greater than 25 percent.[1]

Speculators had often led government officials to confuse modernization with emulation of successful temperate-zone production systems. Still, traditional tropical products, such as cattle (beef, milk, cheese), fish, fruits and vegetables (including roots and tubers), and rice, sugarcane, coffee, and cocoa represented almost three-quarters of total production (see figure 7.1).

Import substitution policies spawned entirely new industries. Government-induced animal feed and the vegetable oil businesses were prominent examples. Likewise patterned after temperate-zone production systems, these industries provided markets for sorghum, hogs, poultry, and oilseeds, which together represented about 25 percent of total agricultural production. More than 75 percent of agricultural production served as raw materials for relatively modern agroindustrial processes. Artificially cheap currency, ample credit, lax government collections, tariff protection, and other government incentives had provided general access to modern machinery and technologies adapted to raw materials produced in other climates. The animal feed industry used the corn and soybean formulation typical of the United States. Sorghum appeared later as a partial substitute for corn.

Despite the emphasis on agrarian reform in the 1960s, farmland remained highly concentrated in large tracts. Compared to the rest of Latin America, there were relatively few small landholders, not only because of Venezuela's small total population but also because of the unusually large migration from rural areas to the cities after the discovery of petroleum. The campesino problem was thus a relatively less explosive issue in Venezuela than in Mexico, Peru, or Colombia.

There were approximately 380,000 farms in production as of 1990, 70 percent of which were smaller than ten hectares (twenty-five acres), representing less than 3 percent of total cultivated land. These small plots were found mainly in the coffee- and cocoa-growing areas. At the other end of the scale, less than 1 percent of all farms accounted for over 50 percent of all cultivated farmland.[2] These big plots of land were typically cattle ranches in the llanos, or plains.

The growing policy concern with satisfying consumers was not reflected in positive nutritional indicators, which had been deteriorating steadily since the 1970s and began to show signs of improvement in 1989. Consumption patterns also reflected the influence of policies that made imports cheaper. Imported wheat products far outweighed locally produced corn and rice, while per capita consumption of poultry grew much faster than the consumption of red meat because the raw materials for feeding poultry were largely imported with the benefit of subsidies. Consumption of local fish products also grew slowly.

### The Government

The government had a sprawling, disjointed network of overlapping institutions addressing food policy. The agriculture ministry was composed of sixteen separate agencies and maintained a payroll of thirty thousand employees. Moreover, the ministry of development, in charge of price policy and agroindustrial regulation, usually dominated its agricultural counterpart. On crucial issues, such as watershed management and rural road building, the ministry would share responsibilities with other ministries of government. In security, housing, and education—

on a wide range of issues—the agriculture minister depended on the goodwill of his cabinet colleagues.

The ample network of agencies provided careers for many ambitious politicians, who tended to compete with ministers who rarely lasted a full year in office. Low pay fostered corruption, and lower-level civil servants "charged" for free services in exchange for permits or certificates. There was a constant incentive to require new permits. In addition, few activities were free of government certifications. For example, truckers were required to secure a *guía* (permit), subject to compliance with a sanitary certification, to transport produce, and slaughtering a cow required showing evidence of the animal's sterility.

The World Bank estimated in 1990 that explicit subsidies to agriculture were on the order of U.S.$1 billion, or 2 percent of Venezuela's GDP.[3] Most of these subsidies were directed at reducing farm costs by making inputs cheaper. Free land, preferential interest rates, and special rates for water, fertilizer, fuel, and storage were examples of these indirect subsidies—as was farm income, which was exempt from income tax.

### The Producer Associations: Lobbyists or Marketeers?

Obtaining government subsidies and securing good prices required the development of organizations with the ability to put pressure on the government. Local associations as well as national federations, with strong ties to the two major parties and therefore to the government, fit the bill. Association leaders were able to obtain permits, preferential currency, and credits for their constituency of farmers. Soon they extended their role in securing permits to the trading, storage, and handling businesses. It is no surprise that serving on the board of an association became an extremely lucrative activity.

Every producing area had its own association. Some were defined according to a particular crop or product, such as sorghum or potatoes.[4] The various associations were affiliated with national federations, such as FEDEAGRO (farmers' federation) and FEDENAGA (cattlemen's federation). The Campesino Federation was unusual in that it was more centralized and more political in character. Created by Acción Democrática, it included all the major parties except COPEI.

### Congress and the Parties

The agrarian "bloc" of deputies was so powerful in the Chamber of Deputies that the finance ministry generally underestimated the bud-

gets for the agricultural sector, knowing that this group of farm supporters would easily receive the appropriations demanded by their constituencies. These funds were often channeled by congressional
deputies to the public works and credit institutions in return for agrarian reform land, credits, and contracts for friendly construction companies. The Agricultural Committee in the chamber spent much of its
time on land questions and other conflicts. If a deputy had requested a
hearing on the complaints of the coffee growers in the Andes, for example, the committee would "invite" or subpoena the minister to answer those complaints.

Following the Communist party structure, the political parties' agrarian bureaus included representatives from all the various state secretariats around the country. The agrarian secretary, who served as chair of
the bureau, was the official link between the party members in government and the government party. In the Betancourt model of party politics, the president was the most important individual in agricultural policy because he or she managed the party network so that all the parts
would work together.

## Big Business

The major agroindustrial firms—producers of corn, animal feed and
poultry, wheat, fats and oils, sugar, milk and cheese, rice, beef, and
pork—were more fragmented and isolated from one another than is
generally the case in more open economies. With the exception of the
meat and pork industries, the typical business was a domestic family
firm. A few of the large international traders, however, developed
beachheads in Venezuela and integrated vertically into animal feed. It
was entirely possible, for example, for the head of an edible oil company not to know the head of an important animal feed firm. For a
small country, with an even smaller and closely intertwined business
elite, this was highly indicative of the sector's fragmentation.[5]

Just as the various industrial sectors were isolated from one another,
the large agribusiness companies generally were not integrated with
their agricultural suppliers, although the tobacco, sugar, and cotton
sectors had institutional linkages. Policymaking by sector clearly differentiated between the industrialist and farmer. State intervention in the
marketing of crops had aggravated conflicts between buyers and sellers
and paved the way for the emergence of political intermediaries em-
bedded in the farmer associations. Establishing the yearly price for a
crop and deciding who would buy how much and when became an
issue that could not be resolved without political intervention and gov-

ernment action. In response, firms established procurement units in their organizations, which spent much of their time courting political intermediaries who often made juicy profits at the expense of the principal buyers and sellers.

## REFORMING AGRICULTURE

In President Pérez's surprising plan for economic reform, the goal of agricultural policy reform was to develop competitiveness in the production and distribution of food so that national products would have better access to national and export markets without forever depending on the government. To achieve this goal required, first, eliminating price-distorting and discretionary government interventions that discouraged private investment and limited competition, and second, investing massively in agricultural research, extension, land titling, animal and plant health, and public infrastructure. The government also proposed to stimulate private investment with special long-term credit funding, strengthen private marketing and financial systems, and maintain direct small landholder financing.

The Pérez government was initially reluctant to make changes in the agricultural sector, but the elimination of preferential exchange rates and controls on prices and interest rates caused food prices to increase dramatically, particularly for products with imported components. Meanwhile, the conversion of indirect subsidies (to producers) into direct subsidies (to consumers) was applied first to fertilizer and agricultural interest rate subsidies. Finally, the new trade policies—the elimination of government monopolies, nontariff barriers and exonerations, and the progressive reduction of tariffs to a maximum of 20 percent— affected the agricultural sector more than any other.

Agricultural policy proper, however, was initially left in limbo. The general trade policy guidelines gave the agricultural sector a year's moratorium to define its own special guidelines, and price controls were maintained for a number of basic food items. Imports continued under the traditional quota systems.

President Pérez was apparently hoping he could leave agriculture outside the economic reform process. He had grown up in a successful family of coffee growers who had lost their land to a trading firm in one of the many world coffee price crises. Pérez had always devoted special attention to the agricultural problem, advocating the use of state power to help small farmers in their relations with more powerful bankers, merchants, and industrialists. He had strongly supported the development of the state-owned marketing corporation, CMA, and wanted it re-created in some form. He had groomed political leaders in the agricultural and agrarian sectors to run the ministry's principal agencies, and he was reluctant to lose them.

Concerned that his macroeconomic program would cause food supply problems, Pérez called on a group of experts to examine whether it was necessary to re-create a government agency of the marketing board type. They correctly predicted that food supply problems would disappear with the elimination of price and import controls and recommended against another CMA. But they also admitted that such an institution might be useful for emergencies.

Food reappeared on market shelves as soon as higher prices were authorized, but consumers balked. Consumption dropped sharply. The demand for milk, chicken, vegetable oil, and wheat products declined the most because they were heavily dependent on imported raw materials that no longer benefited from the exchange rate subsidy. The elimination of the preferential exchange rates had a whiplash effect on processing firms. Their sales and collections dropped sharply just as their debt and raw materials increased in value. Farmers had trouble selling their produce to industries that had earlier spent all their money taking advantage of the last chance to purchase cheap imports. Long lines of trucks full of wet grain formed at the silos. Speculators paid desperate farmers' prices, which were far below the established minimum levels. With this reduction in income and the stiff increases in cost for imported supplies, interest rates, and fertilizers, profits vanished. Farm production dropped more than 6 percent in 1989 (see figure 7.2).

Searching for ways to manage this situation, a ministerial task force discovered that internal prices for almost all agricultural and agroindustrial products were lower than international prices. After eliminating the effect of preferential exchange rates and establishing normal levels of tariff protection, only a few "sensitive" products (cereals, oilseeds, milk, and sugar) ran the risk of being undercut by cheaper imported products. For these products, the task force designed special transition and stabilizing mechanisms.

Upon review of the new policies, the Venezuelan president decided to move forward. In spite of the agriculture ministry's position that "a more thorough study was necessary," the cabinet approved the new guidelines in June 1990. On June 26, Pérez designated me, Jonathan Coles, the new minister of agriculture. As part of the reform, import licenses were eliminated immediately for all but the "sensitive" items, and a transitional methodology for the oilseed and animal feed sectors was announced in December 1990. Price controls on all foods—except

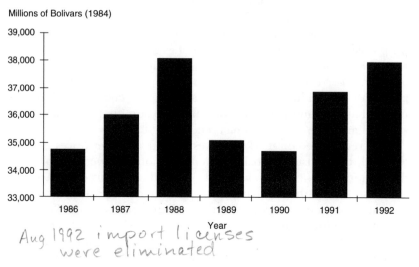

**Figure 7.2
Agricultural production**

Millions of Bolivars (1984)

*Aug 1992 import licenses
were eliminated*

canned sardines—were eliminated by December 1991. By August 1992, all import licenses were eliminated (see figure 7.3). Colombia quickly executed almost identical trade policy reforms, and the two countries easily agreed to liberalize agricultural trade fully between them.

*Political Reactions to Trade Liberalization*

Protests against the liberalization were at first difficult to distinguish from the theatrics that associations staged every year to bring pressure on the government for better prices. After the February 1992 coup attempt, however, associations representing a variety of regions and crops came together in a national protest movement.[6]

   No issue better illustrates the political dynamics of trade reform than the response to the sorghum and feedgrains transition policy.[7] Being one of the most protected sectors, the two industries took the longest to adjust and the change created the most intense reaction. Designed to shift feedgrain imports from license requirements to tariffs gradually, the transition plan proposed to maintain import licensing and the existing minimum price until devaluation reduced the difference between local and international prices to 15 percent, at which point a 15 percent tariff was to replace the licensing system. For an initial six-month period, the ministry was not to issue any licenses at all, in order to allow high inventories to decline to normal levels. The strategy

*sorghum and feed grains transition policy*

**Figure 7.3**
**Nontariff protection as percentage of total production**

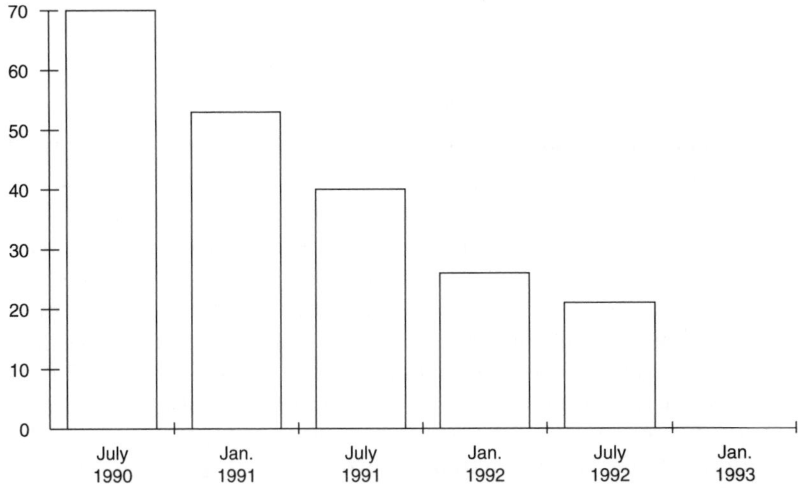

aimed to gain support for the general reform by returning for the time being to an even more protectionist policy than licensing, while at the same time announcing the entire timetable for future policy changes.

In no other crop sector was the activity of the associations and the intervention of government so intense. Although sorghum represented less than 3 percent of agricultural GDP, it seemed to consume all of FEDEAGRO's agenda.

Moving from a policy of licenses to tariffs was a terrible blow to lobbyists and intermediaries whose negotiating power with industry and farmers was based on their access to the government. Bargaining over import quotas and minimum prices served no purpose. As a result, the intermediaries who controlled the farming associations in Guárico decided to mobilize their farmers and, along with others in the domestic feed industry, make a stand against the plan to change the existing system. They reminded the producers that the planning minister had stated that "sorghum was not competitive in Venezuela, and should be replaced by yucca in animal feed rations." And they argued that the new policies would bankrupt sorghum farmers.

The press labeled the subsequent protest the "Cherokee March"—referring not to the native American tribe but to the expensive Jeep Cherokee wagons farmers drove to Caracas during the march against the new policies. The Cherokee episode ended when the feed industry raised the price of sorghum, an increase that extended the transition period by widening the gap between local and international prices. It was clear evidence that the feed industry favored keeping the old system.

*Loans from International Financial Institutions*

By the middle of 1991, the ministry had negotiated with the World Bank and Inter-American Development Bank (IDB) the broad outlines of a U.S.$600 million policy-based investment loan. The ministry had prepared a U.S.$1.1 billion plan to invest in the sector's priority needs: long-term credit, rural roads, electrification, irrigation and drainage, land titling, plant and animal health, and "institutional strengthening," or a training program for government managers.[8] International lending was to finance more than half of the investment proposal. The IDB was scheduled to finance an additional U.S.$129 million program to strengthen research, thus salvaging a previous IDB loan that had foundered due to severe compliance problems with government institutions. The new research project would emphasize training and farmers' participation in determining research priorities.[9]

In the loan covenants, Venezuela agreed to maintain the new commercial and financial policies, restructure a number of institutions, and sell government-owned silos and other facilities. Disbursement of the loans required bank approval of each of the investment projects. Due to dramatic improvement in Venezuela's international reserves position, the banks had switched from rapid disbursement policy loans without earmarks to traditional investment loans for individual projects. Since Venezuela had almost no experience in preparing projects for international financing in the agricultural public sector, this change meant that it would take at least two years to receive new loan money.

Two strategies were developed to accelerate the disbursement of the new funding. The first was to allot more than 40 percent of the funds to term credit for private investment through the private banks. The second was to create a "rapid impact" investment program, funded with government bonds, for repairing the irrigation system. This program helped speed approval of the loans in Congress because it helped friendly AD agrarian bloc members provoke their colleagues' interest in securing immediate funds for public works in the districts they represented.

The World Bank and later the Inter-American Development Bank played central roles in the policy design process. Their technical expertise and knowledge of the adjustment efforts of other countries helped the reform policies gel. Their legal and technical standards for loan and project approval made progress at times slow and difficult, but forced the ministry to achieve higher standards. Although these multilateral organizations were not inflexible or rigidly ideological on policy issues, they were disappointingly narrow at times when the ministry was looking for appropriate reform strategies. At various points, projects were stymied for months by administrative details. When the reforms met strong opposition, the multilateral banks appeared to become more cautious, thus placing additional political burdens on the reformers by delaying the rewards for adjustment costs. In the end, it took far longer for disbursements to begin than the reform team had originally planned.

### Restructuring: The Unpredictable Effects of the Coup Attempts

Restructuring began almost simultaneously in the research fund (FONAIAP) and in the Agricultural Credit Fund (FCA) as a result of the need to convert them into reliable recipients of international financing. The political conditions that sprang from the first coup attempt ironically allowed restructuring to expand quickly to almost all of the agricultural government agencies.

Restructuring FCA was a useful first experience in understanding the politics of reforming government agencies. FCA was created by Pérez during his first presidency to provide long-term credit for crop and cattle farmers. Over the years it evolved into a purely political instrument that provided loans, studies, and projects to friends and allies. Unscrupulous banks could obtain lines of credit for fake "agricultural companies." The FCA board of directors, by tradition, included the heads of all the major producer federations, who tended to act as credit intermediaries for their constituencies.

As a consequence of the reform, FCA's role was switched from one of direct lending to the provision of long-term funding to banks for agricultural loans without the retention of risk. The change allowed the fund to reduce its payroll from six hundred to less than one hundred professionals. Although the detailed restructuring plan was defined early on in agreement with the FCA president and the board of directors, the plan was not actually implemented until the ministry was able to adopt a more radical approach to restructuring.

### The February Coup Attempt

Sensing the government's weakness following the February 1992 coup attempt, FEDEAGRO changed its adaptive strategy to one of frontal opposition. The advisory council's report to the president presented FEDEAGRO's recommendations on agricultural policy as the council's own, without amendment. With this victory in hand, FEDEAGRO's leaders were certain they could force a reversal of the reformist agricultural policies. They organized a national day of protest and demanded from the president the agriculture minister's removal. Congress again voted on a motion to censure the minister in March, and this time the motion carried, one hundred votes in favor, ninety-nine against. The decision was nonbinding, but it demonstrated the power of the agricultural lobby in Congress.

When the internal AD elections for the agrarian bureau were held, the general secretary's candidates surprisingly defeated the president's incumbent group. The victors subsequently presented new candidates for many of the ministry's state offices. The ministry accepted the party's recommendations, but at the same time seized the opportunity to make management changes in all of the agencies and institutes. The ministry was finally able to bring together a cohesive, professional management team to work without hesitation on the reforms. Reorganization of the system as a whole now seemed to be a feasible goal. The rebellious spirit engendered by the February events served as a springboard for the expansion of reform from trade policy and loan negotiations to general restructuring and institution building. The party's internal battle and general public dissatisfaction with politicians had weakened the traditional party networks' control over the ministry and its agencies.

The principal restructuring guideline was to focus the ministry and governmental agencies on pushing operative governmental functions *down* to the municipality level and moving nongovernmental functions *out* of the ministry into the private sector. In addition to general policy formulation, the government planned to pay special attention to information and statistics, public infrastructure, basic research, animal and plant health, and extension and education. Rather than absorb these functions exclusively, the government was to involve private institutions. Instead of hiring veterinarians for vaccination campaigns, for instance, the government would transfer these functions to cattle farmers' associations; instead of creating credit extension and technical assistance departments in public agencies, the government would promote nongovernmental organizations in various regions of the country.

The general restructuring plan proposed to reduce the total government payroll from more than thirty thousand to some ten thousand employees, with opportunities for further reductions in the future. In the highly politicized agrarian reform agencies, restructuring began by redefining the government's role in land and rural credit administration. The government would in effect "finish" agrarian reform by inventorying and titling public lands and selling off properties that had long been in production or overrun by urban development. The funds generated by the sale of lands could be used for rural infrastructure and social programs for small landholders.

Instead of directly administering rural credit at 3 percent interest rates, the government would make arrangements with private banks to cofinance credit for small farmers, leaving the administration of the credit to the private network of branch offices throughout the country. The more remote areas were to be better served by the wider private networks at a lower cost. It was also expected that small landholders would become familiar with modern banking services.

### The November 1992 Coup Attempt and Local Elections

Following the November 27, 1992 coup attempt, the AD agrarian bureau became more aggressive in opposing the agricultural reform policies: the restructuring process was costing party members their government jobs. The agrarian secretary complained to the general secretary that AD would have trouble gaining support for the upcoming 1993 presidential elections if the ministry continued cutting jobs. For the first time, the party was hard on the non-AD minister of agriculture; the reform team was losing one of its major allies. The minister now insisted on resigning and recommended that the vice minister be promoted to his slot in order to guarantee the continuity of the reform program.

The vice minister took office as the new minister of agriculture in January 1993. He faced the difficulties of the 1993 election year, aggravated by the government's fatigue and unpopularity and by the extremely serious fiscal gap that continued to fuel inflation and high real interest rates. In March 1993, when most producers were making their planting plans, the attorney general sent the Supreme Court his request for the president to be tried for graft. Financial markets quickly deteriorated, and the bolivar came under heavy pressure. The minister of finance announced cuts in the budget; investment in public infrastructure was to be drastically cut.

The government delayed the final step of the fertilizer subsidy reduction program and approved an extra duty for yellow corn that allowed the internal price for sorghum to increase almost 20 percent over the previous year. The corn industry announced a more than 30 percent increase in the price of white corn. At the same time, poultry imports from the United States were prohibited following the news of the possible presence of influenza, leading to the reemergence of a concern that sanitation permits would be used as non-tariff barriers.

*NTBs*

### The Outcome of Agricultural Reforms

What were the immediate results of the reforms? Radical changes in agricultural policy promote investments and structural changes that will increase-competitiveness and open markets over time. The early effects of such profound change, however, often cause traumas that can generate a decline in production, particularly when the country is facing political and macroeconomic instability. Early evidence, however, demonstrates immediate improvement in food supply and inflation control, production, and efficiency, as well as success in increasing exports. In addition, consumers enjoyed a full supply of a wider range of food products. Increases in food prices, which had been much higher than inflation in other areas of production under the previous policies, were the same or slightly below the consumer price index (CPI) following the elimination of price controls and implementation of the new policies.

After declining 5 to 10 percent in 1989 and 1 percent in 1990, food production increased by more than 3 percent in 1991 and more than 2 percent the following year, despite adverse macroeconomic conditions and constant political turmoil (see figure 7.2).[10] The 1990–92 increase placed Venezuela in the top quarter of developing countries in agricultural growth. Only one-third of all Latin American countries showed *any* growth in 1990; the same absence of growth was found in the rest of the developing world.

*food trade deficit 1992*

After large dropoffs in 1990 and 1991, the food trade deficit began to increase again in 1992. Exports continued to grow, but imports grew even more as local consumption outpaced local production. The bolivar became stronger in real terms as inflation outpaced devaluation in 1991 and 1992 and made imports relatively more attractive. Despite these adverse macroeconomic trends, the import and deficit levels did not reach those of 1988, when protectionist policies were in full force (see figure 7.4). For the first time in many years, wheat imports had to compete on a "fair" basis with national cereals: they had lost preferential access to foreign exchange and were now paying duties.

With the violent rise in real interest rates, fueled by political instability, crop and cattle farmers faced increasing financial difficulties. Sorghum, sunflower, sesame, corn, cotton, and potatoes all became less profitable. Red meat, fish, tropical fruits, vegetables, coffee, and

## Figure 7.4
## Agricultural exports and imports

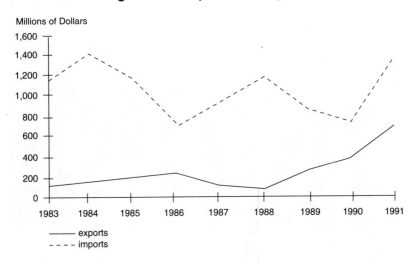

Millions of Dollars

exports
---- imports

cocoa improved in profitability relative to what profits would have been under the previous policies. Profits in poultry and hog production dropped sharply when animal feed prices skyrocketed following the initial exchange shock in 1989, but later began to recover as demand for these products improved. Meanwhile, producers who had made capital investments in land and machinery with preferential interest rates and subsidized dollars found themselves with excess assets, which they resisted selling off. It was difficult for them to find buyers in the country, let alone in the same producing area. Land values remained high, but as in the rest of the economy new investments were slow to appear. The FCA, however, did report strong credit demand for new projects in cattle, African palm, aquaculture, cocoa, fruits, and vegetables.

Farm efficiency increased significantly as production yields per hectare improved. Pressure on profits both pushed out the inefficient producers and focused farmers' attention on improving productivity. Investors who had farms as a pretext for obtaining preferential financing either sold their farms to professional farmers or stopped producing. Moreover, the incentive to falsify production in order to obtain import permits disappeared. The clearest example of these yield improvements is found in rice production (see figure 7.5).[11]

## Figure 7.5
## Rice yield (in kilograms per hectare)

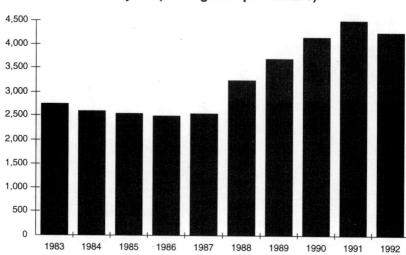

THE LESSONS: HOW TO KEEP SPIDERS
OUT OF THE GARDEN

The agricultural reform experience of 1990 to 1992 provides a number
of lessons—or a review of what worked and what failed—for the management of two major problems: agricultural policy formulation and
implementation, and policy reform. These lessons, in turn, suggest recommendations for the future.

At the expense of the country's dream of reaching sustainable social
and political development, Venezuelan agricultural policies were progressively degraded by short-term political objectives. Petroleum wealth
at first financed a wide array of public investments in physical infrastructure, but later increasingly served to distribute rents and resolve
social conflicts between landowners and campesinos, sellers and buyers
of produce, and producers and consumers. Political actors found their
raison d'être in this rent distribution and conflict intermediation system, and they searched for ways to expand it. To use an apt metaphor,
the state became the great spider in an increasingly complex cobweb of
agricultural policies. The spider's control through many subsidiaries
stunted the development of the social and political skills required for
independent wealth creation and conflict resolution. As petroleum
rents later diminished, these smaller entities tried to maintain their

share of the rent and increasingly exploited the people they were supposed to help progress. A vicious circle was created as the various sectors struggled to maintain their share of a whole made smaller by their
own behavior.        vicious circle

As opposed to supporting laws and budget initiatives that would have
improved the competitiveness of the agricultural sector and strengthened it, politicians left sound initiatives unattended and preferred to
quibble over their respective allotments of funds. Even members of
Congress whose principal area of concern appeared to be general agricultural policy often used their involvement to protect a special interest. Time and again policymakers tried to legislate utopia, without taking into account either the management requirements of different
policies or their ultimate feasibility. At first, this lack of realism was
grounded in inexperience and an honest desire to promote progress;
as time passed, cynics manipulated agrarian idealism for their own special interests. Grand, impractical schemes offered easy prey for the spider. Politicians often said, "The idea was a good one. It just wasn't implemented correctly." Agrarian reform and the state marketing agency,
CMA, were supposed examples of good ideas that were badly managed.
In hindsight, who could have doubted that these programs would become as chaotic as they did? A policy must be judged not only by the
objectives it pursues, but also by its capacity to achieve results.

Policies often had effects directly contrary to the objectives they were
intended to pursue. Protectionist trade policies, for example, generated trade deficits in food by subsidizing imports and cutting off exports. Import substitution policies channeled investments toward technologies and products better adapted to temperate climates. Policies
designed to make the small farmers more autonomous—the Jeffersonian ideal—in fact made them more dependent on the political parties
and governments. Indirect subsidies, to help farmers and impoverished
consumers fight inflation, were captured by the more powerful players
in the system and fueled inflation by aggravating the fiscal deficit.

Agricultural policymakers often thought they could "beat the market,"
either by fixing prices or by controlling imports and exports. The
Venezuelan experience has so far shown that trade reform has not
caused the major problems faced by farmers in the transition to more
open economic policies. Rather, the problems are rooted in macroeconomic instability and political difficulties that have kept real interest rates
at extremely high levels and lowered the real exchange rate. Many of
today's macroeconomic difficulties are the direct result of the rent-dis-
tributing policies that were so prevalent in Venezuela's agricultural past.
Protectionist policies were often justified as a defense against similar poli-

cies in other countries: bad policy was justified "because others do it." Embarking on protectionist wars with countries whose treasuries are richer is doubly destructive. "Winning," apart from being impossible, really means losing.

Years of ample petroleum wealth made Venezuelans unaware of the tradeoffs in policy decisions and clouded understanding of the food system as a whole. The failure to understand that consumers' welfare is crucial to the producer—the consumer is the ultimate market—was the result of the government standing between the buyer and seller. Producer organizations did not realize, for example, that eliminating price controls on consumer products was positive for farmers, that it was the flip side of abandoning minimum prices for farm products. Nor did they realize that discontinuing import controls also meant the elimination of export controls. They mistakenly thought their problems could be "solved" apart from the rest of the system in which they were important participants.

The lessons from these experiences appear obvious: beware of quick, partial solutions; beware of double-talk; beware of those who self-righteously defend "agriculture" in vague, general terms. Agricultural policy must "go back to the basics" by concentrating on the development of lasting skills that reduce the dependency of producers and consumers on the government. If Venezuelans are serious about the strategic importance of food security and the agricultural sector, then they must assign larger proportions of the national budget to investments that will strengthen the system as a whole; they must ensure that the government performs the basic functions that every government must perform for its citizens and farmers. In Venezuela, these functions deteriorated to unacceptable levels owing to the perversions that poisoned agricultural policies. Some of these basic government functions apply to the entire economy, and some are specifically agricultural.

Although not part of agricultural policy proper, the maintenance of sound macroeconomic policies and a legal system that protects life and property is crucial to farmers. Farmers are probably more limited by macroeconomic instability and by the corruption of the legal system than by anything else. In addition, quality education and health services and adequate communications in rural areas are extremely important for improving the quality of life and the productivity of the farm community. These state investments help to distribute income because they benefit entire communities rather than privileged groups.

Failure to achieve the degree of world food security that is now possible is due not to nature but to humans—not as farmers or scientists or extension workers, but as politicians, those among us who use the political process to protect their own interests with little regard as to how others may be affected.[12]

"Special" status for the agricultural sector should be provided in public investment priorities. The obvious priorities in Venezuela's case are: (1) salvaging the impressive but crumbling infrastructure of roads, irrigation systems, and electricity distribution systems; (2) stimulating the recuperation and growth of a strong agricultural research and extension system; (3) creating a reliable land titling and administration system; (4) strengthening animal and plant health administration; (5) fostering the creation of commodity marketing systems that provide liquidity, transparency, and flexibility; and (6) maintaining government funding for long-term credit and for smallholders not covered by private banking. Many of these priorities are most effectively addressed at the local level of government. Continuing the process of political decentralization is a key requirement for future success in agricultural development.

*Policy Reform*

The reform effort was surprisingly successful in expediting changes in agricultural policies and recuperating the sector's lagging behind the economic reforms in the rest of the economy. Although other economic reforms slowed after the February 1992 coup attempt, the agricultural sector was able to continue with the general restructuring of the ministry and its agencies. Was this speedy success achieved at the expense of being able to sustain the reforms? Should the reformers have done less at a slower pace, but with greater consensus?

The experience of managing the reform in two distinct stages offers insight into these issues. During the first stage, the ministry was in constant conversation with the producer associations. Progress was rapid, despite the inexperience of the new team, because the work focused on changing rules and preparing investment plans. This technical part of the reform generated little resistance; producer associations were not concerned about changes in the rules because rules had scarcely been important in a political culture that emphasized exceptions to them. In the second stage, after the producer associations had turned in opposition to the ministry, restructuring gained speed, now because the ministry was spending less time on building consensus. The shift to a hostile strategy by the producer associations was determined more by the general political situation than by the effects of the changes in agricultural policy.

Rapid progress would have been impossible without the experience the minister developed during his year-and-a-half tenure as a commissioner to the president. During this period, he was able to develop a comprehensive plan that already had the support of his future cabinet colleagues, and to learn how the system worked. Securing approval of decrees by the council of ministers required a number of steps that provided multiple opportunities for "sticky fingers" to block or delay approval.

Bringing high-quality professionals into the ministry was another key element of success. The new staff members were change-agents, full of courage and new ideas they were eager to put into effect. Opponents of the reforms underestimated this new team and were sure the system would defeat them, as generally had occurred in the past. The new team had the skill of understanding agriculture as a system, however, a vision that allowed them to develop a flexible-change strategy that could be adapted to the unpredictable events inherent in political life; when progress on one problem was blocked, they could easily take up another. The team never thought it would be in office long enough to implement the restructuring, yet it was able to accomplish its task quickly once given the opportunity.

Although the reform did not advance according to a preconceived sequence of actions, it did follow a set of priorities. Priority one was trade policy and multilateral financing. Second was managing the consequences of the changes, and only then, if time permitted, came institutional strengthening. Progress occurred as opportunities and organizational capabilities allowed. The method of reform is best explained as an effort to do whatever had the best chance of making a major difference and created pressure to do more; it was not a matter of doing one thing at a time or of doing everything at once.

The reform team had very little experience. As is typical with bright young men and women, especially those with degrees in business administration, they tended at first to underestimate the problems they would face, and their plans were often complex and difficult to explain. The programs with the World Bank and IDB, for example, took much longer to implement than originally expected. The ministry's planning group learned quickly to tailor its programs to the limitations of the prevailing institutions. Working closely with the rest of the economic cabinet members made the implementation of the changes smoother and helped defend them when opposition arose. Attacks were much less likely to succeed as a result of this collaboration. A policy implemented by a team was more credible than one defended by one person or one ministry alone.

Experiments with gradual approaches to change were not successful. The sorghum transition policy is probably the best example. When producer associations were given the opportunity to negotiate transition policies, they would direct all of their effort toward making the transition last as long as they could, rather than prepare themselves for the new situation. Considering the attitudes prevalent in the various organizations, the only way to make headway was to move as quickly as possible and maintain momentum—any hesitation would give opponents the opportunity to tangle the process. Opponents argued that the sector needed time to prepare for the new policies, but it is precisely this type of "preparation" that had precluded progress in the past. The pain of fast adjustment was the result and responsibility of those who did not make the changes they should have made in time: the traditional options for procrastination were now no longer available.

The young team of reformers belied the general opinion that only professional politicians could participate effectively in government. The ministry team was able for a time to persuade the traditional "leaders" that it was in their best interest to promote the changes rather than be swept up by them. Only the campesino leaders continued supporting the changes after the events of February 1992, but they were eventually driven from power. FEDEAGRO's leadership may have been similarly dealt with had it not moved over to the opposition.

The ministry underestimated the need to supply information to the general public. Counting too much on its initial good relations with the associations and its support from AD, it did not work out a comprehensive public relations strategy. This omission proved to be a major mistake when the producer associations broke with the ministry and systematically attacked the new policies, putting the ministry on the defensive. The ministry clearly should have made a greater effort to plant the benefits of agricultural policy reform firmly in the minds of the Venezuelan public.

The ministry was consistent in its application of the new policies. Giving special attention to the areas that appeared to suffer most from the new policies would have created pressures in other parts of the country for similar exceptions. The reform measures eliminated practically all of the traditional tools for providing preferential attention to particular groups. The ministry was not ideologically rigid but, rather, concerned with how to make the best use of limited resources and how to attract more.

## CONCLUSION: THE IMPORTANCE OF CONTINUING THE REFORM

So great was the noise created by the conflict between the ministry and its political opponents that it was difficult to tell how much the advantages of reform were understood. One happy result of the controversy was the higher level of attention given to agricultural issues. A higher level of interest in agricultural issues will hopefully lead to more stable policies and institutions, and thus to a stronger agricultural sector and food system.

The reform effort provided an opportunity to improve the quality of the sector by clearing out much of the clutter (the cobwebs) that has plagued it in the past. The new conditions should allow better access to capital, technology, and new markets—all necessary elements to exploit agriculture's obvious potential for healthy growth. If new generations of agricultural leaders do not capitalize on these new opportunities, spiders will again fill the garden with their cobwebs.

Change by shock is never the best way, but it becomes the only way when policies are not adjusted constantly to realities, or worse, are subverted by individual interests. Shocks have sadly been the norm in Venezuelan political and economic history. No sector has been harder hit than agriculture by sudden change, because it has been the least able to understand and take advantage of the events that surround it. Avoiding future shocks will require leadership, forward vision, and dependable institutions. More than the "rightness" of any given ideological formula, the primary lesson of these reform efforts is the need to create and maintain solid institutions that genuinely uphold the public interest.

NOTES

1. These statistics can be found in the United Nations Food and Agriculture Organization 1991 Annual Report.
2. The statistics on farm size and number of farms can be found in World Bank Report no. 9250-VE, *Venezuela Agricultural Sector Investment Project*, November 6, 1991.
3. See World Bank Report no. 9631-VE, *Venezuela Agricultural Research, Extension and Education*, July 31, 1991.
4. There were also hybrid organizations, such as the coffee associations that were partly cooperatives and partly private companies.
5. For a detailed description of the structure of Venezuelan firms and industries, see Moisés Naím, ed., *Las empresas venezolanas: Su gerencia* (Caracas: Ediciones IESA, 1989).
6. The coffee growers' protest occurred on November 13, 1990, and the sorghum farmers' protest, the Cherokee March, was held in early May 1991. After the February coup attempt, a national day of protest against agriculture policies was held on May 7, 1992. The onion growers protested later that year, on July 7. Congress voted to censure the minister of agriculture on two occasions, on March 17 and May 14, 1992; the measure passed the second time. On November 12, FEDEAGRO announced it refused to meet with the president in the presence of the minister. Finally, in January 1993, FEDECAMARAS called for a national meeting in "support" of agriculture.

7. Sorghum is blended with other domestic and imported cereals and oilseed byprod-
   ucts to make animal feed for poultry, hogs, and milk cattle.
8. World Bank Report no. 9250-VE describes the loan project in detail.
9. World Bank Report no. 9631-VE describes this loan project in detail.
10. Due to differences of opinion between the ministry and the Central Bank, growth
    percentages are stated in ranges or represent the lower estimates. Figure 7.2, how-
    ever, is based on the ministry's statistics.
11. The statistics can be found in Maria A. Cervilla, "Documento de base No. 5," *Proyecto
    Venezuela Competitiva* (Caracas: Editiones IESA, 1994); the sources are indicated as fol-
    lows: 1983–88, ministry of agriculture's *Anuario estadístico agropecuario;* and 1989–92,
    Consejo Consultivo Nacional del Arroz.
12. See D. Gale Johnson, *World Agriculture in Disarray* (New York: St. Martin's Press,
    1991), 159.

*Need for solid instiutions*
*up holding*
*public 'interest*

*III*

# The Venezuelan State

# 8

# Legitimacy, Governability, and Reform in Venezuela

## Daniel H. Levine and Brian F. Crisp

Venezuelan politics and organized social life today face what seem to be insoluble dilemmas. The "crisis" that is so often on the lips of ordinary people and politicians and on the pages of the daily press is commonly described as resting on the drastically weakened legitimacy and operative capacity of the political class and its central institutions. To this declining legitimacy, in turn, is commonly attributed the growing sense of ungovernability, manifest most dramatically in the inability of the political class to contain protest, channel participation, and preserve a monopoly on the use of violence. The dilemma rests on the fact that governability is desired at the same time that far-reaching attacks are launched on the central institutions (above all political parties and the state) that have given the system its strength, unity, and governability in the past.

This growing *desfase* or disjunction between civil society and politics situates Venezuela's crisis in a broad comparative and theoretical context. During the last twenty years, many Latin American countries have witnessed explosive growth in associational life, including popular organizations as well as new middle- and upper-class groups and peak associations (organizations composed of the heads or leaders of associations) of various kinds. The emergence of these new social movements came along with basic changes in regime form. Formation of the groups was spurred by the authoritarian closures of the 1960s and 1970s and, as many observers have noted, their activities helped lay the basis for transitions to democracy in the 1980s. In the 1990s, problems have appeared, primarily in the relations between this new "civil society," politics, and the state. The empowerment derived from civil society has only rarely been translated into enduring political organizations (not to mention power). In particular, the popular movement so carefully constructed over twenty years has lost its clear political voice and now lacks allies and clear channels on the national level.

Until the mid-1980s, Venezuela seemed to have little to do with these trends. The state was strong, the petroleum-based economy solid, and politics hinged on a two-party system whose main players dominated and channeled organized social life. This system is now seriously weakened: it is challenged by military conspirators and outflanked by a host of new organizations springing up at its margins. Efforts are being made to formulate new working rules for national politics, but thus far no clear alternative has appeared that seems capable of giving coherent voice to these new energies and molding them into a viable project around which a renewed democracy can be constructed.

How did the democracy created in Venezuela after 1958 decay? Why have the political parties lost their capacity to encapsulate organized social life? To put the matter in more positive terms, what are the defining characteristics of new organizations that together make up a kind of civil society that is not only separate from the established parties, but also markedly hostile to them? What prospects, if any, do these elements of civil society have for creating effective political expressions, capable of transforming democracy in Venezuela so that it can be maintained and strengthened into the future?

This chapter presents an interpretation of Venezuela's recent experience centered on the reconstruction of legitimacy through the elaboration of alternative patterns of state-society relations. Legitimacy can be an elusive concept, but whatever meaning one attaches to the term, it is clear that more is at issue than words, symbols, or rituals, although these are certainly important. But if saluting the flag, appealing to party loyalty, being stirred by the national anthem, and voluntarily obeying laws (to name just a few examples) are to have enduring social effect, these and other behaviors must find expression in regular, routine forms of organized social and political life.

The Venezuelan political system based its claim to legitimacy since 1958 in structures of identity and action closely tied to political parties. Venezuela has been termed a "party system"[1] because the major mass-based political parties effectively penetrated and controlled organized social life, monopolizing resources and channeling political action. After a few shaky years, the party system consolidated as major oppositions were either defeated (the Left or elements in the military) or co-opted. Accepting the legitimacy of this system meant either organizing to work within structures dominated by parties (including their penetration of other groups) or working within a state apparatus they thoroughly controlled.[2] In the half-century test of wills between parties and the military, parties gained the upper hand.[3] Whether through votes or elections or through intermediary organizations, political parties were key. Parties successfully claimed legitimacy on the basis of their ability to advance claims to social justice, political freedom, and utilitarian calculations of interest.[4]

Beginning in the 1980s, challenges to the legitimacy of this system accumulated: growing voter abstention, citizen dissatisfaction and frustration, escalating violence, decaying coherence in the parties, and growing numbers of public protests, work stoppages, and nonlabor-related strikes of various kinds.[5] Concurrently, there have also been sustained efforts at reform that together reflect a search for a new legitimating model, above all one with more citizen choice, greater decentralization, and more information.

Although the discourse of reform has been circulating at least since the mid-1980s,[6] the issue of reform acquired growing urgency and a sense of crisis with three events that punctuated the process: Black Friday (February 18, 1983), when the bolivar collapsed, initiating a long period of hitherto unknown inflation and stagnation; the bloody and traumatic urban riots touched off on February 27, 1989 (27F), which arose in response to the structural adjustment package of the new government; and two attempted military coups in 1992, on February 4 (4F) and November 27 (27N), the first such events in almost thirty years. Together these events point to a weakening of three core pillars of this system: economic strength (Black Friday), social pacts and peace (27F), and control of the military (4F and 27N).

We argue here that the problem of legitimacy rests in a difficult transition from one institutional pattern to another—from dominant state to lesser role, from dominant parties to more heterogeneous forms, from centralization and national control to variety and diversity. By concentrating on these issues, we in no way deny the key role played by economic decay[7] and splits in the military,[8] but those themes are dealt with in other chapters in the volume. This chapter is organized into four parts. We begin with a brief overview of parties and electoral politics, with particular attention to the implications of electoral and organizational reforms. We then consider nonelectoral forms of participation, especially the role played by the state bureaucracy and the dense network of consultative commissions that runs through most organized public life. The third section outlines civil society (both the idea and the reality) as it has emerged over the last decade in Venezuela. We consider its strengths and limitations as a possible source of new political solutions. Reflection on civil society provides an opportunity to examine the extent to which Venezuelan democracy is undergoing not just a crisis with risk of chaos or overthrow but also, and more centrally, a crisis tied to pressures for democratization. How democratic can democracy be and remain effective? We close with brief lessons to be learned from the Venezuelan experience.

## PARTIES, ELECTIONS, AND DEMOCRATIC POLITICS, 1958 TO 1992

Venezuela's political parties have a long and complex history, with roots in the social transformations spurred by petroleum and expressed in massive economic change, migrations, urbanization, and related sociocultural dynamics. These issues have been extensively studied and we will not reiterate those topics here.[9] Instead, we stress the character of parties, changing patterns of electoral politics, and the implications of recent reforms for the future viability both of parties and of the party system that have dominated modern politics in Venezuela.

It has become common lately in Venezuela to talk about the "Leninist" nature of the parties. The name is used to indicate the all-encompassing penetration and control of organized social life that characterizes modern mass parties in Venezuela. Such was their presence that until recently, it was common for contests of all kinds—from elections in trade unions, professional associations, or student groups to elections of beauty queens—to run along party lines. This pattern arose from the fact that groups and parties grew up together: parties were present at the creation of modern Venezuela. In its day, the pattern of party competition within organizations was itself an innovation, intended to avoid parallelism (for example, multiple-union federations) and in this way reinforce the pacts and agreements made to stabilize democracy after 1958.

Parties also provided an indispensable network of identity and communications in a fragmented and for the most part illiterate society. But in the modern democratic period, the country's accelerated modernization has cut the ground from under this pattern. Parties retained control because by now they were ensconced through laws and institutions, but they no longer were indispensable sources of news and guidance.

It is important to distinguish the short-term from the long-term difficulties facing political parties. The major short-term problem is a combination of growing public discredit (discussed later) with incomplete leadership turnover. Neither of the major parties has managed a thorough transition to new leadership generations. Carlos Andrés Pérez won the 1988 nomination against the wishes of his party and for the 1993 election another past president, Rafael Caldera, insisted on being a candidate for the seventh time (and won). In each case, the unwillingness of established leaders to retire gracefully has exacerbated damaging internal divisions. Internal splits and declining coherence among the various sectors of party leadership intensify the structural difficulties posed by the growing incapacity of leaders to control sectors in the party base. This problem has roots beyond the parties themselves, in the emergence of a civil society with organized expressions that have grown up outside party-controlled networks. Together, these short- and long-term problems make for wrenching difficulties of governance. One of the central features of Venezuelan politics since the Pact of Punto Fijo (1958) has been reliance on interparty pacts, agreements, and accords of all kind, both explicit and tacit.[10] After 4F, the immediate response of the political class was to turn once again to pacts, but efforts at putting together a *gran acuerdo nacional* collapsed. The closest the parties came was in the composition of the Consejo Consultativo, but coalition government itself was volatile and short lived.[11] Declining internal coherence, combined with growing dissensus among the parties, made it impossible to reach durable interparty accords or to unite sectors of the parties around them. In the months after 4F, the result was a pervasive sense of paralysis and immobilism.

We note in summary four tendencies that together suggest both the promise and the problem of change in the system.[12] First is a move from electoral dispersion to two-party competition despite a steady rise in the number of parties competing in national and local elections. Second is a transition from tight national control to decentralization, rooted in electoral reforms including the uncoupling of local and regional from national contests. Third is a shift from extraordinarily high levels of electoral participation to growing abstention, especially in state and local contests. Fourth is the visible decay of tight party discipline. This last aspect has been spurred, as we shall see, by new possibilities for interparty alliances, which arise out of decentralization and the uncoupling of national and local elections.

Joint dominance of electoral politics by AD and COPEI is manifest in a growing share of the total vote at all levels, with increasingly even competition across the entire country. Since 1973, the two parties together have regularly garnered more than 85 percent of the presidential and 75 percent of legislative votes. It is important to note that two-party competition in Venezuela was not an artifact of the electoral system. Although all electoral systems skew results in some way, the particular system of proportional representation in force until recently in Venezuela translates votes into seats with little distortion. Two-party competition stems, rather, from the country's own growing homogenization and from the creation of an effective national market for media and communications.[13] Many analysts have pointed to the similarities between the two main parties: both are catch-all parties, interclass organizations rooted in the center that draw members and voters from a broad social spectrum. This pattern of organization dominated from the outset of modern mass politics and, as Teodoro Petkoff, leader of the leftist MAS party, acknowledges, succeeded precisely because it responded to the real contours of a mobile society with no large or distinct working class. Thus, "in Venezuela, in the 1940s, while Acción Democrática tried to interpret the nation and its problems, communists dedicated most of their efforts to singing the praises of the Stakhanovites of Irkutsk."[14]

The two main parties have also dominated local and governorship races. In the 1989 voting, for example, between them the two parties captured 256 of 269 mayoralties and seventeen of twenty governorships. But a focus on this shared electoral success should not obscure a few important underlying countertrends. Decentralization and the uncoupling of regional and local from national elections have given smaller groups a hitherto nonexistent platform for political action. Costly national campaigns are no longer needed for a local election to be contested effectively. Minority parties have been favored, most notably Causa R in the state of Bolívar. Separate elections for governors, mayors, and municipal councils have legitimized these arenas as relevant political spaces. Groups that compete successfully here have acquired greater autonomy and legitimacy within their parties, as well as a basis for questioning domination by national party elites. Interparty alliances were also important in the 1989 voting, building on tendencies visible in earlier national elections that have produced a growing gap between presidential and legislative votes.

These trends continued in the 1992 elections for governors, mayors, and city councils. AD and COPEI remain jointly dominant, with COPEI emerging as the big winner. AD continued to decline on the regional and local level, while COPEI captured over 40 percent of the total vote and more than half the governorships and mayoralties. COPEI also reelected its governors in key states, such as Carabobo, Miranda, and Zulia, giving the party a corps of young governors poised for future national leadership. MAS remained in a stable third place, winning governorships on its own in one state and in alliance with COPEI in several others, and Causa R continued to expand (taking the mayoralty of Caracas). Two further aspects of this election warrant comment here. In line with the hopes of electoral reformers, voters in December 1992 engaged in extensive ticket-splitting voting, leading for example to overwhelming victories for governors of one party but a relatively even distribution of mayors in several states. This suggests a pattern of voting in response to local issues and to the records of those running for office. In addition, new parties and "electoral groups" (organizations formed to compete in this election only) grew.[15] Indeed, this election witnessed the largest number of electoral alternatives ever presented in Venezuela.

The implementation of reforms has generated new dynamics in the party system. A different generation of leaders is emerging, with careers rooted not in Congress and national directorates but rather in success with state and local voters. Politicians now vie to be candidates for governor and mayor, offices that were not even open to direct election ten years ago. These changes, including increased power for local leaders (both within and independent of the parties), have now required party leaders (with much resistance) to begin crafting new rules of the democratic game. At the same time, smaller parties and groups are increasing their participation at lower levels. Within the party system itself, three political and electoral subsystems have emerged, which, despite some overlap, are substantially independent of one another. At the level of presidential elections, the hegemony of AD and COPEI has been reinforced in recent contests, although the election of Caldera in 1993 may be a harbinger of future change. At the level of national legislative elections, their joint control remains but is now accompanied by a growing tendency to voter dispersion, which permits representation by smaller parties and a host of new electoral groups. At regional and local levels, there is more ticket splitting and a wider range of alternatives.

There are now more elections (and elections of different kinds) than ever before. Until 1979, elections were held only once every five years, and the prevailing electoral format radically reinforced the power of national party leaders. The act of voting was simple, with each voter having two choices: one vote for president and another for all other elected offices. This second vote (the "small card") was cast for a closed party list. National leadership made up the list and set the order of candidates within it. The whole system drastically reinforced the power of national party leaders and structures. As a result, even though the electoral system accurately reflected vote results, it also constrained and limited voter choice. Following the reform of legislation governing municipalities, municipal elections were separated in 1979. Later reforms made governors (previously serving at the pleasure of the president) subject to direct election and created the office of mayor, also directly elected. More recently, provision has been made for direct election of individuals (known in Venezuela as the *personalización del voto*) through a complex system that combines direct voting for candidates (*uninominal*) with open party lists.[16]

These reforms responded to public pressure and criticisms of the party and electoral systems that grew in intensity throughout the 1980s. It was argued that the parties suffocated civil society and that they had become pragmatic and corrupt machines beyond the reach of democratic and ethical controls. Proposals for reform sought to further internal democratization of the parties, especially with regard to the candidate selection process. Reformers aimed to establish conditions for fair play in interparty competition, particularly regarding the regulation of campaigns and their financing, and they hoped to make elected officials more accountable and answerable to the voters. This has led to new and often temporary alliance patterns in Congress and state legislatures. Although AD and COPEI remain dominant at state and local levels, there is a shift in favor of smaller parties. New patterns can also be observed in the electorate: abstention grows and political preferences diversify as one moves from the national to local levels. Although smaller parties have exploited the changes vigorously, the electorate as a whole has reacted with apathy. In general terms, the effort to reform the electoral system also responded to changes in Venezuelan electoral behavior that some observers attribute to deficiencies of the electoral system itself. In particular, the increase in abstention over the past several elections is seen as a reason for electoral reform, in the belief that change is needed to bring about greater participation by the electorate. Until recently, Venezuela pointed with pride to its high levels of electoral participation. Nevertheless, since the first election for municipal councils (1979), abstention has increased steadily. In the national elections of 1978 the rate of abstention was 12.4 percent, but in the municipal elections of 1979 this figure climbed to 27.1 percent. Whereas abstention was 12.1 percent in the 1983 national elections, in the municipal elections the following year it reached 40.7 percent. Finally, in the national elections of 1988 abstention was 18.3 percent, and in the 1989 elections for state governors, mayors, and municipal authorities the figure soared to 54.8 percent and remained at that level in the elections of December 1992, although with notable local and regional variations. In comparative terms, there is nothing unusual about abstention in local and regional elections. But in Venezuela, where the act of voting has long been linked both practically and ideologically to support for democracy itself, abstention looms as a real problem, especially given the broader context of criticism of the system as a whole.

There are a few nuances to abstention that raise particular concern. For example, levels of abstention appear to be closely tied to polarization of the vote between AD and COPEI: the greater their joint share, the higher the abstention. This suggests an economy of the vote argument among voters, who cannot see why voting matters. When asked why they abstained in 1989 or planned to do so in 1992, approximately equal proportions of those polled responded that voting was "not worth the effort"; apparently there was little change in opinion on this issue. But more than twice as many respondents cited disenchantment with the parties in 1992 (44.4 percent) as opposed to 1989 (21.7 percent for 1989).

Abstention is best understood in the context of evolving public attitudes toward democracy and its institutions. Mass publics continue to prize democracy, but their commitment is shot through with cynicism about institutions and a growing rejection of political parties. Available survey data show consistently strong support for democracy as a political system and rejection of military or single-party rule and backing for the right of public criticism by the opposition.[17] When it comes to specifics, however, parties are now regularly rated among the institutions that warrant least confidence (along with the police and the unions). The greatest confidence goes to neighborhood associations, the armed forces, and the church, in that order.[18] It is clear that overcoming voter apathy, creating new, enduring bases for political organization, and democratizing the theory and practice of democracy in Venezuela are the central challenges the parties and party system face in the future. Whatever the situation, it would be foolish to count parties out of the political equation in Venezuela.

The preceding discussion of parties and elections raises important issues about the unintended consequences of reform. On the one hand, reforms intended to create new spaces for citizen participation, make leaders more accountable, and in general infuse the system with new enthusiasm have been greeted with apathy and growing abstention. On the other hand, the reforms have in fact stimulated the emergence of a new group of political leaders (governors of major states and mayors of key cities) and made space for the creation of new political alternatives, including local citizens' groups of all kinds. The tendency to divergent voting patterns at different levels appears likely to grow, making it more difficult to build the legislative alliances required to govern.

In the past, the party system has adapted successfully to situations where the party in power did not have a majority. But in a contest where new agents of political power are being created, power can fragment, resulting in a systemic incapacity to form viable governing alliances. Party discipline and party-government coherence have decayed visibly in recent years, with serious implications for the ability of either the executive branch or Congress to act effectively and with reasonable dispatch. Whatever reform does occur cannot be limited to the electoral sphere, but must include reform of nonelectoral forms of participation and power, including the policy-making process. The next section examines these related issues.

## CONSULTATIVE MEANS OF PARTICIPATION

In conjunction with this electoral system, the Venezuelan state has been characterized by the institutionalization of a consultative policy process. Campaigning and elections go a long way toward explaining how parties have linked government with the masses, but we must turn our attention to other institutions and procedures if we are to understand how private groups, especially the Federation of Chambers of Commerce and Production (FEDECAMARAS) and the Confederation of Venezuelan Workers (CTV), have been incorporated into government decision making. These and other interest groups have been included in policymaking through participation in consultative commissions and bureaucratic agencies that formalize the role of minority interests in the governing process.

The Venezuelan state has grown rapidly to comprise approximately four hundred entities in the decentralized public administration.[19] They take on many legal forms, including public enterprises (with varying degrees of state ownership), autonomous institutes, foundations, and regional development corporations.[20] They undertake activities in areas as diverse as agriculture, livestock, and fishing; mining, manufacturing, and electricity; construction; wholesale and retail commerce; transport, supply, and communications; finance, insurance, and real estate; and personal, social, and community services.[21]

Although the creation of these entities was in part dependent on government income, especially during the oil boom of the 1970s, it is clear that they have been used as a general means of responding to private sector demands.[22] As a result, the Venezuelan state has in one sense become highly decentralized. Specific concerns of different groups are addressed by partially autonomous agencies, each with jurisdiction in a particular substantive area, thus obstructing the maintenance of government coordination and efficiency. Several attempts have been made to reform the method of monitoring and controlling the decentralized public administration (DPA), but none has had much success.[23] CORDIPLAN, the Central Office of Planning and Coordination, is incapable of keeping track of these entities, let alone providing centralized leadership. In fact, a supposedly comprehensive 1990 CORDIPLAN list of institutions in the DPA not only lacked basic information on many entities (such as year of creation) but in addition simply failed to account for some agencies.

The internationally induced trend to privatization that is currently sweeping Latin America may signal a reverse in some of these tendencies. The neoliberal rationale argues that large state bureaucracies have been sources of debt and inefficiency and that private enterprises are better suited to carry out many of these tasks. In reality, the role of the DPA in encouraging indebtedness and competing with private sector initiatives is not so clear. In fact, government spending through bureaucratic agencies provides finance capital for private sector initiatives and consumes private sector production.[24] As a result, it is difficult to see the two as completely contradictory.

The growth of the state apparatus has had other less obvious impacts on the structure of civil society. For example, a great deal of government expenditure has been devoted to higher education. The government bureaucracy is a major source of employment for the graduates of this system. Thus the state has encouraged the creation of a larger middle class both by spending to educate more members of the population and by employing them once they graduate.[25] So the bureaucracy has been used not only to respond to civil society demands, but also, at least in part inadvertently, to change the very composition of civil society. Along with economic stagnation, privatization may further diminish the government's ability to respond to private demands placed on it. In the name of efficiency and refinancing of the public debt, the government is sacrificing the mechanism historically used to link it with organized constituencies and to implement its own development programs.

The growth of the DPA has resulted in decentralization in the sense that constituent groups now exist in virtually every area of policy concern. In another sense, this form of responding to policy demands has merely signaled a shift in the nature of the executive branch rather than a change in the broader balance of forces among government branches. Previously, the state spent money through and employed people primarily in government ministries, or in the centralized public administration (CPA). Over the years, however, the executive has increasingly relied less on the CPA and more on the DPA. In 1960, 70 percent of government expenditure occurred through the centralized public administration and the remaining 30 percent through the decentralized public administration. By 1980 these figures had reversed themselves.[26] Although this has meant less centralized government control, it has not shifted power out of the executive branch.

One area that has remained relatively unexamined is the impact these entities have had on direct political participation.[27] While the Venezuelan state is large, its size does not simply indicate power over civil society. Instead, the numerous bureaucracies serve as avenues of participation for organized groups. The majority of these agencies are governed by boards composed of government officials and representatives of socioeconomic groups. Private groups do not act only as "consumers" of these government outputs or constituents of technocrats controlling pertinent resources. They also participate with equal authority in administering government programs. Approximately 80 percent of the entities in the DPA are governed by private law, with the remaining 20 percent governed by public law. Even the agencies that have been designated as the most "public" contain representatives of private interest groups. On the governing boards of the sixty-eight public law entities created between 1959 and 1989, there have been positions for 305 representatives of private groups; the same boards contained 342 government officials. Clearly, the management of state agencies is shared significantly with private interest groups, and this form of policymaking and execution is an extensively used means of direct participation.

The relative level of participation among socioeconomic sectors, however, reflects economic and organizational inequalities. Some sectors are better able to act as a coherent whole than others. Domestic capitalists and organized labor are the two groups most commonly recognized as legitimate actors, and they are most often represented by FEDECAMARAS and the CTV, respectively. But capital is much more successful at resisting pressure from political parties and pressing its case autonomously. Of the 305 private participants on the governing boards, 30 percent were chosen to represent organized labor and 22 percent were chosen to represent private capital. Middle-class professionals were also represented (11 percent), but they are usually chosen for professional expertise rather than as representatives of a self-conscious coherent class (see table 8.1 for details).

In addition, the relative participation among politically active groups is not influenced by electoral politics. As electoral tides change parties and administrations in power, the consultative form of participation marches on with levels of participation across socioeconomic sectors holding fairly steady.[28] For example, the balance between government officials and representatives of private groups may vary from one administration to another, but this cannot be generalized to the party level.[29]

A study of the role played by the agencies, lenders of services, or encouragers of private sector efforts showed no significant variation across

Table 8.1
PARTICIPANTS IN PUBLIC LAW BUREAUCRATIC INSTITUTIONS
CREATED BY EACH PARTY AND ADMINISTRATION[a]

| | Govt. Officials (%) | Economically Defined Groups (%) | Private Capital (%) | Middle-Class Professionals (%) | Labor (%) | Non-economically Defined Groups (%) | Unclassifiable (%) |
|---|---|---|---|---|---|---|---|
| Total | 52.86 | 29.37 | 10.20 | 5.26 | 13.91 | 1.70 | 16.08 |
| AD | 47.51 | 30.85 | 9.70 | 5.22 | 16.42 | 1.49 | 19.65 |
| COPEI | 61.63 | 26.12 | 11.02 | 5.31 | 9.80 | 2.04 | 10.20 |
| Betancourt (AD) (1959–64) | 27.03 | 21.62 | 8.11 | 5.40 | 8.11 | 0 | 51.35 |
| Leoni (AD) (1964–1969) | 43.12 | 42.50 | 12.50 | 5.00 | 25.00 | 1.25 | 13.12 |
| Caldera (COPEI) (1969–74) | 51.09 | 26.09 | 11.96 | 3.26 | 10.87 | 1.09 | 21.74 |
| Pérez (AD) (1974–79) | 50.97 | 25.81 | 9.03 | 5.81 | 10.97 | 2.58 | 20.64 |
| Herrera (COPEI) (1979–84) | 67.97 | 26.14 | 10.46 | 6.54 | 9.15 | 2.61 | 3.27 |
| Lusinchi (AD) (1984–89) | 66.00 | 20.00 | 4.00 | 4.00 | 12.00 | 0 | 14.00 |

[a]Numbers are the percentage of participants from the category, represented vertically, during the time period, represented horizontally.
*Source:* Brian Crisp, "Tyranny by the Minority: Institutional Control of Participation in Venezuelan Democracy," unpublished Ph.D. dissertation, University of Michigan, Ann Arbor, 1992, 163.

parties.[30] If capitalists were highly represented in COPEI-created agencies to encourage private sector efforts, they were highly represented in AD-created institutions of the same type. One must conclude from the extensiveness of their representation and their constancy across time that these groups and their place in the political system are outside of electoral control. This situation calls for a reinterpretation of the way in which the growth of the state bureaucracy has resulted in decentralization. It has diffused decision-making power and made the state accessible at more distinct points, but it has not led to decentralization in the sense of allowing for participation by new and distinct groups. If anything, it has isolated a limited cast of players from pressure by the rest of civil society.

In addition to the DPA, consultative commissions have also been a common means of doing politics in Venezuela during the democratic era. Between the inauguration of Rómulo Betancourt in February 1959 and the end of 1989, the Venezuelan government created 330 advisory commissions with participants named to represent interest groups or entire socioeconomic sectors.[31] These commissions may be either temporary or permanent and have addressed issues as diverse as the location of pig farms to the nationalization of petroleum. Although the decisions of these deliberative councils are nonbinding, they have performed duties as important as drafting legislation, studying issues, and advising policymakers. Given the extensive decree powers of the executive, they open the "legislative" process to organized interest groups. Again, the access created by this form of decision making is characterized by uneven representation across socioeconomic sectors. Economically defined groups representing capital, labor, and middle-class professionals participate more than five times as often as noneconomically defined interest groups (see table 8.2). Among socioeconomic sectors, domestic capital significantly out-participates all others,

Table 8.2
RELATIVE PARTICIPATION IN COMMISSIONS
ORGANIZED BY THE STATE ROLE BEING PURSUED[a]

| | Govt. Officials (%) | Private Capital (%) | Middle-Class Professionals (%) | Labor (%) | Non-economically Defined Groups (%) | Unclassifiable (%) |
|---|---|---|---|---|---|---|
| Producer commissions | 42.55 | 10.64 | 6.38 | 10.64 | 2.13 | 27.66 |
| | (1) | (3/4) | (5) | (3/4) | (6) | (2) |
| Regulator commissions | 57.52 | 17.34 | 9.92 | 8.91 | 2.48 | 4.81 |
| | (1) | (2) | (3) | (4) | (6) | (5) |
| Planner commissions | 63.71 | 16.30 | 9.63 | 6.67 | 0 | 3.70 |
| | (1) | (2) | (3) | (4) | (6) | (5) |
| Service commissions | 57.64 | 8.37 | 11.82 | 9.20 | 4.60 | 8.37 |
| | (1) | (4/5) | (2) | (3) | (6) | (4/5) |
| Encourager commissions | 45.91 | 17.13 | 6.16 | 8.29 | 13.77 | 8.75 |
| | (1) | (2) | (6) | (4) | (3) | (5) |
| General commissions | 65.33 | 17.44 | 3.91 | 7.29 | 2.85 | 3.17 |
| | (1) | (2) | (4) | (3) | (6) | (5) |
| All commissions | 56.67 | 15.51 | 7.45 | 8.06 | 5.95 | 6.35 |
| | (1) | (2) | (4) | (3) | (6) | (5) |

Source: Crisp, "Tyranny by the Minority," 116.
[a]Numbers in parentheses are the rank of each category of participants within that type of commission.
Note: Percentages may be greater than or less than 100 due to rounding.

especially in commissions that regulate the economy and encourage private sector efforts.

The relative levels of participation among socioeconomic sectors have shown some variation across administrations but not parties, thus emphasizing the importance of the executive in Venezuelan politics.[32] Figure 8.1 shows the trends in the creation of both DPA agencies and consultative commissions and the socioeconomic sectors that participate in them. The organizational and political characteristics that give some groups numerically superior influence relative to others in any given commission are multiplied throughout the system because there is no central coordination of this fragmented means of making decisions. Furthermore, the nature of these advisory commissions, their location in the executive branch, and the groups that participate in them all distance themselves from electoral control. These institutions are created to facilitate policymaking among government/party officials, representatives of private capital (especially FEDECAMARAS), and representatives of organized labor (the CTV). In the process, an overwhelming "mobilization of bias" is created as the commissions operate to organize some groups into politics while organizing others out. Through their control of the organizational characteristics of Venezuelan policymaking, the three major groups are thereby able to keep some issues off the political agenda and some actors out of the political arena. At the same time, they maintain balance and fluidity among themselves by creating a host of institutions, each of which provides an opportunity to struggle over relative participation and influence over policy.

Combined, the two arenas of electoral politics and executive commissions characterize the diverse and institutionalized links between civil society and the political system and account for the stability experienced by Venezuelan democracy until recently. The very success of these institutions, however, resulted in their failure to evolve along with civil society. Because they so effectively reflected the status quo of 1958, these arrangements made it possible for key actors to control policymaking and exclude new groups. The end result was ossification of the system and growing difficulty for new groups and issues to acquire legitimacy.

As the social structure evolved, groups that were initially strong became less representative of their given constituencies, and new groups sometimes arose to challenge them. In some sectors, new groups did not emerge for long periods despite the growing distance between political elites and masses. Given the institutionalized position of AD and COPEI in the electoral and patronage arena, and of FEDE-

## Figure 8.1
## Relative participation in commissions and the decentralized public administration

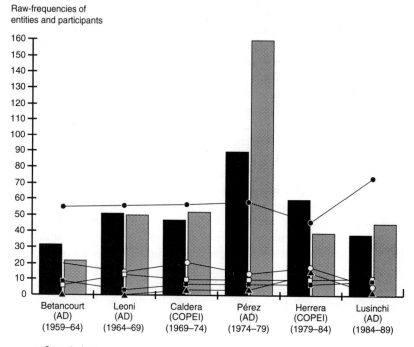

Raw-frequencies of
entities and participants

|  | Betancourt (AD) (1959–64) | Leoni (AD) (1964–69) | Caldera (COPEI) (1969–74) | Pérez (AD) (1974–79) | Herrera (COPEI) (1979–84) | Lusinchi (AD) (1984–89) |

▨ Commissions
■ DPA
● Govt. Officials
○ Capital
■ Professionals
□ Labor
▲ Noneconomically Defined Groups

*Note:* Bars for entities created by each administration within the DPA include both public and private law agencies, while lines representing participation by each socioeconomic subsector reflect commissions and public law entities only.
*Source:* Crisp, "Tyranny by the Minority", 129, 142, 155.

CAMARAS and the CTV in the consultative arena, the political system did not reflect changes in society. As society and the issues confronting government became more complex, the old system of conciliation became increasingly less suitable. For example, the Lusinchi administration created the National Commission of Costs, Prices, and Salaries

(CONACOPRESA) to deal with the economic stagnation and decline of the mid-1980s. This commission was composed of three executive branch officials, a representative of FEDECAMARAS, and a representative of the CTV. After achieving many of its objectives for participating in the commission, namely the increase of government-controlled prices, FEDECAMARAS chose to withdraw, and the government refused to replace the representative with one from FEDEINDUSTRIA, a more nationalist and progressive group, despite the fact that this organization of relatively smaller capitalists had originally been cited for participation in the commission.[33] The government apparently believed that only FEDECAMARAS could speak for domestic capitalists and only this longtime participant could be a legitimate political actor.

It is of serious concern that this form of policymaking may have kept many sectors, or interest groups, from even organizing in the first place. When the legitimate political arena and its participants are identified through formal institutional arrangements of the kind just outlined, this apparent monopoly on the system discourages organization by unrepresented sectors and delegitimizes the system of policymaking and politics among important sectors of the society. In recent years, groups identifying themselves explicitly as "civil society" have pressed vigorously for a change in the rules of the game. The next section considers the meaning of "civil society" in Venezuela and how it relates to the electoral and consultative institutions created since 1958.

## THE EMERGENCE OF CIVIL SOCIETY

*Civil society* is an elusive term that is hard to define with precision. As used in Venezuela, the term embraces groups that are nationally organized as well as a host of regional and local associations. Even a short list would have to include neighborhood barrio movements, cooperatives, human rights groups, nongovernmental organizations (NGOs), private foundations, and a range of groups working to promote coordination and common action among all of the foregoing. The self-conscious effort by elements of "civil society" to present a common front, join forces, and reach beyond specific concerns to achieve a voice in policymaking and politics is one of the new features Venezuelan politics has displayed in recent years. Along this line, one would also have to include a range of recent efforts (also national, regional, and local) to organize new political movements and parties.

The term *civil society* came into wide use in Venezuela only as of the early 1980s as fixation on building institutions that provided for conciliation among the then key players led to a rigidification of the political system that ignored, if not explicitly denied, continuing social change.[34] Society grew faster and further than the political system. Old ways of doing politics were outpaced.[35]

The "emergence of civil society" often has been depicted as primarily defensive. In an impersonal and bureaucratized world, small groups of citizens build circles of intimacy, meaningful relations, and rights. Jürgen Habermas explicitly links this reaction by "life worlds" against systems to problems of legitimacy that in his view arise when the principles and justifications that institutions project no longer find significant response from or correspondence in ordinary life. Habermas further insists on the self-sustaining quality of such actions, in which the free exercise of a claim to reason and of independent judgment acquires "a stubbornly transcending power because it is renewed with each act of unconstrained understanding."[36]

There is much evidence of this process in the origins of what we see as civil society in Venezuela today. For example, the neighborhood movements, in all their many manifestations, clearly began as uncoordinated efforts by urban, middle-class citizens to resist unplanned city growth and to defend their neighborhoods.[37] In similar ways, a number of human rights organizations established in the 1980s began as responses to specific abuses.[38] The women's movement was energized by the reform of the civil code and grew subsequently through the 1980s to establish nets of national coordination. Even cooperatives, by all accounts the most widespread and best rooted of the civil associations, began in many instances as efforts at economic self-defense by small groups of citizens desiring better prices, more accessible capital or credit, better transport, and so on.

But the story does not end here. The vast majority of these movements do more than protest—they also propose, resist, and construct at the same time. The whole process involves an activation of social and cultural energies that for the most part has taken place outside the party-related net of associations.[39] Indeed, a particularity of the discourse of civil society in Venezuela is that political parties tend to be explicitly excluded, and to date (in contrast to cases like Peru or Brazil), no parties or explicitly political movements have emerged out of new civil society organizations. This doubtless is part of the reaction against past party domination or any organized expression of social interests. One need not agree that such movements are the seed of a potential new political culture[40] to accept their importance as a sign of the demystification of politics. Increasingly, the tools of association are in many hands, and politics are no longer the exclusive province of political leaders.[41]

This creative process of growth and expansion is visible in four broad areas: reconceiving the meaning of civil society and of popular action; expanding from a single issue or narrow territorial base; searching for allies and developing explicit coordination structures; and growing interaction with government. Limitations of space preclude a detailed discussion here, but for purposes of illustration we briefly consider the experience of the Centro al Servicio de la Acción Popular (CESAP), Center for Service to Popular Action, and of the neighborhood movements, hereafter referred to as *vecinos*. CESAP is a national organization that began as a service to popular action and has evolved as a broad NGO that combines training programs and a host of short courses for local groups with promotion of small business, operation of officially contracted literacy or child-care programs, and major media efforts. The *vecino* movement began with loose collections of local associations pursuing neighborhood self-defense; it has now evolved into a range of regional and national organizations with important links to media, political reform, and alternative political movements. Both movements are characterized by creative and daring leaders willing to take risks and break established patterns as they reach for a new role.

CESAP, founded in the mid-1970s by a priest who wanted to establish a wholly independent organization that would enable him to work closely with popular groups, evolved into one of Venezuela's major and model NGOs.[42] CESAP and other groups, which had a strong populist tone at the start, slowly yielded to growing interaction with the state. As the state began to shed social welfare functions and international lenders insisted on local involvement in projects, these groups developed confidence, which was reinforced by *articulación* (the bringing of groups together in a variety of meetings); they began to see the state as a partner. The emergence of this new stance and role in policymaking brought considerable criticism of CESAP and similar groups.

After neighborhood associations burst on the scene in middle-class areas of Caracas in the 1970s, they took a few related paths.[43] The Federation of Urban Community Associations (FACUR) was established in 1971 as a coordinating body in Caracas, and would serve as a model as some 15,000 similar associations and federations emerged all over the country. Since their inception, municipal reform (and related electoral reform) have been the central objectives of these organizations. Apart from them, a major development has been the networks centered on the school for neighborhood groups, the School of Neighborhood Communities of Venezuela (EVV). Consolidated on the national level in the mid-1980s, EVV has mounted a regular program of courses for associations and local public officials as well as an active media campaign.

The steady expansion and diversification of the *vecinos* movement has made it a prime target for party penetration. Over the last three years, the three major parties (AD, COPEI, and MAS) have made concerted efforts to work within and perhaps dominate the movement. In response, and as a logical outgrowth of the reform focus that initially spurred the movement, there has been a notable migration of leaders and organized groups into explicitly political vehicles such as Respuesta en Democracia (RED).

Combining themes of civil society explicitly with politics leads to reflection on the democratizing power of experiences like neighborhood organizations or small NGOs. Accommodating new channels for citizen participation and in this way "democratizing democracy" have been central to the reform programs under way for over a decade. As we have seen, pressures for reform have roots that extend well beyond institutional engineering and the details of altered electoral systems. One way to understand these pressures is to see them as the results of democracy itself. They gain strength from an organized civil society that simply did not exist when the party system took on its current form. The defining traits of Venezuelan political parties—centralization, national organization, and a constant effort to penetrate, encapsulate, and control organized social life along party lines—clash increasingly with the existence of a host of groups and movements that have sprung up throughout the social order, independent of party-controlled networks.[44]

It remains unclear how and to what extent groups like these will be able to consolidate and form viable political alternatives. The groups now emerging in civil society and reaching for political expression have many strengths. They are organizationally flexible, are innovative, and have daring and creative leaders. They have few overhead costs and are rooted in a general disposition to organize that makes for great flexibility—if defeated in one form, they can quickly shift terrain and emerge again elsewhere. But there are important weaknesses, too. Success will not be easy, because more is at stake than simply representing new social forces. The task at hand is not simply to represent, but rather to do so in a way that provides reasonable order and governability in democratic politics.[45]

The dilemma, as yet unresolved, is that governability is desired at the same time that attacks are launched on the very elements (the parties and central state institutions) that have provided strength, unity, and governability in the past. The present generation of activists and emerging political leaders in Venezuela will have to figure out how to combine the virtues of decentralization and stimulus of participation with the advantages of unified leadership and strong, disciplined organizations that have been at the heart of politics since 1958. At issue is not so much the formation of new political parties as it is making a successful transition to a more diversified kind of political system where there are more spaces for public participation and greater accountability by leaders at all levels.[46] Amparo Menéndez-Carrión, an Ecuadoran political scientist, argues that the transition is from "a historical style of governability rooted in an authoritarian ethos, to governabilities in which the state and its agents are disposed and required to assume a role of greater accountability to those they represent." This "requires a campaign, unprecedented in the history of the state in Latin America, to return to civil society its condition of citizenship."[47]

Our concentration on new groups in civil society does not mean that old groups will disappear. Obviously, class cleavages and organizations representing labor and capital will be important in Venezuela's future. Any new political formulation will have to take account of business groups and labor unions; in fact, their privileged position in the established hierarchy makes it likely that they will exercise considerable influence over any transition. The same holds true for political parties.

We are returned then to the theme of institutions. Earlier we described how the foundational pattern of institutions in Venezuela after 1958 had served to encourage dialogue among key sectors while at the same time preventing change and isolating the policy-making sphere from organized social pressure. But concluding that old institutions need to change is not enough. The changing organization of civil society—both in terms of new groups and in terms of internal relations within the traditional groups—must be accompanied by a new set of governmental institutions that recognizes and takes advantage of these developments. Currently the executive branch dominates by virtue of its jurisdiction over the enormous state bureaucracy and the decree power it exercises with the help of consultative commissions. This concentration of power in unelected bodies is in part responsible for the rigidity of the old system, and any reformulated process must entail the movement of decision making into bodies that are more available to popular control.

For example, if the two main parties were indeed to become revitalized and more internally democratic, the strengthening of the legislative branch and an increased role for it in policymaking would improve responsiveness. The same holds for decentralization and the transfer of functions and resources to state and local governments, a process only now getting under way on a large scale. Decision making in bodies and at levels where officials are subject to reelection would ensure greater contact with the populace. Likewise, although interest groups would naturally continue to play a strong role, there is already growing diversity among them and their influence could, at least in principle, come under growing public scrutiny.

Other institutional arrangements might further the purpose equally well. For example, the current trends toward privatization, historic inefficiencies, and declining government revenue have forced the state bureaucracy to rely on private groups for delivery of services. This form of decentralization provides a nonelectoral type of participation that strengthens group awareness and confidence. Local communities organize in response to government decentralization as well as to encourage more of it. The government's increasing attention to NGOs, including the appointment of a presidential commissioner for NGOs, signals the state's interest in building new institutional links within a diversifying civil society. No doubt these institutions may seek to control and channel, but they will also provide access to the policy-making process.

Moving power to the legislative or regional arenas would not solve all of the country's problems, however, even if civil society were characterized by more open and democratic organizations. Yet the need for political space for an evolving civil society, regardless of institutional form, is critical. The changes occurring in Venezuela are profound, but results are unclear. It may be that, as posed, the dilemma of governability/legitimacy/reform is insoluble. But if the issues presented here can be addressed successfully, Venezuela will have managed a democratization of its own democracy with important implications for the general process of transition to and consolidation of democracy throughout Latin America.

## WHAT HAVE WE LEARNED?

A few lessons stand out from examination of the Venezuelan experience, the first and most striking of which is that nothing lasts forever. The world can be turned upside down in short order, and what gave stability and unity in the past can present enormous problems for survival in the future. Since the 1960s, scholars have praised Venezuelan politics for their strong parties, powerful state, and leadership capabilities. But these qualities, which long provided the foundation of stability, are now in crisis. Venezuela in the 1990s finds itself at a critical juncture, with issues of governability and legitimacy as real as they were in 1958. If civilian rule and open, pluralistic politics are to survive in Venezuela, it is essential that institutions and connections between elites and masses be rebuilt on new models. Stated differently, the first lesson is that early success is no guarantee of future equilibrium; each situation generates its own dynamics and rigidities.

In addition, we can point to the specific traits that allow civilian rule to be institutionalized in a country that until 1958 was better known for its military *caudillos* than for its civil traditions. These characteristics include the building of strong ties between the elite and the masses through extensive networks of grass-roots organizations knit together on a national scale by the political parties. The history of Acción Democrática is a classic case in point.[48] AD emerged in the 1940s as the expression of change in Venezuelan society, drawing rural and urban sectors together in a coherent program and gradually extending its influence to penetrate professional groups, chambers of commerce, student organizations, and so on. As a result of those organizational links, Venezuelan politics could afford to risk electoral participation while also guaranteeing key sectors (like business, the military, and the church) that such participation would be channeled and would never risk their elimination. This combination of elite consensus with mass mobilization is what made pacts possible after 1958, whereas they had failed in the 1940s when elite agreement was lacking.[49]

On the negative side, we can learn from Venezuela that settling for the art of the possible and stressing stability as a goal in itself can become an excuse for avoiding change. The necessary accommodations of one period all too easily become the axioms of another; rules and procedures freeze in place. It is not only that key sectors ignored the evolution of civil society. More to the point, they were able to do this because the institutional arrangements they had constructed isolated them from the impact of these changes. The channeling role played by parties in the electoral process and their own lack of internal democracy meant that, until recently, declines in voter participation found little response. Likewise, the consultative nature of decision making insulated powerful elites from challenges arising either within their own constituency or from emerging groups.

Would Venezuelan politics have entered a crisis without the economic decline of the 1980s? Such counterfactual conditionals are always difficult to answer, but on the basis of the analysis presented here, we argue that political protest and a search for alternative forms of organization are independent of economic difficulties, although obviously sharpened by them. The emergence of criticisms and reform initiatives, ranging from the *vecinos* to the reform of the state and its relation with the economy, all predate the sense of heightened crisis that arrived after 1989.[50] What arguably makes the crisis after 1989 more of a "crisis" in the common sense of the term is the rising civil violence and the clear discontent in the military, punctuated by the two unsuccessful coups of 1992.

The second lesson is that when potential disaster strikes, it helps to have a reform process under way. Although reform initiatives carry no guarantee of success, in Venezuela it seems clear that the process of political reform during the 1980s provided a point of reference for action, a context for nonviolent citizen activism, and a collection of leaders who rapidly acquired national prominence (for example, Oswaldo Álvarez Paz, governor of Zulia). Indeed, Venezuelans have been continuously engaged in reform initiatives since the mid-1980s, and COPRE was in place before this crisis assumed "crisis proportions." Although COPRE's future role is unclear, there can be no doubt that through its publications, seminars, and workshops COPRE helped to place reform on the national agenda.

A third lesson concerns the importance of publicizing reforms and carefully building political coalitions to support them. Structural adjustment programs carry heavy social costs and have "succeeded" only through careful coalition building. Failure to do so has cost dearly. Party leaders relied on a honeymoon effect from the elections, combined with the power of existing party structures, to contain dissent. But the honeymoon was short, and if anything is clear by now, it is that leadership can no longer rely on party machinery to channel dissent and control unrest.

Fourth, although reform is important in itself, it is no panacea. Reforms have a price and carry unexpected and possibly negative consequences. This is apparent in the case of electoral reform and holds equally for efforts at constitutional change that have generated enormous expectations in Venezuela. At issue is more than the question of whether or not any constitutional reform can possibly satisfy all the hopes placed in it (an unlikely prospect). In more general terms, it is worth noting how legalistic much of the debate about reform has been. There is nothing wrong with legal reform—indeed, a focus on legal reform suggests a willingness to work within standard procedures. Nevertheless, legal reform and institutional engineering have gained prominence in direct relation to the decline in the perceived legitimacy of the party system. As long as the sociological basis of the parties remained strong, parties could provide stability and strength to the political system regardless of formal electoral arrangements or the structure of the state (for example, parliamentary or presidential). With the decay of parties as a model, institutional engineering has moved to center stage, but is likely to work only if basic pillars of the system and in particular links between state and society are reformulated in ways that remain acceptable to broad constituencies. Exaggerated hopes should not be placed on constitutional reform, which ground to a halt at the end of 1992.

The fifth lesson concerns the maintenance of public order and of control over the legitimate use of violence. The first aspect is often ignored in discussions of reform, but is vital nonetheless, given the role that disturbances and a sense of chaos have typically played as pretexts for military action. By itself, repression has considerable risks, for example isolating the government and making it rely too much on the military. Yet maintenance of order, through an uncorrupted police force and a reliable, respected judiciary, is a worthwhile lesson to learn. The more general point linking legitimacy to a monopoly over the use of force is a classic component of any discussion of legitimacy. The events of 1992 raise serious and as yet unresolved questions about the government's ability to identify and control dissent in the armed forces.

A sixth lesson, unscientific though it may be, is that it helps to be lucky. Luck and his characteristic boldness probably saved the day for Carlos Andrés Pérez, who outflanked the insurgents on 4F by addressing the mass media and rallying support. This same boldness and daring, now exercised in the name of fundamental systemic reform, also characterizes many movements in civil society, which have staked their existence on dramatic changes in orientation and expansion of their spheres of action.

The last lesson we can learn from Venezuela is that we are not through learning yet. How Venezuelans deal with the issues of legitimacy that confront them at this time will provide scholars and politicians in other countries with a set of new lessons. The ingredients of a new and more democratic democracy are at hand in Venezuela, but the threat to continued civilian rule is present and clear. The state-society relations outlined here are not the only source of the immediate crisis. That crisis, as depicted and understood in Venezuela, has its roots in institutional decay exacerbated by economic decline and growing military discontent. But the transformations described in this chapter indicate that, in the long term, efforts to stabilize the situation cannot be based on a return to the old formulas. The challenge is to reconstruct legitimacy and readapt politics to social life in creative ways.

The authors thank Margaret Martin, Juan Carlos Rey, Pilar Arroyo, Amparo Menéndez-Carrión, Catalina Romero, and Joseph Tulchin for comments on earlier versions of this chapter.

# NOTES

1. See Daniel H. Levine, *Conflict and Political Change in Venezuela* (Princeton: Princeton University Press, 1973); Daniel H. Levine and Miriam Kornblith, "Venezuela: The Life and Times of the Party System," in Scott Mainwaring and Timothy Scully, eds., *Building Democratic Institutions: Parties and Party Systems in Latin America* (Stanford: Stanford University Press, forthcoming); and Juan Carlos Rey, "La democracia venezolana y la crisis del sistema populista de conciliación," *Revista de estudios políticos* (Madrid), no. 74 (1991): 553–78.

2. In this regard, bear in mind Rómulo Betancourt's famous statement that "the people" in the abstract do not exist—the people are the political parties, the unions, the organized economic sectors, associations, and the like. Betancourt underscored the mediating role of the parties, and as Toro Hardy indicates, suggested that "in other words, what counts is not the citizen considered as an individual, but rather the citizen organized around one of these intermediate structures"; see Alfredo Toro Hardy, "Cual democracia?" *El Globo*, September 8, 1992.

3. See Manuel Caballero, *Las Venezuelas del siglo veinte* (Caracas: Grijalbo, 1988).

4. See Juan Carlos Rey, *El futuro de la democracia en Venezuela* (Caracas: Ediciones Instituto International de Estudios Avanzados, 1989); idem, "La democracia venezolana"; and Diego Bautista Urbaneja, *Pueblo y petróleo en la política venezolana del siglo XX* (Caracas: Centro de Estudios Petroleros, 1992).

5. On demonstrations and disturbances, see the data in Vice Adm. Elías R. Daniels, *Militares y Democracia* (Caracas: Ediciones Centauro, 1992), appendix, tables 2–4; in Programa Venezolano de Educación-Acción en Derechos Humanos (PROVEA), *Situación de los derechos humanos en Venezuela informe anual* (Caracas: PROVEA, 1991, 1992); and in PROVEA, *Boletín de derechos humanos y coyuntura* (Caracas: PROVEA, 1991, 1992). Reliable strike data are difficult to come by, but the growing tension among the government, the party, and the union movement has measurably weakened AD's capacity to count on labor leaders for control. As a high-level AD official told one of the authors, "The situation is very agitated. . . . Nowadays people continuously criticize the union movement—business groups and the Right criticize it a lot, but the fact is that within this consensus I told you about, Venezuelan democracy managed twenty years without strikes. And now they tell me that this is the country that will implement the best economic policy in the world and do it on the basis of strikes, dissent, student riots, deaths of students, and all that! It just isn't possible, no chance"; interview, August 31, 1992.

6. Reform has been carried forward, for example, at the state and national levels by COPRE (Presidential Commission for the Reform of the State), reaffirmed in the Pacto para la Reforma del Estado (signed between the major parties in September 1990), and implemented in significant changes of the electoral laws and related measures, beginning a process of decentralization. In the aftermath of 4F, projects under way (in a congressional commission) to reform the constitution gained some urgency as well, but ultimately came to a standstill. See Miriam Kornblith, "Reforma constitucional, crisis política, y estabilidad de la democracia en Venezuela," *Politeia*, no. 15 (1993). At the same time, a campaign to elect a constituent assembly with wide popular participation that would write a wholly new constitution (bypassing the reform project being drawn up in Congress) failed.

7. See Vanessa Cartaya and Yolanda D'Elia, *La pobreza en Venezuela: Realidad y políticas* (Caracas: Centro al Servicio de la Acción Popular—Centro de Investigaciones Socio Religiosas, 1991), and Gustavo Márquez, *Escaleras y ascensores: La distribución del ingreso en la década de los ochenta* (Caracas: Ediciones IESA, 1990).

8. See Daniels, *Militares y democracia*; Alberto Müller Rojas, *Relaciones peligrosas militares, política y estado* (Caracas: Fondo Editorial Tropykos, 1992); Enrique Ochoa Antich, *Los golpes de febrero: 27 febrero 1989–4 febrero 1992* (Caracas: Fuentes Editores, 1992); and Enrique Ochoa Antich, *Carta a los militares de nuestra generación: Nos alzamos por la constitución: Carta de los oficiales del MBR 200* (Caracas: Fuentes Editores, 1992).

9. See Caballero, *Las Venezuelas del siglo veinte*; Levine, *Conflict and Political Change in Venezuela*; Daniel H. Levine, "Venezuela: The Nature, Sources, and Future Prospects of Democracy," in Larry Diamond, Seymour Martin Lipset, and Juan J. Linz, eds., *Democracy in Developing Countries, Volume Four: Latin America* (Boulder: Lynne Rienner, 1989), 247–89; Terry Karl, "Petroleum and Political Pacts: The Transition to Democracy in Venezuela," *Latin American Research Review* 22, no. 1 (1987): 63–94; Rey, "La democracia venezolana"; and Bautista Urbaneja, *Pueblo y petróleo.*

10. See Eduardo Arroyo Talavera, *Elecciones y negociaciones: Los límites de la democracia en Venezuela* (Caracas: Fondo Editorial CONICIT-Pomaire, 1988); Karl, "Petroleum and Political Pacts"; and Levine, *Conflict and Political Change in Venezuela.*

11. As one AD leader put it, "The real problem that I see as coming before any other in Venezuelan democracy—whether or not its economic model is exhausted and whether or not its models of deepening democracy by making way for reformed parties and new kinds of associations with new goals is realistic—is the fact that none of this can be accomplished on the basis of dissensus, and what we have now is just that, dissensus"; interview, August 31, 1992.

12. For details, see Daniel H. Levine and Miriam Kornblith, "Venezuela: The Life and Times of the Party System," in Mainwaring and Scully, *Building Democratic Institutions* (forthcoming).

13. See Levine, "Venezuela: The Nature, Sources and Future Prospects for Democracy"; Levine and Kornblith, "Venezuela: The Life and Times of the Party System"; and José Enrique Molina, *El sistema electoral venezolano y sus consecuencias políticas* (Valencia: Vadell Hermanos, 1991).

14. Teodoro Petkoff, *Razón y pasión del socialismo en Venezuela* (Caracas: Ediciones Centauro, 1973), 66–67.

15. Because of disputed results in several states, definitive outcomes were not available at the time of this writing.

16. See Levine and Kornblith, "Venezuela: The Life and Times of the Party System," and Matthew Shugart, "Leaders, Rank and File, and Constituents: Electoral Reform in Colombia and Venezuela," *Electoral Studies* 11, no. 1 (1992): 21–45.

17. Voters favor democracy and reject dictatorship, but when asked whether they were satisfied with the current system, less than a fifth said "yes," over half "a little," and more than a quarter "not at all." In the same way, almost 58 percent reported that democracy brought no benefits whatsoever, with 19 percent citing liberty of expression and barely 17 percent social services. The proportion of respondents identifying themselves as militants or sympathizers of political parties has fallen steadily from almost 48.8 percent in 1973 to 38.4 percent ten years later and 25.3 percent in 1991. Over the same period, self-identified independents rose from 19.2 percent to 69.1 percent of national samples. In chapter 3 of this volume, Andrew Templeton demonstrates a long-term decline in expectations of a better life, along with voter conviction that a change in government would make little difference.

18. Data obtained from Consejo Supremo Electoral (CSE), 1991.

19. CORDIPLAN, *Listado de entes ordenados por la naturaleza jurídica* (Caracas: Dirección del Sector Público, CORDIPLAN, 1980).

20. See Alan R. Brewer Carías, "La distinción entre las personas públicas y las personas privadas y el sentido de la problemática actual de la clasificación de los sujetos de derecho," *Revista de la Facultad de Derecho* 57 (Caracas, April 1976): 115–35; Brewer Carías, *Regímen jurídico de las empresas públicas en Venezuela* (Caracas: Centro Latinoamericano de Administracion para el Desarrollo, 1980); Jesús Caballero Ortiz, *Los institutos autónomos* (Caracas: Editorial Jurídica Venezolana, 1984); and Caballero Ortiz, *Las empresas públicas en el derecho* (Caracas: Editorial Jurídica Venezolana, 1982).

21. Miriam Kornblith and Thais Maingón, *Estado y gasto público en Venezuela, 1936–1980* (Caracas: Universidad Central de Venezuela y Ediciones de la Biblioteca, 1985).

22. Bigler, 1981.

23. Janet Kelly de Escobar, "Las empresas del estado: Del Lugar comun al sentido comun," in Moisés Naím and Ramón Piñango, eds., *El caso Venezuela es una ilusión de*

*armónia,* 4th ed. (Caracas: Ediciones, Instituto Internacional de Estudios Avanzados, 1988).

24. Ibid.

25. Carlos A. Sabino, *Empleo y gasto público en Venezuela* (Caracas: Editorial PANAPO, 1988).

26. Kornblith and Maingón, *Estado y gasto público en Venezuela,* 221.

27. See Arroyo Talavera, *Elecciones y negociaciones,* and Brian F. Crisp, "Tyranny by the Minority: Institutional Control of Participation in Venezuelan Democracy," unpublished Ph.D. dissertation, University of Michigan, Ann Arbor, 1992.

28. Crisp, "Tyranny by the Minority."

29. One exception is that AD administrations do seem to favor representatives of labor relative to representatives of capital, and vice versa.

30. Crisp, "Tyranny by the Minority."

31. Ibid.

32. Crisp, "Tyranny by the Minority."

33. See Pedro Guevara, *Concertación y conflicto: El pacto social y el fracaso de las respuestas consensuales a la crisis del sistema político venezolano* (Caracas: Facultad de Ciencias Jurídicas y Politicas, Universidad Central de Venezuela, 1989).

34. Luis Gómez Calcaño, "Los movimientos sociales: Democracia emergente en el sistema político venezolano," in José A. Silva Michelena, ed., *Venezuela hacia el año 2000: desafios y opciones* (Caracas: Editorial Nueva Sociedad, 1987), 337–67.

35. Bautista Urbaneja, *Pueblo y petróleo.*

36. Richard Bernstein, ed., *Habermas and Modernity* (Cambridge, Mass.: MIT Press, 1985), 25.

37. See Nelson Geigel Lope-Bello, *La defensa de la ciudad* (Caracas: Universidad Simón Bolívar Instituto de Estudios Regionales y Urbanos, 1979), and Elías Santana, *El poder de los vecinos* (Caracas: Ediciones Ecotopia, 1983).

38. See Red de Apoyo para la Justicia y la Paz, *Boletín informativo* (Caracas: Red de Apoyo, 1992); COFAVIC; PROVEA, *Situación de los derechos humanos en Venezuela informe anual;* and PROVEA, *Boletín de derechos humanos y coyuntura.*

39. Daniel H. Levine, *Popular Voices in Latin American Catholicism* (Princeton: Princeton University Press, 1992), chap. 3.

40. Levine, *Popular Voices,* and Scott Mainwaring and Eduardo Viola, "New Social Movements, Political Culture, and Democracy: Brazil and Argentina in the 1980s," *Telos,* no. 61 (1986): 17–52.

41. This situation has clear dangers—for example, so much pluralism and activation that fragmentation rules and majorities cannot be constructed; but Venezuela is not at that point yet.

42. Levine, *Popular Voices.*

43. See Geigel Lope-Bello, *La defensa de la ciudad,* and Santana, *El poder de los vecinos.*

44. Note that the key role of the middle class gives such groups a different tone (and greater social presence, e.g., through the media) than has been the case elsewhere in Latin America.

45. The experience of other Latin American countries is not promising. See Nuria Cunill, *Participación ciudadana: dilemas y perspectivas para la democratización de los estados latinoamericanos* (Caracas: Centro Latinoamericano de Administración para el Desarrollo, 1991). Many vigorous social movements created in the 1970s and 1980s failed to create enduring political expression. But for emphasis on the possibilities of citizenship formation over the long term, see Amparo Menéndez-Carrión, "Democracias pendientes y representación política en America Latina: Algunas ideas en voz alta," in Margarita López Maya, ed., *Desarrollo y democracia* (Caracas: Editorial Nueva Sociedad, 1991), 67–91.

46. A good example is the CSE, the national institution in charge of managing elections. The CSE's long-established reputation for fairness and neutrality was called into question in the 1992 elections by charges that it obstructed the process of forming new parties and electoral groups and tolerated practices that encouraged fraud in

the counting and reporting of votes. Both charges have their roots in the fact that the makeup of the CSE at all levels is divided proportionally among the major parties. This provision, logical in light of the party system, is a potentially significant obstacle in the move toward a more open arrangement (see, for example, Clodovaldo Hernández, "El sistema electoral también colapsó en el 92," *El Globo*, December 20, 1992), manifest most recently in charges that the ballot approved for the 1992 elections effectively undercuts reforms.

47. Menéndez-Carrión, "Democracias pendientes y representación política en America Latina," 82–83.
48. See John D. Martz, *Acción Democrática: Evolution of a Modern Political Party in Venezuela* (Princeton: Princeton University Press, 1966).
49. Levine, *Conflict and Political Change in Venezuela.*
50. See Gustavo Coronel, *Venezuela: La agonía del subdesarrollo* (Caracas: Gustavo Coronel, 1990), and Grupo Roraima, *Más y mejor democracia* (Caracas: Cromotip, 1987).

# 9

# Quitting Populism Cold Turkey: The "Big Bang" Approach to Macroeconomic Balance

## Ricardo Hausmann

In their paper on the macroeconomics of populism[1] in Latin America, Rudiger Dornbusch and Sebastian Edwards analyze the devastating effects produced by policies that are based on expanding aggregate demand and real wages but disregard the limits to price and quantity controls and the existence of external and internal constraints.[2] The authors stress, however, that such policies may be part of a longer, four-phase policy cycle in which Latin American countries may have fallen.

In phase I, the government uses the slack and external resources left by the last stabilization effort to embark on an expansionary policy. Growth accelerates, inflation remains relatively low, and reserves are run down. In phase II the economy starts to experience external or internal bottlenecks, and the government reacts through controls, devaluations, and subsidies. In phase III, inflation and the fiscal deficit explode, capital flight and financial instability surface, and real wages fall dramatically. In phase IV, an orthodox stabilization package is adopted, usually under a new government; real wages decline further, falling well below the levels that were present before phase I.[3]

The Venezuelan experience of the last decade follows with some variations this rather sad script. After the 1983–85 stabilization effort, the government decided in 1986 to adopt an expansionary policy in spite of a major adverse external shock, caused by the decline in oil prices. As predicted, the economy reacted with vigorous growth but with increasing external problems addressed through devaluation and exchange, price, and interest rate controls. By early 1989, the economy faced an exploding fiscal deficit, a critical level of reserves, an exchange premium of almost 200 percent, and strong inflationary expectations. Instead of dragging the economy through the nightmares of phase III, the newly elected government decided to *quit populism cold turkey*: it unified and floated the exchange rate, freed prices and interest rates, reduced drastically the fiscal deficit, and embarked on a major trade reform. It soon discovered that the withdrawal syndrome was more painful than expected: nonoil GDP dropped by almost 10 percent while inflation exceeded 80 percent.[4] The trauma of this initial experience would seriously undermine the political capacity of the government to maintain support, even when vigorous growth and investment started in 1991.

In a world where many highly regulated economies in Latin America and Eastern Europe are trying to find a politically and socially tolerable path toward a more market-oriented development strategy, the Venezuelan experience is interesting on at least two counts. First is the question of political economy: What made the government adopt such a big-bang approach to restoring macroeconomic balance before the situation got out of hand? After all, it has been argued that a long bout of high inflation is required to force a democratic political system to adopt corrective measures; that was the case for Bolivia and Israel.[5] Sometimes, as in the case of Chile, the government is overthrown before serious corrective action is taken, while in others, like Alan García's Peru, the government succeeds in muddling through a long period of extremely high inflation. Why then would the Venezuelan authorities adopt such a radical policy package without having first a taste of the impending Armageddon?

Second, what can reasonably be expected from such radical packages? The fact that in Venezuela neither the government nor the International Monetary Fund (IMF) was able to assess the short-term impact of the reform plan is a strong indication that the macroeconomics of the process are not well understood. In this respect, the Venezuelan experience can be considered as the first of a series of big bangs that were implemented in Poland, Peru, and Russia. What then are the macroeconomic effects of such a package and what are its principal transmission mechanisms?

This chapter attempts to address these two issues. The first section sets the scene for the 1989 crisis and analyzes the political economy of the radical package. I argue that the crucial decision was the unification of the exchange rate and give the reasons for its adoption. Interestingly, policy interdependencies made most of the other reforms necessary and even painless at the margin.

The following section studies the macroeconomics of the big bang. I start by analyzing the deviations between the government's plan and its outcomes, then discuss the problems posed by the transition from the dual to a unified floating regime and show that the Venezuelan results are consistent with the recent literature. The recession is explained by several contractionary effects of devaluation, an endogenous inventory cycle, and strong shifts in relative prices. The next section contains analysis of economic events after the reform and assesses the performance of the economy. In the final section I use the benefit of hindsight to assess the big bang strategy.

## THE 1989 RADICAL ADJUSTMENT PROGRAM

This section begins with a brief overview of developments leading to the 1989 crisis.[6] I then analyze the problems faced by policymakers and the reasons behind the adoption of basic policy features. A summary of events is presented in table 9.1, relevant macroeconomic indicators are shown in table 9.2, and an outline of the 1989 adjustment program is presented in table 9.3.

### Venezuela's Road to Macroeconomic Instability

Venezuela's traditional policy regime prior to the oil shocks of the seventies can be characterized by four major principles: a fixed and unified exchange rate, fixed and rather rigid interest rates, fiscal discipline, and a protectionist trade policy.[7] This regime appeared to guarantee high growth and a low inflation rate (1.9 percent for the period from 1950 to 1970). Fiscal balance implied that the exchange rate was viable and interest rates were fixed above world levels, thus securing demand for the instruments offered by the rapidly expanding financial system.

When the first oil shock appeared in 1973, policy discussions dealt almost exclusively with the issue of what to do with the additional fiscal resources. The newly elected government of Carlos Andrés Pérez[8] initially decided to sterilize the windfall revenue abroad "until profitable investments appeared locally." As the five-year presidency progressed, however, expenditures, mainly on public sector companies, rose quickly and oil revenues declined; as a result, fiscal balance was reached in 1976 and a deficit of 14 percent of GDP developed by 1978. Growth initially accelerated to over 10 percent in 1975 and then began to fall, reaching 3.5 percent in 1978, as shortages of labor and infrastructure became dominant.[9]

### From Positive to Negative Shocks: The Treacherous 1980s

By early 1979, the newly elected government faced a rapidly falling reserve level, an exploding foreign debt,[10] and repressed inflation due to

Table 9.1
SUMMARY OF MACROECONOMIC EVENTS IN VENEZUELA

| Period | External Situation | Policy Orientation | Principal Results |
|---|---|---|---|
| 1964–73 | Stagnant oil income | Fixed unified exchange rates<br>Fiscal discipline<br>Import substitution industrialization | High but falling rate of growth (average 6.8%)<br>Very low inflation (1.7%)<br>External balance |
| 1974–76 | First oil shock<br>Higher world inflation | Expansionary fiscal policy<br>Emphasis on publicly owned basic industries<br>Nationalizations and restrictions on foreign investment | Acceleration in growth (9%)<br>Higher inflation but lower than world levels (9%)<br>Large and declining surpluses in fiscal and external accounts; balance achieved in 1976 |
| 1977–78 | Declining oil income | Increase in public spending, mainly in state enterprises<br>Some attempts to cut back spending and credit | Decline in growth (3.5% in 1978)<br>Major external and fiscal deficits<br>Extensive supply bottlenecks: labor and installed capacity |
| 1979–80 | Second oil shock<br>Jump in world interest rates | Strong fiscal contraction (mainly in imports)<br>Price liberalization<br>Wage increase law<br>Some trade liberalization<br>Interest ceilings do not adjust fully for the rise in world rates | Growth falls to zero<br>Unemployment grows slowly<br>Inflation accelerates to record levels (21% in 1980)<br>Real exchange rate appreciates strongly<br>External and fiscal balance achieved<br>Capital outflows begin |
| 1981–82 | Oil income very high, starts to fall | Fiscal expansion in public works<br>Interest rates are freed but monetary policy is expansionary<br>Large deficits in public enterprise sector financed through foreign borrowing | Mediocre growth (1%)<br>High but falling inflation (16%)<br>Large current account deficit and massive capital outflow (8 bolivars to U.S. dollar in 1982) |

## Table 9.1 (continued)

| Period | External Situation | Policy Orientation | Principal Results |
|---|---|---|---|
| 1983 | Fall in oil income<br>Start of debt crisis | Adoption of a multiple exchange rate<br>  regime, average devaluation 30%<br>Import controls<br>Contractionary fiscal policy<br>Monetary policy expansionary<br>Generalized price controls are adopted | GDP falls 5%<br>Inflation kept at 7%<br>Large balance of payments surplus<br>  (4 bolivars to U.S. dollar)<br>Still important fiscal deficit<br>Large expansion in money supply<br>Floating rate depreciates over 200% |
| 1984–85 | Oil income stable at lower<br>  level (13 bolivars to<br>  U.S. dollar) | Devaluation of official rate<br>Maintenance of import controls<br>Fiscal cuts<br>Interest rate controls adopted<br>Price controls are relaxed<br>Debt strategy: simple rescheduling | After an additional contraction in 1984 (–2%),<br>  economy starts to grow in 1985 (3.5%);<br>  unemployment reaches peak<br>Inflation increases to moderate levels (15%)<br>Large fiscal and balance of payments surpluses |
| 1986–88 | Oil income collapses<br>  (8 bolivars to U.S. dollar) | Fiscal expansion adopted<br>Forced financing of imports<br>Major devaluation when situation becomes<br>  untenable<br>No change in interest rate ceilings | Economy grows at 5% average; unemployment<br>  falls back to 7%<br>Major balance of payments and fiscal deficit<br>Acceleration of inflation to over 30%<br>Floating rate depreciates by almost 200%<br>  over the period |

Table 9.2
VENEZUELA: SUMMARY ECONOMIC INDICATORS, 1974–92 (PERCENTAGES EXCEPT WHERE NOTED)

| | 1974–78 | 1979–82 | 1983 | 1984 | 1985 | 1986 | 1987 | 1988 | 1989 | 1990 | 1991 | 1992 |
|---|---|---|---|---|---|---|---|---|---|---|---|---|
| GDP growth | | | | | | | | | | | | |
| Total | 5.8 | -0.2 | -5.5 | -1.1 | 1.3 | 6.8 | 3.0 | 4.2 | -8.3 | 5.3 | 11.1 | 8.8 |
| Nonoil | 8.1 | 1.0 | -4.7 | -1.2 | 3.2 | 7.1 | 3.5 | 4.5 | -9.4 | 3.7 | 10.9 | 11.7 |
| Unemployment rate[a] | 4.5 | 7.2 | 10.2 | 13.4 | 12.1 | 10.3 | 8.5 | 6.9 | 9.2 | 9.9 | 8.7 | 7.5 |
| Oil price (dollars per barrel) | 14.2 | 27.8 | 25.3 | 26.7 | 25.9 | 12.8 | 16.3 | 13.5 | 16.9 | 20.3 | 15.9 | 14.7 |
| Current account (billions of dollars) | 0.0 | 1.4 | 4.4 | 5.4 | 3.1 | -1.5 | -1.1 | -4.9 | 2.5 | 8.0 | 1.5 | -2.5 |
| Exchange rates (bolivars per dollar) | | | | | | | | | | | | |
| Official | 4.3 | 4.3 | 6.0 | 7.5 | 7.5 | 7.5 | 14.5 | 14.5 | — | — | — | — |
| Average (imports) | 4.3 | 4.3 | 5.0 | 6.6 | 7.5 | 8.9 | 11.8 | 15.3 | — | — | — | — |
| Floating[a] | n.a. | n.a. | 13.5 | 14.6 | 15.2 | 24.3 | 31.6 | 40.5 | 43.1 | 50.4 | 61.6 | 80.0 |
| Relative prices (1974–78 = 100) | | | | | | | | | | | | |
| Real exchange rate[b] | 100.0 | 88.4 | 91.7 | 105.9 | 101.4 | 100.2 | 96.3 | 98.7 | 83.9 | 75.5 | 80.5 | 88.5 |
| Importables versus nontradables | 100.0 | 86.9 | 80.7 | 88.5 | 89.0 | 92.8 | 94.1 | 92.8 | 78.9 | 71.0 | 75.7 | 83.2 |
| Inflation | | | | | | | | | | | | |
| Consumer prices[a] | 8.2 | 13.1 | 7.0 | 15.7 | 9.2 | 12.7 | 40.3 | 35.5 | 81.0 | 36.5 | 31.0 | 33.0 |
| Nonoil GDP deflator | n.a. | n.a. | 8.7 | 13.3 | 13.4 | 11.7 | 27.3 | 26.3 | 83.4 | 35.5 | 29.8 | 31.4 |
| Growth rate of money supply (M2) | 28.0 | 14.7 | 28.7 | 8.8 | 8.6 | 16.7 | 24.4 | 18.3 | 41.0 | 64.3 | 33.6 | 31.5 |
| Interest rates | | | | | | | | | | | | |
| On commercial loans | 10.1 | 16.7 | 15.8 | 15.3 | 12.7 | 12.7 | 12.7 | 12.7 | 36.5 | 34.8 | 38.9 | 56.5 |
| On 90-day deposits | 8.0 | 14.2 | 13.5 | 13.0 | 10.5 | 8.9 | 8.9 | 8.9 | 29.2 | 27.8 | 31.1 | 49.1 |
| Public sector surplus (as share of GDP) | n.a. | n.a. | -4.5 | 4.9 | 3.4 | -4.5 | -5.9 | -9.9 | -1.4 | 1.1 | 0.7 | -7.9 |
| Net internal public spending (as share of GDP)[c] | n.a. | 32.6 | 16.5 | 9.2 | 6.3 | 9.1 | 14.8 | 28.8 | 23.5 | 17.3 | 22.3 | 19.2 |

*Source:* Banco Central de Venezuela.
n.a. = not available.
[a]End of period.
[b]Average nominal exchange rate of imports adjusted by inflation differentials.
[c]Internal public spending minus internal taxes, where oil taxes are mostly taken as external income, as calculated in Ricardo Hausmann, "Venezuela in 1987," *Coyuntura Económica* no. 2 (June 1988): 241–78.
— = no official rate.

Table 9.3
THE 1989 ADJUSTMENT PROGRAM

| Policy | Measures Adopted | Date |
|---|---|---|
| Exchange rate policy | 1. Unification of the exchange rate. | March 1989 |
| | 2. Recognition of a fraction of the letters of credit on imported goods at the old exchange rate, to be paid in three years. | April 1989 |
| Interest rate policy | 1. Interest rates were freed on all transactions except for agriculture and preferential mortgages. The Central Bank influences the market through money market operations. | Feb. 1989 |
| | 2. The Supreme Court forces the Central Bank to set rates. Maximum rate on loans set at 37%, minimum rate on deposits at 25%. | April 1989 |
| | 3. Rates increased to a maximum of 42% and a minimum of 30%. | June 1989 |
| | 4. Rates reduced to a maximum of 39% and a minimum of 27%. | August 1989 |
| | 5. A new short-term zero-coupon bond is created to aid as a Central Bank monetary policy instrument. It is auctioned at the stock exchange. | Nov. 1989 |
| | 6. Rates increased to a maximum of 43% and a minimum of 28%. | Dec. 1989–Jan. 1990 |
| | 7. Rates reduced to a maximum of 35% and a minimum of 15%. | March 1990 |
| | 8. Relaxation of controls with a maximum rate of 60% and a minimum of 10%. | April 1990 |
| Trade policy | 1. Elimination of import prohibitions and relaxation of import licensing. | March–June 1989 |
| | 2. Reduction and standardization of tariff rates: maximum rates set at 80% for consumer goods, 50% for inputs. Average rates decline to below 40%. | June 1989 |
| | 3. Adoption of a simplified tariff structure and reduction in rates. Maximum rate was set at 50% for consumer goods, and several tranches at 40, 30, 20, and 10% were created depending on the degree of elaboration. | April 1990 |
| | 4. Liberalization of agricultural imports. | Mid-1990 |

## Table 9.3 (continued)

| Policy | Measures Adopted | Date |
|---|---|---|
| Fiscal policy | 1. Public sector deficit is targeted at 4% of GDP. Increase in gasoline prices of 100%, elimination of tariff exonerations. | Feb. 1989 |
| | 2. Increase in electricity, telephone, and fertilizer prices. Government demands additional expenditures in social sectors and in an employment program. | March 1989 |
| | 3. Government presents to Congress a value-added tax law and a reform to the income tax law. | Sept. 1989 |
| | 4. Congress approves additional spending. | Oct. 1989 |
| | 5. Budget for 1990 approved; it does not include sufficient investment spending. Deficit targeted at 1% of GDP. | Dec. 1989 |
| | 6. Government submits a Public Credit Law to fund additional investments. | Feb. 1989 |
| International financing policy | 1. Government signs letter of intent with the IMF and asks for first and second tranche financing. It stops principal payments on commercial debt. | Feb. 1989 |
| | 2. Government signs a three-year Extended Fund Facility with the IMF and two policy loans with the World Bank: a structural adjustment policy geared at getting public sector prices in line and a trade policy loan to support the liberalization effort. | June 1989 |
| | 3. The IMF board reverses its policy of allowing Venezuela to finance itself through arrears, forcing the country into an agreement with banks to make payments current. Expected bank financing falls short by U.S.$900 million. | Sept. 1989 |
| | 4. A debt-to-equity swap auction is adopted with the intention of converting some U.S.$600 million of debt into private sector investment projects. | Nov. 1989 |
| | 5. Venezuela reaches an agreement in principle with the banks on a menu of options that include interest and principal reductions, new money, interest holiday, and buy-backs. | March 1990 |

severe overheating. It did not foresee the second oil shock, which occurred just a few months later. The state adopted a policy of fiscal cutbacks, mainly on imported goods, and freed most prices.[11] The economy went into a recession led by a contraction in the construction sector and by a fall in importable output due to the rapidly appreciating real exchange rate; the shift in the exchange rate was caused by the gradual return of the overheated economy to its natural rate of unemployment through a rise in real wages. Moreover, political difficulties in adjusting the controlled local interest rates to the jump in international rates led to some capital outflows.

After two years of spending cutbacks (1979–80), and given the apparently permanent character of the second positive oil shock, the government decided to adopt in 1981 an expansionary fiscal policy based on a projected increase in oil revenues of 12 percent per year. As the policy got under way, the first negative shock of the eighties appeared, generating current account and fiscal deficits accompanied by a massive attack on the currency by 1982. In February 1983, after a loss of more than U.S.$10 billion in international reserves, the Central Bank decided to abandon the traditional unified and fixed exchange rate system and to adopt multiple rates. Capital account transactions were left to a floating exchange market, which depreciated by almost 300 percent in the following six months. Fiscal policy turned contractionary and trade policy became more protectionist. The economy went into recession with surprisingly little inflation, a massive depreciation of the parallel rate, and large surplus in both the external and the public sector accounts.

Given these large surpluses and rising unemployment, further austerity seemed unnecessary and a jump in public investment (from 10 to 13 percent of GDP) was approved for the following fiscal year. No change was thought necessary in the other policy areas, which had wide support. In particular, the multiple exchange system was favored by many groups that had become used to living with a foreign exchange premium of 100 percent, and that did not appear to be too painful.[12]

Just when the fiscal expansion started in January 1986, oil income fell by almost half from U.S.$13.9 billion in 1984–85 to U.S.$7.6 billion in 1986. After this steep drop, the government found commercial banks unusually ready to sign the debt-rescheduling agreement that had been under negotiation since 1983 and that had suddenly become impossible to sustain. Hence, in February 1986 the state went ahead and signed a nonviable commercial debt-restructuring accord, which included no new money, a large down payment on principal, and no grace period for amortizations.

For the next three years, the government attempted to maintain its expansionary policy with increasing difficulty, falling progressively deeper into all the traps of populist policymaking. In 1986, the nonoil economy grew by 7.1 percent, but the floating rate went from 15 bolivars per dollar in January to 26 bolivars per dollar in November. The credibility of the official rate, which was fixed at 7.50 bolivars per dollar, collapsed and the government was increasingly unable to manage the exchange control mechanism. In December 1986 it decided to make a "credible" devaluation of 93 percent to 14.50 bolivars per dollar.[13] Inflation accelerated to an all-time high of 42 percent in 1987.

Given the political costs of the December 1986 devaluation and the approaching election of December 1988, the government felt that it could not carry out a fiscal contraction or an increase in the fixed nominal interest rates, in spite of rising inflation. Consequently, real interest rates became increasingly negative. This prompted an escape from the bolivar and the appearance of a parallel interest rate for the first time. In spite of a growing economy, real money declined, the real value of foreign assets increased, and the foreign exchange premium rose rapidly after the large December 1986 devaluation. Consequently, most portfolios had liabilities in bolivars and assets in dollars and benefited from the increasing real depreciation of the floating rate.

To contain the accelerating inflation caused in part by its disregard for monetary discipline, the government fell into the well-known populist trap of price controls and froze prices for agriculture and the public sector. The ratio of nonoil public sector prices relative to the private sector GDP deflator fell to 70 percent of its 1984 level, accentuating the public sector deficit, which reached 9.9 percent of GDP in 1988.

### The Economic Crisis of 1989

The 1986–88 expansion left the newly elected government with four major disequilibriums. First was an external imbalance, expressed in a large current account deficit, a low level of liquid net international reserves (U.S.$300 million), an exploding foreign exchange premium (table 9.2), short-term Central Bank dollar liabilities (recognized official-rate letters of credit) of U.S.$6.3 billion—of which over U.S.$1 billion were overdue—and no international financing plan for 1989.[14]

Second, the fiscal deficit, which had reached 9.9 percent of GDP in 1988, was projected to rise to 12 percent of GDP, mainly due to the impact of rising explicit and implicit subsidies on goods such as gasoline, fertilizers, milk, feed grains, electricity, and petroleum products. More important, although the 1988 deficit was financed through reserve losses, the projected deficit for 1989 would have had to be financed through the inflation tax or new loans. It is at this stage that economies enter phase III.

Third, repressed inflation was causing serious shortages of basic products and massive speculative inventory accumulation. This situation was generated not only by growing pressures on controlled prices, but also by the general perception that a major devaluation was imminent.

Fourth, inflationary expectations in the context of controlled interest rates generated severe financial repression. Strong demand for credit emerged, which was generally used to finance inventory accumulation or capital flight. For the first time, a parallel interest rate appeared, which hovered around 30 percent when the official ceiling was at 13 percent.

These four macroeconomic imbalances can be characterized as implying excess demand for goods, foreign exchange, and domestic credit while money is in excess supply. Since the expansion left the economy close to full employment,[15] this situation also implies real exchange rate misalignment in the sense that, at prevailing relative prices, external balance and full employment are not simultaneously achievable.[16]

*The Making of the Big Bang*

Explosive Change

Under these circumstances, policymakers face rather stark choices. Imbalances have been allowed to gather strength by the postponement of adjustment covered through reserve losses and there may not be much room to finance a more gradual approach. Here, a bomb may be a good metaphor in the sense that the disequilibriums act like an impending explosion, ready to wreak havoc on society. After realizing the damage done, policymakers may find some comfort in the fact that the bomb exists no more.

If the problem is to be avoided in the future, progress must be made on correcting the fundamentals, especially if one is to rely on markets as a means of determining exchange and interest rates. The need to make credible advances in these areas also puts an additional constraint on policy, which may require other abrupt measures. The sudden release of tensions and the attempt at major corrections generates a tradeoff between the havoc created by the big bang and the convenience of having (eventually) a sounder policy environment and better functioning markets. But this tradeoff may be extremely difficult to manage.

The Venezuelan case could be explained either as a stroke of genius in policy design or as just another case of making virtue out of necessity. In the next subsection I argue that the latter interpretation accounts for a good part of the story. Nevertheless, it must be pointed out that lack of courage in accepting the inevitable has often been costly to many countries facing similar problems and is usually decisive when entering phase III.

## A New Government

A new government is in a unique situation for introducing radical changes in policy. It can denounce previous policies in such a way as to shift the blame backward for the consequences of its own decisions. Also, in democratic regimes, it has the best chance of profiting from the longer-term benefits of adjustment, since its planning horizon is at its maximum. Finally, it is most vulnerable to insufficient adjustment, since it is most likely to have to pay for the consequences within its governing period. Thus, when in doubt, it will prefer to err on the side of overkill, since it will be easier to relax policy later instead of tightening it up. By contrast, as the governing period progresses, a change in policy is more likely to be blamed on the regime's own previous mistakes, while the beneficiary of the policy will more likely be the next government. Except in the case of reelection, interpresidential generosity should not be presumed.

## Adjusting the Exchange Rate

Pressured by an unsustainable balance of payments and by strong expectations of devaluation, policymakers had to decide on a way of devaluing the currency. Obviously, now with an exchange premium of 200 percent, only a major adjustment of the official rate could be credible. A wrong guess, however, would require future adjustments likely to erode credibility. With a low level of reserves, there is little room for defending any particular exchange rate peg. A floating arrangement, even a temporary one, becomes an expedient way of solving the problem.

Furthermore, overinvoicing of imports became a serious difficulty. The extensive regulations required to avoid leakages through exports or through inflows of foreign direct investment were blocking development. The productive sector received extremely confusing price signals due to the proliferation of exchange rates. Supply became more rigid because foreign exchange was distributed based on past allocations, so high-growth sectors were being dragged down by low-growth sectors, which could waste foreign exchange.

Nevertheless, the political argument that won the day was corruption. Public opinion had the feeling that rent-seeking activities were being stimulated to such an extent that the whole social and political system was in danger of being corrupted to an intolerable degree.[17] Since a major adjustment to the official rate had to be implemented anyway, why not pay a small extra price and get rid of all these problems at once? If the exchange rate was ever going to be unified again, when would the country find a better moment? The additional cost of unifying appeared small compared to the potential benefits.

Fiscal Adjustment

Both the government and the financial markets recognized that the underlying cause of inflation was the large public sector deficit. If progress was not made on the fiscal front, the markets would move against the currency, causing an acceleration of inflation and putting upward pressure on interest rates, both of which were unwanted developments from the viewpoint of the government. The deficit had to be reduced—but how?

The first important element was the exchange rate policy. Since a major devaluation was about to take place, the fiscal deficit would fall immediately. This is because the public sector, given its oil resources, runs a balance of payments surplus and the real exchange rate affects its terms of trade with the rest of the economy, determining how many domestic goods can be purchased with the oil surplus. The ratio of the GDP deflators between the oil industry and the private sector nearly doubled in 1989. This explains over two-thirds of the increase in the oil surplus (table 9.4).[18] By contrast, interest on debt grew by only a small fraction of this increase.

The second major policy item in fiscal correction was the adjustment in public prices and subsidies. Traditionally these have tended to exhibit a strong political cycle, with binding controls decreed before elections and large adjustments occurring afterward. Since public prices had been frozen in 1987 and had fallen significantly in real terms, the government recognized that they had to be adjusted. Political logic implied that it should be done sooner rather than later.

Tax reform was formulated and submitted to Congress, but no action was taken. In fact, Congress did not seriously consider the proposed taxes until after President Pérez had been separated from his post in May 1993. In 1989, no other important fiscal changes were deemed

Table 9.4
THE DIFFERENCE BETWEEN PLAN AND OUTCOME

| | 1988 | 1989 Proj | 1989 Act |
|---|---|---|---|
| Nonoil GDP[a] | 5.6 | 2.0 | –9.8 |
| CPI inflation[a] | 35.5 | 37.5 | 81.4 |
| Current account[b] | –4.7 | –1.6 | 2.3 |
| Trade balance | –1.1 | 2.3 | 5.8 |
| Exports FOB | 10.3 | 10.5 | 12.9 |
| Oil | 8.2 | 8.4 | 9.8 |
| Other | 2.1 | 2.1 | 3.1 |
| Imports | 11.4 | 8.2 | 7.1 |
| Capital account[b] | –0.2 | 1.6 | –1.4 |
| Public | –0.7 | 2.5 | 0.4 |
| Private | 0.5 | –0.9 | –1.8 |
| Public sector deficit (as % of GDP) | –9.9 | –4.0 | –1.9 |
| Revenue | 23.9 | 27.9 | 25.9 |
| of which: Oil surplus | 11.4 | 16.3 | 17.1 |
| Taxes | 7.4 | 4.3 | 2.8 |
| Expenditures | 33.8 | 31.9 | 27.8 |
| M2 (end of period % growth) | 15.8 | 46.5 | 43.5 |
| Floating rate (year average)[c] | 33.5 | 28.0 | 39.2 |

*Source:* Banco Central de Venezuela: letter of intent.
[a]Percent per annum; [b]Billions of dollars; [c]Bolivars per dollar; CPI = consumer price index; Act = actual (a measure of volume); FOB = free on board; M2 = (growth rate of) money supply; Proj = projected.

necessary. In practice, the 4 percent target for the fiscal deficit of 1989 was surpassed (table 9.4) mainly because of higher than expected prices for oil and foreign exchange and lower spending on transfers.

Deciding on Price Policy

After two years of price freezes in many sectors, despite an inflation rate of more than 35 percent per annum, the pressure to make major adjustments was on. But the situation in 1989 was aggravated by the imminent devaluation, which implied that many more prices had to be revised in a short time. Given anticipated inflation and fixed nominal interest rates, real rates became strongly negative and favored speculative inventory accumulation and generalized shortages. In this context, the cost of price negotiations, industry by industry, became too high to bear. Short delays may cause large cash-flow losses or may imply intolerable supply conditions.

After attempting to manage the process of price increases, but facing severe supply problems, the government decided to free most prices except for a list of eleven items. When this measure was taken, severe conflicts arose between some of the more radical members of the cabinet (who thought price liberalization should be postponed) and those in charge of administering policy (who could not manage a controlled rise in prices). Thus price liberalization was not an element of policy decided on ideological grounds—it was more like a collapse of the price control regime.

### The Rise in Interest Rates

Clearly, exchange and price liberalization increases the cost of maintaining interest rate controls at levels well below expected devaluation or inflation. On the one hand, if the public perceives that interest differentials do not cover expected depreciation, there will be a sudden rise in the exchange rate until the future path of the exchange rate is consistent with covered interest parity.[19] Consequently, not adjusting interest rates implies a heavy political price in the short term, to be paid in terms of higher inflation and exchange rate overshooting. Moreover, if speculative inventory accumulation is important, a rise in interest rates may help burst the speculative bubble, forcing companies to sell their stocks so as to pay back the now more expensive loans. Thus interest rate liberalization may reduce devaluation and inflation in the short run, when exchange and price liberalization is adopted.

### Trade Liberalization

The issue of the right timing and sequencing for trade liberalization has been amply discussed in the literature,[20] analyzed mostly in light of the experience of Southern Cone liberalization attempts in the late seventies. The discussion has centered on the sequencing of current versus capital account liberalization, with the consensus heavily dominated by the current-account-first strategy. Underlying the issue was the need to avoid real exchange appreciation, generated by significant capital inflows, and its negative consequences on tradable production. The discussion usually also involved predetermined exchange rates.

Against this background, the Venezuelan experience will appear odd. Critics could argue that exchange unification implied a capital-account-first strategy, since trade was liberalized more slowly. Why did Venezuela adopt a rather radical trade reform policy, in the midst of an attempt at stabilization? Why did Venezuela not wait for calmer times?

How did the government get away with it? I argue that trade liberalization became necessary and relatively cheap, precisely because the adoption of a unified float had already been decided.

The adoption of a floating exchange rate regime eliminated the most potent protectionist policy in place and implied a return to the pre-1983 tariff structure aimed at industrial development, which had become hopelessly outdated and looked arbitrary. Now (for reasons explained later), the unification of the exchange rate and the pressures for short-run portfolio balance generated real exchange rate overshooting. Trade liberalization was seen as a way to reduce what appeared as an excessive real depreciation. By lowering tariffs, the cost of imported goods would not rise by as much as the increase in the exchange rate because of a partially compensatory reduction in tariffs. With inflation as the principal policy concern and with the government worried about giving too much price freedom to a monopolistic industrial structure, the introduction of some foreign competition in the context of an otherwise excessive devaluation was seen, in net political terms, more like a carrot than a stick in the effort to get economic actors to adjust to reforms. Moreover, the fact that the exchange market was allowed to float and that the country was facing a balance of payments crisis eliminated the argument that the economy would be swamped with imports. If import demand increased, the exchange rate would adjust, providing automatic and unbiased protection to all sectors.

*Ugly Facts Point to Wrong Theories*

The previous section presented the political and economic factors that affected the making of the policy package but did not stress the outcomes that were expected. Table 9.4 presents both the expectations and the actual results. Clearly, the process was much more costly in terms of GDP and inflation than was expected. This outcome may have inadvertently eased the adoption of the plan, because it implied that a healthier policy environment could be achieved without major disruptions. Our interest now is in the macroeconomics of the surprises.

What Went Wrong with the Inflation Estimates?

Year-end inflation was more than double the initial estimate; more important, this deviation cannot be explained away by blaming some unforeseen external event. First, there were no adverse external shocks to the economy—on the contrary, oil exports were U.S.$1.4 billion, or 16.7 percent above target. Second, fiscal objectives were surpassed, mainly due to a shortfall in expenditures.[21] Third, monetary growth remained well within the stated ceilings.

Hence neither balance of payments, nor fiscal, nor monetary deviations can explain the difference between planned and actual values for this variable. There is a clear link, however, between the underestimations of inflation and the exchange rate. As shown in table 9.4, the price of the dollar averaged more than 39 bolivars instead of the expected 28 bolivars, a difference of 39 percent.

Two alternative and contradictory sets of arguments were used at the time to justify these projections. The first view implicitly assumed that the real side of the economy would determine the exchange rate. It indicated that the new rate would resemble the average commercial rate plus some allowance for importers' rents and for a needed real depreciation. Because the average commercial rate for December 1988, including imports at the parallel rate, was 16.4 bolivars per dollar, the figure of 28 bolivars per dollar appeared more than reasonable.

The second view argued that prices already reflected in part the floating-rate dollar, even though only 8 percent of imports took place at that rate. The difference between cost and market price of foreign exchange was a rent to importers that would be passed on to the government through unification, thus reducing the fiscal deficit. Consequently, unifying the exchange rate would have a small short-term impact on the price level and a healthy effect on the underlying rate of inflation.

The available evidence suggests that these two positions were partly right but mainly wrong. The first view may be correct in asserting that an exchange rate of 28 bolivars per dollar was consistent with the projected trade surplus of U.S.$2.3 billion, instead of the higher actual surplus of U.S.$5.8 billion, which occurred given the larger depreciation. But this view shows only that the exchange rate is not determined in the short run by the trade balance and that overshooting is a real possibility.

With regard to the second view, it is true that underlying inflation did fall. After a sudden jump in the consumer price level, the rate of change dropped rather quickly, falling below the rates of inflation that were present before the big bang. In fact, inflation in the second half of 1989 was below that for the same period in 1988, and the trend was maintained thereafter. It is not true, however, that the price level was not significantly affected, or that prices reflected for the most part the parallel rate. On the contrary, prices reflected mainly the official, not the parallel, exchange rate. In short, according to this perspective, the package did not include an adequate theoretical means of determining what the price level and exchange rate would be.[22] I address this issue again later.

As pointed out earlier, instead of the low but positive growth predicted by the program, the economy reacted with its worst recession in memory, with nonoil GDP falling by close to 10 percent and total GDP decreasing by 7.6 percent.

### The Monetary Impact of the Abandonment of the Multiple Exchange Regime

The fact that the results of the plan were a surprise is an indication that the underlying model used to think about its impact was flawed in some fundamental way. Both the authorities and the International Monetary Fund were using the standard IMF-type financial programming model. This approach, familiar to anyone who has had to negotiate a letter of intent, has become more than an analytical framework. It forms part of the agreed principles for the design of loan conditionality and for the training of hundreds of public officials.

The operational procedure runs more or less as follows. Independent fiscal and balance of payments projections are calculated based on government plans and available information. An inflation target is adopted exogenously and money demand is projected, assuming a well-behaved money-demand function. Accounting identities are then used to project the balance sheet of the financial system. This allows testing of the coherence of the fiscal and balance of payments projections with the requirement of monetary equilibrium. If a gap is found, additional measures must be taken to make the program viable. In the end, the agreed program must pass quite a few consistency checks. How then could the Venezuelan program have missed the target by such a wide margin?

### Adjusting the Theoretical Framework

The problem is that this approach, which was designed for fixed or predetermined exchange regimes, fails to take into account the macroeconomics of multiple exchange rate regimes. Moreover, it disregards a crucial element of the policy package: the switch in the exchange rate regime, moving from multiple rates to a single floating rate.

The IMF-style model makes two crucial implicit assumptions: first, that agents hold only domestic money; second, that exchange rate expectations do not enter into the demand for local financial assets.

In contrast, the standard model of a multiple exchange rate regime[23] assumes that all commercial transactions take place at the official exchange rate and that all financial transactions occur at the parallel rate. Imports are assumed to be demand-determined so that their internal price is equal to the world price calculated at the official rate. Agents hold both domestic and foreign assets in a portfolio that is permanently in equilibrium and that depends on the expected rate of depreciation. Given the nominal money supply and expected depreciation, agents would like to reduce their holdings of domestic money in exchange for foreign assets. They are thwarted, however, by the fact that there are no net supplies of dollars at the parallel rate. Portfolio balance is achieved through a depreciation of the parallel rate: domestic currency is worth less and foreign assets are worth more. The parallel rate is the rate at which portfolios are in balance.

When such a system is abandoned in favor of a floating regime, the exchange rate premium obviously disappears.[24] Portfolio balance must be maintained, which requires an exchange rate similar to the parallel rate. This implies that the rate for commercial transactions must rise by the amount of the premium, causing a price shock for tradables which is passed on to the rest of the price system. The jump in the price level reduces drastically the real value of both foreign and domestic financial assets.[25] To reestablish real wealth, agents must generate a higher level of financial savings, which requires a fall in spending. A balance of payments surplus appears and it is used to increase the depleted real stock of foreign assets.

Furthermore, if the change in regime is anticipated, as was the case in Venezuela, any discontinuous adjustment in the parallel rate occurs at the time that the policy is expected and not when the program is actually implemented, since people will try to profit from expected capital gains, thus bringing the change in price forward in time.

The Venezuelan Experience

The Venezuelan experience fits rather neatly into this overall process. The exchange rate became unstable in January 1989, when the program was announced. It had a maximum of 43.25 bolivars per dollar and a minimum of 32 bolivars per dollar. Then it tended to stabilize, with smaller fluctuations and a small appreciation to the range of 36 to 37 bolivars per dollar by March and April. Thus there was a slight appreciation when the program was announced in early January, but when unification effectively took place in early March, there was no discontinuity in the floating exchange rate.

Since the price of tradables was determined mainly by the commercial rate, the unification implied a once-and-for-all price shock to the economy, with measured inflation accelerating drastically in March and April, while the real value of domestic and foreign assets collapsed (see table 9.1). As expected, private spending fell by 6.7 percent of GDP, while private financial savings amounted to 6.5 percent of GDP instead of the 0.9 percent of GDP expected by the program.[26] Also, the capital inflows anticipated by the program failed to materialize (see table 9.4), as predicted in the previous discussion.[27]

*The Real Impact of the Abandonment of the Multiple Exchange Regime*

Many of the effects on output can be understood following the literature on the contractionary effects of devaluation. The seminal works of Carlos Díaz-Alejandro and Paul Krugman and Lance Taylor, however, have pointed out the existence of other effects that may have contractionary implications.[28] Three of them appear to be of particular importance in our case: the real balance effect, the Díaz-Alejandro effect, and the impact of imported inputs.

The Real Balance Effect

As mentioned before, the fall in the real value of both foreign and domestic assets was extremely large and may be a principal cause of the rise in private sector financial savings. Finding themselves with fewer financial assets than expected, agents cut spending in order to replenish their financial stocks. The related fall in demand, given price rigidities, must have had important contractionary effects on output.[29]

The Díaz-Alejandro Effect

Díaz-Alejandro, analyzing the case of Argentina, argues that devaluations may transfer income from groups with a high propensity to consume, such as urban workers, to groups with a low propensity to consume, such as landowners. This distributional effect would thus have an overall contractionary effect on aggregate demand. In the Venezuelan case, the principal beneficiary of the devaluation is the public sector, given its balance of payments surplus due to its oil exports. A devaluation increases the real value of this surplus. Since the government did not spend the increased real value of its oil revenue, but instead used it to reduce the deficit—and in addition cut real public expenditure—it exhibited a negative propensity to consume.

The relative price of the petroleum sector with respect to the nonoil economy went up by 34.3 percent, which, given its share in national income in 1988 of 19.3 percent, implies a shift of revenue to the exporting sector equivalent to 6.6 percent of GDP.[30] This is an amount of revenue extracted from the private sector and is consistent with the fall in private consumption of 6.4 percent in 1989.[31] Part of the increased public income was transferred abroad through the rise in the real value of debt service. According to table 9.4, this amounted to 1.6 percent of GDP.

### Speculative Inventory Behavior

Another effect that explains the collapse in output is an inventory cycle that is endogenous to an anticipated big bang. Since people expect all prices to rise significantly, demand for storable goods (domestic or foreign) jumps before the shock, producing excess demand for goods and credit and a flight away from money balances. In fact, their behavior may well force the government to act.[32]

After the shock, once prices and interest rates increase, the cost of holding stocks goes up while the expected benefit falls with the new lower inflationary trend. Consequently, inventories are drawn down. Companies reduce current assets and pay back their current liabilities, making banks face a major decline in the demand for credit.[33] Households retire temporarily from the goods market and run down their inventories while they use their current income to increase the depleted financial assets. The increased supply of and reduced demand for goods produces a deep but temporary recession. The change in inventory accumulation amounts to 6.9 percent of GDP, which is an amount close to the total fall in GDP of 7.6 percent, indicating the importance of this effect. Of course, once inventories are run down, aggregate demand reappears to the surprise of many.[34] This explains why after the sharp recession of 1989, the economy recovered quickly thereafter.

### The Supply Side: Imported Intermediate Inputs

A fourth effect that may have a contractionary impact on output is the increase in the price of imported inputs. This supply-side effect may be particularly important in Venezuela because the internal prices of final tradable goods were initially above the level consistent with the official rate (given rationing), whereas inputs were coming in at the official rate and were probably overinvoiced. Thus, with unification, the final price of output went up by less than the increase in imported input costs, causing a change in relative prices against most sectors and reducing or reversing the positive effect of the devaluation on competitiveness. The average cost of foreign exchange for imports increased by

154 percent, while the GDP deflators for agriculture and manufacturing rose by only 87.4 and 78.9 percent, respectively. This may explain why output in agriculture fell by 5.7 percent, even though its relative price with respect to the nonoil GDP deflator improved by 11.7 percent, whereas manufacturing declined by 12.4 percent in spite of an improvement in its relative price of 6.6 percent.[35]

Real Effects: A Summary

The Venezuelan experience suggests that the indeterminacy of the elasticity of output with respect to the exchange rate is not produced by the fact that the effects are small, but on the contrary that both expansionary and contractionary effects may be quite large, with an uncertain result: net real exports improved by 7.9 percent of GDP, quite a large amount. However, the impact of the fall in real financial wealth and the transfer of income from the private to the public sector through the Díaz-Alejandro effect produced a drop in private sector spending of 6.7 percent of GDP. Together with an endogenous inventory cycle, which cut demand by 6.9 percent of GDP, and other supply shocks, these effects completely reversed the rather large expansionary impact, producing a major recession. Contrary to a widely held view in Venezuela, fiscal spending appears to be a minor part of the story.

LIFE AFTER THE BIG BANG: ECONOMIC SUCCESS AND POLITICAL FAILURE

The short-term consequences of implementing a big bang approach were characterized by unexpectedly high recession and inflation, features that are common to similar reforms in Poland, Russia, and Peru. After the explosion, however, life goes on and the medium-term benefits of the reform should start emerging. Together with additional reforms in the fields of economic integration, foreign investment, debt restructuring, privatization, and new social programs, the institutional framework of the Venezuelan economy was radically changed.

The new set of relative prices started to generate incentives for efficient output. One clear example was agriculture. The multiple exchange rate system had assigned the lowest, most subsidized exchange rate to agricultural inputs, such as feedgrain and machinery. Feedgrain is used in the production of pork and poultry, but not for beef, because the huge prairies of the llanos provide ideal conditions for cattle raising. The system created an implicit subsidy to the sectors where Venezuela did not have a competitive edge, while dragging down those that did. When the reform was introduced, these distortions were reversed. There were sectors and regions adversely affected and others that prospered.

The inventory cycle that accentuated the 1989 recession had the opposite effect in 1990 and stopped being a factor thereafter. With a simpler, clearer trade and exchange rate policy, integration with Colombia became possible and a single market was created as of January 1992. Exports to Colombia grew by 65 percent in 1992 and were 83 percent higher in the first half of 1993, relative to the same period in 1992. Colombia became Venezuela's second market for nonoil exports and the most dynamic and diversified. The example was instrumental in introducing Ecuador and Bolivia into the agreement and in reaching accords with Chile, Central America, and the CARICOM (Caribbean Community) countries.

In January 1990 a major reform of the foreign direct investment regime—allowing for the free movement of capital and dividends and opening up sectors previously restricted to nationals—enabled the country to attract substantial investment flows. In 1992, a year when the country suffered two military coup attempts, foreign investment surpassed U.S.$1.2 billion. This number must be compared with the 1985–88 average of U.S.$20 million.

The renegotiation of all the commercial bank debt (U.S.$21 billion) through the Brady plan allowed Venezuela to return to the voluntary lending markets while significantly reducing the net present value of its debt service. Privatization, initially concentrated in areas most likely to affect the competitiveness of the exporting sector, such as ports and telecommunications, was instrumental in bringing in capital, increasing the net yearly flows of private investment, and improving service. For example, the privatization of the telephone company implied the sale of 40 percent of the shares for U.S.$1.9 billion. Moreover, a cellular phone band was auctioned off and nineteen other companies were allowed to invest in this previously restricted sector. In 1993, investment in telecommunications exceeded U.S.$1 billion, with the telephone company accounting for U.S.$650 million. This annual figure is more than was invested in the sector during the previous decade.

Targeted social programs were used to substitute for the indirect subsidies previously channeled through distortions in the price system. Cash and kind transfers through the school system and milk subsidies to infants reached over 4.5 million children and channeled more than U.S.$650 million in 1992.

With this policy framework, the economy recovered quickly from the initial recession, with the nonoil economy growing in excess of 9 percent per year during 1991–92. The effects of the Gulf War brought in an unexpected U.S.$4 billion to the country in 1990, establishing confidence in the viability of the program. These resources plus the revenues from the sale of the telephone company in 1991 gave the feeling that the fiscal problem was no longer critical.

In 1992, however, the fiscal situation changed dramatically. The decline in oil revenues and the important increase in costs, linked to depletion, real appreciation, and tax changes, meant that the fiscal tax revenues declined from 19 to 11 percentage points of GDP. Moreover, the February 4 military coup attempt put the government on the defensive and made harsh measures more difficult and costly to implement. A freeze on gasoline and electricity prices was forced on the government by the pressure of public opinion. The turbulence that ensued paralyzed the privatization process.

As the fiscal situation deteriorated, the government tried to change the fiscal stance by cutting expenditures, raising public sector prices, and increasing pressure on Congress to pass a comprehensive fiscal and financial reform. This process was hindered by the government's political weakness and by pressures to increase public sector wages. At a moment when the economy was expanding, creating new jobs, and raising living standards, the government was facing a serious lack of resources and had no room to accommodate the political pressures that were unleashed by the first coup attempt. Nevertheless, a package of reforms was approved in the second half of 1992 consisting of a new Central Bank law that granted independence to the monetary authority, new budgetary procedures and public credit laws that increased control over the deficit, and a new tax code to facilitate collection and prosecution. The tax reform, consisting of a new value-added tax and a new gross asset tax, remained hostage in Congress, however, due to the political parties' unwillingess to support harsh measures.

In 1992, the cut in expenditures and the improvement in tax collection allowed the government to keep the increase in the deficit to just a third of the fall in oil revenues. In early 1993, further cuts in spending and massive increases in prices for electricity, water, natural and domestic gas, Social Security contributions, and tax withholdings were implemented to keep the fiscal situation workable. However, it was impossible to secure a political coalition for the approval of the tax reform, which was required to give viability to the fiscal accounts.

The political uncertainties—prompted by the military coups of February and November 1992, by the disputes over some of the results of the December 1992 local elections, and by the set of events that led to the president's impeachment—caused financial markets to become nervous, prompted a major decline in the demand for money, and caused interest rates to rise. In these conditions, the deficit became difficult to finance internally, and foreign markets remained cautious.

Three important dynamics appear to explain the politics of this process. First, political forces seem to react with a lag over economic events. Thus the military coup attempt of February 1992 took place in the context of an economic boom that was creating modern sector jobs and increasing real wages, but it was prompted by a state of mind that had more to do with the reaction to a thirty-five-year-old political system (more than a three-year-old administration) that allowed traumas, such as 1989, to take place.

Second, the political opposition that was expressed through the attempted coup prompted some politicians, led by former President Rafael Caldera, to realign themselves to cater to the opposition's views. This shift, which became quite explicit, had a destabilizing effect on the political dynamic between the two main parties. The government wanted the taxes approved mainly to improve the economic outlook, since the whole collection process would take time to set up. In normal times, the opposition would have accepted such a move because it would make the next government's (that is, the opposition's) job easier. This time, however, responsible behavior on the opposition's part was exploited electorally by Caldera's group, and setting up a coalition became very difficult.

Third, the Venezuelan experience shows the trap into which tax reform falls in countries where the public sector runs a balance of payments surplus. First, the country starts to run a fiscal deficit toward the end of a government's term of office. Then the fiscal deficit turns into a balance of payments crisis as the administration uses reserves to prevent adjustment from taking place during its mandate. A new regime takes over and must do a major exchange-rate adjustment to correct the external crisis, which was in fact caused by a fiscal crisis. The devaluation wipes out the deficit temporarily, however, since the same number of oil barrels now buys more teachers and nurses. The devaluation also brings with it inflation and recession, which make tax reform less of a priority and weaken the government's support basis. As time goes on, the fiscal advantages provided by devaluation are eroded since teachers and nurses now demand higher wages. The deficit grows again, hopefully in time to be financed through reserve losses until the next election.

The important point in this cycle is that what drives it is the lack of tax reform; but the system generates a dynamic whereby when the system runs into a crisis, it is the exchange rate, not taxes, that moves. The pain caused by this adjustment makes tackling the real problem both temporarily unnecessary and politically difficult.

Finally, the reforms that were implemented in the second half of 1992 made the budget constraint faced by the treasury a truly binding one. With severe restrictions on borrowing, on budgetary revisions, and on Central Bank financing, the problem faced by the treasury is not that a large deficit may produce inflation, but instead that it simply does not have the cash to pay for budgeted expenditures. This predicament implies that a good part of the budgeted deficit is not realized and, to the degree that it does take place, it is financed through arrears, not money creation.

## CONCLUSION

The beginning of this chapter noted that Venezuela was an odd case, because it took on a major adjustment effort before going into the dreaded phase III; later sections described how the authorities adopted such a program unaware of its real consequences. This may have been to the country's benefit. After all, Christopher Columbus was able to embark on his celebrated journey only because he was mistaken about the distances involved. Had the actual outcome been known, it is unlikely that the venture would have ever been realized. But would Venezuela have avoided phase III?

In one sense, the Venezuelan experience highlights the reasons that cause most governments to fall into phase III: they may correctly perceive the short-run costs of avoiding it but commit the opposite mistake by thinking that inaction will not be as disastrous as it usually becomes. If our interpretation is accurate, however, a few of the costs paid by Venezuela in 1989 are not unique to adjustment efforts and may well have to be paid in phase III anyway.

Since even the most populist of governments is forced to devalue, it will suffer the contractionary effect produced by the fall in real financial assets and the rise in imported input costs. Moreover, since the policy environment is correctly perceived as unsustainable, the inventory cycle will appear, causing a contraction once some action is taken.

In hindsight, one can imagine a different policy package that may seem more conventional. The alternative strategy is based on the standard principle: stabilize first, adjust later. It emphasizes fiscal and monetary correction in the short run while leaving exchange unification and trade liberalization for later. As I have shown, however, this strategy is likely to be quite problematic.

It may be that the Venezuelan package was close to optimal, under the circumstances. The problem is that it was too much for the political process to absorb and too little to do the job of stabilization. Venezuela's long-run fiscal picture did not improve enough, given the oil scenarios that developed in the nineties. Thanks to privatization, restructuring, and targeting, some improvement did take place; yet the decline of the oil surplus was a much more important factor, whereas the real exchange rate overshooting provided only a temporary respite.

Here, political economy reenters the picture. Populism is made easier by fixed or predetermined exchange rates and controlled financial markets. A fiscal expansion will be financed by reserve losses until these run out. Meanwhile, the price level will not be much affected and the economy will grow until it hits a balance of payments crisis. By contrast, under a freer exchange regime, society permanently faces the following dilemmas: if it wants lower interest rates, it must accept higher exchange rates and prices (or vice versa). If it wants both lower exchange and interest rates, it must run a tighter fiscal policy. These tradeoffs may make fiscal restructuring politically viable.

It is said that there are two types of government: those that solve problems and those that prevent them. It seems that by preventing the dreaded phase III of the populist cycle, the government of Venezuela may have done a lot of good, but had a difficult time explaining what it had achieved. Governments that allow financial instability to take over may elicit more willingness to adjust and may have an easier job communicating.

The market-oriented reforms carried out in Venezuela since 1989 may guarantee that disequilibriums do not accumulate to the point of generating the type of explosive outcome seen in 1989. If the fiscal deficit is not dealt with, however, the economy may become a simmering hell characterized by a slowly increasing inflationary trend. I hope that the reforms carried out since 1989 at such a cost to Venezuelan society are seen as an investment that set the basis for long-lasting growth. I hope the new authorities see that the road to the future lies in dealing with the unfinished business of tax and fiscal reform and not in reversing what are clearly very sound building blocks for the country's future.

## NOTES

1. Since *populism* is a term invented by political scientists, its use by economists will always be subject to criticism. Here I consider populism not as a movement but as an attitude. It amounts to entitlements without duties, absolute rights with no tradeoffs, and

redistribution without the discipline of a budget constraint. In this context, it is no wonder that a macroeconomic theory that, by emphasizing underutilized resources, does away with budget constraints should sound like music to one's ears.

2. Rudiger Dornbusch and Sebastian Edwards, *The Macroeconomics of Populism in Latin America* (Chicago: University of Chicago Press, 1991), 11–12.

3. Dornbusch and Edwards argue that the fall in real wages is caused by the fact that capital is mobile and leaves the country, whereas labor is trapped; see ibid., 12.

4. The government program expected 2 percent growth and 37 percent inflation; I analyze the reasons for this error in the section titled "The Economic Impact of the Big Bang."

5. On Bolivia, see J. Sachs, "The Bolivian Hyperinflation and Stabilization," National Bureau of Economic Research Working Paper no. 2073, Cambridge, Mass.: 1986; J. A. Morales, "Inflation Stabilization in Bolivia," in M. Bruno et al., eds., *Inflation Stabilization: The Experience of Israel, Argentina, Brazil, Bolivia and Mexico* (Cambridge, Mass.: MIT Press, 1988), 307–57; and A. Carriaga, "Bolivia," in J. Williamson, ed., *Latin American Adjustment: How Much Has Happened?* (Washington, D.C.: Institute for International Economics, 1990), 41–53. On Israel, see M. Bruno and S. Piterman, "Israel's Stabilization: A Two Year Review," in Bruno et al., *Inflation Stabilization.*

6. I lack the space to go into any detail on recent Venezuelan economic history. The pre-1973 policy regime is analyzed in A. Baptista, "Tiempo de mengua: Los años finales de una estructura económica," in P. Cunill-Grau et al., eds., *Venezuela contemporánea 1974–1989* (Caracas: Fundación Mendoza, 1989), 105–56, and in R. Hausmann, *Shocks externos y ajuste macroeconómico* (Caracas: Banco Central de Venezuela, 1990), chap. 10. The reaction to the oil shocks is studied in F. Pazos, "Efectos de un augmento súbito en los ingresos externos: La economía de Venezuela en el quinquenio 1974–1978" (Caracas: Banco Central de Venezuela, 1979, mimeographed); M. Rodriguez, "La estrategia del crecimiento económico para Venezuela," Academia Nacional de Ciencias Económicas, Caracas, Notebook no. 19, 1987; F. Bourguignon and A. Gelb, "Venezuela," in A. Gelb, ed., *Oil Windfalls: A Blessing or a Curse?* (Oxford: Oxford University Press, 1989), 289–325; and Hausmann, *Shocks externos*, chapter 5. Capital flight is analyzed in M. Rodríguez, "Consequences of Capital Flight for Latin American Debtor Countries," in D. R. Lessard and J. Williamson, eds., *Capital Flight and Third World Debt* (Washington, D.C.: Institute for International Economics, 1987), 129–44.

7. Venezuelan policy in this period has been analyzed by Baptista, "Tiempo de mengua," and Hausmann, *Shocks externos*, chap. 10.

8. Presidential elections take place in Venezuela in early December every five years. The new government takes office in the first quarter of the following year. The reader should keep in mind the recurring coincidence of the political and economic cycles: 1979, 1984, and 1989 are years in which newly elected governments take over and also periods in which stabilization programs are adopted.

9. On the impact of the oil windfall, see Pazos, "Efectos de un aumento súbito en los ingresos externos"; Rodríguez, "La estrategia del crecimiento económico para Venezuela"; Bourguignon and Gelb, "Venezuela"; and Hausmann, *Shocks externos*, chap. 5.

10. It is interesting to note that in his inaugural address in 1979, President Luis Herrera Campíns announced that he was receiving an overindebted country and named a commission to study the problem and propose solutions. As a consequence of this initiative, the Public Credit Organic Law was made stricter in 1981 and short-term debt of decentralized agencies was restructured. This move, however, did not stop the fall into the debt crisis, which hit Venezuela in 1983. On this period see P. Palma, "1974–1983: Una década de contrastes en la economía venezolana," Academia Nacional de Ciencias Económicas, Caracas, Notebook no. 11, 2d ed., November 1985; Rodríguez, "La estrategia del crecimiento económico para Venezuela"; and Hausmann, *Shocks externos.*

11. Even though total public sector spending increased by only 0.5 percent in 1979–80, expenditures on nontradables rose by 5.1 percent, while those on tradables fell by

11.1 percent. Consequently, the policy alleviated the balance of payments more than it did the internal imbalance.

12. The dangerous political economy implications of the adopted multiple exchange regime are analyzed in R. Hausmann, "Venezuela," in Williamson, *Latin American Adjustment*, 224–44.

13. The average effective devaluation was 59 percent in 1987 with respect to 1986, because food products, pharmaceuticals, and other goods remained at the 7.50 bolivars per dollar rate.

14. Amazingly, in August 1988 the Lusinchi government adopted a financing policy based on the return to voluntary lending; needless to say, it ended in failure. Only U.S.$150 million were placed in bonds at an implicit rate of LIBOR+5 (London Interbank Offered Rate), mostly among Venezuelan institutional investors.

15. The rate of unemployment reached 6.9 percent in the second half of 1988. This clearly signals a situation close to full employment, since it was the lowest rate in nine years and was also below the 1967–82 average of 7.3 percent.

16. In some extreme cases of populist disequilibrium, the absence of goods on the shelves reduces the incentive to work and causes a decline in labor supply. This has been documented for the economies in Eastern Europe as well as in Tanzania, Angola, and Mozambique; see D. Bevan, P. Collier, and J. Gunning, "The Imploding Economy: Consequences of Generalised Price Controls," unpublished manuscript, Oxford, 1990. I do not believe this is a relevant phenomenon for Venezuela.

17. With imports hovering around 24 percent of GDP, moderate overinvoicing of 20 to 30 percent implies a rent of some 4 to 7 percent of GDP.

18. Besides the improvement in relative prices, the increase in the dollar value of oil exports accounted for 3.2 percentage points of GDP.

19. See R. Dornbusch, "Expectations and Exchange Rate Dynamics," *Journal of Political Economy* vol. 84 (December 1976): 1161–76.

20. See S. Edwards, "The Order of Liberalization of the External Sector in Developing Countries," Essays in International Finance no. 156, Princeton University, December 1984, and D. Rodrik, "Trade and Capital Account Liberalization in a Keynesian Economy," *Journal of International Economics*, no. 23 (1987): 113–29.

21. Higher oil revenues were overshadowed by lower income from other sources given the size of the recession. Spending fell short of target because of lower than expected exchange rate losses and subsidies to individuals. Exchange losses were due to the recognition of part of the outstanding letters of credit (LCs) at the old exchange rate. They were originally calculated at 4.9 percent of GDP but reached only 1.8 percent. Two mistakes were committed on this variable. First, given the rather awkward formula adopted and the lack of adequate information, the total amount of recognized LCs was overestimated. Second, the process of distributing the subsidies was significantly slower than expected. These mistakes overshadowed the fact that the subsidy per dollar was underestimated, given the higher than expected exchange rate. Social programs designed to alleviate the shock were held up in Congress until late in the year.

22. If we assume that **P** is a linear combination of the official and the parallel rate, with a dynamic adjustment process described by a Koyck polynomial, we can test the following equation:

$$\mathbf{P} = \mathbf{a}\,\mathbf{b}\,\mathbf{E}^c + \mathbf{a}\,(1-\mathbf{b})\,\mathbf{E}^f + (1-\mathbf{a})\,\mathbf{P}_{t-1}$$

where $\mathbf{E}^c$ and $\mathbf{E}^f$ are the commercial and the parallel exchange rates, **a** is the share of the commercial rate in **P**, $(1-\mathbf{a})$ is the share of the parallel rate, and **b** is the coefficient of adjustment. An unrestricted estimation of this equation using ordinary least squares with monthly data for the period from January 1985 to December 1989 offers the following (All prices were put as indexes with the base as January 1985. I used the wholesale price index, the average commercial exchange rate as calculated by the IMF, and the parallel rate.):

$$\text{WPI} = 0.173 \ \text{E}^c + 0.029 \ \text{E}^f + 0.789 \ \text{WPI}_{t-1} + 0.023$$
$$(7.6) \qquad (1.1) \qquad (23.7) \qquad (0.6)$$
$$R^2 = 0.998 \qquad \text{DW} = 1.39 \qquad N = 60 \qquad F = 4{,}196$$

This equation estimates **a** to be 0.82 and the speed of adjustment to be 21 percent. In other words, the commercial exchange rate was about four times as important as the parallel market rate in determining the price level. Notice also that the coefficient for the parallel rate is statistically insignificant. See Hausmann, *Shocks externos*, chap. 7, in which I present a model that generates this result. In that model, the price level is affected by the level of imports, which is decided exogenously by the government and is not influenced directly by the official exchange rate.

23. See Dornbusch, "Expectations and Exchange Rate Dynamics," and S. Edwards, *Real Exchange Rates, Devaluation and Adjustment: Exchange Rate Policy for Developing Countries* (Cambridge, Mass.: MIT Press, 1989).

24. The abandonment of the multiple exchange rate regime is studied in José Saúl Lizondo, "Unification of Dual Exchange Rate Markets," *Journal of International Economics*, no. 22 (1987): 57–77; M. Obstfeld, "Capital Controls, the Dual Exchange Rate and Devaluation," *Journal of International Economics*, no. 20 (1986): 1–20; D. Park and J. Sachs, "Capital Controls and the Timing of Exchange Regime Collapse," National Bureau of Economic Research Working Paper no. 2250, Cambridge, Mass., May 1987; and M. Kiguel and J. S. Lizondo, "Adoption and Abandonment of Exchange Controls Regimes," unpublished manuscript, Washington, D.C.; World Bank, 1988. The following two paragraphs of the text present the standard prediction of these models.

25. In this framework, money "velocity" is a questionable concept and is certainly not well used.

26. Such a rise in private financial savings is inconsistent with a fiscal interpretation of the recession.

27. This result was predicated on the assumption that a rise in interest rates would change the incentives to hold bolivar assets, since up to that point the choice between foreign and domestic assets was a rather one-sided game. Average ex-postnominal returns on New York certificates of deposit were well above ninety-day time deposits in Caracas during the period from 1985 to 1988, whereas they became similar in 1989.

28. C. Díaz-Alejandro, *Exchange Rate Devaluation in a Semi-Industrialized Economy: The Experience of Argentina 1955–1961* (Cambridge, Mass.: MIT Press, 1965), and P. Krugman and L. Taylor, "Contractionary Effects of Devaluation," *Journal of International Economics*, no. 8 (1978): 445–56.

29. To get an idea of the magnitude of this effect, I ran a regression between output and real money balances (M2) for 1970 to 1986 using quarterly data. I found a long-run elasticity of output to real monetary balances of 0.39. Given the actual decline in these assets, this effect could explain a drop in GDP of 6 percent.

30. It must be pointed out that this calculation is also affected by the internal price of oil products, which increased more than average prices during the year. Nevertheless, internal sales amount to less than 20 percent of total sales of the oil industry.

31. It should be noted that this effect incorporates the contractionary impact of the fall in real wages.

32. In M. Kiguel and N. Liviatan, "Inflation Cycles in Argentina and Brazil," paper presented to the seminar "Inflation Stabilization: What Have We Learned," Bank of Israel, Jerusalem, January 31 to February 2, 1990, the authors argue that the recent inflation cycles in Argentina and Brazil can be explained in part as the consequence of generalized expectations that the government will rely on price controls to stop inflation. By attempting to increase their prices before the next freeze, agents accelerate inflation and prompt the government to act. Our case may be interpreted as the exact opposite. Agents know that the government will try to maintain the price level as long as possible, but that eventually it will be forced to give way. By accumulating inventories, they force the collapse in policy.

33. A contractionary effect of devaluation, as analyzed in the literature, is the fall in real credit and its effects on supply. See S. van Wijnbergen, "Exchange Rate Management and Stabilization Policies in Developing Countries," in S. Edwards and L. Ahamed, eds., *Economic Adjustment and Exchange Rates in Developing Countries* (Chicago: University of Chicago Press, 1986), 17–41, and S. Montenegro, "Stabilization Policy in Open Developing Economies: The Case of Colombia," unpublished Ph.D. dissertation, Oxford University, 1990. In Venezuela during 1989 the stock of net real bank credit to the private sector fell by 37.8 percent in the real stock. This may suggest that excess demand for credit would appear given the large rise in working capital requirements to be financed through one's own funds. Contrary to what may be expected, the credit market during most of the year was characterized by excess supply, with bank liquid reserves rising quickly. The inventory cycle helps explain this anomaly. Of course, there was also a positive wealth effect for the productive sector due to the fall in the real value of their debt to banks.

34. During 1990, the industrial opinion survey for the first quarter of 1990 carried out by the Council of Industries (CONINDUSTRIA) and published in *El Universal* on May 14, 1990, showed companies facing unexpectedly high demand levels. This surprise is the consequence of the fact that during the worst of the recession, companies tended to interpret current demand (consumption minus inventory use) as current consumption and planned output accordingly. When demand reappears, actual consumption levels do not necessarily go up—they are just supplied out of current output rather than out of existing stocks. For a theoretical presentation of inventory cycles, see O. Blanchard and S. Fischer, *Lectures in Macroeconomics* (Cambridge, Mass.: MIT Press, 1989), chap. 6.

35. For the case of agriculture and some manufacturing sectors, such as agroindustry and pharmaceuticals, the increase in imported input costs was higher because many items were subject to the preferential rate of 7.50 bolivars per dollar, implying a devaluation of 406 percent for products subject to this subsidy.

# 10

# The Question of Inefficiency and Inequality: Social Policy in Venezuela

## *Janet Kelly*

There is no better way to capture the social situation in Venezuela than to arrive at the Simón Bolívar Airport, better known locally as Maiquetía, in the daytime. As your jet circles over the sparkling blue waters of the Caribbean, you first see rising green mountains lifting over a flat, narrow stretch of coastline. Next are the brick-colored foothills, where the tropical lushness gives way to a swath of haphazard housing strewn precariously over the rising land. Finally in the airport, you pass by well-stocked duty-free shops and begin to enter the chaotic world that is modern Venezuela: between airport and city are ambiguous public officials, uniformed porters assisted by a myriad of poorly dressed men and young boys, dispatchers with unclear functions, and taxis more often illegal than not. You will suspect that modernity has arrived unevenly in Venezuela and that in this country of potential, poverty and wealth coexist uncomfortably. And despite the haste of your analysis, you will be right.

The central human problem in most developing countries is the poverty that excludes a significant portion of the population from a decent life. Although in even the poorest countries there are usually enough resources to provide everyone with enough to eat, access to food and essential services is insufficient among the neediest. At the same time, even the middle and upper classes suffer from an inadequate supply of public services—roads, security, water, electricity, parks, and other amenities that are taken for granted in developed countries. Venezuela has not yet solved its social problem even minimally in these terms and thus continues to be classified as a "middle-income developing country." This chapter reviews Venezuela's efforts to develop an adequate social policy during the democratic period since 1958 and analyzes the reasons for its successes and failures along the way. The grand question is whether the current system can provide the impetus to transform the country in the coming years, ensuring both equity and prosperity.

## THE CENTRALITY OF SOCIAL POLICY

The aim of social policy is to intervene in the workings of a community so as to improve the chances of the underprivileged and provide a minimum of decency for those who cannot help themselves for whatever reason. Social policy should also ensure the provision of public goods to all members of the society.[1] Finally, social policy must be designed so that its incentives favor the general development of the system. When social policy fails, many children receive inadequate nutrition, education, and health care and, as a result, grow up to propagate the vicious cycle of poverty. In addition, the middle classes feel cheated of the just products of their labor. When social policy is badly designed, the productive capacity of the country stalls, investment moves elsewhere, and entrepreneurship goes underground. Under these circumstances, politics tends to oscillate between populist excesses and cruel adjustments pushed and pulled alternately by popular resentment and elite resistance.

Venezuela, a country endowed with one of the largest oil reserves in the world, is no exception to the rule that failures in social policy lead to serious weaknesses in the polity itself. Deficient social services arouse the ire of people who do not understand why the government cannot seem to deliver. Poverty has stubbornly refused to cede, despite the sustained social ideology that has characterized all of Venezuela's governments in the democratic period since 1958.

If we accept Richard Titmuss's definition of social policy as choices about the constitution of a "good society," it is clear that social policy is central to the question of development and to the viability of a political system in satisfying the population as a whole. But it is not enough to decide what is the good society; it is also necessary to put it into practice, deliver, or implement it through an efficient social administration. Both aspects will determine the final outcome, and both are considered here.[2]

## WHERE DOES VENEZUELA STAND WITH REGARD TO SOCIAL WELFARE?

It is common sport in Venezuela to complain about the abysmal state of life in general and about the dilapidated condition of public services and infrastructure in particular. The schools are run down, the hospitals are chaotic and lacking in basic supplies, the streets and sidewalks (when they exist) are full of holes, the water (when it flows) is contaminated, the courts and prisons are a disgrace, and so on. Comparisons with Europe or the United States invariably depress even the cheerful, and the idea persists that, somehow, things should be much better than they are. Antonio Francés reflects this public perception when he compares social spending in Venezuela with that in other countries: "The Venezuelan government has not been stingy in the least when it comes to social concerns. But it has been careless in its spending and not at all effective in delivery."[3]

It is unclear why the country is not better off than it is. A widely held belief is that the country's failings have much to do with government waste and corruption, a cause that has supplanted the traditional villains: colonial heritage and imperialist injustice. Venezuela is a country that *should* be rich, but is not; a country that has wealth that never gets to the people. It is not the purpose of this chapter to determine how rich the country should be, because we might suppose that all countries should be at the level of Switzerland or Japan had they chosen some other path a few centuries back. Instead I ask where Venezuela might be if it used its existing resources better.

A simple exercise is instructive. Venezuela's gross domestic product (GDP) per capita in 1990 was U.S.$2,560 according to the World Bank. In the income class up to about U.S.$3,000 per capita, there are almost one hundred countries that have all had to make hard choices about where to invest their resources, including all Latin American nations. In table 10.1, I compare what might be considered the "best possible level of achievement" by all the South American or Caribbean countries in this group with the level achieved by Venezuela.[4]

From table 10.1 we can conclude that in important areas, Venezuela does not have such a bad record in its income class. The most "successful" countries in some cases are not much better off than Venezuela and, in other cases, are anomalies in the group because of some special attention to one social goal or other (medicine in Cuba, university education in Uruguay). Indeed, international comparisons are intrinsically difficult due to differences that can occur in local measurements and should be considered significant only in the case of wide divergences. For instance, while Venezuelans expect to be better off than their Southern Cone neighbors because of officially higher per capita income, another measure of income adjusted for real purchasing power shows Venezuela to have a lower per capita income than Chile, Argentina, Mexico, and even Brazil, although the differences among all

Table 10.1
COMPARATIVE SOCIAL INDICATORS, 1990

| Indicator | Venezuela | Best performance in Latin America/ Caribbean | Country with best performance[d] |
|---|---|---|---|
| Life expectancy (yrs.) | 70 | 75.2 | Cuba |
| Illiteracy (%) | 12 | 5 | Argentina |
| Energy consumption (kg. equiv. of oil) | 2,447 | 1,801 | Argentina[e] |
| Population growth (%/yr., 1980–90) | 2.7 | 1.3 | Jamaica |
| Births per 1,000 population | 29 | 17 | Uruguay |
| Population per medical doctor | 590 (1989)[a] | 333 (1988) | Cuba |
| Infant mortality (per 1,000 births, 1985–90) | 24.8[c] | 11.0[a] | Barbados |
| Calories per day | 2,582 (1989) | 3,052 | Mexico |
| Primary school enrollment (% pop. 7–12 yrs.)[a] | 105 (1989) | 117 (1985) | Ecuador |
| Postsecondary school enrollment (% pop. 20–24 yrs.) | 28 | 50.0 | Uruguay |
| Housing: persons per room in urban area | 1.4 | 1.3 | Chile |
| Urbanization (% pop.) | 84 | 86 | Chile |
| Telephones (persons per line)[b] | 11.3 | 3.9 | Costa Rica |
| Crime (murders per 100,000 pop., 1984)[b] | 8.4 | 0.2 | Argentina |

*Source:* World Bank, *World Development Report* (Washington, D.C.: World Bank, 1992), except the following:
[a](Comisión Económica para América Latina y el Caribe (CEPAL), *Anuario estadístico CEPAL* (Santiago, Chile: CEPAL, 1990).
[b]*Economist, Book of Vital World Statistics* (New York: Random House, 1990).
[c]Oficina Central de Estadística e Informática (OCEI), *Anuario estadístico 1990* (Caracas: OCEI, 1989).
[d]When more than one country has the same level of indicator, only the country with the lower per capita income level is listed.
[e]Trinidad is excluded because its consumption is not comparable. Ecologists might protest that higher energy consumption goes against development, but it is assumed here that energy consumption in less developed countries is a sign of industrialization and access to consumer goods. It is legitimate, of course, to doubt the "goodness" of this indicator.

these countries are slight.[5] Additionally, the intensive attention that one country may give to a single social indicator may prejudice its ability to maintain the level of consumption of social services in other areas.

Can Venezuela be considered clearly deficient in any one of the indicators in table 10.1? Certain health indicators look unusually weak. Infant mortality is much higher than in Uruguay, Argentina, Panama, Costa Rica, Chile, or Jamaica; this seems more connected to high population growth rates (and, probably, high rates of teenage pregnancies with little or no medical control during pregnancy) than to the availability of doctors. Caloric intake also appears to be unusually low compared with countries with similar income levels. On the other hand, educational statistics are comparable to most other Latin and Caribbean countries, although at the secondary level enrollments in Cuba, Chile, Argentina, Uruguay, and Costa Rica are much higher than in Venezuela and the rest of Latin America. At the same time, Venezuela is among the countries with the highest postsecondary school enrollments in the region. It compares favorably with the best-endowed Latin American countries in telephones (11.3 persons per line), but suffers a high crime rate (similar to U.S. levels in murders).

What one can conclude from these comparisons is that Venezuela is not much better or worse off than other countries from the region in its income group, and that some of its more pressing problems are associated with an inability to keep up with burgeoning population growth. The countries with lower population growth have, on the whole, been better able to provide health, education, and nutrition in a virtuous circle whereby a better educated and healthier population also tends to take better care of itself. The birth rate is not important so much in terms of absolute pressure on space or resources as it is in terms of the burden on the working-age population to invest in the young.[6] The so-called dependency ratio that measured the young (under fifteen years old) and old (over sixty-four) populations as a percent of the working age population (fifteen to sixty-four years old) places Venezuela in a disadvantageous situation. In an international comparison made in the *World Competitiveness Report: 1992*, Venezuela figured in the next-to-last position, worse off only than Pakistan.[7]

## WHAT KIND OF SOCIAL ADVANCEMENT HAS OCCURRED?

Venezuela came late to development, mainly because of the lack of development or modernization efforts by dictatorial governments until almost the middle of the twentieth century. In this sense, it may be unfair to compare Venezuela with countries that have much longer traditions in health and education; we must also compare Venezuela with itself and its own starting point in the early 1960s. It is here, perhaps, that indicators will show the most progress.

### Income

Although national income is in principle independent of social policy, social results are to an important extent dependent on the resources available to the society for application to social goals. Income levels are the starting point for social policy and, given the relatively stable pattern of distribution, determine the welfare level that people may achieve apart from policy intervention. Income levels put strict limits, for instance, on access to food and shelter, on the taxing power of the state, and on resources available for investment in social infrastructure, such as water, transport facilities, and electrification.

Income in Venezuela depends strongly on the oil receipts that finance government activity and provide foreign exchange. When oil prices or production falls, as it did in the 1980s, nearly everyone's income in Venezuela falls. The percentage of the population living below the poverty line rose to 40 percent in 1989 compared with about 25 percent in 1981.[8] The rise in poverty—and the decline in nutrition that accompanied it—was popularly attributed to poor economic management and ineffective social policies in the period, particularly to the so-called economic package implemented after 1989, in which price and exchange controls were removed and the currency devalued (see figure 10.1).

Figure 10.1 does not, however, show anything in particular about which policies were successful or unsuccessful. It indicates only that income levels in the late eighties were comparable to those of the early

### Figure 10.1
### Evolution of real per capita income, 1977 = 100

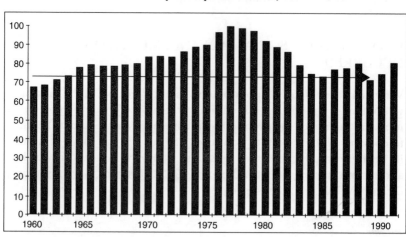

*Source:* Central Bank of Venezuela, *Informe económico*, and Oficina Central de Estadística e Informática (OCEI), 1991.

sixties. Although the 11 percent drop in real per capita income in 1989 did accompany the liberalization policy implemented in that year, growth resumed thereafter. But none of these changes can erase the fact that Venezuelans had begun a downward slide as early as 1978. Real per capita income in 1991 had fallen by 19 percent since the peak of 1977. It should come as no surprise that people felt they were worse off: they had indeed suffered a precipitous decline in welfare that left all social sectors disenchanted with the performance of the system. They tended to blame social policy for the disastrous result, although they might better have attributed their plight to the fortunes of the oil market, where prices had fallen in 1988 to only one-third of their historical high.

*Health and Nutrition*

Whatever health complaints are heard in Venezuela, the citizens today live longer and are better protected against sickness than at any time in the nation's history. Table 10.2 illustrates the progress made since 1960. The figures on health should not be interpreted as meaning that all is well in health in Venezuela, but only that important progress has occurred since 1960. This progress slowed at the beginning of the 1980s, and even went backward in the case of calorie (and protein) consumption, which is associated with the fall in family income suffered in the 1980s. There is a suspicion that in the area of public health, efforts declined in the 1980s as well. While not, perhaps, affecting overall mortality, there has been a worrisome increase in diseases such as malaria, cholera, Chagas's disease, dengue fever, and similar tropical

Table 10.2
HEALTH INDICATORS

| Indicator | 1960–65 | 1965–70 | 1970–75 | 1975–80 | 1980–85 | 1985–90 |
|---|---|---|---|---|---|---|
| Life expectancy | 61.0 | 63.8 | 66.2 | 67.7 | 69.0 | 69.7 |
| Infant mortality per 1,000 births | 72.8 | 59.5 | 48.6 | 43.3 | 38.7 | 35.9 |
| Population per medical doctor | 1,487 | n.a. | 1,120 | n.a. | 850 | 642 |
| Hospital beds per 1,000 population | 3.5 | n.a. | 2.9 | 2.8 | 2.7 | 2.5 |
| Calories per day | n.a. | 2,413 | 2,348 | 2,665 | 2,550 | 2,534 |

*Source:* CEPAL, *Anuario estadístico CEPAL,* 1990.
*Note:* In some cases, data availability required that the figures supplied be for the year or average of years closest to the specified dates. n.a. = not available.

ailments that require public health efforts in fumigation, water purification, education, and the like.

It is widely believed in Venezuela that the quality of health care has declined, although most statistics on health conditions indicate a slow but steady improvement. Opinions about the inadequacy of health care may largely reflect a sense that the population is paying for a service that it does not receive. Mandatory contributions to the Venezuelan Institute for Social Security—which give every wage earner the right to receive care at Social Security hospitals—generally are viewed as lost payments. Social Security hospitals provide a quality of attention below that considered acceptable to the middle classes, who tend to provide themselves as well with private insurance policies to cover their needs at private clinics. At the same time, these hospitals do provide services to those who do not contribute to the system (nonworkers and informal workers and their families). According to one study, approximately one-half of those served by Social Security hospitals are not paying members of the system. Only 7.3 million workers and their families are covered by the system—about 35 percent of the population. In some sense, the rest of the population might be considered to belong to the gray world of the informal economy, where both contribution and access to the publicly supported social network is only partial.

The Social Security system has been heavily criticized, not only because of the inefficiency and irrationality of its hospitals, but also because of the bankrupt state of its pension fund. Its hospitals should be transferred to local government control under the restructuring plan, while the Social Security Institute would limit itself to making payments to those hospitals against services provided to its members. Such a plan would undoubtedly improve the situation for system members, while leaving the nonmember population at the door of other public facilities outside the Social Security system.

*Schooling*

Education receives even sharper public criticism than health, despite the improvement in enrollments, the expansion of the university system, and the extension of public schooling in all categories (see table 10.3). In general, the complaints against the educational system have to do with quality and with the failure to train the population for participation in the labor force in a productive way. However, despite the desperate tone of the critics, things have been steadily improving. Although illiteracy stands at 12 percent, the rate among youngsters ten to fourteen years old was 4.7 percent according to the 1990 census, heavily

## Table 10.3
## EDUCATION INDICATORS

| Indicator | 1965 | 1985–90 |
|---|---|---|
| Preschool enrollment (% of children aged 4–6) | n.a. | 65 |
| Primary school enrollment (% of age group) | 94 | 105 |
| Secondary school enrollment (% of age group) | 27 | 56 |
| University and technical enrollment (% of age group) | 7 | 28 |
| Illiteracy rate (% of population) | 37 | 9 |

*Sources:* Illiteracy: CEPAL, *Anuario estadístico CEPAL,* 1990; enrollments: OCEI, *Anuario estadístico,* except literacy and preschool figures for 1989: OCEI, Census 1990.
*Note:* In some cases, data availability required that the figures supplied be for the year or average of years closest to the specified dates. n.a. = not available.

concentrated in rural areas; among urban youth, the rate is as low as 1.6 percent.[9]

The problem of education in the modern world goes far beyond mere reading ability. Participation in the world economy requires a competitive work force able to handle the demands of the productive system. Ability to read according to literacy standards is not the same as functional literacy for getting along in a world of written instructions. On this count, surely Venezuelans with only primary education—the majority of the population—do not qualify.

One may argue that the Venezuelan education system has been badly designed to provide for the needs of the greater part of the population that will not attend college, but which should still play a central role in the growth of productivity. No country can grow if it lacks good clerks, secretaries, bank tellers, salespeople, machine operators, public servants, carpenters, plumbers, stevedores, or bus drivers. In fact, since the early seventies, it would appear that the system has been designed to produce only engineers, scientists, lawyers, doctors, and other professionals. Most of the emphasis in middle and secondary education has been geared toward academic subjects, based on the sentiment that all should have an equal shot at getting to the university. Unfortunately, the difficulty of such subjects is one of the main factors in promoting school desertion, with few educational alternatives for those students who do not make the grade. The result of the skewedness of the education system is reflected in a study of foreign executives' perceptions of Venezuela as a site for investment: the survey showed that foreign investors were more concerned about the scarcity of skilled labor in Venezuela than about problems they might meet in recruiting managers or professionals.

National discussion of the educational system is beginning to produce a reconsideration of the priorities assigned in the last decades. The national system for trades training, Instituto Nacional de Cooperación Educativa (INCE), underwent a reorganization aimed at decentralized control and private sector involvement under the leadership of an oil industry human resources director and with the collaboration of important private sector leaders. But it will take many years before the status of technical education approaches the levels found in developed countries like Germany or Japan.

At the same time, the political pressure in favor of decentralization of all government functions, the creation of stronger state and local governments (made possible by the direct election of governors and mayors), and the dedication of educational crusaders tend to generate new experiments in education. This is not to suggest that Venezuela should seek out fads; administrators are trying a back-to-basics approach of longer school days (most public schools operate a double schedule such that students attend classes for only half of the school day), more time dedicated to reading programs and mathematical literacy, and teacher upgrading. Unfortunately, it is difficult to measure the quality of education, since there are no standardized tests of achievement administered on the national level.

Education is the key social policy insofar as it affects the productive ability of the population. Venezuela has made much progress in the field, but it would appear that education should be the centerpiece of social policy in the 1990s.

## Housing and Urban Development

The urbanization of Venezuela has imposed a heavy burden on social policy. Much of the urbanization of the country occurred before the 1960s. In 1965, 70 percent of the population was urbanized and by 1990, the proportion had grown to 84 percent. When we take into account the growth of the population in general, this twenty-five-year period represents an increase of ten million persons in cities and towns since 1965. Providing for the infrastructure necessary for this number of people is equivalent to providing for practically one-half of today's total population, or to building ten medium-sized cities of one million inhabitants each. This would be a huge task for any country—virtually impossible for a poor one. Indeed, the growth of the population, and in particular the urban population, has brought chaos, crowding, service failures, traffic problems, and bad humor to Venezuelans over the last decades.

The poor have continued to build their own *ranchos*, houses of blocks with prefabricated roofs, on land to which they often have no property rights. Such haphazard and informal building tends to create extensive areas of unplanned urbanization without the services necessary for a healthful environment. The housing stock of 3.5 million units in 1990 included 444,000 units (13 percent) classified as *ranchos*, although the proportion of inadequate housing is certainly greater than this.[10] By some estimates, in 1991 the country had a deficit of housing units that had reached 1.5 million, affecting 40 percent of the population. The feeling that the government could not keep up with the housing problem led to an innovative effort by the Herrera Campíns government (1979–84) to try to improve the housing condition of existing units and to provide minimum structural standards to new informal units—a policy styled as "housing solutions," meant to provide a cheaper way to upgrade the housing stock.

The succeeding governments of Jaime Lusinchi and Carlos Andrés Pérez tried to combine the orientation of past policies with a radically new policy that established the National Housing Council and aimed at creating a huge new pool of financial resources, via payroll deductions made available through the private financial system, for housing at the lower end of the market. One portion of these funds was reserved for directly funded, publicly constructed housing for the poor, while the rest was available for low-cost housing through private financial institutions that would use a raffle system to ration the mortgage funds. Even such a vast program could not put much of a dent in the housing deficit: in two years under the new system seventy thousand units (not necessarily new) had been financed, constituting about 5 percent of the "deficit." It should be remembered that population growth alone requires the construction of one hundred thousand new units a year just to keep pace. In 1990, only about forty-nine thousand units were built, although construction recovered significantly in the next two years. It is not impossible that the public policy effort of the National Housing Council has merely served to displace savings (from private to public) and to displace mortgage financing (from private sources to public sources), although some figures do show a slow improvement: the number of persons per housing unit declined steadily from 5.7 in 1971 to 5.1 in 1990.[11]

Housing is an area of social concern that is particularly dependent on income levels. The investment required to build a housing unit is huge when compared to the family income levels of the largest part of the population and when compared to public funds available; thus public policy tends to limit itself to lowering the cost of purchase only at the margin. This margin cannot be reduced enough to favor the poor, whose disposable income after food, education, and clothing simply does not meet any standard for credit. In this sense, the alternative of simply bringing services to the poor—water, sewerage, electricity, public telephones, trash removal, and streets and transport—may in the end do more to better their lot than housing programs that reach only the few.

### Transportation

The older generation in Venezuela often looks back to the dictatorial years of the 1950s as the golden age of infrastructure construction, especially in road transport. In those years, crucial intercity routes were turned into modern highways that for the first time permitted Venezuelans to travel about in their own country. The democratic period, in turn, is often characterized as one of little progress in transportation. But if we compare 1966 with 1991, we find that the total kilometers of road service have grown from thirty-nine thousand to eighty-six thousand kilometers, an increase of 120 percent. The increase in concrete and asphalt roads was 132 percent, although in the same period population grew by 106 percent. There was progress, but it was slight. In the meantime, the number of private automobiles increased by almost 250 percent, with predictable results on traffic flow, time lost, and accidents. While there was talk of putting out major highways to bid by potential concessionaires, little progess has been made in improving maintenance or widening the road network.

Public transport in the democratic period became increasingly private, as public bus companies disappeared under the weight of bad management and corruption. Private buses and jeep services at least provided a flexible response to demand, in that new routes could be quickly incorporated to serve new populations, even in remote areas. But the absence of public control of such companies often meant that service would not be provided at times of low demand: nothing could stop drivers of buses and taxis from calling it a day when traffic came to a standstill.

In Caracas, where the worst problems of public transportion and traffic developed, the construction of a new subway system was one of the few initiatives that really made a difference for all social classes. The Caracas Metro is a shining example of effective and popular social policy—a company whose success is often attributed to the vision of a single man, José González Lander, who has been president since its inception and who had the good judgment to extend the first lines from those areas where the poor are concentrated toward the city center, where jobs tend to be. The Metro Company also decided to go into the bus business, offering premium service through feeder lines that carry people to Metro stations.

Public transportation has been and remains dispersed and unsatisfactory. Apart from initiatives like the Caracas Metro, the system suffers from the weakness of transportation authorities to devise and impose rational routes and rates. To an important extent, the deficiencies of public transport and of road construction and maintenance have their origin in social policies aimed at protecting the poor from excessively costly services. Bus and taxi fares were long controlled by the central government, to the point where profits could be extracted only at the cost of quality service and even at the cost of safety. Again, the Metro might serve as an example of a service whose higher price causes few complaints from users who appreciate the quality difference. Yet transport fares are a sensitive issue. The urban riots of February 1989 began with disturbances resulting from fare hikes announced only two weeks after the start of Pérez's government. Clearly citizens require service improvements before they will accept fare increases.

*Equality before the Law*

It is not possible, in this short space, to do "justice" to the legal system in Venezuela. In most countries, the legal system is not even considered to be a part of "social policy"; rather it is taken for granted as a neutral part of the social system. In Venezuela, however, the judicial, police, and prison systems have come to be taken as crucial elements for social development, requiring reforms to ensure justice for all social classes. Some problems are the following:[12]

- Judges are held in low repute and the courts are often characterized as corrupt.
- Police are distrusted by the very people they are supposed to protect because of their reputation for violence and graft.
- Prisons are highly dangerous places, with little internal control of violence.
- Prisoners rarely have contact with public defenders and often serve more time before coming to judgment than the total time of their final sentence.
- Civil cases tend to be resolved, but depend on questionable relationships between lawyers and judges.

The legal system in Venezuela requires an overhaul and, until such a time as citizens begin to have faith in it, will continue to undermine the legitimacy of the political system as a whole. The problem is both economic and cultural. A recent study undertaken by a team from the Simón Bolívar University found that 98 percent of the courts were operating below the minimum standard necessary to carry out their daily business.[13] The costs of providing a decent environment for the courts, added to the costs of clean and efficient jails, may go beyond what the government can allocate to this social subsystem. The cultural problem is just as deep: how to ensure that judges and lawyers have the knowledge and the ethical anchors that are needed for any legal system to function. The legal system constitutes one of the weakest links in the chain of social policy, and it remains to be seen what priority will be given to its reform.

## IS INCOME REDISTRIBUTION NECESSARY FOR GUARANTEEING THE GOOD SOCIETY?

It would be comforting to think that income redistribution alone might resolve the difficulties of the poor. If this were so, however, we would find that countries such as Bangladesh and India had achieved the necessary social parity to reduce the indignities of poverty. Both countries display income distribution patterns similar to those found in Sweden, Japan, and Belgium, the three most egalitarian economies in the developed world, where the poorest 20 percent of the population receives at least 8 percent of total family incomes.[14] But being relatively equal in a very poor country only ensures that one feels well accompanied in one's neediness.

This is not to say that income distribution does not matter, but only that the absolute level of income in a country is a more powerful indicator of the living level of the poorest people than are the statistics on income distribution. Venezuela's income distribution is typical for countries in its income category, yet clearly more skewed in favor of the rich than any of the developed countries. According to the World Bank's Income Comparison Project (which attempts to correct for distortions in exchange rates and buying power), Venezuela's richest 20 percent of families receive just over 50 percent of total family incomes, while the poorest 20 percent receive only 4.7 percent of total family incomes. Among Latin American countries, this constitutes a more equal distribution than that found in most countries analyzed, although in developed countries, typically the 20 percent richest families receive about 40 percent of total incomes and the poorest 20 percent receive 6 percent. Needless to say, in the developed countries absolute levels of income are much higher and tend to provide for basic human needs.[15]

Might we conclude that a more equal income distribution is a semi-automatic product of development? Or does an income redistribution policy act as a spur to development? Should social policy actively redistribute? One difficulty of answering these sorts of questions is that income distribution figures tend not to capture the effects of distributive policies. When governments implement policies aimed at alleviating poverty, family income may not change, even though consumption and access to services improve. For instance, a school lunch program does not increase family income, but it does make possible higher levels of food consumption or, at least, more disposable income available to the family unit that benefits. Even cash distribution programs may fail to be registered as income to the degree that income survey responses ignore supplements not earned.

Some efforts have been advanced to analyze the distributive impact of social spending in Veneuela, in order to go beyond mere cash income comparisons. In general, government spending on social goods and services benefits the rich more than the poor, although, in relative terms, the poor tend to enjoy a greater benefit relative to their own income.[16] One study estimated the redistributive effect of spending in education, health, social security, housing, and other social services, together with spending on other items at the national level, and concluded the same.[17]

Income distribution is one of the variables most resistant to change, short of revolutionary policies aimed at overthrowing the existing order. Despite diverse policies favoring the poor, most countries exhibit stability in distribution. For this reason, many conclude that only policies that affect overall national income reduce poverty levels. This view can be criticized as passive or "trickle down," but it is nevertheless powerful. In Venezuela in the 1980s, a period of sharply declining per capita income, the distribution of the economic pie changed only slightly (table 10.4).

In any case, there are severe practical and political limits to social policies based on simple income redistribution. In Venezuela, the income tax system exempts the greater part of the population. Individuals earning up to the equivalent of U.S.$3,500 per year do not have to declare, while those earning considerably more enjoy enough exemptions to keep from paying as well. There are exemptions for school payments, medical costs, car repairs, utility payments, rent and interest, and so on. Although there is room for increasing taxes on the rich, it would be difficult to reduce taxes on the poor. Individual income taxes, plus Social Security and taxes on goods and services paid in the entire

Table 10.4
INCOME DISTRIBUTION IN THE 1980S

| Families in the: | 1981 | 1987 | 1989 | 1990 |
|---|---|---|---|---|
| Lowest quintile | 5.2 | 4.9 | 4.9 | 5.1 |
| Second lowest quintile | 9.2 | 8.7 | 9.5 | 9.9 |
| Middle quintile | 14.4 | 14.3 | 14.4 | 14.8 |
| Second highest quintile | 22.5 | 21.9 | 22.1 | 22.3 |
| Highest quintile | 48.8 | 49.3 | 49.2 | 47.8 |

*Source:* G. Márquez et al., "Gestión fiscal y distribución del ingreso en Venezuela," study carried out for the Network of Research Centers in Applied Economics of the Inter-American Development Bank (Caracas: IESA, 1991), 7.
*Note:* This table is based on the household survey carried out by the OCEI. The author based the conclusions on a sampling of the survey.

country, do not amount to more than 8.7 percent of total government receipts, versus 58 percent in the United States (where corporate taxes take up much of the rest) and 87 percent in a supposedly low-tax country like Italy, where indirect taxes are important.[18]

Only a negative income tax would make the system more redistributive; in effect, a negative income tax of sorts already exists through direct cash benefits, particularly the so-called *bono alimentario,* or direct food subsidy of U.S.$7.50 per month per school-aged child, which is currently available to people whose children are enrolled in public schools serving low-income areas. The cash subsidy is supplemented by tickets for powdered milk and corn flour, the school milk program, and special arrangements for pregnant women and infants.

It should be obvious from the preceding observations that direct income distribution policies are difficult politically and provide only marginal solutions in the long run. They may be necessary as part of a safety net to prevent malnutrition and help the poorest send their children to school, but they do not create the dynamics for balanced development. They do nothing to improve overall service provision and may even displace more effective long-run policies.

## THE AIM AND CONTENT OF SOCIAL POLICY

The level of per capita income in Venezuela is the underlying cause of backwardness. We have already seen that in some countries it has been possible to maintain better social indicators given similar income levels, but it is not possible to reach an acceptable level of health, social security, or education as long as a country suffers from the absolute scarcities that correspond to a per capita income of U.S.$2,500. This uncomfortable truth should not be taken as a fatal condemnation to long-run poverty, however. The strategy chosen by the country in addressing its social policy is critical in determining the evolution of poverty over the longer term.

*Alternative Strategies*

Social policy would be a relatively easy problem to address if the past experiences in other countries had produced clear results as to which strategies are more effective in which situations. But in two areas at least—education and health—heavy state intervention seems to be a key to explaining higher levels of social welfare. The fact that education and health play a central and positive role is widely recognized because of their dynamic and positive effects on all social variables. Strategy differences appear at the level of how to intervene most effectively in these areas and to what extent other policies must be implemented alongside the core projects.

## THE HERITAGE OF SOCIAL POLICY

Social policy did not start from zero in the democratic period beginning in 1958. The development of the oil industry in the 1920s began to augment the income-producing capabilities of the country and, inevitably, to make possible improvements in health, education, and social infrastructure. Infant mortality fell from 185 deaths per 1,000 live births in 1936 to about 60 in 1960.[19] After the death of Gen. Juan Vicente Gómez, both military and civilian governments began to attend to the demands of modernization. Initial efforts in public health quickly brought results in life expectancy, and the extension of education began to improve literacy levels and to produce university-educated professionals who would gradually transform all organizations, public and private. Two external influences alternately pushed social policy: corporatism and socialism.

In Venezuela, a sort of tropical corporatism certainly informed military governments from 1936 to 1945 and from 1948 to 1958. State resources were used to put in place at least basic educational and health services, while industrialization was stimulated via foreign investment, public construction, and modernization of the state apparatus. Democracy was possible as a subproduct and second stage after the country had moved up the ladder of development; in the meantime, the government knew best what was good for the people. The modernization process itself would produce growth and employment. Indeed, the 1950s saw a transformation of the physical face of the country, as buildings went up, roads connected hitherto isolated sectors, and the population made the transition from rural to urban environment.

In opposition to this underlying corporatist approach, an alternative and more socialist model began to gain support. Although not denying the necessity of public investment in infrastructure and industrialization, this view—represented clearly in Acción Democrática, the leading party—stressed the need for subsidizing the lower classes in a variety of ways, since economic growth would not automatically trickle down to the bottom of society. COPEI, the Christian Democratic party, was likewise imbued with a paternalistic ideology stressing the moral requirement that all citizens have access to health, education, housing, and a fair wage. The consensus on this approach among the major (and minor) parties is reflected in the 1961 Constitution, which provides social and economic rights for all citizens and policies, including the following: the right to health care; the right to education; the right to work and to a just salary; the extension over time of Social Security to all workers, with financial protection against sickness, old age, death, and unemployment; and policies to ensure access to comfortable and sanitary housing.

In the primary areas of health and education, it would be difficult to detect differences of strategy among democratic governments. Even though private investment in schools and clinics was allowed to grow, the state continued its policy of providing services to all comers. In housing, however, there have been important shifts of emphasis. Housing policy dates back to 1928, when the military government created the Worker's Bank (Banco Obrero), converted to the National Housing Institute (Instituto Nacional de Vivienda, INAVI) in the democratic period. Publicly built housing became ever more important in the total housing stock and in new construction after 1958. One expert estimated that by 1978, one-quarter of all urban inhabitants resided in publicly built housing. In the seventies, public construction rose to as high as 48 percent of new urban housing.[20]

In summary, the political and ideological heritage of Venezuelan social policy has driven it inexorably toward the view that the government must assume a central role in guiding its citizens to the good society. There are few areas where its influence should not be exerted. Indeed, both left and right on the political spectrum have shared this conception.

*Traditional Strategies*

Given the high level of consensus about social policy, it should not be surprising that strategies have shown remarkable stability, in terms of the areas considered as most important—health and education—as well as in the kind of approach traditionally applied. Until the end of the 1980s at least, policy took the following forms.

The state never clearly favored growth over distribution, or distribution over growth. Some analysts consider this lack of prioritization to be the primary confusion underlying the society's strategy. Adopting a "guns and butter" approach, the Venezuelan government has usually acted as if there were no dilemma or tradeoff between growth and distribution. In the words of Moisés Naím and Ramón Piñango, this was an important element of the "illusion of harmony," which posited that "there is enough for everything" (*hay pa' todo*).[21] While income was rising quickly, this view was probably not entirely wrong, but as soon as income increases slowed by the late 1970s, hard choices had to be made about how generous the government could be in its distributive strategy, when budget receipts no longer could be stretched to cover the various transfers that social policy had mandated.

As for preferences for the free market versus market intervention, no government shied away from intervention, in the belief that the immaturity of markets required correctional measures. The accumulation of state intervention tended, of course, to bring an accompanying and increasing distortion to all market exchanges. Such policies, usually meant to protect the poor, also led to corruption and illegality as well as to the growth of the "informal" sector of the economy (all those who operated outside the legal structure for companies). Oftentimes, the real effect on the cost of goods and services benefited citizens who were not poor. Rent control is a good example of this tendency, because only the middle classes can muster the legal support for protecting their low rents, whereas the poor must accept what landlords dictate.

The government traditionally preferred indirect over direct subsidies. By this it is meant that on the whole, direct handouts in cash or kind were avoided in favor of subsidies to producers to maintain "social" prices or in favor of government enterprises set up to provide alternative and cheap products to the poor. There is no doubt that this was an extremely costly social strategy in that all income classes might enjoy the subsidization. Rich and poor alike bought milk, grains, flour, and other staples at bargain-basement prices. The only factor limiting access to subsidization was that many subsidized services provided such a poor level of quality or attention that the better off preferred to pay more elsewhere, as certainly is the case for health care. By the 1980s, however, some of these subsidization schemes had collapsed or were collapsing, either because of the breakdown in competent and honest administration (CORPOMERCADEO was the government company with the responsibility for buying and selling subsidized goods) or because the cost of maintaining them had grown to unsustainable levels (fertilizers, milk and other basic foods, public transport, and so forth).

It might seem from the foregoing description that the government would have favored public production over private production in social policy, but the facts do not bear out such a hypothesis. Rather, in many but not all areas, the state pursued a mixed policy in which both the private and the public sector were used for distributive purposes, reflecting perhaps the power of the private sector in preserving its share of productive activity. The state expanded public education but provided stimuli and subsidies to private educational institutions, particularly at the university level. The system of indirect subsidies required transfers to private companies for price reductions to consumers. Companies were required by labor law to provide a severance pay system that substituted for unemployment insurance and, to some extent, for retirement funds. Housing policy was mainly a system of contracting with private construction companies to build certain classes of dwellings. On the other hand, some social services—such as water—remained firmly in public hands, with huge implicit subsidies assumed by the government.

A final aspect of strategy relates to the degree of centralization or decentralization in the application of social policy. Here, there is little doubt with respect to the centralizing tendencies of government efforts. All roads lead to Caracas, one might say, when it comes to social administration. Ministerial offices in education, health, or transport concentrate activity at the center, with little scope for decision making or implementation at other levels or in other localities.

## THE HEROIC FLAWS OF SOCIAL POLICY

The argument thus far is that, contrary to the view of many popular commentators in Venezuela, the country has shown a constant concern with social policy throughout the democratic period. Money and other resources have been poured into the system to raise the standard of welfare, with significant and positive results. Yet in Venezuela, such efforts have failed to satisfy either the elites or the popular classes that a good job has been done. The idea persists that things should be different—the poor less poor and the middle classes better served. The political dissensus that erupted in the late 1980s reflects this dissatisfaction and provides a powerful argument that improvement is needed if the system is to survive. What have been the failures in social policy? Why has so much effort produced so little acceptance?

### The Shotgun Approach: There Is Not Enough for Everybody, after All

Social policy in the democratic period invaded all aspects of life in Venezuela. Constitutional protections were taken to mean that all classes should enjoy the benefits of the just society. Until recently, even luxury hotels were subject to rate controls, so that antisocial price gouging would not occur. Telephone rates were strictly controlled according to the theory that this basic service should be accessible to all. Yet the poor never visited luxury hotels and generally do not have telephones in their homes.

We might call this the shotgun approach to social policy, which in Venezuela reflects a profoundly egalitarian philosophy, even as it implies unequal results. The shotgun philosophy engendered some arcane arguments about the necessity of intervention and subsidization in the most unsuspected fields. For instance, the state erected its own industrial sector in steel, aluminum, petrochemicals, and other products that might otherwise have been left in the hands of the private sector. These industries, which have tended to absorb a significant portion of scarce public resources, have required subsidies far greater than those made directly to the underprivileged.

Practically the entire gamut of government spending was justified as socially necessary, in the interests of the good society—defined as modern, industrialized, and diversified. The gratuity of university education was defended as the mainstay of this good society, although even the constitutional guarantee of the right to education recognized the possibility that those with the ability to pay might be required to do so.

The problem is that the shotgun approach dilutes the availability of resources for the lower classes and disperses the ability of government to deliver social services through its own scarce pool of capable administrators.

### Implementation: The Vulnerable Heel

For diverse reasons, Venezuela has never been able to rely on its public administration to carry out policy in an efficient way. There is no corps of public servants imbued with civic values or system for recruiting and training the bureaucracy. Idealists have come and gone in different ministries and governments, but the public administration has not developed institutionalized forms of rewarding efficiency or punishing corruption.[22]

Any day's newspaper provides a litany of failures to deliver social services in a manner that respects the time or dignity of the beneficiaries. It is taken for granted, for example, that sick people may have to knock at several hospitals before being received, including women in labor who have only a couple of hours left before giving birth.

Social administration is generally based on the premise that no one can be trusted, so the design of programs demands complex paperwork from persons who have little interest in accuracy or speed. Reform efforts are often reported, but frequently forgotten. Complaints are not registered or not responded to, because correction would require that the system work in the first place.

In fact, the choices made about the kind of social programs the country will apply often depend on the belief that the bureaucracy will be unable to deliver goods and services to the needy population. It is at this point that the shotgun approach becomes linked to implementation. If we cannot deliver social services to those we would like to benefit, then we are reduced to social policy that benefits all. The traditional dependence on indirect subsidies, for instance, may result more from the realities of implementation weaknesses than from any ideological preference for them. Where few companies sell a product important in the basket of commonly consumed goods, it may be easier to deal with them than to manage handouts to a million families. In services, the problem of cost might be seen as solving itself, to the extent that the dismal quality of public health services and, to a lesser extent, educational services will ensure that only those who are truly in need will make use of them.

We must next consider the possibility that some of the flaws of social policy and social administration result from deeper causes rooted in the political economy of the country. We should also ask whether social policy affects the wealth available in the society necessary to raise the standards of welfare across the board.

Does the Political System Bias Social Policy?

The Venezuelan political system is based on strong mass parties that have come to adopt pragmatic programs tailored for their multiclass base. That policy tends to include something for everybody is not only a function of the necessities of implementation, but also a result of the political game. Voters may switch sides, from AD to COPEI and back, without suffering serious risk of backing a very different ideological horse. Each party tends to offer something to all classes, so it should not be surprising that social policy reflects this tendency. The party system explains various facts observed here: the consistency of social policy across all governments, the persistence of subsidies to the rich, and the wide range of social subsidy programs directed at an incredibly broad number of human problems. It also explains the lack of attention to the problems of the most marginal elements of the underclass— prison crowding and criminal court abuses of rights, absent security forces, and lack of services in the poorest areas, for instance—where political participation is low and apparently declining.[23]

The nature of the party system also affects social policy in other ways. The parties depend on the associations affiliated with them to provide them with funding. This is true for election costs, but it is also true with respect to the financial supports that party officials and representatives in government require to maintain their standard of living. In particular, links to labor and professional organizations are central; these organizations not only provide funding directly to the parties, but also protect party workers by ensuring them employment that does not interfere with their political activities.

### Do Social Policies Inhibit Growth?

In many developed countries, one concern with social welfare policies is that they act as disincentives to growth because they provide a comfortable safety net that diminishes the necessity to work. I do not examine the validity of such a view in the developed countries, but argue here that such a problem is *not* a factor in Venezuela. In the first place, in Venezuela there is no direct welfare system in the sense of an agency designed to provide income support to poor families. There are, of course, cash transfer programs, but in no case are these considered sufficient to sustain a family. After ten years of economic decline, from 1981 to 1991, the behavior of poor families is an indicator that the poor respond to greater poverty by working harder. During this period, among the poor, labor force participation rates increased significantly, unemployment fell, and family size shrank.[24]

In another sense, however, there is reason to believe that broader social policy aimed at protecting industry, subsidizing prices, and limiting domestic competition in the name of employment and stability had a more insidious effect on the productive capacity of the country, and hence on the total resources available both to the state (for distribution purposes) and to the society (in terms of wage levels and purchasing power). This view corresponds to the (disputed) thesis of Mancur Olsen, which states that productivity stagnates in those countries where entrenched interest groups achieve such sway over policymaking as to accumulate programs that dampen competitive pressures and eventually reduce the wealth of the country.[25] A vague notion that the widespread subsidization of the Venezuelan economic and social system was having such a result informed those who began to question social policy in the last decade.

### The Imperative of Political Stability

A final factor must be touched on to understand social policy. As mentioned at the outset, social policy requires not only that the less privileged be granted a floor of decency and opportunities to better their lot, but also that public goods be guaranteed to the society as a whole. The legitimacy of government depends on providing the basic goods and services that individuals cannot obtain in the market. To the extent that a government fails in this respect, its survival is at stake, because it will lose the essential political support without which no regime can last.

The Venezuelan government has not been particularly effective in providing these public goods. Security is perceived by the electorate as totally lacking, transport and communications are precarious, and private expenditures on schools and recreation are necessary because the publicly provided alternatives are of such poor quality, to cite some examples.

## WINDS OF CHANGE

Such has been the record of social policy in Venezuela: shotgun strategies that benefit the many combined with poor delivery that fails to respond to the demands for improvement. Such, at least, was the record as long as oil income covered the cost. But as foreign exchange income fell in the 1980s, successive efforts to hide the fact that there was simply not enough money to pour into problems increasingly contributed to the fiscal deficit—feeding inflation, eroding wages, and generally causing consternation. That apprehension in turn transformed itself into a questioning of the legitimacy of the system and of the possibility of continuing with the strategies of the preceding thirty years. The situation was extremely perilous, since popular opinion had it that the decline in welfare was the direct result of unfair social policy that favored the rich and of corrupt administration that diverted resources to venal officials and their acolytes.

Confronted with a bankrupt fiscal system and disappearing foreign reserves, the new government of Carlos Andrés Pérez initiated a radical reform of government economic and social policy in 1989. While attention has usually been focused on the economic reforms—floating the currency, eliminating price and wage controls, lowering commercial barriers—social policy was also being overhauled. What was called for was a profound change in the strategy of social policy. In practically all areas, there was a shift to more emphasis on growth rather than redistribution, more reliance on the market mechanism, fewer generalized and indirect subsidies, and a more decentralized system of administration. The new strategy did not imply a shift away from the provision of public goods, however, although it did stress more efficient means to supply them.

Although such a shift had been promoted by technocratic elites in a diffuse way, the true impulse was economic necessity. The fall in real incomes made it ever more important to provide safety nets to the poorest families, but shrinking resources also made it ever more difficult to do so with shotgun strategy and shoddy implementation. The theoretical underpinning did not emerge from a process of domestic soul-searching so much as it arose from international institutions called in to bail out the floundering economy. The World Bank played a crucial role by negotiating a structural adjustment loan, a public enterprise reform loan, and other programs whose quid pro quo was just the change in strategy described here.

The drama of the new social policy linked to economic policy transformation was that the major groups in the country did not really participate in the policy debates. The parties, with their traditional leadership, could scarcely be expected to accept such a profound change in a matter of months or even weeks. The implementation of the new policies was not achieved as quickly as the shifts in economic policy occurred. Thus the government confronted its first test with the riots of February 27, 1989, when protests erupted over transportation rate hikes—long before the new direct-income support program would take effect. Equally, devaluation and price decontrolling were cutting purchasing power brutally, without compensation for the poor.

Yet by fits and starts, the new policy began to take form, despite constant sniping at an "economic package" that was said to fall most heavily on the poor. The idea was to let prices be determined by the free market, with competition from imports acting as a limit on monopolistic practices. While all classes would have to pay the real price of goods, subsidies would be targeted for the poorest groups only and delivered directly to them in cash or in kind. Practically all of the new battery of income supports were aimed at ensuring basic needs for children: cash subsidies were based on the number of children enrolled at specific school districts and complemented with transfers for the purchase of milk and corn flour. In-kind transfers were implemented for school supplies and uniforms, milk and lunch programs for students, and food and vitamin supplements for pregnant and nursing mothers and preschool children. Public transport was subsidized for students and day-care facilities were increased. The bulk of these programs depended on the ministry of education, charged with the administrative control over selecting the beneficiaries.

A new emphasis was made on self-help and private sector contributions to solve social problems. Several programs were instituted to encourage and finance microenterprise, often using private foundations and other nonprofit organizations as intermediaries to improve the quality of implementation. The ministry of the family assumed the responsibility for these programs. The private sector was also called on to cofinance both a new housing program and an unemployment insurance scheme together with payroll deductions. In addition, the government presented a plan to revise the existing system of workers' benefits to convert it into a privately managed pension plan; this policy met strong resistance and was relegated to the back burner.

Another policy, meant to improve service delivery and reduce centralized rigidities, was accepted in principle but not implemented on any scale: the transfer of responsibilities from the central government to the states and municipalities. Some important experiments were carried out in creating municipal police forces with greater control by city administration, which showed promising results.

In the meantime, resources were to be freed up by a privatization program, a more progressive income tax, and, it was hoped, a greater efficiency through the reform of the public administration. But these necessary components of the new policy were not to achieve many tangible results during the Pérez administration. Privatization developed sporadically and would, in any case, require some years before producing visible fruits. Income tax reform was gutted in Congress with a view to saving the middle class from having to pay any substantial taxes. Nowhere did the public bureaucracy appear to be functioning any better, and most plans to improve training or modern information systems remained on the drawing board. The educational and health systems remained virtually untouched, perhaps as a result of the persistence of the political realities described earlier. Reform of the court and prison system first required study of an unfamiliar and complex phenomenon. In short, much still needed to be done and the combination of falling real salaries and evident failures to reform the most troubling problems in health and justice led to public rejection of the government's efforts. The Pérez government's approval rating became almost nil and political instability led to constant doubts that the regime could last.

The grand question is whether these winds of change will bring a lasting and effective change in social policy. Thus far, few results can be documented, and the new strategy requires a certain act of faith in the logic underlying it and a reliance on the counterfactual argument that things might have been much worse had Venezuela not begun the long process of reform. The costs of maintaining the shotgun approach would certainly have included hyperinflationary tendencies, which would again have knocked down both the middle and the lower classes.

But faith and counterfactuals do not consolidate political support. Per capita income growth, already vigorous in 1991–92, is a fragile variable that could be endangered by external shocks or by the macroeconomic imbalances that continue to plague the economy. Large sectors of the population, professional associations, and party leaderships remain unconvinced of the virtues of the new social policy—their unwilling acceptance was achieved only because they lacked alternatives. Success will depend on economic growth that increases real incomes as well as on new solutions that improve daily social administration. Greater equity will demand greater efficiency.

I would like to thank Eduardo Casteñeda for his help in assembling the data included in this chapter.

## NOTES

1. "Public goods" in this text refers to all those goods and services that individuals are unable to provide for themselves in the absence of government intervention because the nature of these services makes it impossible or impractical. Roads are a good example, although there are many others.
2. R. Titmuss, *Social Policy: An Introduction* (New York: Pantheon Books, 1974), 50.
3. A. Francés, *Venezuela posible* (Caracas: Corimon and IESA, 1990), 130.
4. I chose to limit the comparison to other countries in the region, mainly because I consider some other countries to have a cultural or historical tradition so different as to exclude fair comparisons. For instance, in Eastern Europe, countries such as Hungary have birth rates that even become negative and suggest the convenience of a population policy to encourage reproduction.
5. This ranking was published in the *Economist's Book of Vital World Statistics* (New York:

Random House, 1990), 41. A purchasing power parity adjustment allows us to compare what a person can actually buy with his or her income. Some countries have high internal prices that reduce the real income of their residents.

6. Consider a country whose labor force constitutes 76 percent of the population aged fifteen to sixty-four, and where 22 percent of the population is under age fifteen (such as the United States) with Venezuela, where only 58 percent of the population works and 38 percent of the population is under fourteen years old. A much higher percentage of the wage bill must be dedicated to building schools, housing, and service infrastructure, and a much higher percentage of family income must be used to feed, clothe, and shelter children, even though there are fewer wage earners relatively in the country.

7. World Economic Forum and IMD, *World Competitiveness Report: 1992* (Geneva: World Economic Forum, 1992).

8. These statistics reflect an average of estimates made by the World Bank, the Comisión Económico para América Latina y el Caribe (CEPAL), the Inter-American Development Bank, and G. Márquez (whose figures for poverty are lower because of a correction made for underreporting in household surveys carried out by the Oficina Central de Estadística e Informática, OCEI). All sources report a significant increase in poverty in the 1980s resulting from the fall in total national income. See G. Márquez, "Poverty and Social Policies in Venezuela," paper prepared for the Brookings Institution project "Confronting the Challenge of Poverty and Inequality in Latin America," Washington, D.C., 1992, 36.

9. Oficina Central de Estadística e Informática, *Anuario estadístico venezolano* (Caracas: OCEI, 1989).

10. OCEI, 1990.

11. Ibid.

12. The best source on the legal system and its treatment of the poor is found in R. Pérez Perdomo, ed., *Justicia y pobreza en Venezuela* (Caracas: Monte Avila, 1987).

13. *El Nacional,* October 7, 1992.

14. These estimates are based on the International Comparison Program of the United Nations, which attempts to correct income figures across the country for real buying power in local markets. Reported in World Bank, *World Development Report* (Washington, D.C.: World Bank, 1992), 272.

15. Critics of income distribution ratios often point out that these measure only income flows and do not take into account differences in wealth, which tend to be much more pronounced than income disparities. Little is known about wealth, however, since statistics do not currently exist in countries like Venezuela.

16. J. C. Navarro, "El impacto del gasto público en educación en Venezuela," in G. Márquez et al., eds., "Gestión fiscal y distribución del ingreso en Venezuela," study for the Network of Research Centers in Applied Economics of the Inter-American Development Bank, IESA, Caracas, 1991.

17. G. Escobar, "Equilibrio y justicia: El impacto del gasto público en Venezuela," IESA Working Paper no. 21, IESA, Caracas, 1990.

18. International Monetary Fund (IMF), *Government Statistics Yearbook* (Washington, D.C.: IMF, 1991).

19. Francés, *Venezuela posible.*

20. V. Fossi, "Desarrollo urbano y vivienda: La desordenada evolución hacia un país de metrópolis," in M. Naím and R. Piñango, eds., *El caso Venezuela: Una ilusión de armonía* (Caracas: Ediciones IESA, 1988), 486.

21. Naím and Piñango, *El caso Venezuela,* 547.

22. See World Bank, "Public Administration Study" (World Bank, Washington, D.C., 1991, mimeographed).

23. Although in the first decade of the democratic period voter turnout was unusually high in Venezuela, succeeding elections have seen ever lower participation.

24. Márquez, "Poverty and Social Policies in Venezuela," 19.

25. For a corresponding view of this argument, see Mancur Olsen's thesis in *The Rise and Decline of Nations* (New Haven: Yale University Press, 1982).

# 11

# Corruption and Political Crisis

*Rogelio Pérez Perdomo*

In the popular imagination, this story is about a mythical rich country ruled by a king who makes disappear the value of everything he sees or touches outside his palace. Except for those who live in the palace, his subjects become increasingly poor and wretched. The curse that has fallen upon this Midas-in-reverse and this country is called "corruption."

Corruption is regarded as one of the most serious threats to the functioning of the Venezuelan state and one of the principal destabilizing factors of the political system. Not only was it the most important stated reason for the attempted coup on February 4, 1992, but, for the past fifteen years, it has been singled out as one of the most negative features of Venezuela's political regime. Moreover, the word *político* ("political" when used as an adjective, "politician" when used as a noun) has developed negative connotations. In Venezuela, the word traditionally meant courteous or educated, and during the period of the restoration of democracy in 1958 it began to be used to describe someone genuinely concerned about public affairs. This last meaning is actually the one closest to the classical tradition. Today, however, the words *corrupt* and *politician* are practically synonymous, a most unfair turn of events for those politicians who are honest.

Corruption is often described as a deeply rooted trait in Venezuela and other Latin American countries, dating from the colonial period. This commonality will be discussed later, but the interesting point is that such a view contradicts the idea of corruption being a destabilizing factor in the political system *now*, rather than previously. The historical argument is difficult to sustain; that is, if corruption really is such a deeply rooted part of the Venezuelan tradition, why is it creating such immense political problems today? John Noonan's careful study of corruption cases in English and U.S. history documents scandals that are unparalleled in eighteenth- and nineteenth-century Venezuela[1]—one early U.S. example is the Yazoo case of 1795, which involved practically the entire Virginia elite and many important figures in other states—yet only specialized historians appear to remember these cases today, and no one suggests that this legacy is an indication that England and the United States are hopelessly corrupt countries.

This chapter has two basic goals. The first is to show that corruption in public life is a recent problem in Venezuela, attributable not to an increase in corruption as such, but rather to changes in the political system and the perception of the economic situation. The second objective is to advance the idea that the keys to this change are found in the redefinition of the public and private domains and the workings of the system of control.

## CORRUPTION AND THE POLITICOECONOMIC SYSTEM

Broadly speaking, corruption today takes the form of an illegal transfer of public assets into private hands. Public officials who appropriate state-owned assets or collude with a private individual to obtain such assets, or both, in order to benefit from the state's action or inaction, commit acts of corruption. The legislation usually referred to in Venezuela as the anticorruption law is more correctly known as the *salvaguarda del patrimonio público*, or the law to safeguard the public patrimony.

In a hypothetical situation in which the concept of private property is eliminated, such as Plato's Republic, corruption would be impossible. Nor could corruption exist in the Lockean state of nature, in which the concept of public dominion has also been eradicated. Crimes and misdemeanors may be committed between private individuals, but they could not be labeled as acts of corruption.[2] Of course, this is a contemporary definition. In other periods, corruption meant the loss of religiosity, the spread of deviant sexuality, or, in classical Greek philosophy, the illegal exercise of public power. Carl Friedrich has pointed out the parallel between our own concept of corruption and this latter definition.[3] The public and private domains have always been linked in Venezuelan historical tradition, and the connection seems hard to break. Corruption, therefore, depends on the nature of this link, as well as the legitimacy of the political system.

Political scientists and historians have examined the efforts to combat corruption, both in general and in highly specific cases, and the mechanisms used to control the problem.[4] For example, Teresa Albornoz de López has studied corruption in the Audiencia of Caracas; Marianela Ponce, impeachment as a system of control; and María Elena

González Deluca, the business dealings of Antonio Guzmán Blanco.[5] This chapter attempts to draw attention to the fact that the concept of the public weal was so ill-defined in eighteenth- and nineteenth-century Venezuela, and so limited in scale, that the incidents that occurred in that era are hard to comprehend without a strong sense of history. For example, the Audiencia's prosecutor, José Gutierrez del Rivero, was accused of accepting gifts in exchange for favors, but the Council of the Indies was more concerned with his living with two women.[6]

Nineteenth-century constitutions provide a modern definition of the concept of the public domain, but its interaction with a personalized political system meant that in practice no such distinction existed.[7] *Caudillos* and politicians became rich by plundering the limited public exchequer (where this was possible) or by divesting private individuals of their possessions under threat of violence. The limited size of the state[8] and widespread poverty made these exercises in self-enrichment modest by today's standards. Guzmán Blanco appears to have been the only important exception to this pattern, due to his cosmopolitanism and extraordinary ability to mix politics with business.[9] Under Gen. Juan Vicente Gómez's rule (1908–35), the state was organized efficiently, but the general was a personalist ruler clever enough to retain control of political repression. Members of an educated intellectual elite ran the country, making illicit profits with little business acumen or ability to accumulate wealth.[10] Like many of the political leaders under Gómez, they resorted to traditional methods of divesting their enemies of their possessions or appropriating public assets for themselves directly.

When Gómez fell, his successors confiscated the assets of the dictator and his closest relatives, but no effort was made to carry the clean-up campaign further. Gen. Eleazar López Contreras (1935–41) drew up the February Program in 1936, a clear attempt to modernize the state and conspicuous for its appropriateness, conciseness, and realism. Respect for the constitution, the rule of law, and the rights of the individual were the core elements of the program, whereas the reform of the state and the integrity of public officials are mentioned only with regard to the judiciary. López Contreras and Isaías Medina Angarita (1941–45) set out to modernize the country by creating a state that was more active in the promotion of economic activity and by liberalizing the political system. Their moderate and gradualist approach was sharply criticized by Acción Democrática (AD), established in 1941, particularly by its leader and founder, Rómulo Betancourt.

Given their use of the exchequer for personal profit and the limited public benefits of the government's activities, López Contreras and

Medina were regarded by Betancourt as true perpetuators of the Gómez regime. In justifying the 1945 coup (or October Revolution), Betancourt described the mixing of public and private assets as a long-standing Venezuelan practice[11] and praised the efforts of the Court of Administrative Responsibility (Tribunal de Responsabilidad Administrativa), which tried more than a hundred former government officials. The court's verdicts, running to five volumes, "constitute a 'how-to' of the most diverse methods of using public assets for private profit."[12] The total value of the assets repaid to the nation was over 400 million bolivars, more than the average annual national budget during the Medina administration. One of the linchpins of AD's program as presented by Betancourt was the honest administration of public funds. Betancourt himself states that he left office as poor as he came in.[13]

Two other aspects of AD's 1945 program are relevant to the argument of this chapter: the expansion of the government's role in promoting or directly generating modernization, and the mobilization of the people through strong grass-roots organizations (parties, trade unions, and so on). State intervention, an honest administration, and strong parties constituted the common agenda for all political parties when democratic rule was reestablished in 1958. This politicoeconomic program enjoyed considerable success during the 1960s and early 1970s, but the cracks and contradictions that began to appear have become more pronounced in recent years.

The growth of the Venezuelan state and its main areas of action or intervention have been well documented and discussed in terms of the evolution of public expenditure.[14] One hypothesis is that the larger the state, the greater the likelihood of illegal exchanges between the public and private sectors, assuming that a private sector actually exists. Essays on the Soviet Union and other socialist countries suggest the existence of fairly endemic corruption.[15] Nonetheless, the notion that the level of corruption is directly proportional to the size of the state is simplistic; other important variables must be taken into account.

Of all the activities undertaken by the state, the provision of services per se is the one least prone to corruption if the services in question can be easily extended to cover the entire population. The education system and mail services are good examples. Naturally, when shortages occur, whether they be in school admission capacity or the availability of telephone lines, access to services can become negotiable objects, and the discretionary powers of officials acquire considerable economic value. Corruption in this sphere can affect a great many people and becomes a source of resentment against the state, which is committed to providing such services.

Usually, inducements to secure services illegally involve small payments and benefit only the most minor government officials. Some analysts take a tolerant attitude toward corruption of this kind, because it compensates for a low government salary.[16] In the administration of justice, for example, payments made to clerks or other court officials to speed up the routine but requisite matters of any case typically involve small sums and are regarded by repeat-players in the court system, such as lawyers, as simply "surcharges." They can be disconcerting, however, for new lawyers or nonprofessionals who come into contact with the courts.

Of quite a different nature are activities that may be linked to the provision of services (for example, the construction of a hydroelectric power station or the purchase of communications equipment, a building, or military hardware). Often such decisions are made at the highest level of government. Officials' discretionary powers can be of great economic value to companies bidding for contracts. The officials responsible for making the decision are well aware of the size of the profits involved, and the various bidders are prepared to share them. For this reason, much of the effort to control corruption entails attempts to rationalize such purchases or public works, establish a competitive bidding process for the dealers or suppliers, and divide or collectivize decision-making bodies. The success of these mechanisms depends on factors discussed later in the chapter.

Another type of state intervention concerns actions relating to the promotion, fostering, protection, and control of private economic activity. Actions of this kind tend to be complementary: if the state bans imports or establishes import tariffs to protect the manufacture of specific products, provides soft credits, or requires state-owned enterprises to purchase locally manufactured goods, it makes sense also to control the price and quality of such products. Intervention of this sort calls for a regulatory network within which it is impossible to control the discretionary powers of government officials. The state's activity is channeled through legislation or general administrative acts that appear to fall well within the usual public domain (for example, the introduction of import tariffs). Or it may be channeled through lower-level administrative acts, be they general or individual, such as price fixing or certifying a product's quality, where the beneficiaries are even more visible. Controlling corruption is an extremely difficult task, and the incentives for engaging in it are strong. The potential for the transfer of resources to public officials and businesspeople is limited only to the size of the state's resources. A typical example is one of the biggest corruption scandals in Venezuelan history, the notorious affair involving the National Preferential Exchange Office (RECADI), which consisted of supplying dollars for specific types of imports at preferential exchange rates considerably below the prevailing market price.[17]

Finally, there is another kind of state intervention that is actually entrepreneurial activity. In this case, the state compensates for the perceived lack of private initiative in creating businesses and engages in economic activities deemed to be in the public interest. In principle, the incentives for the administrators or managers of these enterprises to commit acts of corruption are similar to those of their counterparts in private firms who commit acts prejudicial to the interests of their shareholders. Thus a manager may make bad deals for his company that are actually secret transfers to himself and to third parties who serve as his accomplices. The difference between public and private enterprises lies in the greater diligence of shareholders in the private sector, the greater potential for political interference in public concerns, and the impact of losses or poor management. In the case of public enterprises, the loser is the state—the community directly. In the case of privately owned businesses, the losers are the shareholders directly and the community indirectly.

This analysis touches on the various kinds of state intervention and the type of corruption that may be occasioned by each of them. It should not be viewed as a criticism of state involvement in any particular activity. But individuals with decision-making responsibilities should bear in mind the potential for corruption and its impact on their plans and the expected results.

A comparison of Venezuela and other countries suggests the existence of basically similar options for intervention, to the extent that the intervention mechanisms adopted in all countries generally follow a similar pattern. The trend toward greater government intervention, like the recent tendency to scale down the state's role, has been worldwide. Such trends probably reflect periods of greater or lesser confidence in public administration or the harmonious effect that private initiatives can have on society.[18] One truth about Venezuela is that among Latin American countries, it has never been an innovator in such matters.

The foregoing argument implies that the types of corruption described are not specifically Venezuelan; they are just as likely to be found in countries such as France, whose state structure and administrative system has long been seen as a model and imitated by many other nations, including Venezuela.[19] The question for analysis, then, is, What are the traits within Venezuelan society that appear to generate relatively more corruption, lead to more corruption scandals, and allow corruption to produce a greater destabilizing effect on the political system? An analysis of the relationship between the state and the political system is crucial in answering this question.

One aspect that may be important to consider is the ethos of the administrators concerned. By *ethos* I mean a set of values shared by a specific social group strongly enough to mold its behavior. The standard representation of the role of the administrator (or bureaucrat) in textbooks on organizational theory is that of the counterweight to the politician or decision maker. The administrator is the executor of political decisions and will perform duties in accordance with established procedures, adopting an attitude of strict neutrality toward the public and making every effort to attain the organization's goals. This normative image is a caricature. It would be hard to find, in any public or private bureaucracy in any country in the world, administrators who adhere strictly to bureaucratic rationality. The traditional distinction between politicians and administrators can also be criticized. The latter also have beliefs and interests that influence their approach to, and the results of, their actions. Nonetheless, some societies are able to produce groups of administrators who share an ethos approaching that of the standard representation. Therefore, even if there are deviations from that standard representation, any changes will be limited (through various mechanisms) by the awareness of a set of responsibilities linked to the administrators' ethos.[20]

The way in which that set of administrators is produced may vary from one society to another and often involves slow processes generated in the course of the development of the state (or the organizations) in question. The mechanisms that produce the group may also vary considerably, ranging from a common education and training to distinguishing social traits afforded by membership in a social stratum. Or cohesion may be the result of the pride administrators take in their work. One manifestation of this ethos is so-called esprit de corps. Countries such as France, Germany, England, Spain, the United States, and Italy have enjoyed varying degrees of success in creating these administrative elites. In some instances the identification is more specific, as in the case of members of the diplomatic service or judges. The group is composed of individuals who identify with each other and serve, or say that they serve, the public interest and are usually aware of their own status and privileges.

It is quite clear that in Venezuela such a body of administrators was never consolidated. Nevertheless, in the first part of this century some individuals seemed to have developed an identification with a functional role or status. Interviews with old bureaucrats or retired people suggest this sense of identity. Unfortunately, I am not aware of any studies conducted on the subject. I believe the failure to develop a public service ethos—or perhaps the destruction of an incipient ethos—in contemporary Venezuelan society is related to the model adopted for modernizing and democratizing the country. One of the central elements of this model was the strengthening of the political parties to a degree unthinkable in other societies, extending far beyond the actual realm of politics. Betancourt, in particular, suggests that there was an ideological commitment to instill a substantive ethos in the party member, identified with a vision of the country.[21] This political ethos was to be much more important than the ethos of public officialdom and it was believed that it could prevent corruption.[22] In practice, membership in the same party created a solidarity and personal links that in the long run actually proved to be much stronger than identification with an ideology, which becomes outmoded over time, or with the formal duties of public servants.

In both the period from 1945 to 1948 and the era after 1958, the parties—first AD, then COPEI and others—took over the administration. Posts were meted out on the basis of party connections, and party loyalties were thus transferred to public administration. In such a situation, assistance for a loyal or disgraced colleague, or preferential treatment for someone who can contribute financially to the party, is probably more valuable than strict adherence to rules or principles that are abstract or difficult to interpret. Regulations on choosing the best offer or the most qualified applicant tend to fall by the wayside.

The impact of the widely held notion of the vast wealth of the country and in particular the state requires consideration. In a state with immense resources, the administrator of public property or state-owned assets does not have to worry about a lack of resources; there is plenty for everyone and everything.[23] This perception became particularly strong in Venezuela in the wake of the oil boom of the 1970s and the huge inflow of cash from foreign loans.

It is significant that leading public figures and scholars drew attention to the dangers of a clientelized public administration without an administrative ethos. Efforts were made to create a school for training public administrators, and the civil service career law was enacted in 1970 with this idea in mind.[24] By and large, these efforts proved to be unsuccessful. Although space limitations preclude discussion of the failures, it suffices to note that the goal of professionalizing public administration clearly ran counter to the clientelistic features of the Venezuelan political system—and still does.[25]

Corruption does not take place in a public sector divorced from the rest of society, where the only private interest that impinges on it is that of the officials concerned. The fact is that promotion and protection activities have a real impact: businesses grow, or spring up and prosper, sometimes at a surprising rate. Certain economic groups are consolidated.[26] The prosperity of these concerns is largely attributable to the massive transfer of wealth generated by the protection of the market or by access to credit. Indeed, some credits were so soft because it was common knowledge that the Venezuelan Development Corporation and the many other state-owned credit agencies would never collect them. Credits of this kind masked actual transfers for which public officials received a commission. It goes without saying that many private businesspeople chose to avoid getting caught up in the web of political clientage or repaid their state-authorized credits on time, but the list of entrepreneurs who profited from such transfers has never been made public.

The link between corruption and poverty is complex. On the one hand, corruption can lead to the concentration of wealth, as when it affects social programs and public services, benefiting a limited number of people. It can, on the other hand, lead to the redistribution of wealth. A case in point is the surcharges and commissions that can augment the often very low salaries of public officials. As far as companies are concerned, this practice can guarantee large profits; however, it can also have the highly undesirable effect of acclimating entrepreneurs and managers themselves to not being overly concerned about productivity and the quality of products and services. Instead, they may channel their energies into obtaining protection or other state-related sales. In the broadest meaning of the word, public corruption can also corrupt the private sector.

State-owned enterprises and government agencies are probably even larger victims, not only of corruption but of the conditions that it produces and permits. The selection and promotion of personnel ceases to be a question of ability, productivity, and efficiency; collective agreements grant enormous privileges that are concentrated in the hands of trade union leaders and the individuals they support. The existence of *reposeros*—people who collect a salary without having to work for it—and overstaffing are the most extreme manifestations of this problem. Many enterprises, both public and private, can be guaranteed monopolies thanks to government regulation or protection, a factor that also can contribute to their low efficiency and levels of production. A key link between corruption and poverty, therefore, is that corruption produces highly inefficient public and private enterprises.

## CRISIS, SCANDALS, AND CONTROL

The Venezuelan political system has achieved one of the longest periods of stability in the country's history. Yet it has also squandered the country's enormous oil revenues with relatively few benefits for the nation as a whole. In the process, the political parties became channels for the aspirations of the people and their representatives. The clientelistic traits of Venezuelan politics are marked, but Venezuelans appear to accept them because the system has afforded them considerable prosperity.[27] Indeed, until the late 1970s, the system showed remarkable stamina: it survived coup attempts by members of the military who yearned for a return to the days of Pérez Jiménez; the latter's subsequent, surprising popularity; the successive splits in Acción Democrática; the guerrilla movements; the election of Rafael Caldera (the main opposition leader); and various other scandals and pressures.

Toward the end of the seventies the pressures increased. Luis Piñerua Ordaz's candidacy for the presidency (the slogan of his campaign was *Correcto*) was a condemnation of the corruption of his own party's administration. The trend continued with the political censure of President Carlos Andrés Pérez (1974–79) by the party's ethics commission and the national congress over the 1979 Sierra Nevada affair.[28]

Manifestations of dissatisfaction with the state and the political system were becoming more evident, and the trend continued and actually picked up momentum in the 1980s.[29] The state's modus operandi, as described earlier, made it a particularly inefficient apparatus, and public criticism of the poor quality of public services mounted. In general terms, this was a result of the failure by administrators to rank efficiency and productivity top priorities in their work. They usually responded to malfunctions by effecting cosmetic changes and making (often substantial) capital investments. Given the interaction between the state apparatus and the political system, however, these were bound to have relatively little, or no, effect. The deterioration in public services reduced living standards of the Venezuelan population and contributed to the increase in poverty.

The two important elements behind the present crisis in Venezuela are (1) the end of the oil boom and the growing poverty, and (2) the loss of legitimacy by the political parties. These problems grew throughout the 1980s but reached a peak—threatening the existence of Venezuelan democracy—during Pérez's second term as president and are still running their course.

The economic crisis and its impact on the populace have been dealt with in far greater detail elsewhere, but bear mentioning here.[30] Oil revenues fell sharply throughout the 1980s and the accrued debt exacerbated the impact of this loss of income. The many state-owned enterprises also added to the problem. Given the political context, all of their losses had to be underwritten with public funds or new loans.[31] As the regulator of change and still the largest dispenser of favors, the state has been able to keep the system going, but there is a growing belief that other Venezuelans are the big losers under this arrangement. The palliative of dealing with the perceived gaps in public services through investment is no longer a viable alternative. Dwindling reserves also make the policy of regulating change unworkable, and the political leadership finds itself faced with an unparalleled political and social crisis.[32] Privatization and spending cuts are common occurrences. The most celebrated politicians have become liberals out of necessity, while others talk of resources that in fact are no longer available.

The second aspect underlying Venezuela's crisis is the bankruptcy of the political parties. As in nearly every political system, the interrelationships between party militants are not horizontal. Client networks are created that are, of course, transferred to the state bureaucracy.[33] The dominance of a strong leader may partially obscure these informal networks, but the community of interests becomes increasingly factionalized when the leader's prestige wanes for some reason, or when the networks become stronger. Intraparty rivalry can surpass interparty competition—and this has been the case in Venezuela since the 1980s.

The Venezuelan people view politicians as being like partners in a marriage who stay together despite constantly squabbling and often hurling serious accusations at each other. They are blamed for the state's poor record and the increasing poverty, as reflected in calls for a reduced state role and for electoral systems that place greater emphasis on the candidates rather than on the parties. To protect themselves, politicians denounce or criticize unpopular policies, which intensifies crises within the parties. With the parties discredited and divided, the lack of popular representation is intensified.

Furthermore, intraparty strife, or one member's displeasure with a leader or public official who has failed to meet expectations (whatever those may have been), increases the likelihood that an individual will blow the whistle or leak information and confidential documents to people in a position to accuse and even slander those involved. There are plenty of whistle-blowers ready to speak out in every party, for it can provide a means of personal advancement, especially for young politicians, as well as being a most valuable weapon.[34]

The media give such revelations plenty of coverage, realizing that corruption scandals generate interest in the newspaper and ensure notoriety for the journalist involved. Politicians and rulers now have much less influence over the media and cannot easily cover up a scandal. The media, then, can be viewed as the amplifiers of scandals. The importance of a scandal is determined by how much coverage it receives, how long it lasts, where it is reported, and the amount of newsprint devoted to it. The size of a government disgrace has little to do with the amount of cash or material wealth transferred into private hands.

The formal recipients of the charges are the judicial authorities, usually the public prosecutor's office and the judiciary. The limited capacity of these bodies to deal with cases of this kind is described later, but suffice it to note here that their actions generate further headlines and fuel the scandal. These officials can also be a source for new scandals.

It is significant that scandal has a dynamic all its own as far as actual corruption is concerned: more corruption scandals do not necessarily mean that more acts of corruption are being committed. Rather, they merely reflect the greater openness of the political and social system, making it more likely that acts of corruption will be made public, that there will be a greater interest in scandals or readiness to be shocked by them, and that a suitable infrastructure for "scandalization" exists. This point becomes clearer through an example from the period when there were no scandals, though the information source in such cases—gossip—is highly unreliable. A rumor dating from Betancourt's presidency (1959–64) indicates that the chief executive was indignant to learn of the corruption of one of his cabinet ministers. He consequently convened a series of top-level political meetings and it was decided that the minister in question should be asked to resign from the cabinet. It was also decided that a scandal should be avoided, as this could undermine the image of the still weak democratic system. Word of the minister's corruption spread in the form of gossip, and the editor of at least one important newspaper was aware of the case and the government's decision, but nothing was ever published. At the time the ruling elite was unified and could exert enormous influence over the media; today the idea of a cover-up would be unthinkable.

The *Dictionary of Corruption* is a compilation of Venezuela's main corruption scandals since 1958.[35] It is, in a sense, a national history of infamy. Chronologically speaking, it reveals a steady increase in the number of cases from one administration to the next. Bearing in mind the foregoing observations, it is unlikely that the growth in the number of scandals reflects a similar increase in actual corruption. The combination of the following factors probably kept the number of cases to a minimum during the first phase of democracy (1958–73): political parties were more closely controlled by their leaders, media organizations were beholden to those leaders, and there was little public interest in the problem. The theoretical premises noted earlier would suggest that the growth of the state and of its entrepreneurial and promotional-regulatory activities accounts for a rise in consumption proportionally greater than the increase in government spending. The de-ideologization of the parties and the decline in the quality of civil service probably exacerbated this upward trend. On the other hand, the policy of rationalizing government controls and privatizing state-owned enterprises—the Great Turnaround of 1989—ought to have brought about a substantial decline in corruption. This effect may have been eliminated by other policies, however, such as export incentives, social programs, and growth incentives in the mining sector.

Carlos Andrés Pérez has repeatedly suggested that reduction of corruption has been one intended side effect of his policies, noting in particular that the scrapping of exchange controls under RECADI removed an important source of corruption. An empirical study on the ethical attitudes of management, conducted among a small group of bosses, suggests that corruption as an issue has ceased to be as important for this group of individuals.[36] The general public, though, continues to regard corruption as an extremely serious problem and gives the government no credit for implementing policies to curtail it.

The explanation for the public's perception of the situation is somewhat complex. The economic policy that was implemented led to a substantial reduction in real revenues, while living standards continued to fall as a result of declining public services. As far as the average Venezuelan was concerned, corruption is to blame for all this. The average citizen of a (mythical) rich country who has personally grown poorer feels that politicians and the businesspeople associated with them are to blame for having taken a disproportionate share of that wealth by illicit means. While the average Venezuelan cannot afford basic medicines, lives in a neighborhood with no piped water, and struggles to find enough to eat, politicians and their friends call on everyone to make sacrifices—but ride in imported luxury automobiles, showing off their cellular telephones. This inequality has become more obvious, and it is attributed to the illegal transfer of public wealth into the hands of a few private individuals. In addition, the press and television bombard the public with revelations of new scandals and mutual accusations by politicians, but no one of importance has ever been brought to justice. This aspect merits closer analysis.

Some specific scandals warrant consideration. Due to the huge sums involved, RECADI is probably the largest corruption scandal in the nation's history, though the literature produced on the subject so far fails to reflect its size. Agustín Beroes offers an account of the scandal from the standpoint of the journalist who played the role of "amplifier."[37] Other commentators defend the economic policy of exchange controls and explain its benefits in macroeconomic terms.[38] They also present a legal analysis of certain trials. Of most interest, however, is the interaction that occurred between the public and private sectors. RECADI made nearly the entire private sector of the economy dependent on certain public servants. Former President Lusinchi and his private secretary (now his wife) played a key role as intermediaries by enabling important executives, including those of media organizations, to obtain the foreign exchange they needed. It was thus an extraordinarily effective political control mechanism, but one that clearly aroused resentment.

Other public officials also enjoyed various kinds of discretionary powers, with respect both to the classification of activities that warranted a specific rate of exchange and to the urgency with which applications were processed. Such discretionary powers could easily be used to extort monies from applicants, as indeed was the case. Equally important was the possibility of fraud. The purchase of foreign currency at preferential exchange rates was authorized for the importation of specific products or raw materials. The regulations required that the recipient demonstrate that the products or materials had actually been purchased at the price and in the amounts and quality specified, imported into the country, and used there. It is unlikely that the Venezuelan bureaucracy possessed the technical expertise and ethical qualities necessary to verify all of these particulars conclusively. It is also unlikely that it had all of the information required to expose overbilling or hidden transfers and, in general, prevent the numerous frauds that could be committed under this system. Although RECADI was repeatedly accused of being a center of corruption during the Lusinchi administration, the foreign exchange system was never reformed because the government's economic policy did not take into account the ethical and political consequences of ongoing behavior.

Two more corruption cases are worth examining, given their similarities: the jeeps and the Florida Crystals scandals. During the Lusinchi administration, a group of one hundred vehicles, most of which were for rural transportation, were acquired through the use of state security funds. The minister of interior relations, José Angel Ciliberto, who should report to the president, was responsible for administration of these funds. Most of the vehicles were distributed to leaders of AD and were used in the party's election campaigns. The jeeps were distributed in the presidential palace by Private Secretary Blanca Ibáñez, who is now Lusinchi's wife. As a result, Ibáñez, Ciliberto, and various other individuals were ordered under arrest. Legal action against Lusinchi requires a pretrial by the Supreme Court, part of a process that is ongoing as of this writing.[39]

The Florida Crystals case involves a luxury building constructed by the Worker's Bank, whose principal shareholders are the Venezuelan state and the Venezuelan Confederation of Workers (CTV).[40] The bank, charged with financing housing for workers in need, was constructing luxury homes in contravention of its stated aims. The scandal erupted when it became public that Deputy Antonio Ríos, president of the CTV and a member of the bank's board, had written a letter requesting that a number of apartments be sold—under exceptionally favorable financing conditions—to his daughter and other persons linked to the CTV. Legal action was taken against Ríos, who was found guilty of influence peddling and imprisoned for a year. Under pressure from his political party, he resigned from the presidency of the CTV.

These two cases involved only a few million or tens of millions of bolivars, or, as former Minister Ciliberto himself put it, "mere trifles" compared with the size of other transactions handled by Ciliberto and Deputy Ríos. Furthermore, none of the individuals accused benefited personally from the events that took place. Compared with cases that are currently making headlines or have recently appeared in the international press (such as those involving Alan García of Peru and Fernando Collor of Brazil), or have enormous economic repercussions (such as the *tangenti* of Milan, the savings and loans crisis in the United States, the Bank of Credit and Commerce International [BCCI], the Recruit Corporation in Japan, and even RECADI), these scandals suggest excessive moralism on the part of the press, the public prosecutor's office, and the Venezuelan public. But they must be seen in context. To most Venezuelans, ten million bolivars is an astronomical sum. Even more important, people believe acts of this kind to be just the tip of the iceberg, that many small deals, or possibly a considerable number of larger ones that are hard to detect, have allowed a group of politicians and politically oriented businesspeople to pocket huge state assets (again, in a reputedly wealthy country), while the average citizen feels increasingly impoverished and abandoned.

These two cases have an important symbolic value. The first involves a clear misuse of government funds for exclusively political ends. In the Florida Crystals case, the activities of the Worker's Bank, occurring within a climate of strong resentment of the illegal transfer of public assets, are as reprehensible as those involving larger sums or the personal enrichment of public officials.

Corruption scandals constitute a real form of punishment for the individuals involved: they are held up to public ridicule, in itself a harsh punishment, condemned without a trial, and have little chance of a defense or of regaining their tarnished reputation. It is for this reason that action by the courts—to distinguish false accusations and slander from actual crimes—is so important.

Venezuelan law in this area is particularly strict. In 1982 a major law, the Constitutional Statute to Safeguard the Public Patrimony, was enacted. It was a clear attempt to relegitimize the political system at a time when the crisis was gathering momentum.[41] The law not only introduced stiffer penalties for traditional crimes against the public patrimony but also established new offenses. It became compulsory for a great many individuals to declare their assets to the controller general's office, and the law reversed the burden of proof in cases of possible visible enrichment. Finally, it created a *jurisdicción de salvaguarda*, or a special procedure and courts to hear cases of this kind, with certain procedural innovations. The enactment of this law was eagerly awaited, but it soon became clear that leading political figures had no intention of putting it into effect. Humberto Njaim, however, has carried out a rigorous analysis of the limitations of legislation in general in the campaign to combat corruption.[42]

No law can enforce itself, and the individuals assigned the task of doing so are also public officials: judges, prosecutors, the police, and controllers. What is usually referred to as the "judicial sector" is in fact a complex system with unique characteristics. The judiciary—the Supreme Court as well as all other courts—is only one of a number of subsystems and is heavily dependent on the input it receives from the public prosecutor's office, the judicial police (an agency of the ministry of justice), and the office of the controller general (an independent branch of Congress).

In theory, irregularities in the management of public funds can be detected by the controller general's office, which is authorized to provide a legal opinion in *autos de responsabilidad administrativa*, or cases with limited effect that can be appealed in the administrative law courts. If the irregularity detected implies evidence of civil or criminal liability on the part of the public official concerned, such cases are forwarded to the public prosecutor's office. If the latter feels there is sufficient evidence to indict, it can take the appropriate action in either the civil or the criminal courts. The judge may seek assistance from the judicial police in gathering or examining evidence or undertaking further investigations, and the procedure is more complicated when senior public officials are involved. The process may also vary somewhat if it begins with a charge brought before an ordinary court. In practice, generally speaking, none of the institutions or agencies mentioned possesses the technical expertise and political autonomy to carry out properly the extremely complex work called for in corruption trials.

The controller general and the attorney general are appointed for five-year terms by Congress and they enjoy independence of operation. These appointments are clearly political and members of the establishment are usually chosen, though there are occasional surprises. In 1975, the controller general resigned on the grounds that the executive was obstructing his work. A warrant has been issued for the arrest of a former attorney general for offenses committed in 1989 under the *jurisdicción de salvaguarda*. The present attorney general, however, appears to be a champion of the fight against corruption, despite his department's obvious limitations. Unfortunately, to the best of my knowledge no studies have been done on the offices of the controller general and the public prosecutor. The judiciary is the ultimate recipient of charges of corruption, and the public expects prompt and stern action against illegal behavior. The key question is whether the judiciary is equipped to take action.

Cases brought under the *jurisdicción de salvaguarda* are tried in the lower courts by criminal court judges. Like all judges, except those in the military (who are linked to the executive), they are appointed, evaluated, promoted, and disciplined by the Judicial Council. Created in 1969, the council is meant, under the constitution, to "ensure the independence, efficiency, discipline and propriety of the courts," and to guarantee the judicial career.[43] In practice, since its creation it has been a political body used to distribute posts and favors within the judicial system.[44] Generally speaking, the 1980 Statute on the Judicial Career has not been implemented due to a lack of political will and technical informational difficulties that could easily have been remedied.[45]

There have been many accusations of corruption within the judiciary. It suffices to mention that the potential impact of a judge's ruling on the freedom or property of an individual means that the incentives for corrupting judges are greater than for any other type of public official. At the same time, a judge's independence and the fact that his or her acts can be justified on polyvalent technolegal grounds make it easy to conceal the motives for a particular decision.[46]

Appellate jurisdiction for prosecutions brought under the *jurisdicción de salvaguarda* was not conferred on higher criminal court judges. Instead, a special court composed of three judges was created. These judges are appointed by the Supreme Court, which, being highly dependent on the political parties, means in effect that they are appointed by the parties themselves. As a result, this special court (Tribunal Superior de Salvaguarda) has an ongoing history of friction among the judges. Likewise, the justices of the full Supreme Court vote on every politically sensitive issue in accord with the views of the parties in Congress that appointed them—hence the widespread talk of the "politicization" of the judiciary.

Corruption and politicization have stripped the judiciary of the capacity to discharge its assigned duties and to legitimize the workings of the political system by correcting its most serious aberrations. The general view is that the political system has no self-regulating mechanisms and that the situation could be corrected only by destroying or transforming it.

One must recognize that what are loosely termed "corruption" offenses are usually white-collar crimes. The perpetrators are well aware of the rules of the game and they possess the intellectual skills, assistance, and time to ensure that they do not leave a trail behind them—that there is no smoking gun. Yet the legal background and training of judges and the principles they share lead them to demand tangible proof that the offense was committed and that everything be clearly set forth in the written case records. In reaching their verdict, judges must observe a procedure consisting of various stages that allows the defense considerable leeway. Public opinion does not take account of the difficulties involved and merely expects to see tough and speedy justice. Corruption and the dispensing of justice on the basis of party loyalties are not, therefore, the only obstacles to bringing corrupt officials to justice. The larger shortcomings of the judicial system are so obvious, however, that it is hardly worth bothering to point out these procedural difficulties. Nonetheless, campaigns to combat corruption should be very clear on the issue.

## WHAT LESSONS CAN BE LEARNED?

Two lessons can be singled out. The first concerns the decision to expand the role of the state. Today it is a common view in the social and economic analysis of law that the costs and benefits of every intervention must be carefully evaluated. In particular, the risk of corruption (called "moral hazard" in the economic literature) must be taken into account. One aspect of that risk needs to be stressed: the most perverse effect is not the material transfers that take place, but the change that occurs in the individuals concerned and the delegitimization of the system over the long term.

This lesson could be regarded as a liberal argument against state intervention, but it is also pragmatic. Taken at face value, it suggests the need for careful consideration of the type of intervention to be undertaken and a realization that even the best-intentioned intervention may spawn incentives for corruption that will pervert not only the particular effort in question, but public life as a whole. Events in the former Soviet Union and Eastern Europe demonstrate the potential impact of the delegitimization of a political system in which corruption likely played an important role. The repression underpinning the system can contain the scandal but not the corruption, which ensures that the political system can survive for a time. But such repression also makes the government's collapse more difficult and often more violent.

The second lesson, which involves strengthening the public sector, appears to contradict the first. The state must carry out many important responsibilities properly, even for markets to operate effectively. The point is that the ethos required of public officials must be strengthened if they are to discharge these duties *well*, in both technical and ethical terms. The idea that political party members should act through their ideologies as control mechanisms is incompatible with the development of a public service ethos. It follows that criticism of the political parties as the greatest corruptors of Venezuelan democracy is not misplaced. Since the parties are central to the workings of a modern democratic political system, the more functions they perform—beyond their roles in the discussion of ideological issues and as mechanisms for electoral association—the more likely they are to contribute to the corruption and delegitimization of the political system.

The public service ethos is a vital control mechanism (particularly where the judiciary is concerned)—an indispensable element of the public domain. As discussed earlier, this ethos is not something purely spiritual or intangible. It involves the right education and experience, the design of professional training courses, and adequate remuneration for the duties involved. The public service ethos can be taken to extremes, however, and create undesirable results, one of which is the development of a mandarinate, though this problem is not the same as corruption.

The literature on the subject leads me to conclude that statements like that of writer Arturo Uslar Pietri—"Either we put an end to corruption, or democracy is doomed"—are indicative, at the very least, of muddled thinking. Just as it cannot fully stamp out crime, no political system can eliminate corruption altogether. The best to be hoped for is that corruption becomes only an individual aberration that is punished in a significant proportion of cases, rather than being part of the logic of the political and economic system. Otherwise, one would have to be a hero or a saint to participate honestly in politics, business, or public life.

It is appropriate to close with a brief note of caution. Relatively little is known about the impact of government intervention on society. Those who created the interventionist state and those who are trying to correct its mistakes have acted with good intentions, convinced that their actions were based on sound judgments. The reality is that they each have opened a Pandora's box.

## NOTES

1. John T. Noonan, *Bribes* (Berkeley: Macmillan and University of California Press, 1984).
2. This is a polemic definition, since the acts that may be committed against large private firms are basically the same as those we class as "corruption." They also adversely affect the public sector as the inefficiency of the companies concerned increases. In my argument I accept that crimes and misdemeanors committed among private individuals are equally serious, but given the specific interaction of the management of the public sector with the political system, it seems prudent to give such behavior a name when the state patrimony is involved. In support of this definition of corruption I cite Albert O. Hirschman, *Shifting Involvements: Private Interests and Public Action* (Princeton: Princeton University Press, 1982), and the work of Arnold Heidenheimer, Michael Johnston, and Victor Le Vine, eds., *Political Corruption: A Handbook* (New Brunswick, N.J.: Transaction Publishers, 1989). A more detailed discussion can be found in Rogelio Pérez Perdomo, "Corrupción y ambiente de los negocios en Venezuela," in R. Pérez Perdomo and Ruth Capriles Méndez, eds., *Corrupción y control: Una perspectiva comparada* (Caracas: IESA, 1991), 1–27.
3. Carl Friedrich, *The Pathology of Politics: Violence, Betrayal, Corruption, Secrecy and Propaganda* (New York: Harper and Row, 1972).
4. See Humberto Njaim, "Costos y beneficios políticos de la Ley Orgánica de Salvaguarda del Patrimonio Público," in *Archivo de derecho público y ciencia de la administración* (Caracas: Universidad Central de Venezuela, 1983), 145–76; idem, "Antecedentes de la lucha contra la corrupción como un problema de política pública," in *Revista venezolana de ciencia política*, vol. 2 (Caracas: 1988); and idem, "Alcance y limitaciones de la ley en lucha anticorrupción," in Pérez Perdomo and Capriles Méndez, *Corrupción y control*, 109–40.
5. Teresa Albornoz de López, *La visita de Joaquín Mosquera y Figueroa a la Real Audiencia de Caracas (1804–1809): Conflictos y corrupción en la administración de justicia* (Caracas: Academia Nacional de la Historia, 1987); Marianela Ponce, *El control de la gestión administrativa en el juicio de residencia al gobernador Manuel González Torres de Navarra* (Caracas: Academia Nacional de la Historia, 1985); and María Elena González Deluca, *Negocios y política en los tiempos de Guzmán Blanco* (Caracas: Universidad Central de Venezuela, 1991).
6. Albornoz de López, *La visita de Joaquín Mosquera y Figueroa*, 125.
7. See Jesús Muñoz Tebar, *Personalismo y legalismo* (Caracas: Fundación Sánchez, 1977); Graciela Soriano de García Pelayo, "Proposiciones metodológicas para el estudio del personalismo político hispanoamericano," draft edition, Instituto de Estudios Políticos, Universidad Central de Venezuela, Caracas, 1988; and Rogelio Pérez Perdomo, "La organización del estado en Venezuela en el siglo XIX (1830–1899)," working paper, IESA, Caracas, 1990.

8. See Pérez Perdomo, "La organización del estado."
9. See González Deluca, *Negocios y política en los tiempos de Guzmán Blanco.*
10. See Ruth Capriles Méndez, *Los negocios de Román Delgado Chalbeaud* (Caracas: Academia Nacional de la Historia, 1991).
11. See Rómulo Betancourt, *Venezuela: Política y petróleo* (Barcelona: Seix Barral, 1979), 268.
12. Ibid., 272.
13. I single out Betancourt not on account of any particular like or dislike of the man, or because he was the first to formulate such ideas. I do so based on his importance as the founder and leading ideologue of Acción Democrática, without doubt the most important political force in contemporary Venezuela.
14. Miriam Kornblith and Thaís Maingón, *Estado y gasto público en Venezuela 1936–1980* (Caracas: Universidad Central de Venezuela, 1985).
15. See María Los, *Communist Ideology, Law and Crime* (London: Macmillan, 1988), and idem, "Los delitos de cuello rojo: Los delitos de la elite en la URSS y Polonia," in Pérez Perdomo and Capriles Méndez, *Corrupción y control,* 69–91.
16. Reisman calls them "transaction bribes"; see Michael W. Reisman, *Folded Lies: Bribery, Crusades and Reforms* (New York: Free Press, 1979).
17. During the presidency of Jaime Lusinchi, RECADI, distributing dollars at preferential rates of exchange to businesses that imported industrial goods and essential items, was a great locus of corruption—monetarily, probably the largest in the country's history. Several ministers and other high-level officials were brought to trial for misappropriation of funds and for having exceeded the foreign exchange budget. In what is a highly complex legal issue, the criminal tribunal of the Supreme Court declared in a divided (3–2) decision that the prosecution did not have standing in the case. The Supreme Court verdict was very unpopular and preceded by a few months the coup attempt of February 4, 1992.
18. See Hirschman, *Shifting Involvements.*
19. See Robin Theobald, "Corruption in Developed Societies, or What Is a 'Modern' Organization?" paper for the Polytechnic of Central London, 1991; various country analyses in Heidenheimer, Johnston, and Le Vine, *Political Corruption*; and Pérez Perdomo and Capriles Méndez, *Corrupción y control.*
20. Theobald, "Corruption in Developed Societies."
21. Betancourt, *Venezuela: Política y petróleo.*
22. The observation by Bill Stewart is germane: "While corruption was widespread under dictator Marcos Pérez Jiménez (1952–58), it has not been a serious problem under the democratic regimes that have followed him. Partly this is a consequence of the wealth of the country: Venezuela has been able to afford relatively good salaries for governmental personnel. A stronger factor may be that of the present political organization of the country. With a highly organized citizenry the parties have been able to use their influence to hold the bureaucracy accountable." Stewart regards the clientelism of the parties as the main instrument for controlling corruption. It is surprising that at the time he did not regard corruption as a serious problem. See Bill Stewart, *Change and Bureaucracy: Public Administration in Venezuela* (Chapel Hill: University of North Carolina Press, 1978), 10.
23. Moisés Naím and Ramón Piñango, "El caso Venezuela: Una ilusión de armonía," in M. Naím and R. Piñango, eds., *El caso Venezuela: Una ilusión de armonía* (Caracas: IESA, 1988), 538–79.
24. An analysis of the general diagnostic and the projects that were under consideration can be found in the work by Brewer-Carías, one of the most consistent analysts and leaders of the reform of Venezuela's public administration: see Allan R. Brewer-Carías, *Cambio político y reforma del estado en Venezuela* (Madrid: Tecnos, 1975). A major indication of the limited impact of the *Ley de Carrera Administrativa* was the reform of 1975, which abolished the *carrera* (career) for all public officials appointed to middle ranking and senior posts. Moreover, the state has lost nearly all the cases brought against it for breaches of the *Ley de Carrera* (information supplied personally by Attorney General Luis-Beltrán Guerra).

25. See Ruth Capriles Méndez, "Racionalidad de la corrupción en Venezuela," manuscript, Caracas, 1992.

26. See Moisés Naím, "Viejas costumbres y nuevas realidades en la gerencia venezolana," in Moisés Naím, ed., *Las empresas venezolanas: Su gerencia* (Caracas: IESA, 1989), 17–55, and Clemy Machado de Acedo, Elena Plaza, and Emelio Pacheco, *Estado y grupos económicos en Venezuela* (Caracas: Ateneo de Caracas, 1981).

27. One example of a particularly successful clientalist policy is in the area of housing. Leaders of Acción Democrática were the main instigators of the squatting of the land on which the *barrios* (shanty towns) were built. Those same leaders then supplied construction materials to upgrade the houses and help of different kinds to improve sidewalks and roads. Utilities were also gradually installed as part of the vote-garnering effort. The allocation of housing built by the Banco Obrero, now INAVI, was also used as clientelism. See Talton Ray, *The Politics of the Barrios of Venezuela* (Berkeley: University of California Press, 1969); Magaly Sánchez, "Estructura social y política de las viviendas en el área metropolitana de Caracas," in Manuel Castells, ed., *Estructura de clases y política urbana en América Latina* (Caracas: Ediciones Sociedad Inter-Americana de Planificación, 1974); and Rogelio Pérez Perdomo and Pedro Nikken, *Derecho y propriedad de la vivienda en los barrios de Caracas* (Caracas: Universidad Central de Venezuela, Facultad de Ciencias Jurídicas y Políticas [FCE], 1979). In Capriles Méndez, "Racionalidad de la corrupción en Venezuela," the author speaks of a *corrupción buena,* or good corruption, in which the social benefits outweigh the costs. Leaders such as Betancourt were probably aware of these practices but no doubt accepted them on account of their social benefits.

28. Ruth Capriles Méndez, *Diccionario de la corrupción en Venezuela,* 3 vols. (Caracas: Consorcio de Ediciones Capriles, 1959–92).

29. Enrique A. Baloyra, "Public Opinion and Support for the Regime: 1973–83," in John D. Martz and David Myers, eds., *Venezuela: The Democratic Experience* (New York: Praeger, 1986), 54–71.

30. Vanessa Cartaya and Haidée García, *Infancia y pobreza: Los efectos de la recesión en Venezuela* (Caracas: Nueva Sociedad, 1988); Gustavo Márquez, "Poverty and Social Policies in Venezuela," draft manuscript, IESA, Caracas, 1992; and Samuel Morley and Carola Alvarez, "Poverty and Adjustment in Venezuela," draft manuscript, Inter-American Development Bank, Washington, D.C., 1992.

31. Janet Kelly de Escobar, "Las empresas del estado: Del lugar común al sentido común," in Naím and Piñango, *El caso Venezuela.*

32. See Moisés Naím, "The Launching of Radical Policy Changes: The Venezuelan Experiences," manuscript, World Bank, Washington: D.C., 1991.

33. Larissa Adler Lomnitz, "Informal Exchange Networks in Formal Systems: A Theoretical Model," *American Anthropologist* 90 (1988): 42–55.

34. Pérez Perdomo, "Corrupción y ambiente de los negocios en Venezuela."

35. Capriles Méndez, *Diccionario de la corrupción.*

36. An ongoing study undertaken by Pérez Perdomo and Ríos at the IESA with middle and senior managers enrolled in courses to develop their management skills; see Rogelio Pérez Perdomo and Javier Ríos, "Percepciones de ética de la gerencia en Venezuela," ongoing work, IESA, Caracas, 1979.

37. See Agustín Beroes, *RECADI, la gran estafa* (Caracas: Planeta, 1990).

38. Héctor Hurtado, Francisco García Palacios, and Eduardo Mayobre, *Las cosas en su sitio* (Caracas: Editorial Unamuno, 1991).

39. The attorney general formally charged former President Lusinchi, and after various procedural moves the Supreme Court declared that the prosecution had standing and communicated that decision to the Senate. The Senate suspended Lusinchi's immunity from prosecution, which is granted to presidents under the national constitution, and he is now subject to arrest (or preventive detention). Lusinchi is in exile at present.

40. The bank, involved in an earlier scandal as well, has been taken over and is largely subsidized by the state.

41. Karin Van Groningen, "La Ley Orgánica de Salvaguarda del Patrimonio Público como un instrumento de legitimación del sistema político," in *Anuario del instituto de ciencias penales y criminológicas*, no. 10 (Caracas: Universidad Central de Venezuela, 1986).
42. Njaim, "Costos y beneficios políticos."
43. National Constitution of Venezuela, Article 217.
44. See Federico Brito Figueroa, *Historia económica y social de Venezuela* (Caracas: Ediciones de la Biblioteca, Universidad Central de Venezuela, 1978).
45. See Mariolga Quintero, "La independencia del poder judicial en Venezuela," in *Libro homenaje a José Melich II* (Caracas: Instituto de Derecho Privado, Facultad de Ciencias Jurídicas y Políticas, Universidad Central de Venezuela, 1983); Mariolga Quintero, *Justicia y realidad* (Caracas: Universidad Central de Venezuela, 1988); Rogelio Pérez Perdomo, "La administración de justicia en Venezuela: Evaluación y alternativas," *Revista de derecho privado* (Caracas), no. 2–4 (1985): 49–80; and Rogelio Pérez Perdomo, "En nombre de la república y por autoridad de la ley: Problemas de legitimidad del poder judicial en Venezuela," manuscript, Caracas, 1992.
46. Rogelio Pérez Perdomo, "Corrupción y justicia," manuscript, Caracas, 1992.

# 12

# Political Crisis and Constitutional Reform

## *Miriam Kornblith*

Recent political science and sociology literature on processes of constitutional reform has called attention in a theoretical and practical sense to the relationship between constitutional reform and political regime.[1] Constitutional change is considered a process in which fundamental, long-term rules are defined for the sociopolitical order. Understood in these terms, constitutional change is a "pre-eminently political act."[2] Democratization of the former Soviet bloc and the return to democracy in many Latin American nations have highlighted the connections between sociopolitical change and constitutional reform. When authoritarian governments succumbed in Peru, Nicaragua, Brazil, and Paraguay, for example, constitutional assemblies were convened in these countries in 1978, 1984, 1986, and 1991, respectively.

In Latin America, several features are common to the relationship between constitutional processes and political regime. On the one hand, since independence in the early 1800s, any number of de facto governments have adopted their own constitutions, using constitutionalism as an ideology to legitimize authoritarian regimes. On the other hand, constitutionalism has been used to strengthen government under the rule of law and respectful of civil and human rights.

Latin American constitutions have generally been programmatic in nature. That is, they are conceived as political programs setting forth the proposals of the sectors that aspire to govern. They typically contain a set of provisions that require a new administrative and legislative apparatus, particularly if the expansion of economic, political, and social rights is a goal.[3] These new institutions, services, and laws usually do not exist at the time of the adoption of a new constitution, but are included in the constitutional mandate nonetheless in an effort to compel future legislators and branches of government to put them into effect.

The programmatic nature of Latin America's constitutions has had a variety of consequences. In the legal realm, it results in lengthy, excessively detailed documents replete with provisions of dubious viability. Effective observance of the constitution and the law accompanying it is also undercut. Profound gaps between law and reality emerge, for as long as the institutional, sociopolitical, and ideological conditions needed to facilitate program implementation do not materialize, the decisions and actions required to put the constitutional principles into practice are temporarily or indefinitely postponed. Meanwhile, the discretionary powers of officeholders, established routine, and suspended decisions all result in actions or the creation of institutions that differ from or even contradict what one would find if the provisions of the constitution were enforced. The lack of correspondence between what is formally written in the national constitution and what is actually put into practice has arisen time and again in the history of the republics of Latin America, and perilously persists to this day.[4]

The programmatic nature of Latin American constitutions also has had political consequences. Since the constitutions attempt to set forth a political program of a particular group or groups, the political struggle shifts to the effort to determine the precise contents of the constitution. The constitutional process becomes an arena for political confrontation, at times marked by sharp debate and often burdened by short-term considerations.

Constitutions generally contain political programs that are spelled out in great detail; each regime change, it is thought, needs to be accompanied by a new political vision, which is set forth in a new constitution. Similarly, the gaps between the text of the constitution and reality are an important reflection of the sociopolitical situation. Aspirations for a more just social order and the need to bring the law into line with reality become a focus of political struggle. But the evidence of a persistent (and sometimes widening) gap tends to produce frustration and to discredit the constitution and the legal order it upholds. A further result is in excessive legal formalism and trust in the virtues of constitutional engineering as a means of shaping and transforming society.

## CONSTITUTIONAL PROCESS AND DEMOCRACY: RECENT VENEZUELAN EXPERIENCE

In June 1989, the Venezuelan Congress voted to create the Special Bicameral Committee for the Review of the Constitution, appointing former—now current—President Rafael Caldera as chair. The establishment of this committee marked the first attempt to undertake a thorough review of the 1961 Constitution, the longest-lived in Venezuela's republican history and, more important, one that has enjoyed the greatest legitimacy and acceptance as a far-reaching, sociopolitical blueprint. Prior to the enactment of the 1961 Constitution, Venezuela's constitutional history was checkered. Twenty-five constitutions had previously been adopted, and although they were not substantially different from each other, their number and the conditions under which they were produced reflect the instability and vicissitudes of the postindependence period of Venezuelan history. The 1961 Constitution, however, incorporates conflicting ideological positions and enshrines their respective—and at times contradictory—aspirations for the country. Only recently has it begun to be challenged by those who object to its excessive tendency toward centrism and state intervention.[5]

Likewise, only recently have the stability and strength of Venezuelan democracy been questioned. Since the events of February 27 and 28, 1989, and especially after the February 4 and November 27, 1992, coup attempts, preserving democracy and restoring national self-confidence once again became top priorities.[6] In addition, the debate on constitutional reform, which had been a back-burner issue, became a key factor of regime stability.

As will be discussed later, political developments in the wake of the attempted coup on February 4, 1992, cast doubts on the acceptability of the 1961 Constitution. As a result, the process of revising the constitution begun in 1989 by the Bicameral Committee produced a draft law for much greater, wide-ranging reform than initially anticipated. Under the pressure of a fierce debate, the constitutional reform process itself was eventually challenged, giving rise to the idea of convening a National Constituent Assembly to undertake the task. Ultimately, the tensions surrounding the process grew to the extent that the reform effort collapsed and was suspended.

This series of events raises several questions: Why was the 1961 Constitution challenged to such an extent that there were calls from some quarters for broad reform and a National Constituent Assembly? Why, in the wake of the events of February 4, 1992, did the constitutional debate in the country become so highly politicized and thus contribute to the attempts at wholesale reform? Coupled with the crisis following the attempted coup, what impact has the constitutional debate had on the stability of the Venezuelan regime? What does the difficulty reaching agreement on crucial constitutional issues say about the current state of the political system? Can a new constitution become as widely accepted as the 1961 Constitution once was? Finally, under what conditions can the debate on constitutional reform reinforce stability of the democratic system, and how can such conditions be achieved? This chapter is dedicated to answering these questions.

## FROM THE SPECIAL BICAMERAL COMMITTEE TO THE CHAMBER OF DEPUTIES AND SENATE

The mechanisms for amendment and general reform of the 1961 Constitution are spelled out in Articles 245 and 246, respectively.[7] Although the difference between these two procedures is not clear-cut and they continue to be controversial, it is generally understood that "amendments" should be sought for issues that do not substantialy affect content, while "general reform" entails significant change in both the doctrine and the fundamental structure of the constitution.[8] In both cases the initiative to propose change must come from Congress.[9] General reform must be approved by referendum; it is effectively the only type of change for which the constitution requires a vote by the Venezuelan public.

The 1961 Constitution has to date been amended on only two occasions, first in 1973, when the immediate concern was to block the presidential aspirations of former dictator Marcos Pérez Jiménez.[10] The second amendment, adopted in 1983, dealt with a variety of issues, including, for example, powers to adopt a special electoral system for municipal elections,[11] the appointment and workings of Congress's legislative committee, and the executive's responsibility to submit to Congress a plan for national social and economic development.

The Special Bicameral Committee for the Review of the Constitution was established in June 1989.[12] Closely paralleling the process adopted in preparing the 1961 Constitution,[13] the decision to reform the constitution in 1989 and the idea of establishing a committee for this purpose originated in Congress. The reform plan enjoyed the support of all the political parties represented in Congress, and all parties were proportionally represented on the committee according to the share of the vote they had obtained in the preceding parliamentary elections. The committee was to conduct a broad review of the constitution with the aim of identifying any aspects of the main text or accompanying legislation that required modernization and adaptation to the country's institutional needs. With this as its ambitious—if somewhat vague—goal, the committee set out to draft a series of *enmiendas*, or amendments.

As in the past, the forum chosen to frame and discuss the reform of the constitution was a small, low-profile committee. For the first time in the history of the Venezuelan republic, however, the goal was not to establish a new political system. Nor was the committee a response to the pressures or strains imposed by the opportunism and fluctuations of Venezuela's turbulent political scene[14].

But the political climate would change in 1992. The committee's initial timetable called for the completion of its work and submission of a report by the beginning of the 1990 parliamentary year. As committee chair Rafael Caldera argued, if some of the committee's recommendations were accepted, they could be discussed that same year and a draft law introduced in both houses of Congress and adopted in 1991[15]. As it turned out, the committee's work fell more than a year behind schedule, partly because for most of 1990 Caldera was preoccupied with drafting a new labor law. The committee eventually completed its work in March 1992, when its report and a draft law, known as the Bill for General Reform of the 1961 Constitution, was presented to the president of Congress. The committee worked systematically to gather the opinions of various figures and organizations, both on specific issues and on the general approach of the proposed constitutional changes. Until the attempted coup on February 4, 1992, the committee's work was carried out with no public controversy and away from the media spotlight.

The scope of the committee's work was first made known and discussed at the Jóvito Villalba Conferences on Constitutional Revision, which were held early in October 1991.[16] At that time, several key articles had been approved "in principle." Still to be approved were recommendations that had yet to be discussed or regarding which no decision had been reached, such as the transfer of power to the regional level, the political rights of naturalized Venezuelans, and military service.[17]

## THE BICAMERAL COMMITTEE AFTER THE ATTEMPTED COUP

Events following the February 4 coup attempt thrust the debate on constitutional reform—and particularly the work of the Bicameral Committee—directly into the public spotlight and influenced the tenor of the final stages of the committee's deliberations. Caldera achieved extraordinary notoriety thanks to a speech he delivered on February 4, the day of the military uprising, during a joint session of Congress convened to denounce the coup attempt. He took a tough line with the government and the status quo, and his stance earned him widespread popular support but strong criticism from members of his own party (COPEI), among others, for both the timing and the contents of his speech.[18] Then, because Caldera was chair of the committee for constitutional reform, the media began attending committee meetings to obtain his opinions on daily political developments and also began taking an interest in the proceedings of the committee itself.

Even more important, the Bicameral Committee soon became one of the few forums considered qualified to frame or discuss solutions to the institutional crisis facing Venezuela. Once the military situation had been brought under control, the political hierarchy became increasingly unstable. Various ideas began to float through the halls of power, such as the resignation of President Pérez (endorsed by, among others, Caldera himself), the shortening of the mandates of all or some of the branches of government, the convening of a constituent assembly, and the holding of early elections for all or some of the branches of government. Reform of the constitution, or the manner of interpretation of some of its articles, had great bearing on all of these options.

Among the general public and in some political quarters, the committee's work was considered the most effective vehicle for formulating solutions to the crisis that had erupted. In addition, as members of the committee began to consider the alternatives just mentioned, the idea of a constituent assembly and the conditions under which it would be convened became the focal point of many of the group's final sessions. The committee, moreover, was forced to examine what its own role might be in such a case.

The president of Congress called on the committee to conclude and report on its work by March 20, 1992. Moving quickly, by March 10 it already had decided to recommend that Congress proceed with a "general reform," pursuant to Article 246. The decision to propose a general reform rather than amendments was influenced by both technolegal and political considerations. The increased scope of the proposed changes[19]—coupled with the need for swift ratification of the measure (which is facilitated under Article 246) in order to provide an institutional forum for debate on constitutional solutions to the crisis— tipped the scales in favor a general reform.[20]

Following a series of intensive sessions during the week of March 16 to 22, the committee voted on and issued a final report composed of seventy articles.[21] The most important innovations of this draft law included the establishment of various referendums for obtaining the electorate's endorsement of government decisions, the creation of the office of prime minister, and a review of the structure and operations of the judiciary. Although the draft law contained important institutional innovations, it failed to suggest any specific solution to the ongoing cri- sis. The committee decided to limit itself to its original mandate: to conduct a thorough review of the constitution, identify any shortcom- ings, and recommend long-term institutional changes.

In the end, the ambiguity of the goals of the constitutional reform characterized the process: the demands for recommendations for solu- tions to the crisis in the short term were coupled with an opposite focus on issues that would effect the institutional framework over the long term and in a global manner. Both sides saw their hopes dashed at some point. Venezuelans who had been hoping for "solutions" to the nation's immediate problems were disappointed, while those who wished to strengthen the country's institutions with improvements suc- cumbed to the pressure of events. This ambiguity, particularly evident during the last sessions of the Bicameral Committee, was manifest throughout and had a profound impact on the constitutional process. If the purpose of the reform process was never made clear, even when the Bicameral Committee was created, the events of February 4, 1992, and the days that followed even further confused the issue of its objec- tives and direction.

## CONSTITUTIONAL REFORM IN THE CHAMBER OF DEPUTIES

The motion to consider the draft law on constitutional reform was ap- proved by Congress in late March.[22] The bill was subsequently debated first in the lower house for three reasons. First, the government opposi- tion hoped to create a coalition in that body (including a dissident wing of the ruling AD party) large enough to press for the resignation of President Pérez or a reduction in his term of office. Congress ulti- mately could have either approved a reduction in the presidential term to four years, included a referendum to recall the present government, or revoked the mandate of every branch of government pending gen- eral elections in December 1992; none of these possibilities, however, came to be.

Second, it was believed that debating the reform law in the Chamber of Deputies precluded Caldera, as a member of the upper house—or as a former president, a senator-for-life—from playing an active and effec- tive role. This view was shared by AD members who supported the gov- ernment and by groups within COPEI who were supporting the presi- dential candidacy of Eduardo Fernández, the secretary general of the party, whose popularity had suffered with his support for the government and with Caldera's rising popularity. Finally, initiating the process in the lower house was the usual procedure for new legislation, so it seemed the most natural course to take.

The motion to introduce the Bicameral Committee's draft law was approved unanimously by Congress in a joint session of the two houses.[23] The first debate ran from April 6 to 22, 1992, and included policy statements on the constitutional process and the current political situation by representatives of all eleven political parties with seats in the chamber.[24] Before the debate's end, the Chamber of Deputies appointed the Special Commission for the Study of the Draft Law to Reform the Constitution, which was charged with submitting a report on the draft law prior to the second debate. The inaugural meeting was convened on April 10. The full commission met on April 20 and assigned the work to the four subcommissions created ten days earlier: Basic Principles; Political Reforms; Reform of the Judiciary and the Office of the Human Rights Advocate; and Territorial Organization of the State and Transfer of Responsibilities. The work was completed on June 16 with the presentation of the "Report of the Special Commission of the Chamber of Deputies for the Study of the Draft Law to Reform the Constitution for the Second Debate."

The subcommissions were able to call on the deputies assigned to them as well as other eminent individuals invited in a personal capacity or as representatives of organizations concerned with the issues to be addressed. Former advisors to the Bicameral Committee and to the Congressional Office of Legal Research and Assistance were also available. To ensure the participation of a greater variety of sectors—and partly to silence critics, who had accused it of conducting its earlier deliberations in secret—the Special Commission invited a number of individuals and organizations to provide their opinions and suggestions concerning the constitutional reform process.[25] Finally, following a detailed review of all of its work, the ninety-article final report was completed.

A source of particular controversy were the sections dealing with the judiciary, referendums, the powers of the states, electoral system, retiree rights, indigenous groups, and naturalized Venezuelans. In response to a request—or warning—from governors, who threatened to reject the reform if their demands were not met, the document as finally approved granted wider powers to the states. The conditions for the convening referendums were tightened, as were the rules governing the operations of the judiciary, and judges in particular.

The second debate in the Chamber of Deputies on the draft law to reform the constitution concluded on July 28, 1992, with the approval of a report composed of one hundred articles. This second debate was highly controversial. It took place on the floor of the House, not in a committee room, although a number of issues were assigned to ad hoc commissions for discussion and recommendations. Many of the sessions were televised; the public—enthralled by the proceedings—was able to follow a large proportion of the debate.

Two issues were the focus of extensive public attention and debate in the lower house: (1) regulation of the private communications media and the referendum initiatives for recall of elected officials, cutting short their terms, and (2) bringing forward the date of the forthcoming elections. This latter debate concentrated and amplified existing tensions among political parties. Although none of the referendum initiatives passed, moments of confusion and conflict over the course of the debate led to a walkout by the minority factions of Congress. These groups felt that the removal of the president was a necessity and one of the clear possibilities of the reform process.

Although the constitutional reform process had ceased to be a quasi-private affair as of February 4, during the second debate in the lower house it attracted a blaze of publicity, primarily due to the discussion of two controversial articles dealing with the regulation of the activities of the media.[26] Up to this point, the most polemic issues had been those relating to the immediate political situation, such as the shortening of the president's term in office, decentralization, and the reorganization of the judiciary. The other key issue, Congress's authority to promote reforms of this nature, was a politicoprocedural matter and had no bearing on the actual substance of the proposed changes. The main focus of attention had been the differences of opinion on these issues, which were also at the root of the most serious clashes —though occurring largely within the political party system and among various government agencies. The articles dealing with the regulation of the media, however, propelled the constitutional debate into uncharted waters and placed it in the public spotlight. Rightly or wrongly, the media reacted angrily to this attempt to regulate their activities. Since that point, the media's strategy has been to involve the general public in the defense of a common right—freedom of speech—which allegedly would have been violated by the proposed revisions of the constitution.

Throughout June and July 1992 the country's political and social environment was especially tense, as reflected in the internal dynamics of Congress. The climate for reform weakened as more and more institutions and individuals publicly stated that they intended to vote against the referendum to reform the constitution.

## CONSTITUTIONAL REFORM IN THE SENATE

During this period, the Senate denied President Pérez authorization to travel abroad twice in a row—to the June Earth Summit in Rio de Janeiro and to the Ibero-American Summit on July 16 in Seville—which is unusual in Venezuela. The denials of travel authorization, together with political party conflicts, general political tensions, and the particular alignment of forces in the Senate, delayed a review of decisions taken in the lower house. Expectations for the Senate debate arose in three fundamental areas: the functioning and structure of judicial power, regulation of the communications media, and once again, recall of elected officials, with the added element that Caldera was expected to be involved in this debate.

On August 3, the Senate appointed its own special commission to study the draft law. As opposed to the procedure followed by the lower house, the upper house's commission, appointed to make recommendations on the *reforma general,* worked parallel to, and simultaneously with, the debate in the Senate. It was on the Senate floor that most of the discussions actually took place, drawing on the observations made by the senators and on the reports of the commission and the ad hoc subcommissions created to study specific issues.[27]

The Special Commission received the findings of its subcommissions, to which the most controversial articles had been deferred, on August 6. It voted to approve the establishment of the freedom of thought, information, and speech and the right of reply, and it decided to work on a more acceptable version of the article on monopolies and the media. Since no agreement was reached on the article dealing with the referendum to recall the president, the Congressional Office of Legal Research and Assistance was asked to submit a text reflecting the variety of views expressed. It was further suggested that the various aspects of the referendum be dealt with under a special law, as proposed in the draft law passed by the Chamber of Deputies.

The debate on the floor of the House, originally scheduled for August 7, occurred on August 11. In the intervening days, beginning on August 7, the national print media, television, and radio associations met with the members of the subcommission responsible for studying the articles dealing with the regulation of the media. A second meeting was held on August 10. The subcommission advocated that a provision on monopolies and the media be incorporated into Article 97 of the constitution, which outlawed the creation of monopolies of any kind. With respect to the right of reply, it was suggested that the position and/or wording of the article be modified without altering the meaning of the right embodied therein. For their part, the media argued that enshrining the right of reply in the constitution would seriously restrict their freedom of action. They requested the adoption of the wording proposed by the Bicameral Committee instead.[28]

Also at this stage the debate on the recall referendum and the various proposals for reducing the term of the president and other elected officials captured public attention and produced friction among the political parties in Congress. These proposals did not prevail, but bitter debates and close votes again accompanied the debate.

The debate concluded on September 4. The Senate's recommendations were referred to the Special Commission for further study and the completion of a draft report on the proceedings. This first stage in the Senate's consideration of the reform was overshadowed by the media's opposition and by the impact of the proposal put forward by Senator Alfredo Tarre Murzi in his speech on August 17, when he suggested that "the debate on the reform of the constitution be deferred until a more propitious moment."[29]

On September 12, given the decisions taken by the Senate on the articles regulating the activities of the media—including provisions prohibiting media monopolies, barring the offense of public decency, and requiring pluralistic representation of views—the print, radio, and television associations mounted a public campaign to block the constitutional reform process. The rest of the month was dominated by discussion of the media campaign and the question of suspending the debate. The Special Commission organized the work carried out in the upper house and completed its activities on September 28. The Senate's deliberations produced a reform bill of 118 articles.

The start of the second debate in the Senate was delayed pending a decision on the suspension of the constitutional reform process. But the Senate as such did not make a formal decision, nor did the political parties define their position on the matter. The future of the debate on the constitution remained in the hands of the senior decision-making bodies of the different parties, who weighed the pros and cons of such a move and assessed the prevailing conditions for their eventual decision.

## OPPOSITION TO THE CONSTITUTIONAL REFORM

The dilemma of whether to suspend the discussions on constitutional reform transcended the immediate resolution of each of the controversial substantive or procedural points raised in the course of the debate.

But the quandary was nonetheless the direct result of the volatility of this constitutional process.

From the outset, the idea of overhauling the constitution had met with opposition from several quarters. First opposition arose from those who questioned Congress's authority to undertake sweeping reforms and assume the powers of a de facto constituent assembly; they proposed convening a constituent assembly instead. This criticism formed part of a broader criticism of party politics in general and of the major, pro–status quo political parties in particular.

The reform package also faced opposition from individuals or groups who felt threatened by it. State governors objected to the centrist bias of the bill drafted by the Bicameral Committee, some aspects of which had been ratified (for example, the powers to dismiss governors to be conferred on the president, the Senate, or both houses). Influential members of the judiciary objected to aspects of the draft law calling for the establishment of a special commission or disciplinary tribunal to dismiss judges whose behavior "brings the dignity of their office into disrepute."[30]

The reform process was also opposed from the outset by influential individuals, such as writer Arturo Uslar Pietri, who, when asked for his opinion of the Bicameral Committee bill, stated that it seemed to be a return to the nineteenth-century belief that by changing the constitution one could change the sociopolitical situation. He felt that given Venezuela's stormy political climate it was not the best moment to institute such an ambitious program of reform. Uslar Pietri went on to criticize one of the bill's most innovative aspects—the inclusion of various types of referendums—on the grounds that it could "create a climate of uncertainty, endless agitation and institutional instability."[31]

Despite the opposition early on, not until the interests of the media were directly threatened did there emerge a coordinated, radical, and systematic opposition movement. The reform process moved in a new direction the moment the media became embroiled in the controversy. The privately owned media organizations pressed on with their campaign against the *reforma mordaza* (gag reform), even though intensive negotiations between media representatives and the Senate produced provisions that were watered down and more ambiguous than the lower house's draft law.[32] The media not only campaigned directly against the reform, but also invited the general public to support them in rejecting the package.

The various sectors opposed to the reforms made some effort to coordinate their efforts, but demonstrated little ability to carry their arguments beyond the ambit of their particular interests or preferences.

Such was the case, for example, of the different institutions and person-alities who at various times pressed for the convening of a constituent assembly. With or without the cooperation of the other sectors opposed to the reform process, however, the privately owned media organiza-tions mounted a persistent, aggressive, and incisive campaign against it.

The political parties and their representatives, barring a few notable exceptions, expressed only timid support for the constitutional reform process. Individuals or groups within all the political parties questioned the wisdom of the constitutional reform process on the grounds of tim-ing, procedure, and substance. Although the parties were the original promoters of the reform, they failed to present an organized and co-herent front, coordinate a solid defense of the substantive innovations of the different bills, or assert convincingly Congress's legitimate right to propose constitutional reform. The political parties appeared bewil-dered and isolated, and failed to defend what was, after all, their own project. Intra- and interparty divisions and pressures, especially in the case of AD and COPEI, are to some extent to blame for the parties' confusion and have served to undermine the reform process. In the end, constitutional reform was put on hold as a result of the lack of in-terparty solidarity in the face of criticism from various quarters and the direct, united opposition of the communications media.

## CONSTITUTIONAL REFORM AND STABILITY OF THE DEMOCRATIC REGIME[33]

During the twenty-eight years between the time the 1961 Constitution took effect and July 1989, when the Special Bicameral Committee for the Review of the Constitution was appointed, Venezuela had dramati-cally changed. Implementation of the macroeconomic adjustment pro-gram[34] and the subsequent social unrest of February 1989, the same year in which the review of the 1961 Constitution was initiated, are per-haps the most obvious signs of major sociopolitical change. Yet the de-cision to rely on the same procedure—the creation of a bicameral com-mittee—used to promulgate the 1961 Constitution suggests that such changes were not fully perceived. The underlying presumption was that the present sociopolitical circumstances did not preclude the methods known to have worked in the past.

The celebration of the Venezuelan constitution's thirtieth anniver-sary in 1991 marked thirty years since the fall of dictator Marcos Pérez Jiménez and the restoration of democratic rule. On its first anniversary the constitution entered into force; this thirtieth anniversary celebrated its coming of age. Despite the apparent continuity, however, the belief that the formulas of the past would work in the present—not only for constitutional reform, but for other sociopolitical processes as well— was only weakly supportable before 1989[35] and continued to be so in the years ahead.

Given this context, the question arises: Why is it so hard to develop consensus solutions on issues crucial for Venezuela's political system? Or, with respect to constitutional reform, why was it not possible to reach basic agreements during the reform process of 1992?

## THE PROCEDURES, CONTENT, AND OBJECTIVES OF CONSTITUTIONAL REFORM

Although the goal of constitutional reform was clearly defined at the outset, the process ultimately generated a wide array of interpretations and expectations. As those who directed, opposed, or closely followed the process interpreted it, each according to his or her own convictions and experiences, the significance of the reform came to exceed the aims of its original proponents.

The variety and ambiguity of the purposes for which the reform was to be undertaken mushroomed after February 4, when the initially vague formulations were turned into objectives, albeit still not very clear ones, tied to the political and economic tensions of the time. The impact on the content of the reform was negative. Subjects were added, some crucial, others secondary; arguments were advanced regarding both short-term and long-term issues. The reform became multifunctional: it was used to address the deficiencies in the text of the constitution, remedy shortcomings in the regular juridical order, and propose immediate solutions to the crisis. The proposed reforms became increasingly wide-ranging and ambitious to the point that their full approval by popular consultation was not feasible. As the reform process broadened in scope, its significance seemed to decline and it became much more likely that many interests would be affected and adversarial relationships created. Consequently, political support for constitutional reform waned.

The procedure chosen for designing, debating, and promulgating the constitution also created problems. Entrusting the constitutional amendments to a bicameral committee that received little public attention produced criticism regarding the lack of broad participation in the process. In contrast to the years following the return to democracy in 1958, today there is little tolerance for removing issues of broad social interest from public debate. Furthermore, in an atmosphere marked by extreme skepticism toward political parties and the political elite, implementation of reform through Congress—given the objections to those who were proposing changes—led many to question the legitimacy of the process itself. General reform, as opposed to the amendment process, meant that enactment of the new constitution would depend on the outcome of a referendum. Venezuela's difficult sociopolitical conditions implied that the referendum would likely be interpreted as a plebiscite on the administration, the regime, or the forces proposing reform more than on the reform itself. Rejection of the proposed reform became the most likely outcome.

The interaction of each of these constitutional decisions produced so many stumbling blocks and areas of conflict that supporters of reform were put in an increasingly weak position. They eventually decided it would be best to suspend the process, rather than insist on heading down a path that would result in further confrontation and rejection of the referendum.

The decisions and the resulting difficulties are more readily understood through examination of the constitutional debate's context. Since it is a process in which the most general and long-term rules of a given society are defined, the sociopolitical context is endogenous to the process. The constitutional process interacts as an independent variable with the immediate as well as the general sociopolitical context; that is, the reform effort has a discernible impact on the sociopolitical order in which it unfolds.[36] At the same time, the constitutional process is shaped by the sociopolitical context; in this sense, it is dependent on it.

## CONSTITUTIONAL REFORM AND THE CURRENT POLITICAL JUNCTURE

Two central questions arise when the relationship between the immediate context and the constitutional process is examined: What impact did the February 4 attempted coup have on the course of the constitutional debate? What was the impact of the constitutional debate on the stability of the government and Venezuelan democracy following the events of February 4?

As was already shown, the sociopolitical dynamic set off by the coup attempt introduced issues and tensions into the process. It made constitutional change visible and relevant, but at the cost of turning it into a debate on the current situation. Long-term institutional design became secondary, or came to be interpreted only in terms of its immediate impact.

Nevertheless, the experience of constitutional reform made it possible to express and process differences under the rules of Parliament, which in turn made it possible to channel or contain political tensions within a democratic framework and within a public and institutional context. With the failure of initiatives like the formation of a national unity government or the Great National Accord, and amid growing social and political unrest and multilateral conflict, the institutional arenas for formulating agreements or resolving differences were losing effectiveness or had lost it completely. Congress served as a sounding board for friction in the overall environment; the constitutional debate became important. It also became the principal and almost only forum for discussion and the development of institutional means to overcome the crisis. Paradoxically, at the cost of the success of the reform effort, the interaction between the short-term political situation and the constitutional debate was focused (in the very short run) on the democratic system.

Constitutional reform was also linked to other aspects of the national sociopolitical situation, as well as to the political parties' internal dynamics, the proximity of the 1992 and 1993 elections, and friction among the branches of government. The proximity of the gubernatorial and mayoral elections gave greater force to the appeals and threats of these authorities. The tensions and coalitions formed for the upcoming 1993 presidential elections, especially within COPEI and concerning the support of minority parties for the presidential aspirations of Rafael Caldera, contributed significantly to the insistence with which the reforms were treated, to the extent that they became the most attractive elements for those sectors. Likewise, international events such as the "self-coup" of President Alberto Fujimori in Peru and the impeachment of President Fernando Collor in Brazil generated analyses of the similarities and differences between these two countries and Venezuela.

## CONSTITUTIONAL REFORM AND THE SOCIOPOLITICAL MODEL

An examination of the interaction between the constitutional reform and sociopolitical model makes it clear that other difficulties and characteristics of the process, albeit having emerged prior to February 4, transcended the events of that day. Additional questions need to be addressed, such as: What is the impact of the crisis in the sociopolitical model with respect to the difficulties experienced in the constitutional reform effort? What is the impact of the success or failure of the constitutional reform process on the observance and stability of democratic rule in the country?

As Juan Carlos Rey has demonstrated, the operation of the populist system of reconciliation of elites, based on recognition of a plurality of social, economic, and political interests (which is how the democratic order is currently organized in Venezuela), has depended on the appropriate interaction among three fundamental factors: the relative abundance of economic resources with which the state has been able to meet demands from a variety of groups and sectors; the relatively limited nature and simplicity of such demands, which made it possible to meet them with available resources; and the ability of political organizations (parties and interest groups) and their leaderships to pull together, channel, and represent those demands, securing the trust of their respective constituents.[37]

An adverse shift in any of these three factors represents a threat to the stability of the system, which could then be addressed. But in the early 1990s the simultaneous fissures in each factor brought the sociopolitical system to the brink of crisis.[38] The existence of these three elements made it possible to reconcile heterogeneous interests and ushered in a decision-making process based on a complex system of negotiation and accommodation of interests. The system was, on the one hand, able to ensure minority but powerful sectors—the armed forces, the Catholic church, business groups, organized labor, and trade associations—that their interests would not be threatened by respect for majority rule in government decision making. On the other hand, the system ensured that most of the population trusted in the mechanisms of representative democracy, construed as respect for majority rule in the process of choosing governmental authorities. Political stability, interelite consensus, and securing the confidence of the population were the main achievements of this model.[39]

As noted earlier, the Venezuelan political system is currently on the brink of collapse. Adverse changes in the three key factors and in their interaction have seriously threatened the system's stability.[40] The country has moved from conditions of relative resource abundance to relative scarcity, and income from oil is not enough to meet the needs and demands of the various social sectors. At the same time, the demands and expectations of the population in general as well as specific groups are greater, more differentiated, and more complex; satisfying them requires increased economic, institutional, and organizational resources.

Finally, the two most powerful parties, AD and COPEI, and the organizations that represent distinct sectors, such as the main business association (FEDECAMARAS) and the Federation of Venezuelan Workers (CTV), lost much of their ability to aggregate, channel, and manage the demands and interests of the sectors they represent. Their constituencies have lost confidence in them. Divisions that have led to a breakdown of internal discipline and provoked questions about leadership have emerged within each of these organizations, reducing their room to maneuver and their representativity. The various sectors need more than one organization to represent them, which increases the number of actors and the differences among them, divides the leadership, and generates more complex, costly, and unpredictable patterns of negotiation.

The mounting difficulties reconciling diverse interests in the decisions that must be made in the name of society as a whole are both an expression and a consequence of the crisis in the "populist system of reconciliation," as is the ineffectiveness of the mechanisms previously designed to manage the conflict and create consensus. Due to the relative success of the previous framework for negotiation and the stability attained with its use, alternative institutional mechanisms for dispute settlement and consensus-building were not developed. When the previous rules and mechanisms became ineffective, amid adverse sociopolitical and socioeconomic conditions that were the cause of various conflicts, Venezuela found that it had no institutional "safety valves" or reliable formal devices for negotiation and conflict resolution.[41]

The constitutional debate expressed and exacerbated this situation, and the confrontation cut across organizations and sectors. Specific differences emerged among different groups (such as indigenous peoples, women, retirees, governors, judges, naturalized Venezuelans, and the mass media) that could not be readily contained or channeled through political parties or interest groups, bearing witness to the inability of the existing organizations to continue representing such interests and satisfying the population's expectations and demands. In addition, interests clashed within the organizations and conventional means of settlement were of no avail. Discrepancies within parties were openly expressed throughout the debate. The confrontations among the branches of government and between the national and regional leadership were expressed in raw form; it was of no use to try to impose the party line.

In several cases the dispute was marked by the struggle for scarce resources. The demands to increase the constitutionally fixed income allotment of the state governors and to include a constitutional provision on the right of retirees to a minimum pension are examples. When the effort to foster negotiation between members of Congress and media representatives failed, the media shifted the conflict to the public arena, in a strong and abusive wielding of its power. The failure of informal means of negotiation between the political sector and the communications industry brought to light the lack of appropriate forums and rules for arbitrating and settling the disputes in question.

Mass discontent with the political and economic situation undermined the support and credibility of the reform effort, giving rise to fears that the constitutional referendum would not pass. The inability of the most powerful parties and organizations to represent a wide array of interests or to generate an active base of support and the weakness of Congress were unveiled for all to see.

The vicissitudes of the constitutional reform effort displayed just how much the forces at work militated against adherence to the organizations, rules, principles, and leadership groups that existed at the time. The interaction of these underlying sociopolitical processes, coupled with the specific tensions that stemmed from the coup attempt and the decisions made in the course of the constitutional reform process, frustrated the effort to reach basic agreements in the course of the debate.

## CONSTITUTIONAL PROCESS AND THE STABILITY OF DEMOCRATIC RULE

Preserving the regime is once again a priority of the Venezuelan political system. This priority involves increasing the likelihood that the basic rules of the democratic game will be respected and accepted. In the short term, it assumes that the elected government will not be overthrown and that elections will continue to be used to select the party in power. In the short and long term, it implies convincing the various actors of the need for these rules and ensuring that they are sincerely accepted as legitimate. Undemocratic solutions must be discarded as both unviable and undesirable.[42]

With respect to the present, the constitutional reform has contributed to government stability and to that extent has contributed to the preservation of democracy in the long run. Nonetheless, more specific observations are needed to assess the possible medium- and long-term impact of success or failure of the constitutional reform process. Deeming the constitutional reform effort a success assumes, at the least, that it will continue and that it will be possible to submit the proposed revisions to a popular referendum and, at the most, that the outcome of the vote on the reform proposal will be favorable. A failure of the process implies a suspension of the process of constitutional review, either for good or indefinitely.

Now that the process has been suspended, its consequences should be examined. A definitive suspension of the constitutional debate would have a negative effect on preservation of democracy in several areas: it further discredits Congress as a legislative body, given its inability to formulate viable and desirable institutional options for the country; it fosters the impression that the effort to use institutions to solve the crisis has failed; it suggests that it is not possible for the main actors in the system to reach basic agreements; it affirms the weakness of the political leadership, especially of the principal parties; it creates the impression that what is apparently popular is to be feared and seems to explain why many politicians oppose submitting the constitutional reform to a referendum; and it leaves the country with the same constitution, important provisions of which have been called into question yet have not been addressed. In summary, a definitive suspension of the reform process would be costly, since it would further discredit fundamental institutions of the democratic system, frustrate the expectations of change generated by the reform, and weaken the legitimacy of the present constitution.

## REFORMULATING THE TERMS OF THE CONSTITUTIONAL DEBATE

Given the impasse in the reform effort, it is neither very likely nor very desirable that the process will continue as initially envisioned. The constitution requires reformulation with a view toward converting it into a vehicle for stabilizing the democratic system. Several questions must be addressed: In what circumstances can the debate on constitutional reform reinforce the stability of that system? What strategy should be adopted and what resources are needed to achieve it? How is it possible to weather the negative climate and opposition generated around constitutional reform?

The constitutional reform effort has faced political, ideological, and legal problems. Political difficulties include, on the one hand, the weakness and isolation of the advocates of reform, in particular the parliamentary factions of AD and COPEI, and, on the other hand, the active opposition of several political, social, and economic sectors. Fragility of the political coalition and the limited conviction and unity with which the political parties addressed the various aspects of and moments in the reform process dramatically reduced its chances of success. Success of the reform requires the active and committed involvement of the political parties, which must become convinced of the need and opportunity for the process and the specific measures proposed.

As the strongest backers of the constitutional reform, the political parties—in particular AD and COPEI—share the greatest responsibility for ensuring that the process strengthens democracy. The contents of the constitutional reform should form a significant part of the political program of both parties. Issues such as participation, the deepening of democracy, decentralization, judicial reform, reform of the parties and the electoral system, and improving the rule of law as a democratic and social concern have been advocated by the parties at various stages of the reform process. Yet these issues have not been unequivocally proposed as ideological banners or as the principal justifications of the reform. Although advocates of the process, the parties fell short when it came to defending the substantive innovations of the reform project they proposed, and they adopted a defensive posture when faced with attacks from adversaries.

The tendency of Venezuelan constitutions to enunciate political programs was exacerbated in the course of preparing the various reform proposals. The large number and complexity of the proposed articles drew attention away from the most crucial aspects of the reform proposal, and made holding a referendum infeasible. The proposed reform should be reworked; this requires examining the proposed articles individually with the aim of determining which reforms, amendments, and statutory or programmatic provisions to be included in the constitution are debatable or problematic. Only those provisions that effectively qualify as substantive reforms should be considered in a general program of reform and subject to a referendum. This procedure would make it possible to overcome the legal difficulties entailed when submitting a voluminous text to a referendum. Likewise, it would help diversify and broaden the arenas of conflict, transferring to a regular parliamentary body the consideration of possible amendments or provisions now pertaining to other legal entities. Diversifying and broadening the scope of conflict and generating other forums for institutional disputes would reduce the pressure that has emerged around the constitutional debate and especially around Congress.

Crucial aspects still undefined include how to bring about the needed agreements between and within the parties; how to channel the opposition of those against the reform; how to create new bases of support for the constitutional reform; and how to generate enthusiasm among the population. Public opinion turned against the reform as a result of the active opposition it faced in other sectors, its advocates' passivity, and the general ignorance of the population as to what it represented. The most controversial provisions need to be studied to determine which elements should be negotiated or reconsidered and which should be staunchly defended; in addition, the cost of such confrontations should be evaluated. A massive information and education campaign on the content and importance of the reform is indispensable. The goal should be the generation of widespread interest and enthusiasm among the public, since the political parties themselves do not enjoy unconditional popular support.

## LOOKING TO THE FUTURE

As of March 1993, the constitutional reform process had come to a standstill. In late 1992, a number of Venezuelans, particularly members of COPEI,[43] came out in favor of continuing the debate after the 1992 elections, yet no decisions were made or initiatives taken in this direction. The constitutional reform was to be addressed once again in 1994 by the new Congress members elected in December 1993. The new Congress will likely have greater credibility than the previous one, given the partially uninominal nature of its selection, although it could meet some objections regarding its representativity and legitimacy.

For constitutional reform to contribute to stability and the restoration of the prestige of the democratic system, the process should be reformulated in political, ideological, and legal terms and involve communication with the public. To this end, its continuation should be part of a strategy to preserve and stabilize democratic rule. Any initiative to restart the constitutional debate will have to bear the burden of the negative image (justified or not) associated with the previous effort. Yet at the same time, Venezuela can benefit from past experience, making use of the effort invested in drafting the various proposed reforms and drawing lessons from the accomplishments and mistakes of the earlier process.

# NOTES

I would like to thank Zuleima Añanguren for her valuable assistance in preparing this chapter.

1. The interrelation between political regime and constitutional reform is discussed in many works, including Donald Horowitz, *A Democratic South Africa? Constitutional Engineering in a Divided Society* (Berkeley: University of California Press, 1991); Terence Ball and J. G. A. Pocock, eds., *Conceptual Change and the Constitution* (Lawrence: University Press of Kansas, 1988); Vernon Bogdanor, ed., *Constitutions in Democratic Politics* (London: Gower, 1988); Jon Elster and Rune Slagstad, *Constitutionalism and Democracy* (Cambridge: Cambridge University Press, 1988); Robert Goldwin and Art Kaufman, *Constitution Makers on Constitution Making* (Washington, D.C.: American Enterprise Institute, 1988); Adam Antal and Heinrich Hans-George, *Society, Politics and Constitutions: Western and East European Views* (Budapest: Bildau Verlag Wien-Koln-Graz, 1987); and Keith Banting and Richard Simeon, eds., *Redesigning the State: The Politics of Constitutional Change* (Toronto: University of Toronto Press, 1985). I have highlighted these connections for the case of Venezuela in Miriam Kornblith, "Concepción de la política y conflicto antagónico en el trienio: Su estudio a través de los debates de la Asamblea Constituyente de 1946–47" (Instituto de Estudios Políticos, Universidad Central de Venezuela, Caracas, 1988, mimeographed); "Proceso constitucional y consolidación de la democracia en Venezuela: Las constituciones de 1947 y 1961," *Politeia*, no. 13 (1989): 283–329; and "The Politics of Constitution-Making: Constitutions and Democracy in Venezuela," *Journal of Latin American Studies* 23, no. 1 (1991): 61–89.

2. Daniel Elazar, "Constitution-Making: The Pre-eminently Political Act," in Banting and Simeon, *Redesigning the State*, 232–48.

3. A constitution has three types of provisions: principles, legal rules, and programmatic provisions. The principles, which constitute the normative basis of the constitution, express the values that the legislators wish to enshrine in the fundamental charter. The legal rules are complete provisions that are immediately and directly enforceable, demandable, and binding with no further legislative enactment. The programmatic provisions are statements that outline various objectives whose attainment is considered imperative to address the country's current situation. These suggest future actions for the various branches of government, but are not immediately demandable, and thus are not legally binding because their enforcement requires the passage of specific legislation. Typically they take this form: "The State shall promote, protect, foster . . . in accordance with the respective law." See Juan Carlos Rey, "Los 25 años de la constitución y la reforma del estado," *Venezuela 86*, no. 2 (1986): 26–34.

4. The classic formulation of this distinction can be found in the lecture given by Ferdinand Lasalle in 1862, *¿Qué es una Constitución?* (Barcelona: Editorial Ariel, 1984). For an influential elaboration and application to Venezuela and Latin America, see Laureano Vallenilla Lanz, *Cesarismo democrático: Estudios sobre las bases sociológicas de la constitución efectiva de Venezuela* (Caracas: Tipografía Universal, 1929). See also Ernesto Wolf, *Tratado de derecho constitucional venezolano*, vol. 1 (Caracas: Tipografía Americana, 1945).

5. See, for example, Emeterio Gómez, "La constitución de 1961 y la creación de una economía competitiva en Venezuela," paper presented to "Seminario 30 años de la Constitución de 1961" (Instituto de Estudios Políticos, Univérsidad Central de Venezuela, Caracas, 1991, mimeographed).

6. A review of the 1989 events can be found in Jesús Civit and Luis Pedro España, "Análisis socio-político a partir del estallido del 27 de febrero," *Cuadernos del Centro de Estudios del Desarrollo (CENDES)*, no. 10 (1989): pp. 35–46; Miriam Kornblith, "Deuda y

democracia en Venezuela: Los sucesos del 27 y 28 de febrero de 1989," *Cuadernos del CENDES,* no. 10 (1989), 17–34; and Luis Salamanca, "El 27 de febrero de 1989: La política por otros medios," *Politeia,* no. 13 (1989): 187–217. On the first coup attempt, see Vice Adm. Elías R. Daniels, *Militares y democracia: Papel de la institución armada de Venezuela en la consolidación de la democracia* (Caracas: Centauro, 1992); Enrique Ochoa Antich, *Los golpes de febrero: 27 febrero 1989–4 febrero 1992* (Caracas: Fuentes Editores, 1992); and Heinz Sonntag and Thaís Maingón, *Venezuela 4-F 1992: Un análisis sociopolítico* (Caracas: Editorial Nueva Sociedad, 1992). On the second attempt, see William Ojeda, *Las verdades del 27-N* (Caracas: Vadell Hermanos Editores, 1993).

7. The procedures for amending and reforming the 1961 Constitution are set forth in articles 167, 168, 245, and 246 (under Title X). See the Venezuelan Constitution in Albert P. Blaustein and Gisbert H. Flanz, eds., *Constitutions of the Countries of the World,* vol. 21 (Dobbs Ferry, N.Y.: Oceana Publications, 1971).

8. In the explanatory statement that accompanies the text of the 1961 Constitution, it is stated:

> In the opinion of the Commission [responsible for drafting the 1961 Constitution], an amendment would be a reform of articles that leaves the original or basic text unchanged, a modification made necessary by the constant changes taking place within society, but which does not alter the integrity and basic meaning of the text. The phrasing does not alter the accepted meaning and conception of the Constitution, so that it remains valid in the eyes of the people, giving the favorable impression of stability. A reform, on the other hand, would be a more radical change of the subject matter of the document, altering the actual spirit of the Constitution, in short, the revocation of the Constitution and its replacement with another.

The discussion of the meaning and differences between both procedures can be found in Allan Randolph Brewer-Carías, *Instituciones políticas y constitucionales,* vol. 1 (Caracas–San Cristóbal: Editorial Jurídica-Venezolana-Universidad Católica del Táchira, 1985), 345–48; Rafael Caldera, "Enmiendas y reformas a la constitución," in *Libro homenaje a Manuel García-Pelayo* (Caracas: Facultad de Ciencias Jurídicas y Políticas, Universidad Central de Venezuela, 1980), 107–23; Oropeza Ambrosio, *La nueva constitución venezolana de 1961* (Caracas: Biblioteca de la Academia de Ciencias Políticas y Sociales, 1986), 142–44; Petzold-Pernía Hermann, "Algunas consideraciones jurídico-metodológicas y filosófico-políticas sobre la revisión constitucional en Venezuela," Second Venezuelan Congress of Constitutional Law, in Miriam B. de Bozo, ed., *Hacia un nuevo orden constitucional* (Maracaibo: Centro de Investigaciones y Estudios Políticos, LUZ, 1992). For a discussion of the thinking that lay behind the creation of the two procedures, see Congreso de la República, *La constitución de 1961 y la evolución constitucional en Venezuela: Actas de la comisión redactora del proyecto* (Caracas: Ediciones del Congreso de la República, 1971), 2 vols.

9. For a comparative study of the constitutions of Latin America and their respective procedures for constitutional reform, see Jorge Mario Eastman, *Constituciones políticas comparadas de América del Sur* (Bogotá: Andean Parliament, Fondo de Publicaciones Collection, 1991).

10. The amendment establishes that "no person who has been tried and convicted by a lower court and sentenced to a term of imprisonment of three years or more for offenses committed in the discharge of public duties, through them, may be elected to the office of President, Senator or Deputy, or Justice of the Supreme Court. No judicial remedy may be presented against the rulings of the competent authorities other than the right of any citizen to appeal to the full Supreme Court of Justice. The Court shall rule within ten days of the presentation of the appeal. Such appeals shall be heard for review only," National Constitution, amendment no. 1

11. This article provided the framework for reform of the Organic Election Act and introduced nominal and uninominal voting in the 1989 and 1992 municipal elections. An analysis of these reforms can be found in Miriam Kornblith and Daniel Levine,

"The Life and Times of the Party System in Venezuela," in Scott Mainwaring and Timothy Scully eds., *Building Democratic Institutional Parties and Party Systems in Latin America* (Stanford: Stanford University Press, 1994).

12. The appropriate bill was introduced on June 6, 1989, by Senator Godofredo González (COPEI) and unanimously approved by the upper house. For a list of the original appointees to the committee, see *El Diario de Caracas*, June 7, 1989. During the course of the debates some new representatives were drafted onto the committee as others resigned.

13. A description and analysis of the procedure followed in debating and enacting the 1961 Constitution can be found in Kornblith, "Proceso constitucional," 298–302, and idem, "The Politics of Constitution-Making," 71–74.

14. Strictly speaking, the twenty-five constitutions before 1961 were not significantly different from each other (many of the changes made were little more than amendments, such as Gen. Juan Vicente Gómez's seven constitutions, enacted to satisfy the dictator's whims regarding the functions of the vice presidents and the powers of the president and supreme commander of the armed forces). The 1961 Constitution has been the most enduring, followed by the 1830 Constitution, which remained in force until 1857 and is, without doubt, the one that has enjoyed the greatest acceptance.

15. Rafael Caldera, "Palabras de Instalación de la Comisión Bicameral Especial de Revisión de la constitución" (Caracas, June 20, 1989, mimeographed), 8. This timetable, Caldera argued, had two advantages: first, the passage of any amendments would coincide with the thirtieth anniversary of the enactment of the 1961 Constitution, and second, the reform process would not interfere with the election campaign.

16. These seminars were sponsored by Congress, COPRE, the Jóvito Villalba Foundation, CUV's Faculty of Legal and Political Sciences, and the Venezuelan Association of Constitutional Law. They were held in Caracas on October 2–4, 1992. The Second Venezuelan Congress of Constitutional Law, held at Zulia University from November 6–8, 1991, was also used as a forum to examine and discuss the committee's progress. By the time these seminars took place, the committee had "in principle" approved articles dealing with the right of information, *leyes orgánicas* (fundamental laws), political parties, the office of prime minister, referendums, the Alta Comisión de Justicia (Judicial High Committee), and the judiciary. See the Jóvito Villalba Conferences on Constitutional Revision, "Propuestas aprobadas en principio por la Comisión Bicameral Especial de Revisión de la Constitución del Congreso de la República" (Caracas, October 2–4, 1992, mimeographed).

17. Other recommendations remaining to be addressed were the power of the houses of Congress and the states; the election of governors; the nationality of spouses; the environment; discrimination against women; indigenous peoples; the forfeiture of assets in cases of corruption and narcotrafficking; economic integration; conflicts of interest for public officials; ownership of mineral, oil, and gas deposits; the irreversibility of the nationalization of the oil industry; contracts affected with a public interest; international treaties; reform of the legislative branch; the nonreelectability of the attorney general; the human rights advocate; the allocation of resources from central to state governments; the procedure for reforming the constitution; and legislative committees. See Comisión Bicameral Especial de Revisión de la Constitución, "Listado de temas pendientes" (Caracas, undated, mimeographed).

18. See Rafael Caldera, *Dos discursos: 27 de febrero de 1989, 4 de febrero de 1992* (Caracas: Editorial Arte, 1992).

19. The initial definition of the issues to be studied with a view to drafting amendments is found in Caldera, "Palabras de instalación," and an undated letter from Ricardo Combellas to Rafael Caldera regarding the agenda of possible constitutional amendments.

20. In the letter that accompanied the presentation of the reform bill, it was argued that

> after lengthy deliberations the Committee agreed to recommend to Congress the adoption of the procedure of *reforma general* contemplated under Article 246 of the

Constitution, instead of the amendment procedure as originally planned. Such a decision is justified in view of the fact that with each passing day public opinion calls for more modifications, and so as to address the basic needs that have arisen in our democracy over the past thirty-one years, along with the proposals that have been put forward by respectable social groups and sectors such as neighborhood associations, the National Association of Journalists, feminist groups, and a number of others, and submitted to Congress via the Committee. Moreover, the procedure provided for under Article 246 is faster than the one stipulated under Article 245 and has an additional advantage in that it ensures the direct participation of the people via a referendum.

Comisión Bicameral para la Revisión de la Constitución, "Proyecto de reforma general de la Constitución de 1961 con exposición de motivos" (Caracas, March 1992), 5.

21. See ibid.; see also Comisión Bicameral Especial para la Revisión de la Constitución, "Borrador de informe final y ante-proyecto de reforma general de la Constitución de 1961 con exposición de motivos" (Caracas, March 1992).

22. See the Venzuelan Constitution in Blaustein and Flanz, eds., *Constitutions of the Countries of the World*, for the procedures envisaged under the constitution for presenting and passing a draft law containing a *reforma general* of the constitution.

23. This and other information relating to the organization of the work of the special commission charged with studying the draft law presented by the Bicameral Committee was obtained from Cámara de Diputados, "Informe de la Comisión Especial de la Cámara de Diputados para el estudio del proyecto de reforma general de la constitución, para segunda discusión" (Congreso de la República, Caracas, June 16, 1992, mimeographed), 2–9.

24. See Cámara de Diputados, *Primera discusión del proyecto de reforma general de la constitución* (Congreso de la República, Caracas, April 1992, mimeographed).

25. For a list of the individuals to whom letters were sent, see Cámara de Diputados, "Informe de la Comisión Especial," 5–9. A fair number of these individuals expressed their points of view to the various subcommissions or to the full commission. I also had the opportunity to participate in this stage of the process, at both the sessions of the subcommission on political reform and those of the full commission.

26. See Articles 25 and 26 in the final version of the draft law recommended by the Chamber of Deputies in Cámara de Diputados, "Reforma general de la constitución" (Congreso de la República, Caracas, undated, mimeographed).

27. The information regarding the course of the debate in the Senate was reconstructed drawing on reports published in editions of the newspapers *El Universal* and *El Diario de Caracas*.

28. The article as proposed by the Bicameral Committee read as follows:

> *Article 20* (modifying Article 66 of the present Constitution). Every person has the right to express his or her thoughts in person, in writing or in any other form, and in doing so make use of any information medium, without prior censure; but any statements that constitute an offense may be punished by law.
>
> The right to accurate and timely information is hereby guaranteed under the principles enshrined in this Constitution.

29. *El Universal*, August 18, 1992.

30. The text of the transitory provision in the draft of the law passed by the Senate can be found in Congreso de la República, "Cuadro Comparativo: Reforma general de la Constitución" (Caracas, undated, mimeographed), 70–71.

31. See Arturo Uslar Pietri, "Carta dirigida a Luis Enrique Oberto, presidente de la Cámara de Diputados" (Caracas, April 24, 1992, mimeographed).

32. The version that emerged as a result of the first debate in the Senate read as follows:

> *Article 30* (replaces Article 25 of the draft law as passed by the Chamber of Deputies). Every individual has the right to express his or her thoughts in person, in writing or in any other form, and in doing so make use of any medium of com-

munication and dissemination, without prior censure. Any statements that constitute an offense may be punished by law.
Anonymity is hereby prohibited. Also prohibited is war propaganda, anything that offends public decency or is intended to incite the public to break the law, though this may not be interpreted as constituting grounds for restricting the analysis or criticism of legal provisions.
*Article 31* (replaces Article 25 of the draft law passed by the Chamber of Deputies). Communication is free, it demands plurality in the media and fulfills a social function. Every individual has the right to receive timely, adequate, and accurate information, under the terms of this Constitution and the law.
The State shall take the necessary steps to prevent the information media from being concentrated in the hands of any single individual.

See Congreso de la República, "Cuadro comparativo," 15–17. The conclusions regarding the right of reply (Article 26 of the draft law passed by the Chamber of Deputies) became Article 26 (modifying Article 22 of the draft law passed by the Chamber of Deputies):

*Article 26* Every individual has the right to preserve his or her personal and family intimacy, privacy, good name, standing, honor, and reputation.
Any individual injured by inaccurate or offensive reports passed by word of mouth, broadcast on television, made in writing or in print shall have the right to a rectification and to reply in the same conditions.

Ibid., 13–14. The ban on media monopolies was included in a new article dealing with monopolies as a whole, which modifies Article 97 of the present constitution:

*Article 45* Monopolies are hereby prohibited. By law, exclusive licenses for a limited period shall be granted only for the establishment and operation of works and services affected with a public interest.
The law shall issue provisions to outlaw any abusive practice that may obstruct or restrict competition or the exercise of the freedoms of information and speech.
The State may set aside specific industries, operations, or services affected with a public interest on the grounds of national expediency and shall be predisposed to create and develop basic heavy industry under its own control.
The industries promoted and run by the State shall be regulated by law. The law shall take special steps to prevent any monopolistic or oligopolistic practice in any information medium (passed in the first debate and referred to the Commission).

Ibid., 21–22.
33. The following considerations are based on Miriam Kornblith, "Reforma constitucional, crisis política y estabilidad de la democracia en Venezuela," *Politeia,* no. 15 (1993).
34. For an assessment and analysis of this program see, among others, Moisés Naím, "The Launching of Radical Policy Changes, 1989–1991," in Joseph Tulchin with Gary Bland, eds., *Venezuela in the Wake of Radical Reform* (Boulder: Lynne Rienner, and Washington, D.C.: Woodrow Wilson International Center for Scholars, 1993), 39–94; Juan Carlos Navarro and Roberto Rigobón, "La economía política del ajuste estructural y de la reforma del sector público en Venezuela" (IESA, Caracas, July 1992, mimeographed); Marisela Padrón Quero, "Venezuela: Crisis, ajuste y política social," in *Primer encuentro Latinoamericano y del Caribe de primeras damas* (Caracas:1991).
35. See Pedro Guevara, *Concertación y conflicto: El pacto social y el fracaso de las respuestas consensuales a la crisis del sistema político venezolano* (Caracas: School of Law and Political Science, Central University of Venezuela, 1989).
36. One study that considers the constitution an independent variable in the shaping of the political process is Peter F. Narduli, ed., *The Constitution and American Political Development: An Institutional Perspective* (Urbana: University of Illinois Press, 1992).
37. See Juan Carlos Rey, "El futuro de la democracia en Venezuela," in Juan Carlos Rey, *El futuro de la democracia en Venezuela* (Caracas: Colección IDEA, 1989), 249–323, and

idem, "La democracia venezolana y la crisis del sistema populista de conciliación," *Revista de estudios políticos,* no. 74 (1991): 533–78.

38. Rey, "La democracia venezolana," 565–66.
39. See Rey, "El futuro de la democracia," 273, and idem, "La democracia venezolana," 543.
40. I have developed this idea in Miriam Kornblith, "La crisis en Venezuela: Características, determinantes y perspectivas," (paper prepared for the Andean conference on comparative perspectives for resolution of the crises of democracy in the countries of the region, sponsored by the Democracy Program, Department of Political Science, Universidad de los Andes, Santa Fé de Bogotá, February 24 and 25, 1993, mimeographed).
41. See Moisés Naím and Ramón Piñango, "El caso Venezuela: Una ilusión de armonía," Moisés Naím and Ramón Piñango, eds., *El caso Venezuela: Una ilusión de armonía,* 3d ed. (Caracas: Ediciones IESA, 1986), 559–63.
42. See Rey, "El futuro de la democracia," 265–67.
43. According to COPEI Secretary General Eduardo Fernández, on October 26, 1992, the National Committee of COPEI unanimously agreed to seek backing for a "national accord" based on five points deemed necessary for continuing the process of constitutional reform: adopt absolute uninominality; reach agreement with the media, remove the right to reply, and retain only constitutional points; reform the judiciary so as to guarantee independent and efficient justice; create a prime minister to render management of the executive branch more effective; and ensure further decentralization and regionalization. COPEI thus proposed to the political organizations represented at Congress to resume debate of the constitutional reform. *El Diario de Caracas,* October 28, 1992. Luis Enrique Oberto, Speaker of the Lower House, said that the constitutional reform was helping to solve medium- and long-term problems and that debate on the reform should conclude in the upper house and the proposed revisions should be put to the public in a ballot initiative at the earliest feasible date. *El Universal,* November 8, 1992.

*IV*

# The World Arena

# 13

# A New Approach to the World?
# The *Gran Viraje* and Venezuelan
# Foreign Policy

*Andrés Serbín*

From the overthrow of the dictatorship of Marcos Pérez Jiménez and the establishment of a democratic regime in January 1958 until the unleashing of the external debt crisis and the devaluation of the bolivar in 1983, democracy in Venezuela was progressively consolidated thanks to the distribution of wealth made possible by the nation's abundant oil revenues. Throughout that period, these two elements—democratic consensus and oil revenues—set the Venezuelan system and its growing political stability apart from the prevailing political regimes in the rest of Latin America.[1]

Furthermore, these two distinctive characteristics have done more to shape the priorities and objectives of Venezuelan foreign policy over the past three decades than the platforms or ideologies of the respective political parties under successive administrations, the personalities of the various presidents, or the conditioning factors dictated by the international system. In addition to these two basic characteristics—democracy and oil—others emerged at specific points in the country's development as an American, Andean, Caribbean, Amazonian, developing, and debtor nation.[2] These varying emphases in the projection of foreign policy have given rise to a debate among Venezuelan analysts as to whether there has been real continuity in government policy despite the successive changes of government,[3] or whether the effect of these changes has been to introduce a lack of consistency and continuity into Venezuelan foreign policy.[4]

In fact, the origins of these characteristics, the influence of which has extended to the priorities of Venezuela's foreign policy, are to be found in the qualities of the political system that has been in place in Venezuela since 1959: a populist system of conciliation based on con-

sensus, consultation, co-optation, and power sharing by the elites—
built around a democratic system underpinned by the political parties
in which the state has played the leading role—and a populist, if unequal, distribution of the revenues generated by oil production. Furthermore, these oil revenues have afforded the state easy access to fiscal resources and foreign exchange, which have fueled national
development historically based on the import substitution model.[5]
Some analysts have argued that it has been the domestic political system, rather than external conditions, that has historically determined
Venezuelan foreign policy.[6]

Over the past decade, however, the country has become far more
sensitive to external factors, particularly due to the crisis unleashed by
falling international oil prices and the external debt. Consequently,
the dividing line between domestic momentum and changes in the international order has become increasingly blurred. The country has
become vulnerable both to changes in the global economy in general
and to oil prices in particular and, as serious domestic problems have
arisen associated with the country's insertion into the world economy,
to issues such as reconversion, the diversification of the oil industry,
the privatization of state-owned enterprises, the restructuring and reduction of the external debt, and efforts to make the economy competitive and diversified.[7]

In addition, although during the first decades of democratic rule
public opinion was indifferent to foreign policy issues (border disputes excepted), a marked change in this attitude has developed in
recent years. There are a couple of reasons for this change: first, the
crisis in the populist system of conciliation and in the established
rules of political consensus regarding foreign policy agenda and priorities, and second, the growing external pressures being brought to
bear on the country. These factors have led to greater public awareness of issues such as economic liberalization, the refinancing of the
debt, economic growth and diversification, and subregional integration, which have been added to the long-standing concern over border disputes.

During the course of the most recent Pérez administration a series of
domestic reforms and a major shift in foreign policy were debated and,
in some cases, instituted. Given current domestic and international economic conditions, these represent an especially difficult challenge for
Venezuela and have raised questions about the future evolution of
foreign policy and the country's regional, hemispheric, and global
insertion.

## THE EVOLUTION OF FOREIGN POLICY: STAGES AND CHARACTERISTICS

At this point it is worth examining briefly the underpinnings of Venezuela's development during the democratic period, the different emphases given to its external projection, and how these relate to the global evolution of the Venezuelan political system and foreign policy.

Under the administrations of Rómulo Betancourt and Raúl Leoni between 1959 and 1969, the combination of the domestic political situation and the external conditions imposed by the cold war and Cuba's links with local guerrilla movements led to emphasis on the country's credentials as a democratic, Western nation (exemplified by the so-called Betancourt doctrine) and as an oil producer. In addition to the country's role in the creation and development of OPEC, the accent was on relations with the United States, the chief market for Venezuelan oil products and its key ally in the context of the subregional impact of the East-West confrontation.

Between 1969 and 1979 the country was governed first by Rafael Caldera and then by Carlos Andrés Pérez. Though the ideologies of these two presidents differed, the growing independence in the world order of countries producing raw materials accentuated Venezuela's credentials as a developing nation as well as its common interests with other developing world countries. Throughout this period this image was promoted in different international forums, ranging from OPEC to the United Nation's Conference on Trade and Development (UNCTAD), the Group of Seventy-seven, and the creation of the Latin American Economic System (SELA). This emphasis was facilitated by the country's oil bonanza during that same decade, which enhanced Venezuela's influence at the world level and enabled it to develop an energetic foreign policy in Latin America and the Caribbean in particular, and the developing world in general. This policy was sharply criticized by some analysts on the grounds that it represented an overextension of the country's true capabilities and resources.[8] In addition, efforts were made at the domestic level to channel the resources generated by the favorable international conditions into the implementation of an ambitious development strategy.[9]

During this stage oil began to play a leading role in Venezuelan foreign policy, affording the country a level of international projection in promoting its regional, hemispheric, and global geopolitical interests beyond its true capacity and importance. A good illustration of this phenomenon was the use of oil revenues to assert Venezuela's presence in the Caribbean basin. Venezuela assumed significant roles in the Caribbean Development Bank and the cooperation programs of the Venezuelan Investment Fund (FIV), the Special Fund for the Caribbean, and the Program for the Caribbean (PROCA), all of which helped consolidate its influence in the islands. Another example was the Pact of San José (providing oil supply assistance), which involved the entire basin.[10] Nonetheless, even during that same period some analysts began to question the limitations of a development model based on oil revenues and import substitution.[11] Cracks began to appear in a political system that was increasingly unresponsive, in need of renewal, and basically geared to a regulatory and interventionist state role.[12]

The third stage began in 1979 and lasted until 1988. Under the administrations of Luis Herrera Campíns and Jaime Lusinchi, owing to the impact of the external debt and the economic crisis and to the consequent strengthening of U.S. ties, the country once again assumed the role of a democratic and Western nation and a reliable oil supplier. This posture was coupled with Venezuela's image as a debtor nation and a good neighbor, in the latter case with particular reference to the Caribbean basin.[13]

During this period Venezuela not only maintained an active presence among the Caribbean islands, but also stepped up its involvement in Central America, with mixed success. Under Lusinchi's presidency, the state initially adopted a tough anti-Communist stance in line with U.S. policy in the region. Then, following the Malvinas-Falklands War, it changed its position and became more involved in the regional pacification process through the Contadora Group.[14] The era was further marked by the exhaustion of the prevailing development model and the need to modernize the political system due to the demands imposed by the external debt crisis, the fall in international oil prices, and the growing demobilization of the masses in a democratic system controlled by the political elites entrenched within the political parties and the state apparatus (also increasingly perceived as being too big).

Throughout these successive stages, however, Venezuelan foreign policy continued to emphasize the country's credentials as a democratic, oil-producing nation and maintained the following objectives: (1) to safeguard and defend the established political order; (2) to participate, to the extent that international conditions allowed, in international politics as an independent actor; (3) to preserve intact the territorial integrity of the nation and sovereignty thereover; (4) to defend the price of, and markets for, the nation's oil production; (5) to ensure the stability of neighboring regions; and (6) to participate actively in international organizations. These formal objectives were tied in with several specific objectives: to maintain a flexible relationship with the United States, the main market for Venezuelan oil and a country with which it shares a number of important common political interests that are more important than any temporary differences; to contain any possible expansion of Cuban influence in Latin America and the Caribbean; to preserve the integrity of the nation's borders; and to guarantee the markets for the nation's oil production.[15]

Set against the backdrop of an international system characterized by strategic polarization, these objectives moved geopolitical issues to first place on the Venezuelan foreign policy agenda, despite the economic crisis and declining oil prices. In the realm of international diplomacy Venezuela tended to favor the peaceful resolution of conflicts—both with Cuba, its geopolitical rival at the subregional level, and with neighboring countries with which there were unresolved border disputes (such as Guyana and Colombia) and Central American countries through active participation in the Contadora Group.

The individual stamp of each administration notwithstanding, and despite Venezuela's limited size and real influence on world affairs, the country pursued an active foreign policy throughout the three stages mentioned, and particularly from the governments of Rafael Caldera and Carlos Andrés Pérez onward. As a result, Venezuela played an active role not only in traditional hemispheric and world forums such as the UN and the Organization of American States (OAS), but also in the forums of developing countries, such as the Group of Seventy-seven and UNCTAD, and in the promotion of specific bodies, such as OPEC, SELA, and the Contadora Group. Relations of this kind established a long tradition of Venezuelan involvement in Latin American and developing world affairs, and in the international system as a whole. This was demonstrated clearly by Venezuela's serving as head of the North-South Conference in Paris from December 1975 to January 1976, the AD's role in the International Socialist, and the country's growing involvement in Latin America during the 1970s. Furthermore, this high profile in international affairs not only drew on the country's democratic characteristics but also attempted to project its "democratic model" abroad, particularly at the subregional and hemispheric level.

## EXTERNAL PRESSURES AND DOMESTIC CRISIS: THE *GRAN VIRAJE*

A fourth stage was initiated in 1989 when Carlos Andrés Pérez took office for the second time, an era catalyzed by the impact of the debt crisis and external pressures. This stage was marked by a major change of policy by the government that came to be known as the *gran viraje* (great turnaround), reflecting the need to reformulate domestic economic policy on account of the impact of the external debt crisis, falling oil prices, and dwindling international reserves[16] that brought the rent-seeking economy to an end, and to adapt the political system to the new conditions. It was also indicative of the need to adjust foreign policy to the challenges presented by the global and hemispheric changes already under way.

Since 1989 the world order has undergone a series of important revisions. The changes precipitated in the strategic-military domain by perestroika in the USSR and the ripple effect throughout Eastern Europe signaled the end of the cold war and the disappearance of the bipolarity that had underpinned the international order for four decades. Furthermore, the process of growing economic globalization and interdependence has been accompanied by the emergence of three world economic blocs and centers of power (the European Community, North America, and Japan and its Asian partners), giving rise to a multipolar international economic order.[17] More specifically, this multipolar international order is composed of a single strategic-military hegemonic power—the United States—and three hubs of economic dynamism centering around the three major international blocs.

The ending of the cold war also altered the priorities of the international agenda, with long-standing security concerns being replaced by global economic questions that have emerged as important aspects of the new world setup.[18] At the hemispheric level there were different initial reactions in North and South America to these changes. Nonetheless, all responses reflected a growing trend toward regionalization, manifested both in the emergence of the North American Free Trade Agreement (NAFTA) and launching of the Enterprise for the Americas Initiative by President George Bush in June 1990, and in the acceleration of economic liberalization and integration in Latin America and the Caribbean through existing mechanisms (Andean Pact, the Caribbean Community [CARICOM], Latin American Integration Association [ALADI], Central American Common Market [CACM]) as well as new structures (Group of Three, Southern Cone Common Market [MERCOSUR]). Latin America wanted to avoid being left behind by the international system.[19]

The combination of changes in the world and hemispheric order and the growing evidence of exhaustion of the economic model based on oil revenues led to the initiation, in 1989, of an orthodox economic adjustment program and the demand for political reform and modernization in Venezuela.[20] This phase in the evolution of the Venezuelan system has been characterized at the domestic level by a series of radical initiatives, particularly in the economic field, producing a drastic program of restructuring of public expenditure reductions, the phased elimination of direct and indirect government subsidies, hikes in the prices of gasoline and services, deregulation, privatization, reconversion, and the lowering of customs duties in order to reduce the fiscal deficit. The program also included the liberalization of exchange and interest rates, price controls, and the opening of the economy to international trade and competition. This radical shift was part of a new development strategy based on the promotion of externally oriented growth, the liberalization of trade, reform of the state, and the modernization of the political system so as to encourage its decentralization and democratization.[21] This general process marked a fundamental change of course for the domestic economy and politics and has unleashed a series of important political and social consequences.

These changes and the resulting social and political ramifications triggered a radical reaction from various sectors of society that led to the *caracazo* (street riots) of February 1989, shortly after President Pérez took office, and the ill-fated military coup on February 4, 1992.[22] This phase has also seen the emergence of new foreign policy priorities for Venezuela with regard to the nature of the country's insertion into the world order, given the declining importance of oil. As was noted in one recent work, there has been a change not only in the international and national context, which has had a major impact on the values and rules of the political game, but also in the foreign policy agenda, which has become more fluid, extensive, and complicated. The organization of this policy has become more complex as well, with the incorporation of new spheres of activity and actors.[23]

On the one hand, as part of the economic measures and liberalization of trade fostered by the new growth model, efforts are being made to implement an aggressive trade policy aimed at boosting traditional and nontraditional exports and creating expanded economic opportunities through free-trade agreements. In this respect, the Eighth National Plan clearly outlines a new development strategy that would create the conditions for a more advantageous role in the world order, based on: (1) the aggressive insertion of Venezuela into the world arena; (2) a foreign policy designed to support the objectives of economic liberalization and the defense of the principles of free trade, Latin American integration, and the strengthening of democracy worldwide; (3) a new approach to regional integration, fortification of cooperation- and integration-promoting institutions, the fostering of agreements for the liberalization of trade and the coordination of macroeconomic policy, and strategic alliances in different fields (technology, culture, and policy); (4) aggressive bilateral and multilateral trade diplomacy to bolster the growth in Venezuelan exports; and (5) membership in the General Agreement on Tariffs and Trade (GATT) and the creation of effective channels of communication between Venezuela and institutions advancing international cooperation and integration.[24]

On the other hand, efforts are also being made to attain these objectives by developing a three-pronged trade policy based on the liberalization of trade, the hastening of economic association and integration processes, and the promotion of exports. It is on the first front that the most notable headway was achieved during the recent Pérez administration; the administration instituted a radical program to reduce tariffs and then accelerated it in 1992 to bring the tariff ceiling down to 30 percent. On the second front, rapid progress has been achieved in economic integration with Colombia, to the point where the Venezuela-Colombia axis is more advanced than either the Andean Pact (which is experiencing difficulties) or the free-trade agreement being promoted by the Group of Three (composed of Mexico, Colombia, and Venezuela)—Mexico has been dragging its feet in the negotiations due to the delay in launching NAFTA. Finally, on the third front, export bonds have been abolished, some of the paperwork required for exports has been expedited, and drawback mechanisms have been set up. The administration has promoted the privatization of the nation's ports, and the creation of a foreign trade bank has been debated. Apart from these limited measures, however, there has been no major restructuring effort to increase the competitiveness of Venezuelan products, diversify the economy more comprehensively, or promote more investment in research, development, and technology. Significantly, it is the government that has taken the initiative in this process, whereas the private sector (with the important exception of the integration process with Colombia) has largely remained on the sidelines.[25]

Furthermore, efforts have been made in the geopolitical and diplomatic domains to reinforce this strategy through a variety of subregional, regional, and hemispheric alliances, capitalizing on the experience acquired and the links established during the previous stages. In this context, economic ties with the United States, the chief market for Venezuelan oil exports, have become a key issue. At the same time, to strengthen the country's bargaining position and fill a growing geopolitical vacuum in the Caribbean basin, links with countries in the area and Latin American nations as a whole are being enhanced through mechanisms developed during the earlier stages, such as relations with CARICOM and Central America and membership in the Andean Pact and ALADI. The latter two alliances are coupled with new political opportunities such as the Rio Group and concerted action in the subregional economic and political sphere through the Group of Three. This trend is being reinforced with a more active role in the Group of Fifteen and the Comisión Sur, reactivating South-South ties with a view to strengthening the country's bargaining power with the industrialized North in general and the United States in particular.[26]

In other words, the foregoing limitations notwithstanding, the thrust of the *gran viraje* is an active development strategy for the nation's insertion into the world economic system by reinforcing, in the medium and long run, both the comparative advantages offered by the oil industry (despite the difficulties and obstacles that may be experienced in the international system) and the promotion of the growth of nontraditional exports. Consequently, the geopolitical and security issues that traditionally figured in Venezuela's foreign policy agenda and were previously associated with elements of the country's main identity[27] are being superseded increasingly by economic priorities such as the liberalization of trade, subregional integration, and the diversification of exports, free markets, and sources of investment and technology. In addition, the country is engaged in an aggressive search for alliances that could strengthen its international negotiating position with regard to these economic objectives, capitalizing on the good relations and links it developed during a period when Venezuela enjoyed a higher international profile.[28]

Finally, it is worth repeating that, in what marks a major change of attitude, the public is beginning to demonstrate increasing interest in these issues. This shift has caused the executive branch to rethink radically its handling of foreign policy, in a domestic context in which the reform process has seriously undermined the political consensus long associated with the democratic system in Venezuela.

## LESSONS, LEGACIES, AND UNRESOLVED ISSUES IN A CHANGING WORLD

Current Venezuelan foreign policy objectives are dictated by the fallout from previous foreign policymaking efforts during the democratic era and by a set of adverse external conditions that raise serious questions about the future evolution of this aspect of government.

First, overdependence on the production of petroleum and natural gas creates a series of specific problems. As a comparative advantage (and despite the fact that it is increasingly incapable of generating revenues due to lower prices and rising production costs), oil remains the cornerstone of the country's economic growth. This will continue to be the case even if there is a downturn in the market or an oil glut—aside from the need for increased investment and technology to maintain efficiency. As one analyst has pointed out, "no other industry today—and we doubt in the near future—could generate the same kind of net revenues as the production of oil and its derivatives."[29] In this respect, the linchpin of the nation's economic strategy is still the need to boost Venezuela's status as an oil producer and to "pave the way for industrialization by developing its comparative advantages associated with natural resources."[30] The expansion and internationalization of the oil industry is intended to guarantee markets and distribution systems and exploit the experience the nation has accrued to promote progressive diversification in the use of its natural and energy resources.[31]

Nonetheless, this strategy runs counter to present global production and trade trends, which tend to favor producers of advanced technology over exporters of raw materials with no, or little, added value.[32] In addition to the worldwide search for alternative energy sources, environmental groups are stepping up their efforts to limit the use of hydrocarbons, which are associated with high carbon dioxide emissions that are harmful to the earth's atmosphere. The United States is also faced with growing pressure from several quarters for a gasoline tax aimed at encouraging greater fuel efficiency and reducing pollution.[33]

In addition, the Venezuelan strategy calls for investment and related technology that will be forthcoming only if there is political stability, which paradoxically could be undermined by the economic adjustment program currently being implemented. Likewise, modernization and economic reform would open the way for greater direct foreign investment. The deepening of this strategy and the use of the nation's energy and natural resources could similarly hinder the prospects for export diversification, which calls for changes in the economic rules of the game, the incorporation of nongovernment players, and a privatization process that challenges the state's traditional role as the manager of the Venezuelan economy. In fact, despite the initial upsurge in nontraditional exports following the measures adopted under the *gran viraje*, they experienced a marked downturn in 1990 to 1991.[34] This was due, among other reasons, to continued bureaucratic obstacles[35] and the protectionist barriers that remain in place in some industrialized countries, affecting products such as aluminum and cement in particular.[36]

Coupled with these difficulties is the impact of the external debt burden with its continued adverse effect on both investment prospects and the state's capacity to redistribute wealth. Indeed, the negotiations with the international banking system in 1990 did not resolve the debt problem, but merely postponed it until the middle of the decade,[37] thus jeopardizing the success of the current development strategy.[38] In some ways, the external debt crisis could actually be said to have had a positive impact. For example, the negotiations with international creditors and financial institutions (in addition to Venezuela's gradual economic decline) were a key factor in the government's decision to change its tack on economic policy and also helped to secure the domestic support needed to follow through.[39]

Third, both the debt legacy and a development strategy geared toward optimizing the country's competitive advantages impose constraints on the distribution of wealth that strike at the very heart of the populist system of conciliation and at the mechanisms for consensus achieved during the period of democratic rule, dependent as they are on the distribution of fiscal revenues. As recent events have shown, the social and political costs of the new development strategy are putting considerable strain on the political system that has been in place since 1958, while future economic and fiscal policies may not do much to alleviate the profound disequilibrium caused by the rentist economy.[40] Built around political parties and underpinned for the past three decades by the (albeit unequal) sharing of wealth facilitated by oil revenues, the pluralist democratic system is exhausted and requires a thorough overhaul if the needs of the varied sectors of society are to be met.

The combination of new economic conditions, the external debt legacy, and a basically nonproductive economy, however, all make it unlikely that a political settlement between the various social actors will be achieved, except through a zero-sum process that creates winners and losers, which would involve a high cost for many of them, the poorest sectors in particular. Just as in other Latin American countries, the situation has had an impact both on the recasting of relations between the nation's political elite and the business sector, and on the ability of other sectors of society to withstand the imposition of the social costs associated with the strategy in question.[41]

Furthermore, a technocratic response (as opposed to political negotiation) would encourage unilateral government action in this field. But imposing Hobbesian solutions would raise doubts about the validity of the democratic solutions traditionally applied under the existing political system.[42] One of the criticisms most often leveled against the *gran viraje* is that it facilitates technocratic decisions and policies, to the detriment of democratic political action that would afford the various national political and social actors a more active role in the economic restructuring process.[43]

The prospects for consensus being reached on new domestic and foreign policy issues under these conditions are increasingly slim and have led to a radical reappraisal of the traditional political rules. The differences of opinion over the process of integration with Colombia are a case in point. The issue put the private sector and the government technocrats who support the process at odds with the nationalist and conservative groups that demand that border disputes be settled first.

Fourth, the overextension and organizational complexity of the foreign policy system in Venezuela, developed originally under more favorable international conditions, undermines the coherence and continuity of this strategy at the international level. The complex framework of government agencies and units involved in the foreign policy process, reinforced by the existing bureaucratic clientelism, actually limits the executive branch's historically preeminent role in foreign policy and creates ambiguities, redundant mandates, and contradictions in policy implementation.[44] This is demonstrated by the rivalries and duplication of decision making and policy implementation between Petróleos de Venezuela, S.A. (PDVSA) and the ministry of energy and mines and between the ministry of development and the Institute for Foreign Trade, particularly with regard to trade and economic policy.

The state's omnipresence is also an obstacle to the participation of nongovernmental actors. Historically, the private sector in particular has been placed in the ambiguous position of being dependent on state favors while hostile to the political elite.[45] This point was underlined by the recent disagreements over private sector participation in the negotiations for the establishment of a free-trade agreement among the Group of Three.[46]

Fifth and finally, one must bear in mind not only the constraints imposed by the changes in the international system (the importance placed on the flow of investment, technological breakthroughs, and the creation of blocs that undermine the competitive advantages of a country whose economy is heavily dependent on energy and other natural resources), but also the specific momentum that these changes impose on hemispheric and subregional conditions.

On the one hand, Venezuela's chief trading partner—the United States—has refused to acknowledge the country as a reliable and stable supplier of petroleum and gas products. It may also postpone indefinitely the negotiations called for under the agreement of principle signed in 1991 for the creation of a free-trade agreement within the framework of Bush's Enterprise for the Americas Initiative.[47] In the global push to create trading blocs, the establishment of NAFTA could ultimately result in the exclusion of several developing countries in the region and affect Venezuela specifically. Hence the attempt to use the Group of Three (G-3) to establish a linkage with the North American free-trade bloc (using Mexico as a bridge) and to increase Venezuelan clout and bargaining power in its efforts to secure a free-trade agreement with North America under the umbrella of the Bush initiative. This new dynamism would also foster externally oriented economic growth through increased economic ties with Venezuela's foremost Latin American trading partner, Colombia.

The prospect of a free-trade agreement with Mexico within the framework of G-3, however, also carries with it an inherent danger. There are economic similarities between the two countries and competition in certain specific sectors, particularly in the case of nontraditional exports such as petrochemicals. This economic overlap is magnified by the difference in the pace of macroeconomic change between Mexico on the one hand, and Venezuela and Colombia on the other hand,[48] and by both of their respective relations with the North American bloc.

Following the brief possibility of a role as an oil supplier to MERCOSUR, and in light of the growing frustration with the Andean Pact (where the increasing economic dynamism between Venezuela and Colombia is the linchpin of the integration process), Venezuela now appears to be placing its hopes on the Caribbean basin, including CARICOM, G-3, and, to a lesser extent, the CACM. Here the interest is attributable to both trade opportunities and geopolitical considerations, as well as to the prospect of gaining greater leverage with North America. In this respect, the Caribbean basin holds not only the prospect of expanded markets and trade links, but also the opportunity to exploit traditional Venezuelan political influence in the subregion through its cooperation programs.[49]

In view of the trade and financial links that already exist, it would appear that part of Venezuela's future lies in throwing in its lot with the subregion, regardless of whether economic integration mechanisms such as ALADI or forums for concerted political action such as the Rio Group can be developed at the Latin American level. Despite the importance of the investment flowing into the country from European trading partners of the stature of Holland and Great Britain (the latter of which recently mounted a financial and trade offensive in Venezuela) and a major Japanese financial presence particularly related to the development of new sectors of production,[50] the question of other markets and sources of funding is at present taking a back seat.

Attention is focused at the subregional and hemispheric levels on existing geopolitical advantages and on the priorities established previously by the nation's foreign policy.[51] Nonetheless, the European Community continues to be a key option for the increased market diversification sought by the country.

## DEMOCRACY: AN IMPORTANT ASSET OF VENEZUELAN FOREIGN POLICY?

Venezuela has an important asset at its disposal: a legacy of foreign policy achievements during the previous stages of democratic rule. This asset should be viewed as the political culture associated with the development and international projection of the democratic system. As one analyst noted in 1983, Venezuela's democratic political system has at times been characterized by a "compulsive pursuit of consensus,"[52] negotiation, and compromise. This attribute was transmitted to the nation's foreign policy with the aid of the democratic image often projected by the country.[53] Indeed, recent Venezuelan history has shown a distinct bias in favor of the peaceful resolution of conflicts, international negotiation, the abandonment of the use of force as an instrument of foreign policy, and a trend toward cooperation (at times misunderstood by its beneficiaries). This tendency has become deeply ingrained in the public mind-set and re-creates the "idealism derived from the Bolivarian vision" that Venezuela only supports the overthrow of tyrants and promotes the unification of Latin America,[54] which is associated with the mythification of the country's heroic past as reflected in the figure of the Liberator, Simón Bolívar.[55]

This approach is reinforced by the attitude adopted by Venezuela toward the border disputes with Guyana and Colombia (about which the public believes national territory has been lost); the peaceful demarcation of maritime limits with the United States, France, and the Dominican Republic; and Venezuelan support for independence movements and the struggle against racism since the 1960s. It is also repeatedly echoed in official pronouncements, both for domestic consumption and in international forums.

As Carlos Guerón points out, as far as security and the diplomacy associated with it is concerned, "the security and defense of Venezuela and its political stability were based not only on the training and effectiveness of the armed forces but also on recourse to the regional system of collective security sanctions when it came under direct attack (Cuba and the Dominican Republic). Even at times of extreme tension, such as the incursion by Caldera, the government continued to prefer the direct, peaceful approach to the resolution of disputes that has characterized its management of foreign policy in recent decades."[56] This tack is evident not only in the case of relations with Colombia, but also with regard to the resolution of the territorial dispute with Guyana over the Essequibo territory: first the dispute was shelved for twelve years after the signing of the Port of Spain Protocol, then the two countries agreed to place the selection of the dispute resolution mechanism in the hands of the UN secretary general. Moreover, since the Lusinchi administration, cooperation programs with the Caribbean basin have stressed "joint responsibility" as a constituent element of both bilateral cooperation programs and regional programs such as the Pact of San José, a joint arrangement with Mexico whereby oil supplies are guaranteed to several Central American and Caribbean nations.[57]

These traits of Venezuelan political culture—the peaceful resolution of conflicts and regional cooperation linked to the public's own perception of the country as a promoter (more defensively than offensively) of decolonialization, democracy, and international cooperation—and their projection internationally as part of the country's democratic credentials have become especially important because cooperation mechanisms are a key factor in the changes in the international, and particularly the hemispheric, system.[58] They also constitute an important point of reference for Venezuelan mediation in internal conflicts in other countries of the region (Colombia, El Salvador, Haiti, and Suriname are cases in point). Aside from the recent changes in the geopolitical situation in the Caribbean subregion, these characteristics are also important for Venezuela's international extension, given the difficulties now being encountered with the democratic process in some Latin American countries and given that the Venezuelan political system has hitherto been conspicuous for its stability.[59]

The democratic component of the Venezuelan identity and the attributes of the political culture associated therein are some of the most important political resources inherited from the previous stages of Venezuelan foreign policy.[60] They not only are a factor in maintaining a Venezuelan presence on the regional and international stage, but could also be important bargaining chips in securing international alliances and support, as was demonstrated in the cases of the external debt negotiations[61] and the reaction of other countries to the events of February and November 1992. Despite the adverse international conditions, these characteristics also generate a key element of external pressure aimed at preventing the suspension of the rule of law, and they reinforce the reorientation of a foreign policy that has been based on the projection of its democratic credentials, particularly at the hemispheric and subregional levels.

Nonetheless, in these changing times it is clear that these attributes alone are insufficient for an active projection into the international arena and fail to resolve the present contradiction between activism and a defensive attitude—that is, between the overextension of the nation's foreign policy and the tendency to resolve conflicts through diplomatic or legal channels[62]—which Venezuelan researchers have on occasion ascribed to their country in the world arena.

In this respect, it is important to distinguish between the democratic identity historically associated with the country's image and the use of this identity to project democracy as an "export model." Essentially, in the short and medium run, the historical identity is contingent on the ability of the political system to adapt to the suspension of the existing consensus and the fragmentation of the political elites, along with the emergence of new social and political actors who reflect the demands of the changes in the domestic situation. The projected identity, however, is seriously limited by falling oil revenues and the necessary reduction in the scope of Venezuelan foreign policy.

In short, the present Venezuelan domestic situation and the pressure to improve the democratic system raise doubts about whether Venezuela's democratic credentials can continue to be a key and enduring attribute of its foreign policy during the current transitional phase— particularly after the suspension of the existing consensual rules of the game and the recent tendency on the part of some military and civil sectors to resort to violence as a means of resolving the nation's problems.

## A CLEAN SLATE? THE IMPACT OF THE INTERNATIONAL SCENE

What, then, are the prospects for Venezuela and the traditionally extolled virtues of its political system and their international projection in view of the challenges imposed by the new world conditions? It is clear that the most important elements of Venezuela's identity and the objectives associated with it will continue to be its credentials as an oil producer and a democratic nation—unless, of course, there is a suspension of the established constitutional order as a result of social and political tensions. It is not merely a question of historical inertia. These elements have become an intrinsic part of the process that has supported Venezuela's economic and political development over the past thirty-five years. Despite the necessary reorientation of both the economic development strategy and the political system in response to the new domestic and international conditions, oil and democracy (albeit under new conditions and with different nuances) will continue to be the hallmarks of the nation's international identity because they are key elements of the political culture.

The historical articulation of these two basic characteristics, so as to promote a positive image and political model of the country in its foreign policy, is no longer a valid proposition, however. Venezuelan democracy in its present form and with its relevant characteristics has ceased to be an exportable model, owing to both the country's domestic problems and the wave of democratization that has been sweeping the continent. Nor can oil serve any longer as the cornerstone of a foreign policy geared to the projection of this image, given the economic crisis facing the country, the slump in oil prices on the world market, and the need to adapt the nation's development strategy to these external conditions. In the current regional economic and political climate, other identities could persist or emerge in the short term to give continuity to the foreign policy objectives and priorities of the Venezuelan state; examples include the identities of a debtor nation and, essentially, a Caribbean and Gran Colombian nation. In any case, regardless of the identities that appear and the conditions they impose, the past suggests that the short- and medium-term formulas and objectives that emerge from them will have to be revised constantly to meet the realities dictated by the momentum of the world system. The international arena is having an increasingly decisive impact on the evolution of the domestic economy and national politics.

Whether the present identities continue to exist or change as a result of a drastic reshaping of the Venezuelan political system, it is clear that since 1989 Venezuela—like many Latin American countries—has entered a new phase in its foreign policy, tied to the country's future economic and political development and to the urgent need to insert itself competitively and effectively into the international system. The government is not able to adopt a consistent policy that can provide continuity to new identities. Rather, this new phase is characterized by a restructuring of the nation's economy and by the social and political repercussions of this process, all of which will have a strong impact on Venezuela's political system and its external posture. As seen in the months following the coup attempt of February 4, 1992, the present context is contributing to the redefinition not only of the role of the president in international affairs but also of the high international profile that the country enjoyed during earlier phases.

In conclusion, the earlier overextension of Venezuelan foreign policy with the help of the country's oil resources and its ability to project its democratic credentials abroad is now coming under increasing pressure. It is likely, however, that some of the historical objectives and priorities established for certain recurring issues will continue to form part of the foreign policy agenda, particularly the need to strengthen ties with traditional trading partners (especially the United States and Colombia) and to optimize Venezuela's foreign policy by exploiting the wealth of experience and influence acquired at the regional level (especially in the Caribbean and Central America).

This short-term focus on the subregion and the hemisphere raises questions about the country's long-term ability to achieve a more diversified insertion into a new world order dominated by economic and trade issues. Venezuela will need to be less dependent on its historical comparative advantages associated with the production of hydrocarbons and its abundant energy resources. Beyond their immediate scope and limitations, the economic and political changes taking place in Venezuela are likely to impose a more moderate foreign policy profile, increasingly dominated by economic and trade issues and linked to the restructuring of the economy. That profile is also likely to be designed to keep the country within the economic and political confines of the new domestic situation and changes in the international system, while optimizing its economic, institutional, and human resources.

In the process, progress needs to be made not only with the economic reforms that could enhance the country's efficiency and competitiveness, but also with the modernization of the political system and foreign policy mechanisms and instruments, keyed to new objectives and priorities. Otherwise, Venezuela could fall prey to either a conservative parochialism nourished by the self-perception originating from the past oil boom and rent-seeking economy or the equally dangerous appeal of an unrealistic cosmopolitanism, also rooted in the glories of a bonanza that has run its course and in the overextension of the country's external approach.

If Venezuela is to cope successfully with the domestic challenges that lie ahead and achieve its necessary and inexorable insertion into the changing world context, it must develop a realistic strategy, resisting both of these temptations and adopting a more pragmatic and flexible vision of the country's true economic and political capabilities. Venezuela's policy must be commensurate with the more complex and demanding international environment.

## NOTES

1. See D. H. Levine, *Conflict and Political Change in Venezuela* (Princeton: Princeton University Press, 1973), and Juan Carlos Rey, "El sistema político venezolano y los proble-

mas de su política exterior," in Instituto de Estudios Políticos, ed., *La agenda de la política exterior de Venezuela* (Caracas: Ediciones de la Biblioteca de la Universidad Central, 1983), 60–68.

2. Eva Josko de Guerón, "La política exterior: Continuidad y cambio, contradicción y coherencia," in Moisés Naím and Ramón Piñango, eds., *El caso Venezuela: Una ilusión de armonía* 4th ed. (Caracas: IESA, 1980), 350–75, and Eva Josko de Guerón, "Cambio y continuidad en la política exterior de Venezuela: Una revisión," in Carlos Romero, ed., *Reforma y política exterior en Venezuela* (Caracas: INVESP/COPRE/Nueva Sociedad, 1992), 41–75.

3. See Josko de Guerón, "La política exterior"; idem, "Cambio y continuidad"; Elsa Cardozo de Da Silva, *Continuidad y consistencia en quince años de política exterior venezolana 1969–1984* (Caracas: Universidad Central de Venezuela/Consejo de Desarrollo Científico y Humanístico [UCV/CDCH], 1992); and Carlos Guerón, "La política de estado y el estado de la política," *Política internacional* (Caracas), no. 23 (July–September 1991): 4–10.

4. See Alfredo Toro Hardy, *Venezuela, democracia y política exterior* (Caracas: Proimagen, 1986), and idem, "La política exterior de Venezuela durante los ultimos 15 años," in P. Cunill Grau, *Venezuela contemporánea* (Caracas: Fundación Eugenio Mendoza, 1989), 315–19. As one of the participants in the debate has pointed out: "In a democratic society, government foreign policy must be capable of generating the broadest consensus, but be open to discussion, with fixed goals but a flexible approach; in other words, with continuity of purpose but constant adaptation to the demands of the changing environment, commensurate with the ultimate objectives and adjusted to the short-term conditions, with a clear appreciation of which factors can be controlled and which cannot, with priorities ranked according to ongoing interests and goals, and flexible priorities as far as objectives are concerned. In short, a government policy that takes account of the status of that policy"; Guerón, "La política de estado y el estado de política," 10.

5. Rey, "El sistema polítco venezolano," 60–68; and Josko de Guerón, "Cambio y continuidad," 41–75.

6. Aníbal Romero, "La situación estratégica de Venezuela," *Política internacional*, no. 1 (January–March 1986): 10.

7. Elsa Cardozo de Da Silva, "Política exterior en tiempos de turbulencia: El desafío de responder al cambio," *Política internacional*, no. 27 (July–September 1992): 8–12.

8. Aníbal Romero, *La miseria del populismo* (Caracas: Ediciones Centauro, 1987).

9. Pedro Palma, "La economía venezolana en el período 1974–1988," in *Venezuela contemporánea*, 157–248.

10. Elsa Cardozo de Da Silva, "La política exterior de Venezuela 1984–1989: Entre las vulnerabilidades económicas y los compromisos políticos," *Política internacional* (April–June 1989): 1–14, and Demetrio Boersner, "Cambios de énfasis en la política exterior venezolana, 1958–1978," *Política internacional*, no. 8 (October–December 1987): 1–14.

11. Palma, "La economía venezolana," 157–248.

12. Josko de Guerón, "La política exterior," 350–75.

13. Josko de Guerón, "Cambio y continuidad"; 41–75, Cardozo de Da Silva, *Continuidad y consistencia en quince años;* 87–130, and Elsa Cardozo de Da Silva, "Las relaciones Venezuela–Estados Unidos y el comercio," paper prepared for the workshop "Acuerdos de libre comercio y su impacto sobre el ambiente" (INVESP/North-South Center, Caracas, July 8–10, 1992).

14. R. D. Bond, "Venezuela, la cuenca del Caribe y la crisis en Centroamérica," in Centro de Capacitación para el Desarrollo-Centro de Investigación y Docencia Económica (CECADE-CIDE), eds., *Centroamérica, crisis y política internacional* (Mexico City: Editorial Siglo XXI, 1982), 253–68, and Marisol de Gonzalo, "La significación del Grupo Contadora," in *Política internacional*, no. 3 (July–September 1986): 16–23.

15. Carlos Romero, "Las relaciones internacionales y la política exterior de Venezuela en tiempos de crisis," manuscript, INVESP, July 1992, 9.

16. These symptoms had already appeared, with different emphases, during the two previous administrations but had been ignored for the sake of the stability of the political system; based on the redistribution of wealth, the administration chose to overlook the fact that its resources were exhausted. See Palma, "La economía venezolana," 157–248, and Antonio Francés, *Venezuela posible* (Caracas: Corimon/IESA, 1990), 63, 83–89.

17. Barry Buzan, "New Patterns of Global Security in the Twenty-First Century," *International Affairs* (London) 67, no. 3 (July 1991): 431–51; Andrés Serbín, *Caribbean Geopolitics: Towards Security through Peace?* (Boulder: Lynne Rienner, 1991); Andrés Serbín, "The U.S., the Caribbean and Latin America: Menage à Trois ou Partouze?" *Caribbean Affairs* 5, no. 2 (April–June 1992): 70–80; and Andrés Serbín, "Liberalización comercial e integración subregional en América Latina," paper prepared for the workshop "Acuerdos de libre comercio y su impacto sobre el ambiente."

18. Serbín, "Liberalización comercial," 12–17.

19. Andrew Hurrell, "Regionalism in the Americas? Latin America and the New World Order: A Regional Bloc for the Americas," *International Affairs* 68, no. 1 (January 1992): 124–31; Serbín, "The U.S., the Caribbean and Latin America"; and Serbín, "Liberalización comercial," 12–17.

20. One analyst recently pointed out that

> the diagnostic undertaken by the new government revealed a country with profound macroeconomic imbalances of a structural and cyclical nature caused by a domestic demand largely stimulated by public expenditure, with artificial rates of exchange for a clearly overvalued currency and negative interest rates in terms of the spiralling levels of inflation. These macroeconomic imbalances generated balance of payments deficits with outflows of foreign exchange that drained the international reserves, public sector deficits running into the billions, and financial markets subject to constant fluctuations. . . . The new government therefore implemented an adjustment and stabilization program in February 1989 in an attempt to slash the deficit, alter the course of the economy so as to achieve a balance in the macroeconomic values that had been distorted by artificial practices, and prepare the economy and society for economic growth in the medium term.

FUNDAFUTURO, *Cuando Venezuela perdió el rumbo: Un análisis de la economía venezolana entre 1945 y 1991* (Caracas: Cavendes, 1992), 114–15.

21. For the incongruities of the adjustment program, see a recent critique in José Toro Hardy, *Venezuela: 55 años de política económica 1936–1991: Una utopía keynesiana* (Caracas: Panapo, 1992), 152–55.

22. Andrés Serbín, "Venezuela: Reversal or Renewal?" *Hemisphere* 4, no. 3 (summer 1992): 24–27.

23. Cardozo de Da Silva, "Política exterior en tiempos de turbulencia," 8–12.

24. CORDIPLAN, *El gran viraje: Lineamientos generales del VIII Plan de la Nación* (Caracas: CORDIPLAN, 1990), and Elsa Cardozo de Da Silva, "El proceso de toma de decisiones en la política exterior de Venezuela: Una revisión," in Romero, *Reforma y política exterior en Venezuela*, 5.

25. Eduardo Ortiz Ramírez, *La política comercial de Venezuela*, Colección de Estudios Económicos, no. 16 (Caracas: Banco Central de Venezuela, 1992), 12–16.

26. Serbín, "The U.S., the Caribbean and Latin America"; 70–80; Serbín, "Liberalización comercial"; and Lourdes Cobo, "Prioridades de la política exterior de Venezuela para el año 2000," in Romero, *Reforma y política exterior en Venezuela*, 239–63.

27. Carlos Romero, "El marco intelectual de la política exterior de Venezuela," in Andrés Serbín, ed., *Venezuela y las relaciones internacionales en la cuenca del Caribe* (Caracas: Instituto Latinoamericano de Investigaciones Sociales/Asociación Venezolana de Estudios del Caribe [ILDIS/AVECA], 1987), 195–210.

28. Laura Rojas, "Aspectos económicos de la política exterior de Venezuela," in Romero, *Reforma y política exterior en Venezuela*, 145–71, and Guerón, "La política de estado y el estado de política," 4–10.

29. Luis Zambrano, "Perspectivas macroeconómicas de Venezuela, 1992–1996," paper prepared for the workshop "Acuerdos de libre comercio y su impacto sobre el ambiente," 6–9.
30. Rojas, "Aspectos económicos," 153.
31. Luis Herrera Marcano, "La internacionalización petrolera," *Política internacional*, no. 3 (July–September 1986): 7–8.
32. Rojas, "Aspectos económicos." 145–71.
33. David Pumphrey, "Energy Policy in the Western Hemisphere," Latin American Program Working Paper no. 195, Woodrow Wilson International Center for Scholars, Washington, D.C., 1991.
34. Oficina de Promoción de Exportaciones (PROMEXPORT), *Evaluación de las exportaciones no-tradicionales 1989–1991* (Caracas: Oficina de Promoción de Exportaciones, 1992), 26–28.
35. Ibid.
36. Zambrano, "Perspectivas macroeconómicas de Venezuela," 22.
37. Ibid., 14.
38. As Zambrano points out: "In the short run, debt-servicing will consume around $13,000,000,000 over the next five years. If it cannot be refinanced, this will represent an outflow equivalent to the entire international reserves and/or a contraction in consumption levels, even if the oil sector were to show substantial signs of improvement over its recent performance"; ibid., 15–16. For the continued importance of the debt in the economic restructuring and adjustment of Latin American countries, see documents of the recent annual consultative meeting of SELA, Caracas, September 1992.
39. Josko de Guerón, "Cambio y continuidad," 63–64.
40. Zambrano, "Perspectivas macroeconómicas de Venezuela," 23–24.
41. William C. Smith, "Neoliberal Restructuring, Distributional Struggles and Scenarios of Democratic Consolidation in Latin America," paper prepared for the seminar "Liberal Strategies of Refoundation: Contemporary Dilemmas of Development," Latin American Social Science Council/Rio de Janeiro University Research Institute (CLACSO/IUPERJ), Rio de Janeiro, August 19–21, 1992, 10.
42. Carlos Acuña, "Política y economía en la Argentina de los 90 (o porque el futuro no es lo que solía ser)," paper for the seminar "Democracia, mercados y reformas estructurales en América Latina," Buenos Aires, March 25–27, 1992.
43. Toro Hardy, "Venezuela: 55 años de política económica."
44. Carlos A. Romero, "La complejidad organizacional en el sector externo de Venezuela," in Romero, *Reforma y política exterior en Venezuela*, 209–38; and Cardoza de Da Silva, *Las relaciones Venezuela-Estados Unidos*, 17–20.
45. Francés, *Venezuela posible*, 98–108.
46. Regarding the constraints imposed on the president in implementing foreign policy, see Josko de Guerón, "Cambio y continuidad," 41–75 and Guerón, "La política de estado y el estado de política," 4–10. See also the recent recommendations made by the ministry of foreign affairs' Comisión de Restructuración.
47. Hence the recent remarks by the current Venezuelan minister of foreign affairs—who insisted that "oil should play an important role" in any free-trade agreement with the United States—and the references to and expectations surrounding a possible hemispherewide energy alliance promoted by President George Bush's National Energy Strategy. Fernando Ochoa Antich, "Discurso ante la cámara venezolano americana," *Zeta*, no. 908 (July 29, 1992). Venezuelan efforts to promote an energy community with the United States, guaranteeing supplies of oil and gas products to that nation, can be traced back as far as the 1960s. They began with the proposals put forward by Minister Juan Pablo Pérez Alfonzo (before the creation of OPEC), which conflicted with global U.S. foreign policy priorities and specifically its involvement in the Middle East. More recently, the energy department undertook a study on possible cooperation on energy in the Western Hemisphere, an idea that has met with opposition from some quarters on the grounds that it could make the United States more

energy dependent, undermine the diversity of the nation's energy sources, and create serious environmental problems. See Pumphrey, "Energy Policy in the Western Hemisphere," 1–11. In addition, Venezuela takes the view that its support for the United States in the form of guaranteed oil supplies during successive crises from World War II through the Gulf War has never been properly reciprocated by its northern neighbor. See chapter 14 in this volume, by Norman Bailey: "Venezuela and the United States: Putting Energy in the Enterprise." See also the recent statements of U.S. Ambassador Michael Skol, to the effect that Venezuela is still not in a position to enter into a free-trade agreement with the United States; *El Diario de Caracas*, September 15 and 16, 1992.

48. Andrés Serbín and Carlos Romero, eds., *El grupo de los Tres: Asimetrías y convergencias* (Caracas: INVESP/Friedrich Ebert Stiftung-Columbia [FESCOL]/Nueva Sociedad, 1993), 11–40.

49. Serbín, "The U.S., the Caribbean and Latin America," 70–80 and idem, "Liberalización comercial," 12–17.

50. Francés, *Venezuela posible*, 165–69.

51. This is an area little studied by Venezuelan academics and analysts that merits greater attention.

52. Rey, "El sistema político venezolano," 60–68.

53. As a document from the ministry of foreign affairs' Comisión de Restructuración notes, "We do the same domestically as we advocate externally." A discussion of the limitations of this attitude in Venezuelan foreign policy is found in Romero, *La miseria de populismo*, 79–184.

54. Boersner, "Cambios de énfasis."

55. Aníbal Romero, *La miseria del populismo*, 185–296.

56. Guerón, "La política de estado y el estado de política," 8.

57. Serbín, "The U.S., the Caribbean and Latin America," 70–80 and idem, "Liberalización comercial," 12–17.

58. Luciano Tomassini, "Estructura y funcionamiento del sistema internacional y sus repercusiones sobre la solución de conflictos especiamente entre países pequeños y medianos," in L. Tomassina, et al., *Integración solidaria para el mantenimiento de la paz en América Latina* (Caracas: Universidad Simón Bolívar/OAS, 1989), 21–61.

59. Instituto de Relaciones Europea-Latinamericanas (IRELA), "Venezuela en crisis: Raíses y consecuencias," Dossier no. 39, Madrid, June 1992.

60. Romero, "Las relaciones internacionales," 7–9.

61. Josko de Guerón, "Cambio y continuidad," 350–75.

62. Romero, "Las relaciones internacionales," 7–9.

# 14

# Venezuela and the United States: Putting Energy in the Enterprise

## Norman A. Bailey

The triumph of political democracy and economic liberalism in Latin America is a recent and fragile phenomenon, as graphically demonstrated by the military coup in Haiti, the presidential coup in Peru, and the failed 1992 coups in Venezuela. In this struggle, modernizing forces must maintain their forward momentum if they are going to prevail ultimately. A powerful retrograde movement could easily sidetrack liberalizing tendencies and return a large part of the region to its multisecular authoritarianism.

All the countries of the hemisphere are important in this regard, but two are of special significance: the United States and Venezuela. In the case of the United States, its leadership as *primus inter pares* is essential, given its economic and strategic weight in the region and in the world. Yet the rest of the hemisphere is of equal importance in this great mutual task. Among these countries, Canada cannot play a leading role because of its divergent traditions and ethnic clashes. Mexico and Chile are playing positive roles, but neither has traditionally had much influence over the rest of the continent. In South America, Colombia has terrible internal conflicts, Brazil is finding the road to political and economic liberalization strewn with obstacles, and liberalization in Argentina is recent and tentative.

Without losing its momentum, the rhythm of progress can endure minor setbacks, such as the coups in Haiti and Peru, if the tendency does not become general. On the other hand, the failed coups of February and November 1992 in Venezuela caused all proponents of liberalization to tremble. If that country—relatively prosperous and with the longest democratic tradition of the larger countries of Latin America—could not continue the trend, the future looked bleak indeed.

From this analysis two conclusions can be drawn: the forces of economic and political liberalism in Venezuela must be strengthened at all costs and the ties between Venezuela and the United States must also be strengthened in all areas, but especially in the fields of economic integration of the hemisphere and assistance to democratic forces in the region. Instead of being simply sellers and buyers of petroleum and its derivatives, the two countries must forge a close collaboration that will have more influence on the future of the hemisphere than any other single factor. Failure of leadership on the part of either country will doom the processes of hemispheric economic integration and liberal convergence. The North American Free Trade Agreement must be quickly broadened and deepened by the application of the principles and programs of the Enterprise for the Americas Initiative proclaimed by the Bush administration in June 1990, ratified by the U.S. Congress, and reiterated by President-elect Bill Clinton in December 1992.

## BACKGROUND: GETTING AWAY WITH COUNTERPRODUCTIVE STRATEGIES (FOR A WHILE)

During the last decade of the nineteenth century, a border conflict between Venezuela and Great Britain (over the boundary with the colony of British Guiana) was the occasion for the proclamation by the United States of its paramount domination over the Western Hemisphere (the Olney Doctrine of 1895). Nevertheless, Venezuela was essentially ignored by the United States until the 1920s, when large quantities of Venezuelan oil began to be produced and exported. Even then, United States–Venezuelan relations were left in the hands of the great oil companies, which had their own interests to protect and defend. It is only during the past decade or so that the wider implications of U.S.–Venezuelan relations have come to be recognized. Still, the checkered and somewhat conflictive past can become prologue to a significantly more cooperative and productive future if the two countries will collaborate in many areas, especially on establishing energy security programs as an additional pillar of the Enterprise for the Americas Initiative.

The United States is an oil-deficit country surrounded by oil-surplus countries, especially Canada, Venezuela, and Mexico, as well as Trinidad and increasingly Colombia, where there have been major new discoveries. One could therefore easily assume that the energy security policy of the United States would base its oil strategy on reliance on these sources to supplement domestic supplies. One could also assume that Venezuela, with the largest actual and potential surpluses in the region, would act to maximize first its own advantage, and second that of its hemispheric neighbors. Both assumptions are incorrect.

The United States has made great efforts and spent enormous amounts of money and political capital to establish, maintain, and solidify its dependence on a source of oil thousands of miles away in one of the most unstable regions of the world, the Middle East. Consequently, the United States has been putting a proximate and remarkably loyal source of abundant energy, Venezuela, in a disadvantageous position.[1] For its part, Venezuela, between bouts of helping the United States at times of crisis without any reciprocation, has unintentionally strengthened the position of its rival producers and engaged in a series of domestic measures that have crippled its own ability to compete. The historical and technical background of this story has been extensively covered elsewhere; the facts are well known and documented. The results of the policies adopted by the two countries in the energy field are only too obvious, culminating in the Persian Gulf crisis and war of 1990 to 1991. Yet neither country appears to have learned much from the experience.

## THE CURSE OF OIL

As a general rule, the discovery of modest quantities of oil or even large quantities of oil in countries with relatively complex economies has not been problematic. Oil in large quantities in undeveloped economies, such as those of the Gulf states, has had pernicious effects but cannot be said to have been seriously destructive because there was little to destroy. In the case of countries in intermediate stages of development, however, the effect of large oil strikes has been extremely destructive. This has been true, for example, in Nigeria, Indonesia, and certainly Venezuela. Among these effects has been an artificial urbanization and abandonment of the rural areas, "decomplexation" of the economy, gigantism, waste and corruption on an epic scale, and erosion of the work ethic.

Even with recent efforts at diversification, oil in Venezuela represents 24 percent of the country's gross national product, over 80 percent of its foreign exchange, and 83 percent of its tax revenues. Recent discoveries have raised Venezuela's proven reserves to over 60 billion barrels, to which must be added at least 20 billion barrels' equivalent of natural gas and about 270 billion barrels of recoverable extra-heavy Orinoco crude. Reserves of normal crudes put Venezuela in second place in the world, after Saudi Arabia, in amount of reserves. If the Orinoco tars are included, Venezuela is number one by a wide margin.

Production of Venezuelan oil rose steadily until 1970, then declined until 1985 and has been rising again since (see table 14.1). Production now averages between 2.1 and 2.5 million barrels per day. Exports represent about 15 percent of U.S. imports of crude petroleum and products, and about 68 percent of Venezuelan exports go to the United States. Most important, Venezuela has always, without exception, supported the United States whenever a crisis of oil supply occurred, as in World War II, 1956, 1967, 1973, 1978 to 1979, and 1990 to 1991. Even the formation of OPEC, often blamed on Venezuela, took place only after then oil minister Juan Pablo Pérez Alfonzo's suggestion of a North American energy community was ignored by the United States.

Internally, oil development took place in a chaotic fashion and the revenues were misused in various ways. Venezuelan energy policy remains counterproductive in many respects, including the strict application since 1988 of OPEC quotas to overall production rather than to exports, as other OPEC members still do. In addition, the government taxes the state oil company, Petróleos de Venezuela, S.A. (PDVSA) at a punitive rate of 82 percent and maintains domestic oil prices at artificially low levels.[2]

Table 14.1
VENEZUELAN OIL PRODUCTION (1980–96)

| Year | Millions of Barrels Daily (average) | Percent Change from Previous Year |
|------|------|------|
| 1980 | 2.2 | — |
| 1981 | 2.1 | −5 |
| 1982 | 1.9 | −10 |
| 1983 | 1.8 | −5 |
| 1984 | 1.8 | 0 |
| 1985 | 1.7 | −6 |
| 1986 | 1.8 | 6 |
| 1987 | 1.8 | 0 |
| 1988 | 1.9 | 6 |
| 1989 | 1.9 | 0 |
| 1990 | 2.1 | 11 |
| 1991 | 2.5 | 19 |
| 1992 | 2.4 | −1 |
| 1993 | 2.5 | +1 |
| 1994 forecast | 2.6 | +1 |
| 1995 forecast | 2.8 | +1 |
| 1996 forecast | 3.0 | +1 |

*Sources:* U.S. Department of Energy and Petróleos de Venezuela, S.A. (PDVSA).

# THE UNITED STATES: FIXATIONS AND OBSESSIONS

Questionable Venezuelan energy policies were reciprocated in spades by the United States. Venezuelan cooperation was rewarded by the United States in the form of tariffs and quotas at various points from 1932 through 1973. Preferences were given frequently to Canada and Mexico, but never to Venezuela. In the period since 1973, the United States has systematically maintained and strengthened its strategic dependence on imported oil, particularly on Gulf oil, through its refusal to apply a reasonably high gasoline tax and its massive subsidization of "low" Gulf crude prices.

The reason usually given as to why North America (defined to include Venezuela and Colombia) is increasingly a net importer of oil is that it cannot match the Gulf producers' low costs. In fact, the U.S. government spends considerable sums under federal defense, diplomatic, security, and energy programs that enable the Gulf producers, at American taxpayers' expense, to out-compete North American oil producers. What the North American consumer does not pay when he or she purchases energy is paid in higher taxes—an arrangement that undermines the domestic productive base as well as the federal budget. Four categories of primary annual expenditures are made by the federal government to sustain a buyers' market: energy policy, military, intelligence and diplomatic, and security assistance.

The discrepancy between the normal price for Arab oil and the real price is summarized in table 14.2; the figures represent highly conservative estimates and thus are likely to err on the side of caution. "Real price" is the total cost to the United States as importers per barrel of Arab OPEC oil, including the military, diplomatic, intelligence, security assistance, and energy program costs as well as the commercial purchasing outlays in any given year. For all the years under comparison (1973 to 1990), what U.S. consumers actually pay per barrel of Arab oil is between two and five times higher than the nominal spot price (the price for a transaction that occurs immediately) for Saudi light oil. The figures demonstrate that if the prices that U.S. consumers have been paying for oil were free-market prices rather than prices resulting from taxpayer subsidies to Gulf producers, U.S. and neighboring oil producers would have been prospering and producing taxable wealth. The result would have been both higher federal revenues and lower federal expenditures.

It is too late to recover the vast resources expended to maintain counterproductive energy policies of the past, but appropriate policies and resource reallocation in the future can easily and quickly ensure

Table 14.2
COMPARISON OF THE NOMINAL AND REAL PRICES FOR
ARAB OPEC OIL, 1973–90

| : Year | Nominal Price (dollars per barrel) | Real Price (dollars per barrel) | Percent Discrepancy between Perception and Reality |
|---|---|---|---|
| 1973 | 2.81 | 22.58 | 803 |
| 1974 | 10.98 | 34.33 | 312 |
| 1975 | 10.43 | 29.18 | 279 |
| 1976 | 11.63 | 24.34 | 209 |
| 1977 | 12.57 | 24.20 | 192 |
| 1978 | 12.91 | 27.30 | 211 |
| 1979 | 29.19 | 35.48 | 121 |
| 1980 | 36.01 | 52.85 | 146 |
| 1981 | 34.17 | 70.72 | 206 |
| 1982 | 31.76 | 103.46 | 325 |
| 1983 | 28.67 | 109.15 | 380 |
| 1984 | 28.10 | 82.19 | 292 |
| 1985 | 27.55 | 115.41 | 419 |
| 1986 | 14.10 | 48.89 | 346 |
| 1987 | 17.02 | 48.96 | 282 |
| 1988 | 11.36 | 34.88 | 307 |
| 1989 | 17.07 | 38.12 | 223 |
| 1990 | 14.17 | 44.84 | 316 |

*Source:* Center for Strategic and International Studies, Washington, D.C.

that these costs do not continue to be incurred. If the recent Gulf War
and the end of the cold war teach nothing else, they clearly demonstrate that continued reliance on volatile and uncertain Eastern Hemisphere energy sources cannot be justified on any grounds—economic,
political, or strategic. Those who would maintain current policies must
be able to argue credibly that Saudi Arabia, Iran, Iraq, Kuwait, and the
United Arab Emirates are somehow more strategically important to the
United States than Canada, Mexico, Venezuela, Texas, or Alaska.

## THE CURRENT SITUATION

The current energy situation in Venezuela is an amalgam of good and
bad news. The good news is concentrated in the state oil company,
PDVSA, and its affiliates. PDVSA is a well-run, imaginative, and aggressive oil company, integrated horizontally and vertically. Despite OPEC
quotas and damaging government policies, PDVSA is profitable and

able to invest in production, refining, and distribution of crude oil and derivatives worldwide. Production averages about 2.25 million barrels per day and is refined in a series of domestic, offshore, and foreign refineries, including facilities in Curaçao, Louisiana, Texas, and New Jersey, as well as Germany, Sweden, and Belgium. Venezuela's exports of about 1.3 million barrels a day of crude and products to the United States place it third in volume worldwide (after Canada and Saudi Arabia, and ahead of Mexico).

In addition, PDVSA has invested heavily in research on the use of Orinoco extra-heavy crude, which also has a high sulphur content and is difficult to transport and refine. The 270 billion barrels of recoverable Orinoco crude, however, is the largest hydrocarbon reserve in the world. One outcome of this research has been an emulsion of Orinoco crude and water, or "orimulsion." Exempt from OPEC quotas, orimulsion can be used to replace diesel oil in power-generating facilities below the cost of diesel fuel and with a modest refitting cost (usually ten to fifteen million dollars). Several supply contracts have already been signed and others are being negotiated. In addition, a process known as hydrocracking-distillation-hydrotreatment (HDH) can turn extra-heavy crude into good quality crude at a cost that would be competitive with out-of-area crudes, if market prices prevailed as noted earlier.

To maintain and enhance its position in the market, PDVSA needs to make heavy investments in the next few years. The country's investment needs are outlined in table 14.3. PDVSA could easily finance these needs from internal capital generation and its borrowing power were it not for the bad news: government policy.

Table 14.3
INVESTMENT NEEDS OF THE VENEZUELAN OIL INDUSTRY,
1991–96

| Investment Sector | Cost (billions of dollars) | Percent of Total |
|---|---|---|
| Production | 16.7 | 47 |
| Domestic refining | 10.1 | 29 |
| External refining | 4.2 | 12 |
| Exploration | 1.7 | 5 |
| Tankers | 1.2 | 3 |
| Domestic marketing | 0.9 | 2 |
| Other | 0.7 | 2 |
| Total | 35.5 | 100 |

*Source:* PDVSA.

Not all Venezuelan government energy policy is misguided. Foreign investment is permitted, indeed encouraged in every area of the industry, except ownership of the oil in the ground. As a result, large investments are being made in natural gas liquefaction, activation of abandoned oil fields, and coal. But the government would greatly enhance its comparative advantage internationally by raising domestic gasoline prices to a level three to four times what they are now, abandoning OPEC, and reducing its punitive taxation of PDVSA (now at 82 percent of profits, which covers about 70 percent of federal government costs).

Again, counterproductive energy policies in Venezuela are matched and surpassed in the United States. It is still U.S. policy to enhance a growing dependence on Gulf oil, as exemplified by the Gulf War, and consequently to penalize domestic and hemispheric producers. If the United States is not willing to counteract this bias with a tariff on non-hemispheric crude, it should at least impose a minimum fifty-cent-per-gallon tax on gasoline, which would simultaneously enhance energy conservation, help improve the environment, and reduce the budget deficit.

## CONCLUSION: IS SENSIBLE COOPERATION POSSIBLE?

Working together in a number of areas, Venezuela and the United States can provide a major impetus for the continuation of the liberalizing impulse essential to the future prosperity of the hemisphere. In the energy field, together they could provide an example not only for the hemisphere, but for the world as a whole.

North America, as previously defined, is registering an overall energy deficit, almost all of which is centered in the United States (see table 14.4). And all of that deficit is found in only one source of energy: oil. A gas and coal surplus in the region is more than offset by the oil deficit. The North American deficit is the equivalent of some 2.5 million barrels per day; the imbalance between crude oil produced within the region and crude oil consumed is 5.4 million barrels per day. As explained previously, this petroleum deficit is not caused by any inadequacy on the part of the region's natural resources, but rather by the pricing regime of the world crude oil market. One can better appreciate this reality by examining the annual behavior of the crude oil deficit during the 1980s. The turning point came in 1984. From 1980 to 1984, the crude oil deficit was being correspondingly reduced—assisted in part by the first Reagan administration's deregulation measures.[3] From 1984 to 1989, the crude oil deficit increased every year. From its lowest level of –3.205 million barrels per day in 1984, the gap grew by over 100 percent to

–7.308 million barrels per day in 1989. By 1990, it was at –6.87 million barrels per day as crude oil consumption fell during the recession. This dramatic growth of the region's energy deficit corresponds roughly to the new era in the politics of the Arabian Gulf OPEC partners. Under Saudi hegemony, OPEC shifted to emphasizing "market share" as a major policy instrument, which led to the collapse of world oil prices to artificially low levels, in turn depressing production in the Western Hemisphere. Events during the subsequent 1990–91 period exacerbated the pattern as U.S. military power was lavishly used to subsidize these artificially low Arabian Gulf prices. Since 1973, U.S. international oil policy has been extremely costly; except for the first Reagan term, it has had the effect of consolidating Gulf dominance of oil production, marketing, and pricing as well as discouraging non–Middle East production and conservation efforts.[4]

In the course of 1990, presidents Carlos Salinas de Gortari of Mexico, César Gaviria of Colombia, and Carlos Andrés Pérez of Venezuela all called for the formation of some form of Western Hemisphere en-

Table 14.4

1992 SUMMARY OF ENERGY PRODUCTION AND CONSUMPTION
FOR SELECTED WESTERN HEMISPHERE NATIONS
(in Quadrillion British Thermal Units)

| Country | Production | | | | | |
|---|---|---|---|---|---|---|
| | Total | Oil | Gas | Coal | Hydro | Nuclear |
| Canada | 14.36 | 3.40 | 5.23 | 1.61 | 3.25 | 0.88 |
| Mexico | 7.76 | 5.87 | 1.48 | 0.12 | 0.25 | 0.04 |
| United States | 66.68 | 15.22 | 20.67 | 21.62 | 2.51 | 6.65 |
| Colombia | 2.05 | 0.97 | 0.18 | 0.61 | 0.29 | 0.00 |
| Venezuela | 6.80 | 5.24 | 1.13 | 0.08 | 0.34 | 0.00 |
| Trinidad | 0.51 | 0.30 | 0.21 | 0.00 | 0.00 | 0.00 |

| Country | Consumption | | | | | |
|---|---|---|---|---|---|---|
| | Total | Oil | Gas | Coal | Hydro | Nuclear |
| Canada | 10.97 | 3.28 | 2.61 | 1.25 | 2.95 | 0.88 |
| Mexico | 5.12 | 3.72 | 0.98 | 0.12 | 0.25 | 0.04 |
| United States | 82.19 | 33.51 | 20.34 | 18.88 | 2.81 | 6.65 |
| Colombia | 1.12 | 0.43 | 0.17 | 0.22 | 0.29 | 0.00 |
| Venezuela | 2.18 | 0.85 | 0.96 | 0.03 | 0.34 | 0.00 |
| Trinidad | 0.27 | 0.04 | 0.23 | 0.00 | 0.00 | 0.00 |

*Source:* U.S. Department of Energy, *International Energy Annual* (Washington, D.C.: U.S. Government Printing Office, 1992).

*Note:* Discrepancies in totals due to omissions and rounding.

ergy community. The U.S. Department of Energy responded with a study indicating that such a community might make sense and should be considered.[5] The idea was rejected by the rest of the U.S. government on the grounds that formation of such a community would be contrary to free-market principles—as if OPEC, OAPEC (Organization of Arab Petroleum Exporting Countries), the IEA (International Energy Agency), strategic petroleum reserves in the United States, Japan, and Germany, and the great international oil companies represent a free-market environment.

Venezuela has pursued an energy policy that includes the following elements, none of which can be faulted, except for membership in OPEC (with the withdrawal of Ecuador, Venezuela is now the only OPEC member in the Western Hemisphere):

- An integrated strategy of development of oil, gas, and coal, all oriented toward exports;
- Research and development of the Orinoco extra-heavy crudes;
- Vertical and horizontal oil integration, from exploration to retail sales, in South and North America as well as Europe; and
- Joint ventures and strategic alliances with domestic and foreign energy companies.

All of these measures are excellent and appropriate. What is missing is a major fiscal reform to reduce Venezuelan dependence on the oil industry in financing the national budget. This in turn would permit a reduction in the tax burden on PDVSA, so that it could finance investment and expansion without resorting to loans. Finally, increasing gasoline prices to world levels would place a greater tax burden on petroleum consumption rather than production.

A North American energy community, especially with recent large discoveries in Colombia and Venezuela and the huge reserves of Orinoco heavy crude in Venezuela, could rapidly enhance energy security and reduce or perhaps eliminate reliance on sources in what is one of the most unstable regions of the world. At a minimum, such a community could adopt meaningful emergency plans, in lieu of the inoperative plans of the IEA, and enhance the Strategic Petroleum Reserve. At a maximum, the vast region from the north slope of Alaska to the southern border of Colombia could be indissolubly united by the strong bonds of energy trade.

The choice is clear: the nations of the hemisphere can either regress to a past of exclusiveness, control, and conflict—as is happening in too much of the former Soviet bloc—or move forward together in a future of ever greater cooperation and freedom.

# NOTES

1. See Norman A. Bailey and Criton Zoakos, "The Case for a North American Energy Community," Center for Strategic and International Studies, Washington, D.C., December 1991. See also, by the same authors, "An American OPEC," *International Economy* (March–April 1993): 50–51.
2. See Henry Schuler, "The Venezuelan-U.S. Petroleum Relationship: Past, Present and Future," Center for Strategic and International Studies, Washington, D.C., Significant Issues Series, vol. 13, no. 11, 1991; and U.S. General Accounting Office, *The Energy Sector in Venezuela* (Washington, D.C.: U.S. Government Printing Office, 1991). Also useful is the occasional publication of the Venezuelan embassy in Washington, D.C., *Venezuelan News and Views.* Nonoil governmental revenues provide only 5 percent of GNP. Raising domestic gasoline prices, now the lowest in the world, would alone raise a yield for the government of 2.5 percent of GNP.
3. See Bailey and Zoakos, "The Case for a North American Energy Community." In February 1981 Ronald Reagan abandoned long-standing U.S. price and allocation regulations, and in March 1982 he vetoed the establishment of a standby price regulatory agency. As a result, domestic exploration and drilling surged until the change in Saudi policies mentioned herein later.
4. See Daniel Yergin, *The Prize: The Epic Quest for Oil, Money and Power* (New York: Simon and Schuster, 1991). See also Bailey and Zoakos, "The Case for a North American Energy Community."
5. U.S. Department of Energy, *National Energy Strategy 1991/92* (Washington, D.C.: U.S. Government Printing Office, 1991), 83.

# Epilogue: Nostalgia as a Roadblock to the Future

A month after the conference in which the preliminary versions of the chapters in this book were discussed, the military coup attempt of November 1992 almost succeeded in overthrowing the Venezuelan government. It was the second such attempt in less than ten months in a country that had experienced more than three decades of uninterrupted democracy. Although both coups failed, they succeeded in unleashing social and political forces that dramatically and irreversibly changed the country's political, institutional, and economic landscape.

Certainly, the second coup attempt called into question the notion of a consolidated democratic state and highlighted the weakness of Venezuela's civil society. Events since 1992 suggest that many, if not all, of the elements of Venezuela's political system are deeply flawed. Alfred Stepan describes the Venezuelan state as bloated, its political society as distorted, and its civil society as underdeveloped.[1] The political regime supporting the state was put into place by the 1958 Pact of Punto Fijo between political leaders and military officials. The two coups underscore the need to revitalize or, better yet, reassess the bases on which the pact was established. Not only the nature of Venezuelan civil-military relations, but also the nature of relations between Venezuela's political society and its civil society must undergo change to fit the realities of the present.

The state—the set of formal institutions charged with carrying out essential national functions in the public interest—became the instrument of political parties (*partidocracia*) and their elites (*cogollos*). Such relationships effectively disregarded the interests of the vast majority of Venezuela's citizens.

Political society—that part of the political system that aggregates the interests of the larger society and makes policy decisions—was so distorted that it represented the interests of only a small portion of the Venezuelan populace. As described throughout this volume, *cogollo* politics meant that special deals were arranged for the traditional party elites, for economic interests allied with the top levels of party leadership, for the highest-ranking military leadership, and for social groups closely linked to them. The cohesive behavior of these groups provided the basis for political stability but not for the evolution of a democratic political system. This situation resulted in mid-level military officers, rank-and-file labor, the middle class, and other disenfranchised citizens supporting attacks against the ruling coalition.

Venezuelan civil society, which includes nongovernmental organizations representing the varied interests of the citizenry, lacked both the complexity and the comprehensiveness required in a consolidated democratic political system. It was only after the 1992 gubernatorial elections that a coalition of nonparty-affiliated voter groups emerged to explore the traditional manipulation by the political parties of the Supreme Electoral Council (CSE). Similarly, it was only after the first coup attempt in February 1992 that citizens' associations assumed responsibility for their own political agendas and began to consider vehicles for expression other than the traditional political parties. These flaws in the Venezuelan system—in the state, political society, and civil society—set the stage for the rapid unraveling of what had been perceived as a stable, consolidated democratic regime.

After the second coup attempt, in November 1992, one unprecedented event followed another at a dizzying pace. The state and local elections that took place, as previously scheduled, in December 1992, confirmed that the two main political parties, AD and COPEI, had lost the grip they had held over the electorate since the first popular election was held in 1947. New political groups—such as Causa Radical (also known as Causa R), a leftist labor party—consolidated their political standing by winning many important elected positions, notably that of the mayor of Caracas. This was a reflection of the more general disaffection with traditional political parties. In a survey taken in January 1989, one month prior to the inauguration of the second Pérez administration, 53 percent of those questioned indicated their adherence to AD. By January 1994 that percentage had dropped 36 points to 17 percent, while adherence to COPEI dropped from 25 percent in January 1989 to 17 percent in January 1994. Those declaring themselves "politically independent" more than doubled from 12 percent in January 1989 to 26 percent in January 1994, while Causa R's support jumped from 1 percent in 1989 to 15 percent in 1994.[2]

In large part, this dramatic shift was due to the impact of the simultaneous opening of Venezuelan politics and economics. Economic liberalization and adjustment created a harsh, unprecedented—and mostly unexpected—economic reality. By itself, the harshness of the new reality would have created a climate of hostility toward the government. But to compound the difficulty, political liberalization produced a much freer environment in which long-simmering dissatisfaction with the way traditional elites had managed the country could be expressed. Naturally, opposition to the government, its economic policies, and especially President Pérez escalated. The coups and the generalized perception of the weakness of the government galvanized an assorted, albeit inchoate, coalition that rejected Pérez and everything he had come to symbolize, from market reforms to traditional politicians to corruption. The opposition to Pérez ranged from the president of his own AD party, who openly and constantly expressed his repudiation of market reforms, to a variety of middle-class groups fed up with politicians, corruption, and declining living standards. Naturally, the anti-Pérez coalition also included the many enemies accumulated by Pérez in his long political life, many of whom occupied important positions in Congress, the media, and the judiciary.

By mid-1993, the attorney general had succeeded in persuading the Supreme Court to put Pérez on trial for embezzlement from a discretionary fund traditionally provided to Venezuelan presidents. As a result, Pérez was forced to step down to await trial and was replaced by Interim President Ramón J. Velásquez, appointed by Congress to complete the remainder of Pérez's term, until the scheduled general elections at the end of the year. For the first time since 1958, an elected president did not finish his constitutionally mandated period. In May 1994, Pérez was arrested and sent to jail.

## THE ELECTIONS OF 1993: A RETURN TO THE PAST OR A DETOUR TO THE FUTURE?

The 1993 general election campaign was like no other in the country's history. COPEI held an "open primary" in which any Venezuelan could cast a ballot to pick that party's presidential candidate. As a result, Eduardo Fernández, COPEI's general secretary, who had been considered by most as the next president, lost to Oswaldo Álvarez Paz, the governor of the oil-state of Zulia. Álvarez Paz then briefly became the front-runner, until COPEI's founder, former president Rafael Caldera, announced that he intended to run for the presidency and broke with the party, running on a coalition with the MAS, the Communist party, an assortment of small political groups, and his own small party, Convergencia, an electoral launching pad. Against the wishes of the party's traditionalists, AD chose Claudio Fermín as its candidate, who then had to spend part of the campaign in jail on charges that were later found to be baseless. Andrés Velásquez, the Causa R presidential candidate, staged an aggressive campaign denouncing corruption and Pérez's neoliberal reforms.

The same tack was taken by Rafael Caldera, who centered his winning campaign on his reputation for honesty and on offering voters what opinion polls indicated they wanted: a rollback of market reforms and the reassurance that painful economic measures were not really needed. The strategy paid off. Caldera was elected with 1.71 million votes, equivalent to 30.5 percent of the total. The three other main candidates trailed Caldera by 7 to 9 percent of the votes, with AD's Fermin placing second (with 1.33 million votes or 23.6 percent), COPEI's Álvarez Paz third (with 1.28 million or 22.7 percent), and Causa R's Andrés Velásquez fourth (with 1.23 million or 21.9 percent of the total vote count). Another first for the 1993 election was the abstention rate, which, at almost 40 percent, was the highest in Venezuelan history.[3]

The new Congress was more fragmented than ever before. Instead of the two-party domination that had existed throughout the democratic era, at least five blocs emerged, none with a clear majority. Also, with party discipline greatly eroded and with many Congress members elected in their own electoral districts and not as a result of having been included in a party list by its authorities, allegiance to the party became blurred.[4]

Political instability and economic uncertainty converged to deepen the generalized crisis that shattered most of the political arrangements on which the country's institutions had been based in prior decades. Almost all traditional power centers lost their influence. Political parties, private sector conglomerates, labor unions, the military high command and even the presidency, not to mention a Congress generally despised for corruption and incompetence, had to scramble to survive the onslaughts of new leaders and new groups. These were spurred and emboldened by an electorate apparently willing to support any initiative aimed at getting rid of the country's political past or promising to bring back the years of economic affluence. Thus, at the same time that preparations for the jailing of Carlos Andrés Pérez were under way, President Caldera pardoned all the military and the civilians who had taken part in the two failed coups and proceeded to dismiss the minister of defense and the high command that had fought against them. Once pardoned, Lt. Col. Hugo Chávez, one of the leaders of the revolt, did not waste any time to start campaigning across the country, savoring the acclaim of adoring masses and announcing that his Bolivarian Revolutionary Movement (MBR-200) was determined to bring about a new era based on "a return to the ideals of Simón Bolívar, to the restoration of true Venezuelan values and . . . the defense of the country's sovereignty against the encroachment of foreign financial powers."[5] Chávez also lost no time in warning President Caldera that his pardon did not buy his subservience and that, unless his administration showed real commitment and progress in bringing about the radical changes that the people expected, social chaos and political turmoil would ensue.

Politicians and generals were not alone in facing unprecedented challenges. Since the first coup attempt in early 1992, the Pérez administration had lost whatever capacity it had left to continue with its economic reforms and complete its proposed changes in fiscal policy and the financial sector. As a result, with oil prices reaching their lowest point in a decade, no income from privatization, mounting losses from state-owned enterprises, insufficient tax collections, and no further room to cut public budgets, the fiscal deficit soared. The Central Bank, which gained its administrative autonomy and political independence in 1993, had to adopt a severe monetary policy to compensate, at least in part, for the inflationary pressures caused by the disarray in public finances. Interest rates ballooned and, as the private sector fell behind in servicing its debts to local banks, the weaknesses of the country's financial sector became apparent. In 1994 the government replaced the Central Bank president and induced the bank to establish currency controls and limits on interest rates.

Before the financial crash of 1994, many years of lax credit policies, almost nonexistent government supervision, and widespread corruption among bankers accustomed to using deposits to make dubious loans to their own corporations in different sectors of the economy— mostly real estate—made the financial sector highly vulnerable. The economic crisis that resulted from the prolonged political turmoil led many banks already weakened by corruption to collapse.

In Venezuela, high finance had always coexisted with politics and amid the deep crisis the financial sector entered at the end of 1993, politics was again present. The second largest bank in the country, Banco Latino, was closed by monetary authorities at the beginning of 1994. Although almost a third of all Venezuelan banks had exhibited the same sorry state of affairs as the Banco Latino, they were bailed out by the government through the injection of massive doses of governmental cash and were not closed. The much harsher way in which Banco Latino was treated undoubtedly owed more to political calculations than to technical considerations. In these political calculations, factors like the dirty wars which large oligopolistic groups waged with each other[6] and in which Latino's rivals gained an upper hand (through their alliance with the government and Latino's active involvement in electoral politics and alleged links with the military) certainly played a part.[7] By mid-1994 the country was facing a deep financial crisis, many traditional economic groups were on the verge of collapse, and those that were able to survive came out with a fraction of their erstwhile political influence and market power.

## NOSTALGIA, RESENTMENT, AND LYNCHING AS DETERMINANTS OF POLITICAL BEHAVIOR

The demise of the political arrangements on which the country had relied for many decades was accelerated and its consequences compounded by an external economic shock. In fact, from 1990 to 1993, the government essentially lost half of its revenues to the decline of oil prices. Attempts at increasing government revenues through taxation clashed with the belligerent attitude of a population that had never paid taxes, that was convinced that every cent paid to the government was lost to corruption, and that in daily life had to endure dismally inefficient public services that appeared to be constantly worsening. Furthermore, opinion polls indicated that 11 percent of those who voted for President Caldera did so on the basis of his promise that his administration was going to reverse a value added tax that the interim Velásquez administration had adopted thanks only to special emergency powers accorded to it by Congress.

These points illustrate the essence of Venezuelan political economy in the middle of the 1990s. The economic policies required by international and domestic realities clashed head-on with political realities driven by a population whose political attitudes made the necessary policies difficult to adopt and almost impossible to implement for any sustained period. Political attitudes and behavior were determined by nostalgia, resentment, and the mood of a lynch mob. The nostalgic longing for a perceived past of generalized affluence was complemented by the conviction that the country's hardships owed less to misguided economic policies than to the corruption of politicians, government officials, and businesspeople who had plundered the riches of the country. An ugly, pervasive lynching mood was a natural and perhaps understandable outcome. Unfortunately, together with the confusion and a lack of leadership, Venezuela became mired in the politics of fragmented, relatively small groups, each with enough power to prevent its rivals from imposing their views but with no single group having the capacity to steer society out of its debilitating gridlock. Under these circumstances, the obsessive search for scapegoats became more important than the search for solutions, since factional politics made them difficult to implement regardless of their value.

Moreover, finding solutions when economic and political realities are at such odds also creates incentives to eschew the public debate about options that could help in building a modicum of consensus. According to an opinion poll at the beginning of 1994, 90 percent of the population rejected the value added tax, 85 percent wanted the government to impose a compulsory increase in salaries in both the public and the private sectors, 80 percent of the population wanted generalized price controls, 70 percent favored subsidizing farmers, and 65 percent supported the establishment of foreign exchange controls,[8] whereas only 40 percent supported the privatization of state-owned enterprises and a scant 10 percent agreed with "a small increase in the price of gasoline."[9] These were the answers in a country where in mid-1994 gasoline sold at less than the equivalent of twenty cents per gallon; where the losses of state-owned enterprises drained from public budgets the money to run hospitals; where tax collection as a percentage of GDP was the lowest in Latin America and one of the lowest in the world; where state capacity had been devastated by years of harsh budget cuts, yet the fiscal deficit loomed as a large inflation-inducing threat; and where a state apparatus plagued by corruption and lack of resources that had proven incapable of performing even the simplest of tasks was expected by the population to manage prices, decide on the allocation of foreign exchange, and oversee all international financial transactions at a time of instant electronic transfers across the globe.

Obviously, any government would be hard-pressed to manage adequately the Venezuelan economy under such a clash between political and economic realities. The challenge for the Caldera administration, however, was made even more complicated because it won the election by appealing to these contradictory expectations.

## CONCLUSION: WHAT HAVE WE LEARNED?

In Venezuela, as in many of the other countries of the region, the old models of economic development and political comity ran out of gas at almost the same point in the road and at the very moment when the cold war was coming to an end. Suddenly, command economies were held in ridicule, and a neoliberal model of growth and international exchange was being promoted by the international financial institutions and the governments of the dominant developed nations and being enthusiastically implemented by most governments in the world. Although it is certainly an exaggeration to argue that the governments of the region that assumed office in the 1980s had no choice in making macroeconomic decisions, it would be fair to state that their range of choice was severely limited by the local failures of previous macroeconomic programs and by the pressure of exogenous factors. In Venezuela, as in most Latin American nations, the economic restructuring programs were rushed through without much public debate and without full appreciation of the potential political impact the changes might have.[10]

The Venezuelan case suggests that eventually, however reasonable or constructive, macroeconomic policy must be able to pass through the political system. In a democracy, that means compromise, delay, and reordering of priorities. Economic reform, it appears, can be realized only in conjunction with a deepening of democracy, but such democratic deepening further complicates the process through which economic policies are formulated and economic objectives attained.

Finally, the Venezuelan case suggests that social tensions accumulated through decades of misguided economic policies are bound to become powerful obstacles to the implementation of macroeconomic reforms aimed at correcting the sins of the past. Despite the risk of complicating economic policymaking, taking all possible steps to buffer the impact on the poorest sectors and soften the negative political impact of austerity is indispensable to the viability of the reforms and to the reinforcement of the legitimacy of the democratic system. In this regard, nongovernmental organizations, often organized to protect groups of citizens against the state, can serve as important instruments of political representation and as a key medium of articulation of interests within the political system. Furthermore, state decentralization in Venezuela, which has been implemented to a limited degree since the late 1980s, also may facilitate the means of addressing the social costs of economic restructuring.

The central point is that the process of improving the quality of life of the people of Latin America requires more effective integration into the world economy and the world system more generally, and that such integration requires a process of reform to make the economies of the region more open and more competitive. The problem is that the reform process cannot be considered as a matter of macroeconomic policy alone. The Venezuelan case demonstrates, above all, that macroeconomic policy must be part of the broader process of a democratic consolidation that requires attention to political relations among all segments of the political system.

## NOTES

1. See Alfred C. Stepan, *Rethinking Military Politics* (Princeton: Princeton University Press, 1987), chap. 1.

2. Consultores 21, S.A., "Informe analitico de resultados," Caracas, January 1994.
3. Of the 9.7 million officially registered voters, 5.83 million Venezuelans went to the polls. After eliminating null and void ballots, 5.62 million votes were considered valid and actually counted by the Supreme Electoral Council. For a complete analysis, see William Perry, "The Venezuelan General Elections of 1993," Institute for the Study of the Americas, Washington, D.C., February 1994.
4. Of a total of fifty-two senators, eighteen belonged to AD, fifteen to COPEI, ten to Caldera's coalition, and nine to Causa R. In the Chamber of Deputies, AD received fifty-five seats, COPEI fifty-four, Caldera's coalition fifty (twenty-four to Convergencia and twenty-six to MAS), and Causa R forty.
5. Interview with Lt. Col. Hugo Chávez, Weekend Magazine, *El Diario de Caracas*, April 17, 1994.
6. In letters published in the Venezuelan press, Banco Latino's chief executive officer explicitly acknowledged that it was common practice for banks and other large private corporations to use "hired pens"—journalists specialized in spreading disinformation and false accusations against the business rivals of their clients and against government officials. Controlling television and radio stations as well as newspaper and other media companies became a paramount objective for the more politically inclined—and more powerful—business conglomerates.
7. The management of Banco Latino was accused of organizing and financing a defense minister's trip to Washington in 1992 to coordinate with the U.S. government actions to be taken by the military in case of a leftist coup. Both the minister and Banco Latino's officers have denied the accusations, but it is widely believed that it was an important contributing factor in convincing the government to close the bank. The decision was later reversed, and the bank was reopened under a government-appointed administration, while arrest warrants were issued to all of its former directors and top management.
8. The question was, "To what extent would you support that foreign currency could be bought only with a special permission granted by the government?" See Consultores 21, S.A., "Informe analitico de resultados," 12, note 1.
9. See ibid.
10. See Moisés Naím, *Paper Tigers and Minotaurs: The Politics of Venezuela's Economic Reforms* (Washington, D.C.: Carnegie Endowment for International Peace and Brookings Institution, 1993). For a discussion of the exogenous forces affecting Latin American governments, see Joseph S. Tulchin, "The United States and Latin America after the Cold War," in Augusto Varas and Joseph S. Tulchin, eds., *Global Transformations and Peace in the Western Hemisphere* (Boulder: Westview Press, forthcoming 1994).

# INDEX

abstention rates (in voting), 41, 225, 227, 230–31, 401

Acción Democrática (AD): cooperation of, with COPEI, 3, 339; and corruption, 90–91, 313–14, 324; criticism of, 60, 68, 75, 131; economic policies of, 127–28, 209, 400; history of, 32–51, 124, 130, 144, 153–54, 195, 227–28, 245, 300, 313–14, 320, 369; labor and peasant ties to, 38–39, 125–26, 195, 200; and military promotions, 57; multiclass composition of, 126, 304; National Executive Committee [CEN] of, 36, 38, 46, 50; and neighborhood groups, 242; in *1992* and *1993* elections, ix, 228–29, 400–1; Pérez's independence from, 50, 84, 125, 127, 226; power of, 15, 33–34, 120; weakening of, 8, 17, 22, 69, 72, 99–100, 115, 228, 230–31, 351, 353, 399. *See also* Betancourt, Rómulo;˙ elites; Pérez, Carlos Andrés; political parties

accountability: importance of, in stable governments, 13–14, 16–17, 20, 243; lack of, in Venezuela, 175, 176, 243; public's desire for governmental, 9, 12, 142, 230

adeco, 37

Agrarian Bank (BAP), 195–96

Agrarian Reform Law (1960), 195–96

Agricultural Credit Fund (FCA), 207, 211

agriculture: vs. oil, 87, 193–219 reform of, 22, 193–219, 273–74; research in, 195–96;

Agüero, Felipe, 19, 21, 136–62

air force, 48, 65, 71

ALADI (Latin American Integration Association), 370, 373, 377

Albornoz de López, Teresa, 312–13

ALCASA, 174

Alfaro Ucero, Luis, 44

Alfonsín, Raúl, 152, 158n15

Álvarez Paz, Oswaldo, 61, 135n22, 246, 400–1

Andean Pact, 174–75, 370, 372, 373, 377

Añez, Ciro, 52n22

anti-narcotics operations, 64, 73–74

*apertura*, 32, 40–41

Argentina, 90, 286, 287, 387; corruption in, 13; decentralization attempts in, 17; economy in, 11, 15, 285; military in, 19, 146, 152, 158n15, 159n28

Arias Cárdenas, Lt. Col. Francisco, 65–68, 70, 74–75

Aristide, Jean-Bertrand, 64

Armed Forces Polytechnical Institute, 148

army, 48, 61

*arsista*, 39

Asociación Pro-Venezuela, 46

Australia, 83

AVEX (Venezuelan Association of Exporters), 179

Aylwin, Patricio, 18

Bailey, Norman, 24, 387–97

Baloyra, Enrique A., 32, 92, 94, 101, 116

Banco Comercial de Venezuela, 171

Banco de Caracas, 171, 172

Banco de Comercio, 175

Banco de los Trabajadores, 175

Banco de Maracaibo, 171, 172

Banco de Venezuela, 171, 172

Banco Latino, 402

Banco Nacional de Descuento, 175

Banco Obrero, 300, 325, 332n27. *See also* INAVI

Bangladesh, 296

Bank of Credit and Commerce International (BCCI) scandal, 325

Barrios, Gonzalo, 37

Baruta (Caracas), 122–23

Bastardo Velásquez, Gen. Juan, 61

BAUXIVEN, 168

Belgium, 296